SCOTLAND:
THE MAKING AND UNMAKING OF THE NATION
c.1100–1707

SCOTLAND:
THE MAKING AND
UNMAKING OF
THE NATION
c.1100–1707

VOLUME 4: READINGS
C.1500–1707

Edited by
Bob Harris and Alan R MacDonald

DUNDEE UNIVERSITY PRESS

In association with

THE OPEN UNIVERSITY IN SCOTLAND

First published in Great Britain in 2007 by
Dundee University Press

University of Dundee
Dundee DD1 4HN

www.dundee.ac.uk/dup

ISBN 10: 1 84586 029 2
ISBN 13: 978 1 84586 029 5

British Library Cataloguing-in-Publication Data
A catalogue record for this book is available on request from the British Library

Typeset by Hewer Text UK Ltd, Edinburgh

Printed and bound in Great Britain by
CPI Antony Rowe, Chippenham and Eastbourne

Contents

Preface

This volume and the series of which it is a part represent the completion of a project which began in the mid 1990s to facilitate the study of Scottish History in Scotland and beyond. A milestone was reached in 1998 with the launch of a module in Modern Scottish History – Modern Scottish History: 1707 to the Present. This module, and the five volumes which accompany it, have won consistently high praise from the students who have taken it, as well as strong commendation from many professional academics. Appropriately perhaps, with the project's completion in 2007, the 300th anniversary of the parliamentary union with England, anyone who wishes to will be able to study Scottish history from c.1100 to the present day by distance learning.

In 1998, the editors said that it was a particularly appropriate moment to bring Scottish history to a new and wider readership and audience. This reflected, in the first place, the outcome of the 1997 Referendum, but also the evident depth of contemporary interest, expressed in a large variety of ways, in the Scottish past. It is no less true today. Indeed, if anything, the need and desirability of doing so are only greater with the first flush of post-devolution excitement over and the place of Scottish history in universities and schools not necessarily any stronger than it was a few years ago. And while popular history books are being written and published, and from 2003 *History Scotland* has been available on newsagents' shelves, long established myths and preconceptions about the Scottish past still exert a very firm grip on general opinion and even on those who really should know better. Scottish history and Scotland deserve better than this.

These volumes aim to present recent academic research to a wider readership. As such they should be of interest to anyone with an interest in knowing about the Scottish past as well as the essential historical background to many present-day concerns and issues. They also provide a way for readers to develop their own skills as students of history, focusing on issues relating to the use (and abuse) of primary sources and the conceptual questions and challenges raised by specific topics. While we have left out some of the overtly pedagogical material which was included in the Modern Scottish History volumes, there is still plenty of discussion on sources and methods for interested readers to follow up.

The potential scope of these volumes is enormous, and this despite the fact that the sources and scholarship for the medieval and early modern periods are considerably less abundant than for the modern one. Any decision we might have taken about how to present the history of periods as long as c.1100–c.1500 and c.1500–1707 would have involved some awkward compromises. The first two volumes, comprising new essays by expert authors, start with a number of broadly chronological chapters, furnishing readers with a basic narrative. These chapters are followed by a range of more thematic ones. All the chapters are designed to offer a reasonably comprehensive introduction to recent work and, as importantly, a context or contexts for further reading and investigation. You will find there is some overlap between the chronological and thematic chapters, which offers scope for comparison between authors and for looking again at topics and themes from alternative perspectives. Some themes span the two volumes – for example, the Highland-Lowland divide, urbanisation, Scottish identity, Anglo-Scottish relations – so they can be traced over the 'long durée' and across conventional period divisions. There are no separate chapters on gender. Rather this theme has been deliberately blended in with other themes and topics. Some will not find this to their taste, but the aim is to present an inclusive, broad vision of the Scottish past, not one which segregates particular experiences. We have also chosen to include greater coverage of areas of cultural history than in the modern volumes. In part, this reflects recent trends in the writing of history – the so-called 'cultural turn' in historical studies – but also the wealth of scholarship which exists on such topics. It may also reflect something of an emancipation of scholars from the primacy of documentary sources, but then this is no new thing for medievalists. Throughout both volumes a key theme which emerges, in terms of how we study the Scottish past, and also the patterns and meanings present in that past, is the importance of Scottish relationships and involvement in a broader European past. Let's hope the anniversary of the Union does not mask or detract from this theme, and the great strides which have been made in recent decades to recover this dimension to the Scottish past. The third and fourth volumes contain selected readings to accompany the topic/theme volumes, and should prove a great resource for those wishing to explore further a particular subject. The fifth volume is a collection of primary sources for the history of Scotland from c.1100 to 1707 designed to accompany the other volumes. It makes accessible documents of both local and national importance, quite a few of which have been specially transcribed for this volume. All students of history should want to read primary sources for the uniquely rich insight they furnish into the past. We also hope that they may encourage some readers to make their own forays into local archives.

This book represents a further product of the University of Dundee–Open University collaboration to offer modules in Scottish history to distance learning students. The modules are offered at honours level for undergraduates. However, all the volumes are designed to be used, singly or as a series, by anyone with an interest in Scottish history. Our hope is that they will inspire and deepen enthusiasm for the investigation of the Scottish past, perhaps even encouraging some to examine aspects of their own community history based on themes covered in the volumes.

From the outset, this project has depended on the efforts and enthusiasm of many people, and there are several major debts to acknowledge. Financial support for the development of these volumes was provided initially from the strategic fund of the Faculty of Arts and Social Sciences at the University of Dundee under the guidance of then dean, Professor Huw Jones. His successor, Professor Chris Whatley, has been a constant supporter, and has contributed his expertise to these volumes, as well as being an editor and contributor to the Modern Scottish History volumes. The

Strathmartine Trust generously provided further vital financial support to facilitate the production of these volumes. Within the Open University, invaluable supporting roles have been played by Peter Syme, Director of the Open University in Scotland, and Ian Donnachie, Reader in History at the Open University. It is the shared commitment of individuals in both institutions, stimulated by the success and quality of the Modern Scottish History course, which has driven forward the continued development of the project. John Tuckwell, who published the Modern Scottish History volumes, and who commissioned the present volumes, has been a sage and an encouraging adviser to the editorial team. The authors produced their contributions to agreed formats and, for the most part, to agreed deadlines. While they are responsible for what they have written, they have also been supported by other members of the writing team and our editors. Particular thanks are also due to Mrs Johanne Phillips, the secretary and administrator of the Modern Scottish History course; to her successor Elizabeth Bryant, and to Mrs Helen Carmichael and Mrs Sara Reid, secretaries in the Department of History, University of Dundee for their administrative support. Thanks are also due to Jen Petrie who typed many of the texts for inclusion in the articles and documents volumes.

USING THIS BOOK

The readings in Volumes 3 and 4 were chosen by the authors of the chapters in Volumes 1 and 2 respectively. Some of the readings provide an alternative view of the period or topic, others look in more detail at a particular aspect of it. They are intended to complement the original essays and should be read alongside them.

Series Editors

Acknowledgements

Grateful acknowledgement is made to the following sources for permission to reproduce material in this volume.

N Macdougall 2001 'Indian Summer: 1517–1560', Chapter 6 of his *An Antidote to the English: The Auld Alliance, 1295–1560*, Tuckwell Press; J Goodare 2000 'Scottish Politics in the Reign of James VI' *in* J Goodare and M Lynch (eds), *The Reign of James VI*, Tuckwell Press; J Scally 1996 'Constitutional Revolution, Party and Faction in the Scottish Parliaments of Charles I' *in* C Jones (ed), *The Scots and Parliament*, by permission of Edinburgh University Press, www.eup.ac.uk; IB Cowan 1989 'The Reluctant Revolutionaries: Scotland in 1688' *in* E Cruickshanks (ed), *By Force or By Default? The Revolution of 1688–89*, John Donald; RL Emerson 1995 'Scottish Cultural Change 1660–1710 and the Union of 1707' *in* J Robertson (ed), *A Union for Empire: Political Thought and the British Union of 1707*, Cambridge University Press, reprinted with permission of the author and publisher; A MacKillop 2001 'Clans of the Highlands and Islands: 1610 Onwards' *in* M Lynch (ed), *The Oxford Companion to Scottish History*, Oxford University Press; AI Macinnes 1996 'Clan Support for the House of Stuart' *in* PGB McNeill and HL MacQueen (eds), *Atlas of Scottish History to 1707*, reproduced by permission of the Atlas Committee of the Scottish Medievalists and the author; J Dawson 1994 'Calvinism and the Gaidhealtachd in Scotland' *in* A Pettegree, A Duke and G Lewis (eds), *Calvinism in Europe 1540–1620*, Cambridge University Press, reprinted with permission of the author and publisher; A Grosjean 2000 'General Alexander Leslie, the Scottish Covenanters and the Riksråd debates, 1638–1640' *in* AI Macinnes, T Riis and FG Pedersen (eds) *Ships Guns and Bibles in the North Sea and the Baltic States, c.1350–1700*, Tuckwell Press; JR Young 2001 'The Scottish Parliament and European Diplomacy 1641–1647: The Palatine, the Dutch Republic and Sweden' *in* S Murdoch (ed), *Scotland and the Thirty Years' War, 1618–1648*, with permission of Brill Academic Publishers; M Lynch 1984 'Whatever happened to the medieval burgh? Some guidelines for sixteenth and seventeenth historians' in *Scottish Economic and Social History*, 4, Edinburgh University Press, www.eup.ed.ac.uk; extracts from MHB Sanderson 2002 *A Kindly Place? Living in Sixteenth Century Scotland*, Tuckwell Press; extracts from RA Dodgshon 1981 *Land and Society in Early Scotland*, Oxford University Press; ID Whyte 1995 'Before the Improvers: Agricultural and Landscape Change in Lowland Scotland c.1660–c.1750', in *Scottish Archives*, I, Scottish Records Association; ID Whyte 1998 'Poverty or Prosperity? Rural Society in Lowland Scotland in the Late Sixteenth and Early Seventeenth Centuries', in *Scottish Economic and Social History*, 18, Edinburgh University Press, www.eup.ac.uk; extracts from FJ Shaw 1980 *The Northern and*

Western Islands of Scotland: their economy and society in the seventeenth century, John Donald; extracts from TM Devine 1994 *The Transformation of Rural Scotland: Social Change and Agrarian Economy, 1660–1815*, John Donald; A MacKechnie 2000 'James VI's Architects and their Architecture' *in* J Goodare and M Lynch (eds), *The Reign of James VI*, Tuckwell Press; M Bath 2003 'A National Style', chapter 1 of his *Renaissance Decorative Painting in Scotland*, National Museums of Scotland; extracts from DJ Ross 1993 *Musick Fyne: The Art of Music in Sixteenth Century Scotland*, Mercat Press; extracts from M Lynch 1993 'Scottish Culture in its Historical Perspective' *in* PH Scott (ed) *Scotland: A Concise Cultural History*, Mainstream; extracts from RA Mason 1982 '*Rex Stoicus*: George Buchanan, James VI and the Scottish Polity' *in* J Dwyer, RA Mason and A Murdoch (eds) *New Perpsectives on the Politics and Culture of Early Modern Scotland*, John Donald; extracts from JE Howard 1986 'The New Historicism in Renaissance Studies' in *English Literary Renaissance 16*.

Indian Summer: 1517–1560

Extracted from N Macdougall 2001 *An Antidote to the English: The Auld Alliance, 1295–1560*, East Linton (Tuckwell Press), 121–42.

Like earlier Franco-Scottish treaties, the Treaty of Rouen of 1517 was an offensive and defensive alliance directed against England, differing from its predecessors not so much in its terms as in the fact that both contracting parties were in France. John, duke of Albany, 'the Scot who was a Frenchman', signed and sealed the treaty on behalf of the infant James V, while Charles, duke of Alençon, did the same for Francis I of France. In many respects, the treaty recalled those made two hundred years previously, Corbeil in 1326 or perhaps even Paris–Dunfermline in 1295–6; for like the latter, the Treaty of Rouen contained a matrimonial clause, albeit a rather nebulous one. Thus Francis I agreed that, if the promise of his eldest daughter – whether Louise or Charlotte is not specified – made to the king of Spain or his brother did not take place, then at a suitable age she would be married to the king of Scots; alternatively, if the Spanish marriage went ahead, and Francis I had the good fortune to have another daughter, that daughter would be married to James V.

A treaty of this kind put the Scots firmly in their place in the matrimonial stakes and diplomatic pecking order. The truth was that the European diplomatic map was changing with remarkable speed in the early sixteenth century, and that many of the certainties which had long sustained the Auld Alliance were being undermined. France's entry into the Italian wars from 1494 had certainly provided a lifetime's employment for soldiers in the service of Charles VIII, Louis XII and Francis I. However, in place of the old Franco-Burgundian and Anglo-French struggles of the fifteenth century, there arose a far more formidable enemy, the greatest power ever seen in Europe, the Emperor Charles V. In 1519 Charles, already king of Spain for three years, was elected Emperor in succession to Maximilian, thus adding to his kingdoms of Spain, Naples and Sicily (and Spain's New World wealth) the Netherlands, Germany, Flanders, Artois, Franche-Comté and Austria. French fear of encirclement led Francis I – temporarily – into alliance with Henry VIII of England, whose feeble shy at restarting the Hundred Years' War in 1512–13 was by 1520 safely behind him, if not for ever.

The mutual antagonism of the leaders of Europe's super-powers, Charles V and Francis I, and a new Anglo-French amity, did not seem to augur well for the Franco-Scottish alliance. However, peace between England and France ran counter to hundreds of years of history, and Henry VIII's alternative was to try to build an imperial alliance with Charles V. His concern with Scotland was and remained her ability to open a 'second front' in the north if England were embroiled in war with

France; and this concern was in no way diminished by Surrey's victory at Flodden. After all, the Treaty of Rouen of 1517 stipulated that should the king of England make war either on Scotland or France, the French king would give to the king of Scots a payment of 100,000 *écus* and the services of 500 mounted spearmen, 500 infantry and 200 archers. The French king's fear of encirclement by potential or real enemies was mirrored, on a smaller scale, by that of Henry VIII.

Thus English diplomacy in the north tended towards a mixture of promises and threats: that is, offers to the Scots of English marriage alliances coupled with demands that they break the French connection. However, Henry VIII unwittingly compounded his own difficulties, and gave the Scottish kingdom a status in Europe quite out of proportion to its size and importance, when in the early 1530s he rejected papal authority and declared himself Supreme Head of the English church. For a generation thereafter Scottish foreign policy had a clear, consistent direction – the pursuit of an often lucrative French alliance underpinned by an adherence to Catholicism which acquired a new importance given the existence of a heretic England. Far from being relegated to the status of a distant sideshow, therefore, in what proved to be its final years the Auld Alliance experienced an Indian summer, with the French providing three royal marriage alliances, troops to fight in Scotland, and wealth to support them on an unprecedented scale. And the period which had opened with a Frenchman in charge of government would end with a Frenchwoman as Regent.

From Rouen (1517) to St Quentin (1536)

Unravelling the politics of the long and fractious minority of James V (1513–1528) would try the patience of a saint; thus far, saintly patience has been granted only to Ken Emond, whose scholarly thesis on the subject has yet to appear in print. However, amidst the general gloom of powerful magnates jockeying for position, changing sides frequently in order to improve their fortunes or even to acquire temporary control of government for their families, certain issues stand out clearly.

The most striking of these is the ability of John, duke of Albany, governor for nine years from his first arrival in Scotland in May 1515 until what proved to be his final departure to France nine years later, in May 1524. As the steadfast representative of the Franco–Scottish alliance, above all as the man who had negotiated the Treaty of Rouen, Albany was of course anathema to the English, who saw him as a French agent in Scotland. The Scots had a different view, best expressed in parliament at Edinburgh in February 1522. Henry VIII, who had managed to have Albany kept in France for over four years from 1517, was alarmed at his return to Scotland in November 1521, and demanded that the Scots dismiss him as governor. The estates' resolute response to Henry VIII is worth quoting at some length:

> We will with his [Albany's] presence take our adventure of peace or war as shall please God to send it; assuring your grace that . . . we neither may nor will, at the request of your grace, nor any other prince, consent nor suffer in any manner

that our said Lord Governor depart furth of this realm during the king our
sovereign lord's minority . . . And if, for this cause, we happen to be invaded,
what may we do but take God to our good quarrel in defence, and do, as our
progenitors and forbears have been constrained to do, for the conservation of
this realm heretofore.

This reply by the chancellor and three estates of Scotland goes beyond a mere refusal
to dismiss Albany; indeed the Scots were concerned to show their approval of the
governor, remarking that 'he is chosen by us all, and so lovably has exercised [his
office of governor] during all the time of his being in this realm, that no creature may
reasonably lay reproach or dishonour to his charge'.

   There is, perhaps, a pardonable exaggeration on the part of the Scots in suggesting
that Albany had been chosen as governor by them all. Certain powerful political
players, above all the Queen Mother, Margaret Tudor, her husband Archibald, sixth
earl of Angus, and James Hamilton, first earl of Arran and second in line to the
throne after the governor, had their own individual agendas, and their intrigues were
fomented by Henry VIII in order to destabilise the Albany government. But the
various brief alignments and realignments of powerful individuals opposed to
Albany hardly merit the collective title sometimes accorded to them of an 'English
party' seeking power in Scotland. There was nothing new in treasonable activities by
disaffected magnates during royal minorities. In 1491 Archibald, fifth earl of Angus,
had been involved in a plot to remove the 18–year-old James IV from the control of
his Hepburn guardians and to become the liege man of Henry VIII of England; over
a generation later, in 1526, Angus's grandson, the sixth earl, would be involved in
the retention of the person of the 14–year-old James V in order to place the Angus
affinity at the heart of government *and* because he was acceptable to the English as a
man with whom they could do business. And there was always Margaret Tudor,
moving swiftly from her 1514 marriage to Angus – 'a young witless fool' in the
opinion of his uncle – to divorce and remarriage to Henry Stewart, Lord Methven;
indeed, Margaret's capriciousness was so notorious that her brother Henry VIII was
moved to write to her warning her about the damage to her reputation which might
result from too many marriages. So she continued, politically a floating iceberg
during her son's minority, but thereafter a much less significant figure until her death
in 1541.

   None of these individuals had a coherent or consistent policy in their domestic or
foreign affairs. Albany had both. At home he proved himself an honest and firm
regent; and even during his long absence in France (1517–21) he contrived to use his
influence in favour of the Scottish crown and merchants. Thus in January 1519 he
managed to have the pope renew an indult whereby the Scottish crown was
guaranteed the right to make nominations to important ecclesiastical benefices;
and a bull of June 1520 took Scotland and its king into papal protection and
confirmed Albany's authority as governor. In May 1518, on Albany's request,
Francis I of France granted a concession freeing Scottish traders from duties laid on
foreign goods at the French port of entry of Dieppe.

These practical demonstrations of the worth of the Auld Alliance – and above all of having a powerful advocate abroad – help to explain its continuing popularity with the Scots. And their desire to retain Albany as governor, so forcefully expressed by the three estates in 1522, may in part be a reflection of a collective desire to avoid the mayhem which occurred when he was abroad, most notably the 'Cleanse the Causeway' incident of 1520, when the Hamiltons had driven the Douglases out of Edinburgh.

The price which the Scots had to pay for Albany's good governance was to become involved in war on the borders against the English. In the late summer of 1522 an English army invaded Picardy, and Francis I required the Scots to open a second front. Albany duly mustered the host at Roslin in Midlothian, and an act was passed, recalling the Flodden campaign of 1513, freeing the heirs of those who lost their lives in the campaign from the onerous feudal payment of relief on the estates which they would inherit. The Scottish objective was Carlisle on the west march; the army was a large one, and it seems to have advanced to within five miles of Carlisle. At this point a truce was made between Albany and the English warden, Lord Dacre, and the Scots host withdrew. Much – probably too much – has been made of the Scots' reluctance to cross the border in the interests of France – though if Cardinal Wolsey's letter to Henry VIII describing the campaign is accurate, the Scottish army was already over the border when the truce was made – and the ubiquitous 'Flodden complex' has been advanced as a reason for the host's failures in 1522, and again in 1523. In 1522, however, Francis I, committed to supplying armies in Picardy, Gascony, and Italy, and prevented by an English blockade from sending ships from Breton ports, may have been telling the Scots no more than the truth when he pointed out to their ambassadors that he could not give greater help at present. Thus the Scots, in 'scaling' (disbanding) their army, may have been responding to the letter rather than the spirit of the Treaty of Rouen.

In the autumn of 1523, however, French aid was duly forthcoming in the shape of 4,000 footmen, 600 mounted troops, artillery, money and supplies. During the summer and early autumn English forces had crossed the border and burned Kelso and Jedburgh; Albany's campaign was a response to these raids, and his target was Wark Castle, just south of the River Tweed. In this case, it was bad timing rather than any 'Flodden complex' which made the campaign a failure. It began extraordinarily late in the season, with French reinforcements reaching Dumbarton only in mid-October, and the combined Franco-Scottish forces of Albany, Argyll and Lennox reaching Wark at Hallowe'en, about the same time that the earl of Surrey arrived at Belford in Northumberland, an easy day's march from Wark. Albany bombarded Wark for two days; but with Surrey in front of him and the Tweed in spate behind him, the Governor wisely withdrew on 3 November. He had done his best, personally summoning the host as soon as he arrived back in Scotland on 24 September. The season and the weather, rather than the reluctance of the Scots, were against him.

On 20 May 1524 Albany departed for France for the third time since his initial arrival in Scotland in 1515. In the event, he would not return; but it should be noted that his reason for going was not so much disillusionment with the Scots – on many subsequent occasions he would propose returning – as the illness of his wife, the duchess Anne, who died in June 1524. It is of course true that prominent Scottish magnates – Angus, Arran and Lennox among them – were glad to see the back of Albany and an end to the strong guiding hand which he had provided for the young king; and they were quick to ignore, to their own profit, the provisions which the Governor had made for the safety of James V during his absence. Ill luck dogged Albany to the end, for the French troops brought to Scotland for the 1523 campaign, attempting to return home, were shipwrecked in the Hebrides and many were drowned, a fact reported by Lord Dacre, with considerable satisfaction, to Cardinal Wolsey.

It would be a mistake, however, to equate the failure of the two autumn campaigns of 1522 and 1523 with any lasting change in attitude towards the Auld Alliance on the part of the Scots. Certainly there was a temporary break in the mid- and late 1520s, occasioned as much as anything else by Francis I's capture by the Imperialists at the battle of Pavia in 1525, and the subsequent conclusion of Anglo-French treaties in April 1527. It is also true that some Scottish merchants were concerned to keep open profitable English markets for Scottish wool and fish by avoiding war with England. And Anglo-Scottish union had a persuasive advocate in John Mair (Major), whose *History of Greater Britain* dates from 1521. However, these straws in the wind had been blown away by the end of the decade; and it should be noted that John Mair's dark inferences about Albany's supposed ambitions as heir presumptive to the young king hardly qualify the writer as an impartial observer of the politics of his times.

In time, it would be Albany's able tutelage of the king which would bear fruit; if Bishop Lesley is to be believed, the governor spent his last Sunday in Scotland at Stirling with the 12-year-old James V, talking to him at length about his duties and responsibilities. When James took charge of affairs in 1528, it would be to Albany that he would turn for advice and assistance in the negotiation of foreign marriages; unsurprisingly the duke continued to advance the claims of potential French brides, and if the Franco-Scottish alliance had faltered in the 1520s, it prospered mightily thereafter.

Yet though Albany's matrimonial negotiations were valued by James V, it was the absent duke rather than the ever-present governor whom the king cherished. James had no more desire than the English to see Albany back in Scotland; the former governor would be an embarrassment to an adult king. Whether Albany himself wished to return is another matter. Certainly the English, in the late 1520s, had an almost paranoid fear of the duke's return, and spread a story that Albany was hiring ships to sail to Scotland early in 1528, assisted by Robert Stewart, Lord of Aubigny. Nothing of the sort happened. Albany stayed in France, a diplomat and soldier, conducting a voluminous correspondence with James V and other Scots, dying at his castle of Mirefleur in the Auvergne on 2 June 1536. In terms of the furtherance of the Auld Alliance, the duke's importance equals that of his fellow Franco-Scot, Bérault Stewart of Aubigny. But Albany's crucial role as Governor for James V gives him a quite unique status among French 'écossois'. That status also made him a target, in his own day and later, for scandal perpetrated by his enemies, with English diplomats well to the fore in efforts to blacken his name. However, rumours of a sexual liaison between Albany and Margaret Tudor may be discounted; and later tales that the governor, when in a rage, used to throw his hat into the fire, if true, simply reflect the problems of a man charged with the unenviable task of governing Scotland in the post-Flodden era.

Albany's young charge, James V, rapidly showed himself an able pupil. Having endured four years of government by groups of magnates, the king escaped from Edinburgh to Stirling Castle at the end of May 1528. He was sixteen; he was backed by a magnate coalition including eight prominent earls; and he was determined to free himself from control by the Angus Douglases, who had ruled since June 1526 on the strength of their possession of the person of the king. This dangerous game had certainly brought the family short-term gains: Angus himself became chancellor, his uncle Archibald was made treasurer, and his brother George master of the royal household. If the English had regarded Albany as a French agent, it can at least as accurately be argued that Chancellor Angus was an English agent, encouraging James V to abandon the French and put his trust in 'his good uncle of England'. James appears to have simulated compliance with the pro-English faction for a time, but he was well aware of the fact that a majority of the Scottish nobility and clergy favoured the French alliance. Even James Hamilton, earl of Arran, who argued for an English treaty, was clearly moved by the fact that, with Albany excluded from Scotland, he was one step nearer to becoming James V's heir presumptive. From an English standpoint, however, there was no doubt that Angus was 'better than five earls of Arran'; the only English concern was Margaret Tudor, who loathed her former husband and was likely to join any coalition that would bring him down.

The English were right to be concerned, for it was to Queen Margaret's castle of Stirling that James V escaped between 27 and 30 May 1528, returning to Edinburgh in strength on 6 July. Angus had prudently withdrawn from the city four days previously; within a week the king had summoned him for treason, and he was duly forfeited in parliament the following September. At the age of sixteen, earlier than any of his Stewart predecessors, James V had taken control of his kingdom.

For the adult James the immediate problem, having forfeited Angus, was how to get rid of the earl. A botched royal siege of Angus's great East Lothian stronghold of Tantallon in the late autumn of 1528 did not solve the problem, for the earl simply retired to Coldingham, and subsequently to the north of England, and for a few years the possibility of his return with English assistance concentrated King James's mind and influenced his policies. Following the king's coup of May 1528, a greater subtlety on the part of English diplomats might have better served their cause. Instead they seem to have gone out of their way to alienate James V. In the autumn of 1528, the earl of Northumberland saw no hope of redress of breaches of the truce on the borders 'unless the earl of Angus be put in authority again'; and in January of the following year Thomas Magnus, the English ambassador, meeting James in Edinburgh, warned him in no uncertain terms about the dangers of 'young counsel', telling him that 'the fall and destruction of King James the Third, his grandfather' had been caused by that king's being 'totally advised, ruled and governed by a light and young council'.

This was not only threatening but also quite inaccurate. If it was designed to woo James back into the English fold, it failed signally. In the early 1530s, Henry VIII moved to the rejection of papal authority and the assumption of the title of 'Supreme Head' of the English church; and a conciliatory, rather than threatening, approach to a staunchly Catholic Scotland would have been appropriate. For the young James V found himself with the ability to deal to his profit with the major European powers and with the papacy. The Emperor Charles V, who was the nephew of Katharine of Aragon, Henry VIII's discarded wife, was alienated from England, and was keen to have an ally against the spread of Lutheranism in the Empire and elsewhere. He was prepared to pay for James V's support with projected marriage alliances, favourable commercial treaties, gifts of cannon and ammunition, and the Order of the Golden Fleece, conferred on the Scottish king in May 1532. Francis I of France, though still loosely bound by the Anglo-French treaty of 1527, was sufficiently concerned about a possible alliance between James V and Charles V as to offer sweeteners to the Scottish king – the Order of St Michael (in 1536) and a series of marriage proposals, though Francis continued to prevaricate over Scottish requests for the hand of his daughter Madeleine for James V, excusing her on grounds of her youth and frailty.

As for Pope Clement VII, he faced in James V a young man with a very old head on his shoulders. James might impress Clement by promising 'to banish the foul Lutheran sect' from Scotland, but there was a price to be paid for his orthodoxy. With Henry VIII leading England into heresy in 1532, King James's influence with the pope increased; he used it to confirm royal privileges over the church, to screw money out of his own clergy and to have Clement VII acquiesce in the appointment of four of his bastard infant sons to major Scottish benefices. It was all polite blackmail, driven perhaps by material rather than spiritual considerations; but it was extremely effective in augmenting Scottish crown revenues.

Thus when Henry VIII came to negotiate seriously with James V, he was dealing with a Scottish king who had acquired firm control of church and state in a remarkably short time. In 1530, still fearing an English attempt to re-impose Angus on Scotland, James had taken the precaution of warding most of the border lords; there was no backlash, apart from the young and foolish Patrick, third earl of Bothwell, who in December 1531 offered to assist Henry VIII in an invasion of Scotland. The earl was punished by warding (temporary custody) followed by exile. By February 1535, therefore, when Henry VIII conferred the Order of the Garter on James V, James had no need to respond to his uncle's blandishments. He was well aware that Henry hoped to prevent him from contracting a French or Imperial marriage; but really Henry had little to offer by way of alternative. His marriage to Anne Boleyn in 1533 raised the possibility of male heirs and would affect James V's place in the English succession; and Henry was not willing to respond to James's request for the hand of his daughter Mary. Later Henry recommended to his nephew that James should follow his lead and dissolve the monasteries; but James was already milking the Church financially to such an extent that the idea, even had he wished to pursue it, would have brought him immense problems and little, if any, additional wealth. In effect, by the mid-1530s, the English diplomatic cupboard was bare; and with the breakdown of the Anglo-French alliance and Henry VIII's subsequent pursuit of an understanding with the Emperor from 1536 – a diplomatic revolution, as Gordon Donaldson calls it – the effective renewal of the Franco-Scottish alliance was only a matter of time.

On September 1536 James V set sail from Kirkcaldy in a fleet of six ships headed by the *Mary Willoughby*, taking with him trusted members of his household including David Beaton, abbot of Arbroath, the privy seal and an escort of 500 men. Probably as a matter of prudence, the king also had with him the young James Hamilton, second earl of Arran, his heir presumptive since Albany's death at the beginning of June. For the first time in over two hundred years a Scottish king was voluntarily leaving his kingdom – not as a refugee, but to have a nine-month holiday in France at the French king's expense and to contract a prestigious French marriage. It says a great deal for James's – justified – confidence in his strength and authority in Scotland that he could appoint six vice-regents to rule in his absence, and was in no hurry to return.

The marriage proposed was to Mary of Bourbon, daughter of the duke of Vendôme. The negotiations had been entrusted to the duke of Albany, in what proved to be his last public act on behalf of his nephew; and the marriage contract had been drawn up in March 1536, at the same time as James V was duping Henry VIII by agreeing to a meeting with the English king in the autumn. In the autumn, however, King James was already in France, landing at Dieppe on 10 September and heading due east to the duke of Vendôme's court at St Quentin in Picardy, to inspect the prospective bride. Reports that Mary of Bourbon was physically less than attractive are perhaps confirmed by the fact that the Scottish king, on seeing her portrait, demanded a pension of 20,000 *livres* on top of the dowry of 100,000 crowns.

James V's trip to France marked the end – or almost the end – of a tortuous period of matrimonial negotiations which stretched back to 1516 and involved the consideration of no less than seventeen brides. Four were Danish, two were proposed by the Emperor, one was Scottish, James's mistress Margaret Erskine, one Italian, Albany's niece Catharine de Medici, and one English, Henry VIII's daughter Mary; but no less than eight were French, a clear indication, in spite of the greatly changed Europe in which it was functioning, of the durability of the Auld Alliance.

Two Weddings and a Funeral (1537–42)

A later commentator remarked that 'there was nothing but merriness, banqueting and great cheer' at St Quentin. But there was no wedding. James V inspected Mary of Bourbon (whether he did so in disguise or not is a moot point), and returned to Rouen, the Scottish headquarters in France during the visit. James was in pursuit of a richer prize than even the duke of Vendôme's daughter, the bride promised to him before her birth as part of the Treaty of Rouen of 1517. By 15 October 1536, French sources were already suggesting that James V would be marrying Madeleine, Francis' daughter. The details were presumably arranged during a tour of the Loire valley – Moulins, Amboise, Châtelherault and Blois – in October and November. On 26 November a new marriage contract was drawn up, and on New Year's Day 1537, James V married Madeleine of France in the cathedral of Nôtre Dame in Paris.

The Scottish king was in no hurry to return home. February 1537 found the royal couple at Chantilly and Compiègne, where James received marks of papal favour – a ceremonial sword and hat – together with an admonition to support France against heretic England. James V, enjoying himself drinking Bordeaux wine and spending 1,100 crowns on a diamond for Madeleine's 'spousing' ring, probably needed no such admonition. At Rouen on 3 April, shortly before his 25th birthday, James issued his Act of Revocation, allowing him to revoke all grants of land and offices which had been made during his minority, and even those made 'by evil or false suggestion' since his assumption of power in 1528. The fact that James could do this in France, where he had already spent close on eight months, without fear of repercussions at home, is a clear indication of his mastery within his own kingdom; and he was now the son-in-law of the king of France.

But not for long. Francis I had probably meant it when he repeatedly excused his daughter from the Scottish match on account of her frailty. Already, in March 1537, she had been ill at Rouen. She left Le Havre with her husband on 10 May, arriving at Leith nine days later. But on 7 July, aged only 17, Madeleine died at Holyrood Palace. The premature death of 'the flower of France and comfort of Scotland' was duly lamented in a long poem by Sir David Lindsay of the Mount, who saw Madeleine as 'the confirmation of the weill keipit ancient alyance maid betuix Scotland and the realme of France'. Lindsay's 'Deploratioun' contains not only formal praise of Madeleine, but lengthy lamentations over what might have been, the Renaissance pageantry surrounding the queen's formal entry into Edinburgh, for which Lindsay as a royal herald would have had a major role in planning. He was, however, to be compensated for his disappointment in less than a year.

For James V wasted little time in plunging back into the European marriage market, on this occasion with a much clearer focus than ever before. During his French holiday he had met Mary, duchess of Longueville, daughter of Claud of Guise-Lorraine, duke of Aumale. Mary of Guise, as she is popularly known, was widowed about a month before James V; her obvious attractions included Catholic orthodoxy, maturity, her birth into one of the great houses of France, and enormous wealth. The Scottish king would have no second trip to France; negotiations were conducted by David Beaton, soon to become archbishop of St Andrews, whose forceful diplomacy won him the small bishopric of Mirepoix in the south of France, and – eventually – a cardinal's hat in December 1538. A ruthlessly ambitious career cleric, Beaton may be regarded, a generation on, as a more successful version of Andrew Forman.

Beaton's success lay partly in negotiating the Mary of Guise marriage in the face of strong competition from James V's uncle Henry VIII, who was once more a widower following the death of his third wife Jane Seymour. The marriage contract was drawn up in January 1538. A proxy marriage took place in May, and Mary of Guise sailed for Scotland early the following month, landing at Balcomie, near Crail in Fife, on 10 June. Sir David Lindsay had his chance at last, arranging the festivities for the queen's entry into St Andrews on Whit Sunday, and taking part in the more formal celebrations for her entry into Edinburgh the following month. On 22 February 1540, already six months pregnant, Mary of Guise was crowned at Holyrood. James V, who must have been more comfortable than his wife, used the occasion to wear the newly remodelled and enriched Scottish imperial crown.

The king was certainly comfortable financially as the result of his two French marriages. Together the dowries for Madeleine and Mary of Guise amounted to £168,759 Scots, dwarfing James IV's paltry £35,000 for Margaret Tudor in 1503–5. And the Stewart dynasty appeared secure through the prompt births, in 1540 and 1541, of two legitimate sons, James and Arthur, to offset the king's illegitimate brood by no less than six mistresses.

In some ways, the years 1537–42 marked the zenith of the Auld Alliance. James V's 'imperial' pretensions are demonstrated not only in the remodelled Scottish crown, but also on his superb gold coinage, the 'bonnet piece' of 1539, and on the contemporary portrait of the king and Mary of Guise. Above all, King James's determination to show that he was a ruler of European significance found expression in architecture. To some extent, he was following the example set by John, duke of Albany, who had used French workmen to add to Holyrood Palace and Edinburgh Castle. But James V's most remarkable creations – a Renaissance palace at Stirling and a remodelled and extended palace at Falkland in Fife – were probably inspired by his tour of the Loire valley with Francis I in the late autumn of 1536. The Falkland ranges have been compared with Francis I's château of Villers-Cotterets, started in 1533, while the portrait roundels in Falkland's north range bear comparison with many French buildings, including the Hôtel d'Alluye in Blois, which James would certainly have seen. At Falkland, and probably also at Stirling, the Scottish king employed French masons, including Nicholas Roy and Mogin Martin. The accounts of the royal master of works survive for this period, and show an expenditure on royal buildings of at least £41,000; Mary of Guise, suitably impressed, declared Linlithgow the finest palace which she had seen.

Thus the French alliance provided James V with European prestige, money, and legitimate male heirs. Its principal disadvantage was that it provoked an increasingly frustrated Henry VIII into bitter enmity. Fears of encirclement by a hostile Empire and France, backed by Scotland, led him to put increasing pressure on the Scots. He proposed a meeting with James V at York in September 1541, and made the long journey north; but James did not appear, probably because of his council's fears that he would be kidnapped by Henry VIII. This would have created a very dangerous situation, because in the spring of 1541 James had suffered the double blow of the loss of both his sons, James and Arthur, and in September had no surviving heir. The Anglo-Scottish war of 1542, however, only followed after a further eleven months of tortuous negotiations. The danger to Henry VIII from a Franco-Imperial alliance had abated somewhat by 1541, as the two great powers had once again turned against each other and both were looking for England's aid. Thus the immediate cause of war between England and Scotland in the autumn of 1542 was Henry VIII's failure to obtain an assurance from James V that he would not support Francis I in the event of an English attack on France. In some ways, it was 1513 all over again.

The results of the autumn war were mixed. In August the earl of Huntly, Scottish lieutenant in the temporary absence of James V's half-brother Moray, who was sick, won a victory over an English invading force under Sir Robert Bowes at Hadden Rig in the east march. A further English army, led by the duke of Norfolk, crossed the border, burned Kelso Abbey, and would have been opposed by the Scottish host under James V himself, who called for a muster of part of the army at Lauder in October; but Norfolk fell ill and disbanded his army at Berwick at the end of the month. James had moved to Peebles by November; he was not present when, in a sideshow on the River Esk on 24 November – subsequently described as Solway Moss – a Scottish raiding party under Lord Maxwell was out-manoeuvred by Sir Thomas Wharton, the English warden-depute, and, caught between a bog and a river, 'lighted at the water's side and fought valiantly' (according to a contemporary English account), subsequently surrendering as an alternative to drowning in the Esk.

By 28 November 1542, James V was back in Edinburgh, giving orders for the further defence of the west march. In early December entries in the treasurer's accounts indicate royal preparations for a renewal of the war in the spring. On 8 December, at Linlithgow Palace, Mary of Guise bore the king a daughter, Mary. However, six days later, at Falkland Palace, James V died, possibly of cholera. He had been ill many times during the personal rule – in 1533, 1534, in Paris in 1536 and in 1540 – of complaints variously described as fevers of the pox. He was thirty years of age.

With the single exception of the recent scholarly biography of the king by Jamie Cameron, James V has not been treated kindly by historians; and a myth has grown up about his character and policies which is the more durable for having started within a generation of his death. A combination of benefit of hindsight – the Protestant Reformation of 1560 – and wishful thinking on the part of contemporary English diplomats created a picture of James V as a 'priest's king', a man out of step with his nobility – indeed conducting something akin to a reign of terror against them in his last years – who stubbornly adhered to the French and papist alliance and was very properly abandoned by his own subjects in time of war. Plunged into melancholy at the end – the birth of a daughter being the last straw – he muttered about the imminent end of the dynasty, turned his face to the wall, and expired. This myth of James V found its most persuasive modern advocate in Gordon Donaldson, who remarked with something approaching Old Testament severity that 'however far the views of sixteenth-century narrators and modern psychologists might go to explain James V's character, they do little to lessen the revulsion with which he must be regarded'.

It would be inappropriate to replace Donaldson's moralising with propaganda on behalf of James V. Unlike his popular father, he was not generous in his patronage to his supporters; and he could be ruthless in pursuit of those guilty of treason, as the execution of the Master of Forbes and the burning of Lady Glamis in 1537 clearly showed. But though on occasions he employed what Jenny Wormald has aptly termed 'sharp practice' against some of his nobility, he was no more guilty in this respect that the popular James IV; and it is significant that he was widely supported throughout the 1542 war. Even Lord Maxwell's raid, which ended in failure at Solway Moss, was an example of a Scottish force crossing the border, seemingly unaware of the 'Flodden complex' with which they were supposedly afflicted.

Equally unconvincing is the portrayal of James V as a 'priest's king'. It is of course true that he spent much of the reign screwing money out of the first estate, and that the clergy contributed hugely towards the cost of the 1542 war. But there was really nothing new in this; James IV, furthering his policy of 'liturgical nationalism', had raised huge sums from the clergy for a popular war in 1513. The difference between 1513 and 1542, it is argued, is the advent of the European Reformation and the spread of Lutheranism amongst James V's subjects. This is difficult to quantify. Certainly parliament had passed an act as early as 1525 – a mere eight years after Luther's protest – forbidding the importation of Lutheran books into Scotland. But the spread of heresy does not seem to have constituted a major problem for James V; in the thirty years after 1528 there were only twenty-one executions for Protestant heresy. In the 1570s the Protestant laird Robert Lindsay of Pitscottie made much of the appointment of the king's familiar, Sir James Hamilton of Finnart, as a judge to try heretics; Finnart, he claimed, promised James V that he would give heretics 'hott ersis for his pleasour and the kirkis'. Given the numbers involved, Finnart can have had very little job satisfaction.

In the post-Reformation era, James V's crimes were to have been an orthodox Catholic and the father of Mary Queen of Scots. The first of these attributes made him a consistent, though not uncritical, supporter of the Auld Alliance; but it did not involve him in the compilation of a 'black list' of heretics – 360 of them, including the earl of Arran and most of the major magnates – which was most likely a fabrication, possibly by Arran himself, early in the next reign. As to the latter, the birth of a daughter provided wonderful copy for Protestant chroniclers, including John Knox, an heretical priest turned reformer, who combined a sure instinct for self-preservation with a remarkable talent for creative writing. On his deathbed, according to Knox, the king had thoughts only of the fate of his favourite Oliver Sinclair of Pitcairn, at Solway Moss; after that defeat, sneered the reformer, James had visited a whore; and appropriately his last words were 'All is lost'. Pitscottie, by contrast, recounts James's most famous – and inaccurate – deathbed prophecy: 'It came with a lass, it will pass with a lass', referring to the Stewart dynasty's descent from Marjorie Bruce and likely extinction with Mary Queen of Scots. It was left to the staunchly Catholic bishop John Lesley to supply James V's most convincing last words: 'Scotland suld be afflicted with the Inglismen shortlie, and sourlie'.

James V died much too early; but he died a rich man, leaving around £26,000 in his treasure chests at Edinburgh Castle. And he died a committed supporter of the Auld Alliance. In the 1540s, this was not a perverse diplomatic stance. As Jamie Cameron reminds us, 'Henry VIII was the maverick monarch in 1542; James, like Charles V and Francis I, represented the prevalent orthodoxy'. Thus his premature death struck a tremendous blow to his dynasty and his kingdom. Early in January 1543, after James V's body had been brought from Fife across the Queensferry to its final resting place in Holyrood Abbey, and following an elaborate funeral devised by Sir David Lindsay of the Mount, there must have been many who had grave fears for the future.

'Extreme Necessity': the End of the Auld Alliance (1543–1560)

In what proved to be the final two decades of its formal existence, the Franco-Scottish alliance was strained to its limits and beyond by a bewilderingly rapid sequence of political, military, dynastic, and religious changes in those countries most directly affected by its terms. The Scots had lost their king; certainly they had an able and well-connected queen dowager in Mary of Guise, but she was still finding her way in the morass of Scottish politics. James Hamilton, earl of Arran, the heir presumptive to the infant Mary, was an inept and inconstant governor whose only loyalty was to the Hamilton interest; Cardinal David Beaton, archbishop of St Andrews, was a ruthless and committed supporter of the orthodox status quo; and at the centre of this political witches' brew was the life of a frail child whose marriage was nevertheless a matter of vital diplomatic concern in the first year of her existence.

Scotland's ally France, of little or no value to her in 1542, found herself faced with a bellicose Henry VIII and an Emperor anxious to renew the war. Fears of encirclement led to a renewed French interest in the old ally, and this proved to be an extremely expensive investment. The death of Francis I at the end of March 1547, two months after his rival Henry VIII, brought Henry II to the French throne, and commitment to Scotland increased hugely, mainly through the influence of Mary of Guise's brothers – Francis, duke of Guise, and Charles, cardinal of Lorraine – upon the new French king. The wars initiated by Charles VIII when he had invaded Italy in 1494, and which had continued intermittently ever since, were brought to an end by the peace of Cateau-Cambrésis (March–April 1559); and as part of the peace, Henry II's elder daughter, Elizabeth, was to marry Philip of Spain. At the beginning of July 1559, the wedding celebrations proved fatal to the French king; taking part in a joust with Montgomery, captain of the *Garde Ecossaise*, Henry II was pierced in the eye by a lance splinter and mortally wounded, dying on 10 July.

Scotland's enemy, the England of Henry VIII, was likewise afflicted with swift and bewildering changes. Henry died in 1547, to be succeeded by his three offspring in turn – the sickly Edward VI (1547–53), under whom Protestantism flourished; Mary (1553–8), who sought a *via media* and whose early years were fraught with religious and dynastic difficulties. Thus as regards Anglo-Scottish relations between 1543 and

1560, the death of Henry VIII in 1547 was an important turning point. It removed from the scene an aggressive ruler whose view of Scotland, at the beginning and end of his reign, had been that the northern kingdom was a client, or even vassal, state which must be coerced into submission; significantly the issue of overlordship was raised in both 1512 and 1542. Henry's death and the gradual dilution of his more bellicose policies, coupled with an inevitable weakness at the heart of an English government which lurched from support of radical Protestantism to Catholic orthodoxy and part of the way back again, provided obvious opportunities for England's enemies. France was one of the winners; Calais, the last English stronghold across the Channel, was lost to Francis, duke of Guise – Mary of Guise's brother – on 7 January 1558.

A Scotland united and strongly led would certainly have been able to take advantage of many of these changes. But the death of James V was rapidly followed by political chaos; a coup removed Cardinal Beaton, the head of the pro-French and papal party, and replaced him with the earl of Arran, who was acknowledged as Governor in March 1543. Arran had the support, for what it was worth, of the 'assured lords'; Scottish prisoners of Solway Moss who, in order to secure their release, agreed to further English interests in Scotland. In practical terms, what this amounted to was a recommendation, speedily adopted, by the most distinguished of the Solway Moss lords, Robert Lord Maxwell, that the scriptures should be issued in the vernacular.

The March parliament of 1543 was however responsible for authorising a step which went much too far for many Scots – the opening of negotiations with Henry VIII for the betrothal of the infant Queen Mary to the English king's son and heir Edward. Within a month Cardinal Beaton, who had been placed in ward, was free and had joined together with John Hamilton, abbot of Paisley, Arran's half-brother and the future archbishop of St Andrews, to reverse the governor's policy. Arran was reminded by the Scottish clergy that his legitimacy, and therefore his claim to the throne, depended upon ecclesiastical authority; that authority had annulled his father's first marriage, and could, if it chose, set aside his legitimacy. At the same time Matthew Stewart, fourth earl of Lennox, was brought over from France; as heir presumptive if Arran were declared illegitimate, Lennox in Scotland would surely help to concentrate the governor's mind.

Thus the summer of 1543 saw a remarkable volte-face in Scottish politics which set the Franco-Scottish alliance on its final course. Arran, having negotiated the Treaties of Greenwich (Anglo-Scottish alliance and marriage agreements, 1 July 1543), dithered and then ratified them towards the end of August, repudiated them almost immediately, renounced his policy of ecclesiastical reform and came to an understanding with Beaton (who, significantly, required the delivery of Arran's son as a hostage for the governor's good faith). By the end of a chaotic year, a Scottish parliament, meeting in December 1543, had denounced the Greenwich treaties, reaffirmed the laws against heresy, and cited Henry VIII's violation of the peace through the arrest of Scottish merchants and the seizure of their goods as a reason for abandoning the entire English package. Meanwhile Cardinal Beaton, who had transferred both the infant queen and her mother from Linlithgow to the relative safety of Stirling during the summer, was able to organise the coronation of Queen Mary, now nine months old, in the Chapel Royal of Stirling Castle on 9 September 1543. Thirty years to the day after the battle of Flodden, another Scottish government looked to repudiate an English alliance in favour of an accommodation with Scotland's longstanding but often fickle ally.

Henry VIII's predictable reaction was one of fury; and from May 1544 to the end of his life and beyond he sought to terrorise the Scots into accepting the repudiated English marriage; these 'Rough Wooings', recently graphically described by Marcus Merriman, were conducted by Edward Seymour, earl of Hertford, and consisted of English invasions in 1544, 1545, and 1547. The destruction caused, though not as frightful as suggested in Hertford's instructions before he set out, resulted in a devastated south-east, with the great border abbeys – Melrose, Jedburgh, Dryburgh and Kelso – and the more vulnerable abbeys of Newbattle and Holyrood all burned, together with the burghs of Haddington, Edinburgh, Leith, Craigmillar, Musselburgh, and Dunbar; in Fife Kinghorn, St Monans, Pittenweem, and Burntisland were all attacked. At the end of the fourteenth century Richard II had torched the border abbeys on the grounds that the Scots, as supporters of the anti-Pope during the Great Schism, were heretics and schismatics; now, 160 years later, the lieutenant of Henry VIII, former Defender of the Faith and now himself a heretic and schismatic, did the same thing. *Plus ça change* . . .

The challenge presented by the 'Rough Wooings' revealed hopeless splits amongst the Scots themselves. Some of this can be explained by the spread of Protestantism – first Lutheranism, then Calvinism – in some areas of the country, though its extent and its influence on Scottish politics have always been a source of controversy among historians. In some rural areas – Ayrshire, Angus and the Mearns, Fife and parts of the Lothians – reforming opinions are apparent from an early stage, supported by local members of the nobility but in no sense forming a national movement; in the burghs Protestantism was weaker still. As Michael Lynch has pointed out, as late as Easter, 1561, eight months after the Reformation parliament had abolished the mass, only 1,200 – that is one in six adults out of Edinburgh's population of 12,500 – went to John Knox's new Protestant communion. But numbers alone do not make a revolution; what mattered was the attitude of the leaders of society – magnates, lairds, and burgh councils – to reforming opinions, for these were the groups who had the power to promote change.

When considering an age in which the Most Christian King of France could make an alliance with the infidel Turkish Sultan against his co-religionist, the Emperor Charles V – as Francis I did in 1536 – it is perhaps dangerous to be too dogmatic about the extent to which the leaders of European society were moved primarily by religious considerations. In the case of the higher nobility in Scotland, politics – local and national – and dynastic considerations often seemed to dictate which side individuals favoured in the pre-Reformation decades. Thus Arran's dynastic rival, Matthew, earl of Lennox, invariably sided with opponents of the governor; Angus, the bane of James V's existence, was understandably an 'assured lord', loyal to

Henry VIII, in the early 1540s; but he changed sides in 1545, winning a victory over the English at Ancrum Moor, a few miles north of Jedburgh, in February of that year. Arran himself, taking advantage of the unpopularity of Cardinal Beaton and the French interest, proposed that Queen Mary should remain in Scotland and be married to his son. Thus as the '40s advanced there emerged powerful advocates of every conceivable shade of political opinion in Scotland, right across the spectrum from those who were prepared to take Henry VIII's money to others who were totally committed to the French alliance; those who blamed Henry VIII for the 'Rough Wooings', others who held Cardinal Beaton responsible for them; those who were attracted by Protestantism, and by extension, by amity with England, others who favoured Catholic reform, and some, like Beaton, who advocated, and sought to promote, the extirpation of heresy. The Scottish kingdom, lacking a king or even a capable regent, had not been so weak and divided since the 1290s.

On 29 May 1546, a few Fife lairds – opponents of the Cardinal, pro-English and pro-Reformation in outlook – broke into St Andrews Castle and assassinated Beaton; they then retained possession of the castle, called for English help, and – quaintly named the 'Castilians' – withstood an inept siege by Governor Arran – whose son was a hostage in the castle – for more than a year. However, in July 1547, a French fleet and expeditionary force invested St Andrews Castle; it fell at the end of the month, and the Castilians were either imprisoned in France or sent to the galleys.

This temporary success was followed by an appalling reverse only six weeks later. Edward Seymour, earl of Hertford, Lord Protector of England since Henry VIII's death the previous January, shattered a huge Scottish army assembled by Arran at Pinkie, near Musselburgh, on 10 September 1547. Divisions amongst the Scottish leadership may have been as much responsible for the defeat as anything else: Arran had little in common with Angus, and the Scottish clergy saw themselves as conducting yet another crusade against heretics and schismatics. The Scottish losses were enormous; worse, unlike the aftermath of Flodden, Pinkie was followed by a widespread English garrisoning of strongpoints in the south-east and east, with their main centre at Haddington and troops posted as far north as Broughty, near Dundee. And many Scots, especially in the east, began as a matter or urgency to look to peace with England as essential, outweighing any possible loyalty to an ancient alliance whose principal supporters could not defend the country, or, for that matter, capture St Andrews Castle without French help.

Therein lay the problem for any Scottish government acting in Queen Mary's name. The choice lay between English or French domination; for the new king of France, Henry II, was prepared to intervene on the side of his old allies only on his own terms. After Pinkie, it is unsurprising that the Scots accepted these with little negotiation. Queen Mary, then in her sixth year, had been sent for safety to the priory of Inchmahome, on an island in the Lake of Menteith, during the Pinkie campaign. In January 1548 Arran, who was so unpopular that he did not dare to set foot on the streets of Edinburgh, agreed that, in return for a French dukedom for himself, he would secure Scottish parliamentary consent for Queen Mary's marriage to the dauphin Francis, and would arrange for the infant queen to be conveyed to

France. Arran, putting the Hamilton interest first as ever, also acquired the marriage of the elder daughter of the duke of Montpensier for his son and heir, and an agreement that he would not be pursued for financial claims arising out of his period as governor; he had had the advantage of the use of James V's sizeable monetary legacy for a few years, and may have misappropriated some of it to feather the Hamilton nest. In February 1549 Arran secured his own prestigious bolt-hole, the dukedom of Châtelherault.

Arran's machinations provided the background to the last formal renewal of the Auld Alliance. Unquestionably, Henry II of France regarded Scotland simply as a pawn – though an important one – in his wars with England, and initially believed that the Scots could hold on against what Gordon Donaldson colourfully describes as England's 'action for breach of promise'; but Pinkie and its aftermath changed all that, and French fears of an Anglo-Scottish union based on the marriage of Mary to Edward VI produced a sensational French financial and military commitment – at least £1,000,000 Scots and 6,000 troops – to the defence of Scotland. In his demand for a huge *aide* to finance the war, Henry II spoke of Scotland's 'extreme necessity' and urged the maintenance of an alliance which stretched back for centuries to 'le Roy Charlemaigne'. His view of Scotland, however, cogently expressed in September 1550, was not one which would have found favour with many Scots, whatever their political or religious affiliations. Commenting on his recent success in the war, Henry II remarked: 'I have brought peace to Scotland which I hold and possess with the same order and obedience that I have in France.'

The first French forces in Scotland arrived at Leith, and a joint Franco-Scottish army immediately laid siege to Haddington. On 7 July 1548, in the nunnery outside the town, the formal acceptance by the Scots of their queen's marriage to the dauphin Francis was enshrined in the Treaty of Haddington. Thereafter south-east Scotland became a cockpit for an Anglo-French war in which the English were not dislodged from Haddington by Franco-Scottish assaults, but rather by news of events on the continent, where the English garrison was expelled from Boulogne.

The 'Rough Wooing' was over; and already Mary Queen of Scots had reached the comparative safety of France. After lying off Dumbarton for a week at the beginning of August 1548, waiting for a fair wind, the young queen sailed for Brittany in the ship of Nicolas Durand, lord of Villegaignon, arriving at Roscoff by 18 August. Thereafter she was escorted overland at an easy pace, reaching St Denis in the middle of October. Her life for the next decade was spent at the French court, a travelling circus which moved regularly among the royal palaces of St-Germain, Fontaine-bleau, Blois and Chambord. Educated together with members of Henry II's family, Mary was reunited with her mother only once, when Mary of Guise visited France in 1550–51; but Guise influence was constantly present in the shape of Mary's grandmother Antoinette, and her uncles, the duke and cardinal of Guise. On 24 April 1558 the last great ceremony of the Auld Alliance took place in front of the cathedral of Notre Dame in Paris: Mary, Queen of Scots, aged fifteen, was married to the fourteen-year-old dauphin Francis. Twenty-one years before, Mary's father had married the daughter of the king of France on the same spot; but James V had been an adult sovereign in full control of his realm. Mary was a minor in the pocket of the Guises.

Her absence from Scotland during the 1550s left her mother, Mary of Guise, as the principal political player, more than a match for the earl of Arran, who was finally removed from the governorship, and Mary of Guise appointed regent, in the parliament of April 1554. The Queen Mother played her political cards skilfully, displaying toleration towards the Reformers, buying support through liberal distribution of pensions and, where appropriate, the Order of St Michael; and she had the good fortune to take control when, in England, the radical Protestantism of Edward VI had been succeeded by the firm Catholic orthodoxy of Mary Tudor.

Yet Mary of Guise may have been swimming against the tide. Already in 1552, with France and the Empire once again at war, the Scots had refused to resume hostilities on behalf of their ally, or to send troops to serve in the French army. So much for Henry II's boast that he had brought Scotland to order and obedience. And there is no doubt that the Frenchmen on whom the Queen Mother relied for counsel – De Roubay, the Vice-Chancellor, Villemore, the Comptroller, and perhaps above all D'Oysel, the resident French ambassador – were disliked by more than those whose political positions they usurped.

In the end, it was events outwith Scotland which broke the alliance. On 17 November 1558, Mary Tudor died and the English succession went to her sister Elizabeth, whose administration moved cautiously towards a Protestant stance. The death of Henry II of France the following July made his sickly son king of France as Francis II; and Mary, Queen of Scots, his wife, became queen of France, and, on the basis that Elizabeth was illegitimate (a view taken by many English Catholics), Francis II and Mary assumed the titles and arms of sovereigns of England. The new English queen, fearing that the French – freed from war in Europe by the Treaty of Cateau-Cambrésis – would use Scotland as a base to launch an attack on England, was prepared to give some cautious support to the Scottish Reformers. Aware that Mary, as queen of France, was unlikely ever to return to Scotland, Elizabeth sought her deposition there; but who could possibly succeed Mary? Her half-brother, Lord James Stewart, James V's eldest surviving bastard, could perhaps be the power behind the throne, but he could never sit on it. The alternative, hardly a popular one, was Arran in his new role as Châtelherault, and temporarily reconciled to Protestantism.

Scottish civil war had broken out between Mary of Guise and the Protestant 'Lords of the Congregation' in 1559; the Queen Mother, who was well served by professional French soldiers, would probably have won the day if there had been no outside interference; but English troops entered Scotland in March 1560, and an English fleet had already entered the Firth of Forth to blockade the principal French stronghold of Leith. Once again an Anglo-French struggle was being fought out in south-east Scotland. Its outcome, however, was decided when Mary of Guise, who had steadfastly refused to negotiate on any terms but the insurgents' return to their allegiance, died of dropsy in Edinburgh Castle on 11 June 1560.

At a stroke Guise influence was removed from Scotland; English and French commissioners moved to Edinburgh and concluded the Treaty of Edinburgh on 6 July. English and French troops were to withdraw from Scotland; it was suggested that Mary Queen of Scots, absent in France, should give up use of the English arms and thus recognise Elizabeth's title as Queen of England; and the selection of a Scottish council was to be entrusted jointly to a parliament and to Mary herself. That parliament, meeting in August 1560, abolished the mass and adopted a reformed Confession of Faith, but did nothing to inhibit the jurisdiction of the leading Catholic clergy within their benefices.

Neither the Treaty of Edinburgh nor the statutes of the 'Reformation' parliament would be ratified by Francis II and Mary Queen of Scots. The Scots had carried through a dubious political and religious revolution which had left them in a kind of limbo, at odds with their sovereign yet having no alternative to Mary but Châtelherault, and no clear future save as an English client state. But any Scottish search for security in England suddenly became irrelevant on 5 December 1560, when Francis II, Mary's adolescent husband, died of an ear infection in spite of frantic Guise threats against his physicians and public prayers for his recovery. Guise influence at the French court collapsed in December 1560, just as it had failed in Scotland six months earlier with the death of Mary of Guise. And the Auld Alliance, arguably long obsolete in the changed European world of the mid-sixteenth century and sustained only by a French commitment to the domination of Scotland, was at an end.

Scottish Politics in the Reign of James VI

J Goodare 2000 *in* J Goodare and M Lynch (eds), *The Reign of James VI*, East Linton (Tuckwell Press), 32–54.

The minority of King James VI ended on 12 March 1578. The regent, the earl of Morton, was forced to resign by a hostile aristocratic coalition, and James was declared to be of age. Morton had helped to lead the English-backed 'king's party' to victory in the civil wars of 1567–73 against the supporters of James's mother, the deposed Mary; he had governed as regent since 1572. Although he had done quite an efficient job, Morton had made many enemies, who now elbowed him aside.

But James was still far from being able to govern Scotland himself. he was not yet twelve years old, and remained at school in Stirling Castle, under the charge of Alexander Erskine, master of Mar. Six weeks after James's 'acceptation' of the government, Morton's faction staged a counter-coup (26 April) with the aid of Erskine's nephew, the young earl of Mar, who had been a schoolmate of the king and was now aged about seventeen. There was a fight in the great hall of the castle, with the terrified king looking on; several men were killed, including Erskine's son. A parliament was summoned to ratify the change of regime; it met on 15 July in the great hall. It was against tradition for parliament to meet inside a castle, and there were complaints that there was no free access for the subjects to give in their petitions. James was brought in to declare, prompted by Morton: 'Least any man sould judge this not to be a free parliament, I declare it to be free; and those that love me will thinke as I think.'[1]

I

This chapter is about patterns in the politics of James's reign in Scotland, and the part the king played in them. Politics is about seeking power about winning power, and about using power. In order to act politically, people have to enter into associations. Although the monarch may be 'absolute' – James certainly said that he was – this still applied to him. He had to work with the people he agreed with and who would support him, in order to get what he wanted against the people who wanted something different.

So it is necessary to look for patterns of consensus between people who joined together to seek a common aim – such as the control of Stirling Castle. The pattern here was that nobles and their followers joined together against other nobles and *their* followers. Rivalries were horizontal ones, between nobles of roughly equal status, and the disputes did not have to be about different political programmes. No obvious principles linked the leaders of the anti-Morton faction in 1578, the earls of Atholl, Argyll and Montrose; indeed Atholl and Argyll had only recently ended a quarrel in order to join against Morton. They simply felt that they could get more power by displacing Morton than by co-operating with him. As for the dispute within the Erskine family, between Alexander Erskine and his nephew the earl of Mar, it was entirely about personalities. Disputes within families, however, were unusual, for one of the basic patterns of traditional politics was that families would stick together to seek advancement against rival families.

Consensus can be sought at a deeper level, by finding out what the rules of the game were. Both factions in a political struggle may recognise the same rules. This was certainly so on 26 April 1578: when Alexander Erskine was confronted by a group demanding the keys of the castle, his immediate reaction was to grab a halberd and attack them, while they were equally well prepared for a fight. Both sides knew that their political position depended on the force they could command. The demand for the keys did have some colour of legitimacy, based on the claim that Erskine's nephew, the earl of Mar, was the hereditary and rightful keeper of the castle. Erskine could have replied that it was a royal castle and that the keepership had been granted to him personally; but there were no authorities who could adjudicate this dispute peacefully.

Patterns of conflict also have to be identified. It is obvious enough that there were conflicts between rival nobles at the outset of the reign, and we can look at how nobles became enemies. There could be disputes over local spheres of influence: nobles and their families often sought to dominate a particular territory. Once a noble had asserted a claim to some property or other rights, the conventions of honour demanded that the claim be vindicated – by force if necessary – whether or not it was legally well-grounded. Not only had honour to be upheld, but insults to it had to be revenged; disputes thus led to bloodfeuds that were sometimes carried on for years or even generations.[2]

These feuds were often simply miniature private wars, fought out in the locality, with no reference to central authority. Sometimes the dispute did involve the crown, either directly or indirectly. Atholl's quarrel with Argyll arose over his office of royal lieutenant, giving him a jurisdiction over Argyll's lands that the latter resisted. But nobles' feuds were usually settled by resort to violence; royal justice, if involved at all, usually did no more than ratify the outcome. If Argyll had defeated Atholl, the crown would have had to help settle the feud by revoking the latter's lieutenancy: anything else would have been politically impossible. Settled, however, bloodfeuds always were, for as well as a readiness to fight, the Scottish nobles had traditions of negotiation, compromise, and compensation for injuries done. Historians used to deplore this pattern of politics as the 'turbulence' of a 'lawless' nobility; nowadays we are more likely to see it as a functional system of autonomous dispute-settlement. But if we take a benign, or at least neutral, view of the bloodfeud, James did not; when he grew up, hostility to it would become a cornerstone of his policies.

While most rivalries between nobles were purely local, those that were played out on the national stage constituted national politics. The normal pattern of politics in the 1570s was that of factionalism – as it had been for generations. A faction was a group within the government or ruling elite, usually headed by a leading noble. The faction sought more power for itself by elbowing aside its rivals. In a monarchical state like Scotland, this was done by a combination of persuasion and mild coercion, directed at the king; the faction either persuaded the king of its value, or made itself indispensable, whereupon it could demand the removal of its opponents. Sometimes rival factions espoused different policies; thus the 'king's party' in the civil war had staunchly upheld the English alliance (on which they depended for support), while the 'queen's party' had sought French or Spanish aid. But that was an unusually deep political rift; the factions could not even agree who should be the monarch. Factions did not have to have policies. Often the rivalry was simply about who would have access to the king and to a share in royal power.

Factions were held together by personal ties between lords and followers. Traditionally, nobles recruited followers through kinship and land tenure: they had a network of lesser landed kinsmen in their territory. The follower might hold land directly from the lord, who was then his feudal superior, although that was not essential. This was what anthropologists call a gift-exchange relationship, not a contractual one: the lord gave free gifts (of land or other resources) to his followers, who in return recognised his overlordship and generosity, and served him freely out of gratitude. The system of lordship worked because it benefited both lord and follower.

This system could also use patronage. Here, a lord used his court influence to procure grants of *crown* land or government office for his followers, thus strengthening their faction's position. This was also a gift-exchange relationship, in which clients were grateful for the benevolence of their patrons. Although the follower held his grant from the crown, his primary loyalty was still to his patron. This was one of the reasons why a faction wanted to win favour: it could gain rewards for its members.

Lordship in the traditional sense was largely independent of the crown. Nobles in the 1570s wielded much the same kind of power whether in or out of favour. They used their locally-based client networks, with which they could offer to serve the crown (or not). As a result, there was a danger that factional crises could lead to noble revolts. If two factions came into such serious conflict that they could no longer tolerate one another's presence, each would try to get the other ejected from court, and this could lead to fighting. The king might wish to be served by both factions, but they would try to force him to choose between them.

By the 1570s, some broader principles had begun to make inroads into these traditional patterns of politics. Scotland had become an officially Protestant country in 1560; a few nobles were determined to reverse the Reformation if they could, while another group were committed to the maintenance and extension of Protestantism. For most, however, the religious status quo was broadly acceptable without arousing fervent passions. The nobles *would* have resisted any threat to their possession of secularised church property, but any such threat was at least as likely to come from radical Protestants (who sought a better-endowed church) as from Catholics.

A related question of principle was that of Scotland's international allegiance. The 'auld alliance' between France and Scotland, based on mutual hostility to England, had collapsed in 1560, and a Scottish regime sympathetic to England had been installed by English arms. This was bolstered both by direct intervention (English armies again entered Scotland in 1570 and 1573) and by the fostering of a pro-English party among the Scottish nobility. This was linked to religion, because England was Protestant, France Catholic; the Protestant party and the supporters of the so-called 'amity' with England tended to overlap. Others, however, resented Scotland's dependence on England; in the 1580s and 1590s, they turned increasingly to Spain, now the premier Catholic power.

As a result, these essentially *ideological* questions could form the basis for factions, or could at least influence factions. If ideology should come to be dominant it would produce a different pattern of politics. People would not take orders from their patrons as powerful protectors whom it was honourable to serve and dangerous to disobey; they would do so because they believed in the cause. This pattern emerged only gradually, but it will need further attention later on.

II

After James's 'acceptatioun' of the government in 1578, there were still seven more years before he finally emerged from tutelage. These were years of constant factional turmoil, with at least six palace coups, five of which were successful. In August 1582, a pro-English faction kidnapped the king in the so-called 'Ruthven Raid' and ruled for ten months against his will.

Political patterns sometimes stand out clearly in a snapshot of the political community in action, such as is provided by meetings of parliament. Scottish parliaments were gatherings of the entire political community, the 'three estates' of clergy, nobles and burgesses. They took or at least ratified, most of the big, contentious political decisions. Parliaments also made new laws and imposed taxes, but these were not common until the later 1580s. Along with parliaments, the Scots also held 'conventions of estates', which were parliaments in almost all but name, and were particularly useful for taking political decisions.

Two examples will illustrate patterns of politics early in the reign. The first is the convention of estates of June 1578 that granted Morton the 'first rowme and place in counsale', setting the seal on his political comeback.[3] The convention was not ratifying a decision already made elsewhere, for there was actually a vote – a rare occurrence in this period; Morton's faction won by 25 votes to 23. The spiritual estate was made up of eight bishops and eight 'commendators' of monasteries.[4] The noble estate consisted of nine earls, eleven lords and two lords' sons. There were nine burgesses for the burgess estate. Most of those present – and almost all of the nobles, the group who really counted – were active members of one faction or the other, as can be seen by comparing the attendance and voting records with contemporary lists of 'malecontentes' (Atholl's group) and 'biencontentes' (Morton's).[5] The whole convention was a struggle between two factions for supremacy, in which there were few innocent bystanders. It failed to convince the defeated faction; next month, Atholl, Argyll and Montrose raised an army in an attempt to regain power, while Morton did the same in order to keep it. There was no fighting, and a new compromise was reached – without a convention this time;[6] the anti-Morton faction was eventually crippled by Atholl's death in April 1579, and Morton enjoyed another eighteen months in power.

A different kind of parliament was held towards the end of James's tutelage, in May 1584. The dominant man in the government was now James Stewart, earl of Arran, who had risen to power after the collapse of the Ruthven regime. Arran's parliament, much better attended than the 1578 convention, amounted to more than a meeting of two rival groups.[7] But factionalism was still apparent in the attendance. One group was conspicuously absent – those among the Ruthven lords who had carried out the failed Stirling Raid the previous month; the parliament forfeited them. There were several former Ruthven Raiders, but they were mostly lesser figures. No Ruthven supporters were chosen to be the lords of the articles, the key committee that managed parliamentary business. By contrast, four Catholic earls were at the parliament;[8] all were on the Articles, showing that the regime's centre of gravity was conservative. Arran, himself a Stewart, seems to have attempted to construct a Stewart connection: there were eleven Stewart nobles and commendators present.

The 1584 parliament was also significant for what it *did*. It did not just ratify Arran's possession of power; it enabled him to do new things with that power. The church, which had been organised independently of the state since the Reformation of 1560, had used that independence to back the Ruthven faction; it was now to be brought under government control. A series of statutes (dubbed the 'Black Acts' by critics) asserted royal supremacy over the church and ordered that it was to be governed by crown-appointed bishops, not by presbyteries.[9] There was to be a new royal guard, funded on a lavish scale from the revenues of the monasteries (which were largely in nobles' hands). Censorship was tightened by an act banning speeches contemptuous of the king or his council.[10]

Arran fell from power in November 1585, removed by a noble coalition backed by the English government and including a number of former Ruthven Raiders. The king, aged nineteen, was now in a position where he could begin to govern for himself. The transition was a smooth and gradual one. Arran's regime had based itself upon the monarchy and the institutions of the state, rather than manipulating them in the interests of specific families. This explains not only why Arran was overthrown so easily – his officials, like the secretary, John Maitland of Thirlestane, were primarily loyal to the crown and not to him – but also why the regime that succeeded him, now under the leadership of James himself, continued his policies: enhancement of state authority, particularly over the church, but also over the autonomous power of the nobility; and closer connection with England.[11]

From 1585 to 1589 there was a temporary political consensus – or perhaps simply a lull in the intensity of factional conflict. This facilitated some progress in the extension of state authority. James's leading adviser here was Maitland, who became chancellor in 1587. Arran had begun a new use of parliament, using statutes as weapons to coerce recalcitrant subjects into religious conformity. James and Maitland used parliament more intensively than ever before. Legislation was called for on many topics, since the law was not intended to settle disputes that formerly had been settled through feuds. Parliamentary taxation was extended, to support more intensive government. All this was achieved through parliaments that were broadly based, not simply the weapons of a faction. One change masterminded by Maitland was the admission of lairds to parliament in 1587, as shire commissioners. The obvious intention was to offset the power of the nobility by granting those below them an independent voice in central government. It was probably also hoped to create a wider political consensus for government decisions. Taxation would be hard to collect if the political community had not been seen to consent to it. This bolstered the regime, but it also stored up problems for the future.

The issue of international allegiance was settled, finally as it turned out, in 1586, when James signed a treaty with England and accepted a regular subsidy from Elizabeth. This was not universally popular, but it ended English destabilisation of the kind that had damaged Arran. The price was the acceptance of Scotland's status as a satellite state: although still independent, it had to defer to English wishes on important matters. This fitted with James's personal interests: he had a good claim to succeed Queen Elizabeth on the English throne, so he had to stay on good terms with her while she lived. If he occasionally negotiated with her enemies, this was largely a gesture to increase his value to her.

Apart from the English succession, James's main concern up to about 1598 was his authority over the nobility. He felt that he could not rule effectively if the nobles pursued their own disputes without reference to his authority. Factionalism at court, if he could not control it, posed the same problem. One of James's earliest declared intentions was to be a 'universal king' – to rule without being beholden to any one faction. He probably did not think he was innovating here; he merely aimed to establish himself as the respected and obeyed king of an orderly kingdom.

In fact, James *was* innovating. Past monarchs had always had to deal with nobles who were effectively autonomous, and who co-operated with the crown for what they could get out of it. Some monarchs – particularly James IV – had cultivated good relations with their nobles, and had reduced the problem of factionalism. But a state in which noble revolts were *impossible* would be a different kind of state from one in which king and leading nobles happened to be friends. All James's Stewart predecessors had faced noble revolts.[12]

James had no wish to get rid of the nobles; he was keen to have them as his courtiers and servants. This respect for an ideal of nobility, together with a dislike for much of what the nobles actually got up to, can make James's book, *Basilicon Doron*, seem contradictory. Nobles, he advised, were to be maintained at court and used in the 'greatest affaires', but there was a vagueness as to whether they were actually to be officers of state, running the government. Financial officers, at least, were to be 'meane, but responsall men'. He praised the severe justice of James V, but warned that too much contempt for the nobility (the same thing as his severe justice, in fact) 'brake the king my grand-fathers heart'.[13]

From 1589 until 1598, it sometimes seemed as if James was following in his grandfather's footsteps. Pressure on the nobility led to two active problems, and a third one in the background.

The active problems were two dissident earls: Huntly, a Catholic and anti-English schemer, and Bothwell, a Protestant and pro-English maverick. Both were hostile to Maitland, for whom it was fortunate that they were also hostile to one another. There was a factional crisis at court early in 1589, when Huntly attempted to eject Maitland from court, but failed and had to leave court himself. Thereafter he and two other Catholic earls intrigued with Spain – England's leading enemy – and used his great regional following in the north-east to lead several rebellions until his surrender to a royal army in 1594. Huntly was leniently treated; James, who himself had occasional contacts with Spain, felt that a well-established conservative magnate might be of service to him, though in the end Huntly proved incorrigible and was never trusted with governmental responsibility after his rehabilitation. As for Bothwell, who was no great magnate, he unluckily fell out with James in 1591, outlawed, he spent three years on the run, conducting daring raids on the royal palaces, before being forced into exile in 1595.

The background problem – the only one, indeed, that made the plottings of Huntly and the escapades of Bothwell serious – was the fact that most other nobles were disenchanted with the Maitland regime, which in the early 1590s was doing more to curb the nobility than *Basilicon Doron* (written in late 1598) might indicate. Lairds, as we have seen, had been officially admitted to parliament in 1587. The captaincy of the guard, Huntly's old job at court, was given to a laird in 1590. There was an effort to reduce nobles' role in the privy council and in parliamentary commissions; the exchequer – a largely noble-free institution – was given an expanded role in government. There was even an attempt to deny the nobles automatic access to the king's chamber. As a result, although few nobles joined Huntly or Bothwell, many sympathised with them. After Huntly's forfeiture in 1594, it was hard to find anyone who would go north and administer his estates; several nobles refused the task, and James had to appoint Huntly's brother-in-law, the duke of Lennox, who ensured that Huntly's interests were protected.[14] But, although nobody knew it at the time, Huntly's rebellion of 1594 was the last regional rebellion ever to take place in Scotland – except in the Highlands, which were not fully integrated into the state. To that extent, the regime of James and Maitland succeeded.

All this time, James had had fairly good relations with the church. After Arran's fall in 1585, Maitland discovered that it was possible to work with the radical presbyterians who had opposed him. This group had come to dominate the general assembly and had built a popular following in several key towns, including Edinburgh. They did not fit the traditional pattern of politics; the ties that linked them were based on ideology, not clientage. The presbyterians proved willing to co-operate with the government in return for the abandonment of bishops; without official support, the episcopal system shrivelled, and was formally abandoned in 1592. But the presbyterians were demanding partners. They wanted complete godliness from the king personally, from his queen, and from his government; exclusion of the ungodly, and especially any suspected Catholics, from royal service; and more generous funding – *much* more generous funding – for the parish ministry.

By 1594, the king's efforts to give the impression that he might be able to deliver all this were becoming increasingly strained; and after Huntly's surrender, the presbyterians were no longer so necessary as a counterweight to the Catholic earls. But it took them some time to realise this, and they were anyway too doctrinaire to be able to adjust to their new political position. Conflict was inevitable. The showdown came on 17 December 1596, when there was a religious riot in Edinburgh; the king fled, leaving the radicals apparently in control of the town. They appealed to godly noblemen such as Lord Hamilton, to back their cause – no insurgent movement at that time could survive without noble leadership – but were unsuccessful;[15] within days the king was back in control, and the leading presbyterians had to flee from the royalist clampdown.

From then onwards, committed presbyterians were systematically excluded from the political consensus. At first, James merely insisted that his authority should be recognised, which isolated the radical leadership. But he soon served notice that he intended to reintroduce bishops. It was this on which he had most to say in *Basilicon Doron*, and on which he spent most of his efforts to restructure the church. The presbyterian principle of 'paritie' in the ministry was also relevant to the secular government, 'for if by the example thereof, once established in the ecclesiasticall government, the politicke and civill estate should be drawn to the like, the great confusion that thereupon would arise may easily be discerned'.[16] A better argument to detach the nobility from the presbyterians could scarcely have been devised; but episcopalianism had long since lost its universal acceptability and had become, like presbyterianism, a divisive and confrontational ideology.

In June 1598, James would finally bring his nobles to accept that their disputes would have to be submitted to royal justice – the most significant turning-point in his reign, and the culmination of a long process of pressure and negotiation. James himself put much effort into mediating between his feuding nobles, while the church preached against the code of morals that sustained the bloodfeud. But one thing that speaks louder than words is money.

To explain the role of money in ending the bloodfeud, we must glance at the royal finances. James's government was innovative in its gathering of revenue, even though the king himself took no interest in it – money, to him, was something to be spent. Maitland, however, saw money as a political tool. He had launched a revitalised organ of central government, the permanent exchequer, in 1590; it involved itself in politics as well as managing the royal finances more actively. Maitland's involvement in finance may have been overlooked by historians who have treated him simply as a politician.[17] The exchequer became still more important, and more political, after Maitland's death in 1595. Power fell in January

1596 to a committee of eight exchequer auditors who became known as the Octavians. They exercised full control over the revenues, and attempted to reduce expenditure on the royal court – and on handouts to the nobility. This triggered off a new pattern of political factionalism, in which discontented nobles and courtiers combined to try to shake the Octavians' control of the purse-strings. They succeeded at a convention of estates in June 1598, where a deal was struck between king and nobles. The permanent exchequer – the Octavians' power-base – was abolished. In return, the convention passed a measure that the king had long sought in vain: an act agreeing that feuds would be submitted to justice in the royal courts.

The writing had been on the wall for feuding nobles since 1594, if not before; the crown was now too strong to be coerced by a noble taking up arms, even a great magnate like Huntly with foreign backing and a large local network of supporters and allies. Feuding did not end overnight, but gradually the serious feuds were patched up, while few new ones started. By 1612–13, it was possible for two peers who had committed vengeance killings (Lords Sanquhar and Maxwell) to be executed for murder, which had never happened before. The ending of noble violence and the acceptance of state authority transformed the behaviour of the nobility; to the extent that they retained their networks of kinsmen and dependents, they would use them in the peaceful service of the crown. Here, the abolition of the permanent exchequer was compensation: it promised continued noble access to the king and royal patronage, with no administrative limits placed on royal giving. The only question – admittedly a big one – was whether the finances could afford the kind of royal spending spree that the deal envisaged.

III

The year 1598 marked a shift in the politics of the reign. After it, James and his government were as active as before, but the target had shifted. The nobility had been reconciled; the church, however, was more disaffected than usual. But since the collapse in 1596 of what he had deemed an insurrection, the king held the initiative on religious matters. Another issue, a hardy perennial, was money. Indeed, now that the Octavians' retrenchment policy had been jettisoned, it was far more of an issue than before.

Gradually, a new pattern of politics was stabilising. The courtiers who had ousted the Octavians emerged to take over the government; two gentlemen of the chamber, Sir David Home of Gospertie and Sir George Home of Spott, became respectively comptroller (1600) and treasurer (1601). They were soon ennobled as Lord Scone and earl of Dunbar. Several former Octavians joined the new regime, particularly Alexander Seton, lord president of the court of session, who became earl of Dunfermline. The watchword was consensus, not conflict; ministers co-operated with the king to advance policies agreed between them. Sometimes there were disputes, but they were minor. There was never again a faction crisis remotely as serious as the struggle of 1589 between Maitland and Huntly.

The major issue for the regime was financial. Despite the Octavians, James had been sinking into bankruptcy for some time, and had periodically defaulted on some of his debts. There was a particularly serious bankruptcy in January 1598, when the king's officials froze payments to the goldsmith and financier Thomas Foulis, who had taken on responsibility for most of the royal finances as the culmination of his years of lending to the crown. The Foulis debt hardly began to be paid off before 1606, and payments were still being made in 1625.[18] And yet this was a regime that had abandoned the Octavians' policy of controlling expenditure, because this had alienated the nobility. The only solution was a drive to raise more revenue.

This had begun under the Octavians; parliament in 1597 had voted a larger direct tax than ever before, and had also imposed general customs duties on imports for the first time. The new regime went further, debasing the coinage and searching desperately for new sources of cash. One scheme was for a sales tax on cattle and grain; the English agent, George Nicolson, thought it would lead to civil war, and it had to be dropped in March 1600.[19] A more important and sophisticated project was to revise the tax assessment system: the traditional assessments were too uneven to tap the country's wealth effectually. In 1599–1600, lengthy efforts were made to cajole a series of wary conventions of estates to agree to this. Provisional approval was given in April 1600, and the final decision was to be made in June. The result of the June convention of estates, however, was an outright defeat for the government; the atmosphere was so hostile that the proposal could not even be put to a vote. The king, who had argued passionately for the proposal, was publicly humiliated by the disaster. What had gone wrong?

One thing that had *not* gone wrong was James's newly-established rapport with the nobility, for most nobles backed his scheme. Instead, it was the shire commissioners and burgesses who destroyed it – and this is a vital clue to the newly-emerging pattern of politics. Of the few opposition nobles (most nursing personal grievances), the most significant was probably the earl of Gowrie, an enigmatic figure linked to the presbyterian party.[20] As on 17 December 1596, the opposition needed noble leadership, but the bulk of its support came from the other groups more distanced from the court. This was probably what Nicolson had in mind when he reported in February 1600: 'Such is the malcontentment here as, if any should take [the leadership] upon them, the country I fear would all back them against this government, so much is it here repined at now.'[21]

That the 'country' might be something distinct from the court and government was a new idea. The central concept of sixteenth-century political discourse had been the 'commonweal', an ideal in which the political nation was united under enlightened royal leadership by a shared common interest. The ideal of the 'commonweal' had made good sense when there had been strong vertical ties linking nobles with their followers, and when political divisions between noble factions had had such a low ideological content. Commentators thought that the nobles simply had to make friends with one another and with the king, and the 'commonweal' – the political nation – would become united and harmonious. By 1598, James had largely achieved this, as far as the nobles themselves were concerned – but it was beginning to be clear that he had not carried the rest of the political nation with him. The nobles had got their handouts, and their place at court, but the whole gravy train was funded by increased taxes on the country. Direct taxes had been few and small before the 1580s; now, the 'country' was a nation of taxpayers.

As for the presbyterians, they had to devise a mode of politics appropriate for the wilderness. Here, they had the advantage of giving their allegiance not to a court patron, but to an ideology. Presbyterianism provided an all-encompassing way of looking at the world, and issued a call to action. It looked in two directions. Backwards, in anger – to the alleged purity of the Scottish church before 1596, the sullying of which was so clearly the king's responsibility that it was difficult to avoid calling him a traitor to God. But also forwards, in hope – to the approaching millennium, the personal reign of Christ, to which the present political arrangements were a mere prologue. This could seem near at hand, particularly in the apocalyptic European wars of the 1620s. The presbyterians built links with the Continent, aided by the exile of several of their leaders; they agitated in those parishes they still controlled; and they hoped for better times.

The country opposition, which first began to emerge in the late 1590s, was a heterogeneous collection of politically involved people who were sceptical about some of the directions taken by the current government. They were spread unevenly throughout Scotland; the court did not control the localities directly, so some areas were loyalist, others seed-beds of dissidence, as local patterns dictated. Their motives varied. For committed presbyterians, the desire to free the church from impurities was paramount, while more secular-minded folk were concerned about their tax bills, and the trading classes had further worries about monopolies and other government restrictions on commerce. But in parliament they all tended to vote the same way. Some may have had ideas of what *they* would do if in government; most just wanted the government to leave them alone. But with the government intervening in a wide range of areas, from religion to trade, those who were unhappy about one aspect began to see the links with other issues – as we shall see.

Meanwhile, the paramount duty of a courtier was to be happy about everything, and to serve the king loyally by implementing his government's agreed policies without question. The presbyterians, when at court in the early 1590s, had offered what they saw as outspoken but friendly criticism of the king; this was no longer tolerated. The new atmosphere was captured by Peter Blackburn, bishop of Aberdeen, writing to James to defend himself from 'hard information which your majestie received anent my carriage in the effeiris of the church and your majesties service', and declaring that 'at this present parliament I have not been deficient in any goode service'.[22] This was not a serious faction struggle, rather an example of the way in which loyal ministers vied with one another for the best means of serving the king.

As they did so, they began to recognise a novel distinction between themselves, as loyal servants, and the world outside. In 1598, Alexander Douglas (one of the general assembly commissioners, newly appointed by the king to help control the assembly) wrote to James complaining of a local injustice he had suffered: 'this I am informed is done to me becaus I am your majesties man'. Patrick Galloway urged the king to pay Peter Hewat's pension in 1607, 'to put difference betuix those that ar your majesties owne men and others'. To the government, the Perth general assembly in 1618 was divided into two groups: 'the opposites' and 'the weel affected'.[23] These terms did not need to be explained; such a duality was taken for granted. James himself endorsed the view that parties had arisen in the political system, telling his English parliament in 1604 that 'if Scotland should refuse' the proposed Anglo-Scottish union, 'he would compel theyr assents, having a stronger party there than the opposite party of the mutiners'.[24]

Apart from finance, the main concern for James and his government between about 1598 and 1610 was the drive to control the church through re-establishing bishops. It was an easy task at first, for the radical presbyterians were just one party in the church; after the riot of 1596, there was a rallying to the government, and the radicals lost their grip on the general assembly. In 1597 the assembly had to accept a set of 'commissioners', nominated in practice by the king; from 1600 bishops, answerable to the crown alone, were appointed; and in 1606 and 1610, the assembly was persuaded to grant these bishops authority over the church in their dioceses, while this was enforced in the localities by royal commissioners. Meanwhile, general assemblies met with declining frequency; James often got what he wanted from post-1597 assemblies, partly through gerrymandering, but he did not trust them and preferred to operate through the bishops.

As the government manipulated its way to the muzzling of the assembly and the restoration of episcopacy, and as the appalling reality of heavy taxation began to dawn, the presbyterians recovered their confidence in the first decade of the new century. They were not winning the battles, but they were consolidating their support. In 1606, many people were shocked by a rigged show-trial (for treason) of six presbyterian ministers who had helped to organise an unauthorised general assembly in Aberdeen. The presbyterians began to make links with the country opposition. The contemporary presbyterian historian and pamphleteer, David Calderwood, had much to say about the delinquencies of the new bishops – and one of his main complaints was their leading role in persuading parliaments to vote unpopular taxes. And while Calderwood was primarily concerned with religion, he was just as sceptical of James's Highland policy as he was of his religious policy.[25]

The re-establishment of bishops made Scotland more like England, and this was one of James's intentions. After he succeeded to the English throne in 1603, he wanted a closer union between his two kingdoms, a union of institutions that would be more than a dual monarchy. This would have been a real upheaval in politics; but it never happened. The English refused to countenance closer union, and the Scots never had to debate the scheme seriously. There was friction at court between Scottish and English courtiers yoked together unwillingly by their unionist king; in Scotland itself, however, the institutions of government continued unchanged. All Scottish politicians accepted the link with England, and a few courtiers could now hope for careers there; but they had accepted this link long before 1603, and it is hard to see much really changing in the structure of politics when the king went south. The realignment in Scotland's foreign allegiance had occurred in 1560, and the union of crowns merely confirmed it. James himself was rather less involved in the government – after all, he had England to govern as well – but policy was still made in the same way, by Scottish ministers supervised by their monarch. James had to take English interests into account, but this was hardly new; he had governed for years in Scotland with English ambassadors at his elbow. The year 1603 was not the political watershed it is sometimes made out to be. Its main result was to solve the fiscal crisis, for the departure of James's court to England lifted the heaviest burden from the Scottish treasury. Payments of pensions to nobles and courtiers could now expand comfortably.

Union also had an effect in the peripheral regions of Scotland – the Highlands and Borders. The latter were savagely and effectively subdued by a military force operating on both sides of the Border, ending the advantage that had been enjoyed by cross-Border families in the days of separate jurisdictions. International links were equally important in the Gaelic-speaking Highlands, which had connections with Ulster. Here, James exploited Elizabeth's victory in Ulster in the Nine Years' War (1594–1603); from the 1610s, expropriated Ulster lands were systematically settled with Englishmen and Lowland Scots. But union was not everything, even here. In Ireland, the English had half a century of experience with such plantations, while a smaller version had been tried also in Scotland when the island of Lewis was colonised in 1598 by a group of Lowland 'adventurers'. The Lewis experiment ultimately failed, the colonists falling victim to local resistance, and the island was granted in 1610 to a compliant clan chief, Kenneth Mackenzie of Kintail. Compliant clans were used on a larger scale in the south-west Highlands, where the MacDonald heartland of Kintyre (close to the Ulster MacDonnells) was taken over by Campbells, headed by the earl of Argyll. None of this was politically contentious, since the victims of the policy – the traditional governing elites of the Highlands – had never been incorporated into the Scottish political system.

The seal was placed on James's episcopal policy by the parliament of 1612, which ratified the decisions of the 1610 general assembly. There appears to have been no open opposition. The parliament did, however, see a major row about taxation; the tax voted was less than half what the government asked for. This was partly caused by a minor factional dispute between the bishops (led by John Spottiswoode, archbishop of Glasgow) and a group of nobles supporting Chancellor Dunfermline. The bishops, always ultra-royalists (for they owed their position to the crown alone), argued for a tax of £800,000, but parliament was 'so wilful and opposit as it was a labour of muche busines'. Dunfermline's supporters claimed (wrongly) that James had said he wanted only £120,000. Eventually parliament agreed on £240,000. This was a victory for the Dunfermline group, though they got into trouble with the king afterwards. But behind them we glimpse the country party, who did not just want a lower tax (£240,000 was, in fact, a similar rate to the last tax) but would have 'maid it nothing, it if had ben in thair power so to do'.[26]

Between 1612 and 1617 there were fewer contentious political issues. Maurice Lee, whose detailed account of the politics of this period is indispensable, attributes this to the moderating influence of Dunfermline, who as head of the privy council had a consensual style of government. By contrast, he explains the controversies of the years 1606–10 by reference to the abrasive personality of Treasurer Dunbar, who was allegedly dominant in politics until his death in 1611.[27] But other explanations of this new-found calm are possible, and indeed are surely necessary to explain the remarkable harmony among James's ministers throughout this whole period. After about 1601, hardly anyone in the government lost their job through faction struggle.[28] The point about 1606–10 was not Dunbar's personality, but the fact that newly-appointed bishops were being forced down the throats of local elites all over Scotland, sometimes meeting fierce resistance. As for the harmony of 1612–17, this was largely because there happened to be a relative lull in religious innovations, and because there were no parliaments to cause trouble.

Why this lull occurred, we shall see in a moment. But it is also worth observing that Dunfermline's ascendancy may have seemed quite confrontational from some points of view: it was just that the victims were politically marginal. There were national government campaigns against overcharging maltsters; against usurers taking more than the statutory 10 per cent interest; and against the outlawed MacGregor clan and their supporters in the eastern Highlands. There was the destruction of the last semi-independent earl of Orkney, executed in 1615. This was hardly consensual, but it did not generate the heat that religion or taxation were capable of doing.

Harmony ceased abruptly in 1617, when James visited his ancient kingdom for the first and only time since 1603. The visit itself was welcome, but he used the occasion to unveil a renewed programme of religious innovations. Having completed his episcopal programme, the king had now turned to the question of worship in churches. Indeed, he and the bishops had been at work on this for some years, drafting new forms of service;[29] the harmony of the Dunfermline years was thus due to the fact that the scheme only now became public. It was natural, thought James, that in a hierarchical church and society in which people revered their superiors, people should worship in a formal and ceremonial way. This upset the presbyterians, who favoured a plain church service focused on a lengthy sermon. Some proposed innovations (like confirmation by bishops or the celebration of Christmas) were denounced as unscriptural; others (like ministers wearing elaborate vestments) were condemned as too close to Catholic practice. The most contentious proposal, affecting every worshipper directly, was the requirement that communion should be received kneeling, rather than seated round a table in imitation of the Last Supper.

While in Scotland, James held a parliament. In order to avoid trouble, he had to withdraw a proposed statute that would have allowed him to introduce these innovations by royal edict. Later in the year, he had the proposals placed before the general assembly – and they were rejected. The king, furious, ordered another assembly, threatening that another rejection would have dire consequences for all concerned. The assembly, held in Perth in 1618, duly passed the proposals, which became known as the Five Articles of Perth.

Implementation of the Five Articles (particularly the requirement to kneel at communion) proved a nightmare. The presbyterians' years of struggle now paid off, and it became clear that they had solid local support in much of Lowland Scotland. Only in the remote north-east could the Articles be implemented properly. The key battles were fought in the east-central regions of Fife and Angus, and in Edinburgh, where a determined effort was made to force ministers to worship in the new way. There was some success, but at a heavy price: hostile congregations, bitter divisions and the emergence of an organised underground resistance network run by presbyterian diehards. Over most of the rest of southern Scotland, the authorities gave in, making little attempt to implement the Articles.[30]

In the parliament of 1621, the presbyterians rallied. Parliament was the one forum in which the opposition could still find a voice; although the crown had an inbuilt advantage in parliament, which had increased since the restoration of bishops, it never controlled that body automatically. The result was a titanic struggle over both the Five Articles and a new tax scheme. Opposition to both proposals came from the same group, in which a prominent role was played by Lord Balmerino and the earl of Rothes. The ratification of the Articles came close to defeat, which would have been catastrophic for the regime. The government majority came largely from bishops, nobles, courtiers and their clients, while most of the Central Belt of Scotland supported the opposition. James's policy was in tatters; it was clear that he had gone too far.

Nor was there any obvious way for him to retrieve his position. He seems never to have considered the unheroic option of cancelling the Five Articles, which would have left him little credibility. Indeed, in 1624 he was planning another campaign to enforce them.[31] But bishops and privy council, exhausted by the effort, could do no more to overcome the mass resistance. By now, the Five Articles could be implemented only sporadically and in a token way. This was not a carefully planned tactical withdrawal, as is sometimes said, but an outright defeat for the crown in the localities.

After 1621, the most significant political event of the last four years of James's reign was the one that did not happen. Defeat did not lead to a change of direction, or the disgrace of the ministers responsible – mainly Archibishop Spottiswoode, with his ally, the earl of Melrose, lord president and secretary. Spottiswoode was passed over for the chancellorship when Dunfermline died in 1622, but he did not lose favour, and there was no faction struggle at court. On the contrary, Melrose formed an alliance with the treasurer, the earl of Mar, who had opposed Spottiswoode in the 1612 parliament.[32] All three retained office well into the next reign. This was an unhealthy sign, because it meant that an important strand of opinion in the country was denied representation at court. Early modern monarchs could govern more effectively, and keep more of their options open, if their court represented a wide spectrum of political opinion. James had known this in the 1590s; he had tried to keep Huntly at court in order to keep the pro-Spanish option open, and to wean the pro-Spanish nobility away from open revolt. But where were the presbyterian nobles in the 1620s? None were at court, if the voting record of the 1621 parliament is anything to go by.[33] Surrounded by yes-men, James was unaware of the trouble brewing, or unable to change course to meet it.

IV

This polarisation of politics was not something that anyone intended. The opposition themselves hoped that a more consensual style of politics would return – if not in James's reign, then perhaps in the next one. The news of James's death reached Scotland on 31 March 1625.[34] On 14 April, the earl of Rothes (who had led the opposition in the 1621 parliament) wrote anxiously but with determined optimism to Sir Robert Kerr of Ancrum, a gentleman of the bedchamber, on a matter which 'may import the good or misery of our stat'. He sought 'sum notice from you of the disposition of our master [King Charles] touards such courses as uas intended in this countray, which you micht perseav did bread greit grief and miscontentment amongst the best both in plac and knawledg [Rothes and his friends]'. The grievances were: authoritarian practices in the privy council; 'the imposing of certain novations upon the Kirk, which bread such caus of miscontentment', in other words the Five Articles, and possibly also episcopacy; 'and the impairing of the libertys of the nobility, both in Counsell and Parliament'. Rothes continued that Kerr had told him that nothing could be done in James's reign, but Rothes

> Did hop quhen itt suld pleas God to bring his majestie to his father's plac there suld be a mitigatioun of thos extremitys . . . Now the tym being precious befor the stamp of any bad impression which thos quho uar exalted and beneficed be the former corruptiones uill preas to imprint,

He exhorted Kerr to work for a 'pacification of thos extermitys', offering the prospect of the 'good of the stat of this nation' and its affection to the new king.[35] In effect, he was trying to restore an older pattern of politics in which he would create a faction with a voice at court – a voice that would gain the sympathy of the king. By the 'libertys of the nobility', he probably meant the ancient right of the nobility to offer counsel to the monarch, and he certainly had in mind the restrictions on parliamentary debate that had been introduced to stifle opposition in 1621.

Rothes was to be sadly disappointed in King Charles, but at the time he had grounds for his optimism. Charles had gone against his father's foreign policy in 1624, and by pressing for war against Spain had even seemed to be courting the radical Protestants in England. He was known to be at odds with the old king's Scottish councillors, who had frustrated his plans as prince of Scotland in 1624.[36] Early in the new reign they were reduced in influence, though not removed. But the result was just another authoritarian regime from which the voice of the country was still excluded.[37] In general, Charles continued James's policies. He was just as keen on taxation. He also introduced a major revocation, following on from his father's revocation of 1587, but more far-reaching in practice, with the aim of restructuring landed property; this caused endless trouble. On the other hand, despite his well-advertised preference for ceremony in religion, he did surprisingly little to revive the Five Articles; probably he and his ministers preferred to focus on projects where they could hope to make more progress. For tactical reasons, the opposition under Charles sometimes referred selectively to the 'great wisdom' of James's rule – after all, the things that Charles was doing were things that James had never got around to doing, so it could be argued that he had been *against* doing them.[38] But those who objected to Charles's own innovations (such as more elaborate vestments for ministers) objected equally to James's (such as episcopacy or the Five Articles).

This last point is important, since some historians make excuses for James's unpopular policies that they do not extend to his son's. Charles is convicted out of hand of political incompetence and allowed no remission of sentence. But James, we are told, stayed within the limits of what was possible. He *talked* about absolute monarchy, but acted consensually. He knew the Scottish nobles personally, and got along well with them. Now, the last point is relevant only for those who assume (as I do not) that all problems stemmed from noble disaffection; while the others are not true. The Five Articles were well beyond the limits of the possible, and were introduced with no significant consultation. Some of the consultation that did take place was just window-dressing: government business in the 1621 parliament was managed secretly by a hand-picked group, while the full council and nobility were ostentatiously summoned to discuss minor matters, to prevent them 'suspect[ing] that conclusions wer made by a few number, and they neglected'.[39] James's determination to push unpopular measures through parliament with a numerical majority – a new feature of the early seventeenth century, since previously voting had been rare – showed a reckless lack of concern for consensus.

During James's long reign, a long-term shift can be detected in the deep structure of Scottish politics. At the beginning, there was *factionalism* – horizontal disputes between regionally-based magnates and their followings. Political disputes at national level followed the same form as local feuds, usually concerning access to resources rather than ideology. At the end of the reign, a vertical division had opened up between *court and country*. The structures of politics were more linked to the court, rather than to local client networks; people with no significant local base could wield great power nationally. Some factional potential continued – competition among courtiers was part of the structure of absolute monarchy; on the whole, however, faction struggles after 1598 were subsumed in the unity of the court. The paradigm was not the feud spilling over into court politics, but court decisions impacting on the localities.

There was also a third pattern, driven by *ideology*. Traditional faction disputes were not about rival ideas; factional conflicts were structured by a chivalric code of honour, loyalty and vengeance which was shared by all participants. The concepts of court and country did involve rival ideas, with the 'country' placing local interests first and resenting interference from a court that it suspected of various forms of corruption.[40] But there were sharper and more sophisticated ideological systems. Presbyterianism was one, and we have seen how confrontational it could be. Its ideological bite was sharpened by adopting secular ideas of limited monarchy and the subjects' right of resistance, an example of the inseparability of religion and politics in early modern Europe. Meanwhile the presbyterians' opponents (headed, of course, by James himself) became equally confrontational. To their high-flying episcopalianism they added the divine right of kings – the secular ideology of European absolute monarchy.

Unlike the vertical court-country split, these were horizontal divisions between incipient parties. The term 'party' should not be taken to imply much in the way of formal organisation. The efficiency of the presbyterian underground movement should not be discounted, but on the whole we should be thinking of informal groupings of like-minded people. The rival ideological positions attracted committed supporters on both sides, within both the court and the country – except that the episcopalians controlled the court and did their best to exclude their opponents. The court-country split and the presbyterian-episcopalian split were different, both in their origins and their structure, but they tended to overlap.

Two contrasts may illustrate how far the regime had travelled. The first parliament of James's majority, that of 1578, had been the weapon of a faction, and had simply endorsed that faction's possession of power without enacting any significant policies; the last, that of 1621, was a forum for the whole political nation, but also the weapon of the court in forcing through two crucial measures against bitter opposition. The chancellor in 1578 had been the earl of Atholl, a regional magnate and faction leader; in 1625 it was Sir George Hay of Kinfauns, the second son of a minor Perthshire laird, who had risen in royal service, first as a gentleman of the bedchamber, then as clerk register (1616) and finally chancellor (1622). Some courtiers did have local links: Hay's patron, the marquis of Hamilton, lived in England but wielded influence through his extensive Lanarkshire estates (he could not, however, control the burgh of Lanark, which voted against the government in 1621). Such links cut across the court-country division to some extent, since clients in the localities recognised their connection to a courtier. But many courtiers had no significant local base, and some, like the earl of Nithsdale, were *unpopular* in their localities.[41] Further research may reveal more about clientage links to the court, but few of the dissident shire and burgh commissioners had such links in the 1621 parliament. Others, such as the magistrates of Edinburgh, had to co-operate with the court out of fear; but that does not reduce the significance of the court's unpopularity in Edinburgh, indeed it underlines it.

It has been argued that James's early experience of ruling Scotland gave him advantages as king of England after 1603, even if the English rarely appreciated the fact.[42] This review of Scottish political patterns suggests that other interpretations are possible. The main things that James learned from his experience of ruling Scotland were the need to stamp out dissidence and to unite the nobility in obedience to his government. In his last years in Scotland, he had a fair degree of success in this; but it is questionable if he ever realised that trouble might come from another direction. He built a powerful regime that not only ended magnate revolts but also recruited the nobles as docile, tax-subsidised courtiers – a remarkable achievement. But by allowing the formation of an excluded opposition group, drawn largely from those below the nobility, James left his son a malign legacy.

NOTES

1 *History of the Church of Scotland by Mr David Calderwood* [Calderwood, *History*], ed. T. Thomson (Wodrow Society, 1842–49), iii, p. 414.

2 K. M. Brown, *Bloodfeud in Scotland, 1573–1625* (Edinburgh, 1986); J Wormald, *Lords and Men in Scotland: Bonds of Manrent, 1442–1603* (Edinburgh, 1985).

3 *The Acts of the Parliaments of Scotland* [*APS*], eds T Thomson and C Innes (Edinburgh, 1815–75) iii, pp. 120–1.

4 These were laymen, since the monasteries had been secularised at the Reformation.

5 *Calendar of the State Papers relating to Scotland and Mary Queen of Scots, 1547–1603* [*CSP Scot*], eds J Bain *et al.* (Edinburgh, 1898–1969), v, 295–6. Cf the vote in council on sending an ambassador to England, 18 June 1578, *ibid.*, p. 301.

6 Articles between James and the lords, 13–14 Aug. 1578, *CSP Scot*, v, 316.

7 *APS*, iii, 290–2. there were eight bishops and thirteen commendators; one duke, thirteen earls and fifteen lords; and twenty-three burgesses.

8 Crawford, Eglinton, Huntly and Morton; the latter was the eighth Lord Maxwell, nephew and enemy of the late Regent Morton.

9 Presbyteries (committees of parish ministers) had begun to be set up in 1581, following a programme launched in 1578. They aimed to take over control of the church at local level. Since the Reformation, the church had been run by an *ad hoc* combination of bishops, superintendents, and temporary commissioners from the general assembly of the church. During the 1570s the ideas of presbyterianism and episcopalianism became more formalised, and it began to be realised that conflict between them was inevitable.

10 *APS*, iii, 292–313, cc 1–6, 8, 13, 20, 22, 31.

11 Even the royal guard scheme continued: for its enforcement in Jan 1587, see *The Register of the Privy Council of Scotland* [*RPC*], eds. JH Burton *et al.* (Edinburgh, 1877–98), iv, p. 134.

12 Fewest revolts were faced by James IV, at least after the initial turbulent years of his reign. After 1495 there were no revolts in the Lowlands, although there was a small group of discontented nobles (supporters of the overthrown James III) in traitorous correspondence with England: N. Macdougall, *James IV* (Edinburgh, 1989), pp. 127–9.

13 J. P. Somerville (ed.), *Political Writings: King James VI and I* (Cambridge, 1994), 29, 37, 24.

14 A. I. Cameron (ed.), *The Warrender Papers* (Scottish History Society, 1931–2), ii, 269–70; *APS*, iv, 99.

15 Cf H. G. Koenigsberger, 'The organization of revolutionary parties in France and the Netherlands during the sixteenth century', in his *Estates and Revolutions* (London, 1971).

16 James VI, *Basilicon Doron*, in *Political Writings*, p. 26.

17 He acted informally as a financial officer between 1589 and 1593, handling nearly £229,000 received from England and Denmark: British Library, Maitland's accounts, 1589–93, Add MS 22,958.

18 J. Goodare, 'Thomas Foulis and the Scottish fiscal crisis of the 1590s', in W. M. Ormrod *et al.* (eds), *Crises, Revolutions and Self-Sustained Growth: Essays in Fiscal History, 1130–1830* (Stamford, 1999).

19 Nicolson to Cecil, 6 Feb. 1600, *CSP Scot*, xiii, II, 621; same to same, 9 Mar. 1600, Historical Manuscripts Commission [HMC], *Calendar of the Manuscripts of the Marquis of Salisbury* (London, 1883–1976), x, pp. 59–61.

20 Denis Campbell to Nicolson, July 1600, *CSP Scot*, xiii, II, 670.

21 Nicolson to Cecil, 6 Feb 1600, *CSP Scot*, xiii, II, 621. Nicolson's use of the term 'country', which was then beginning to be a recognised term in English political life, may indicate that he saw parallels with England.

22 Blackburn to James, n. d. (1612?), 'Extracts from the manuscript collections of the Rev. Robert Wodrow, 1605–1697', in J. Stuart (ed.), *The Miscellany of the Spalding Club* (Spalding Club, 1841–52), ii, pp. 158–9.

23 Douglas to James, 22 June 1598, *Warrender Papers*, ii, 357; Galloway to James, 7 Apr. 1607, in B. Botfield (ed.), *Original Letters Relating to the Ecclesiastical Affairs of Scotland*, (Bannatyne Club, 1851), i, 83; Lord Binning to James, 27 Aug 1618, 'Extracts from the manuscript collections of the Rev Robert Wodrow, 1605–1697', *Spalding Misc*, ii, 159–62.

24 J. Bruce (ed.), *Report on the Union of England and Scotland*, 2 vols (Edinburgh, 1799), ii, p. xxii.

25 Calderwood, *History*, vi, p. 247.

26 The bishops to James, 25 Oct. 1612, W. Fraser, *Memoirs of the Maxwells of Pollok*, 2 vols (Edinburgh, 1863), ii, pp. 61–3.

27 M. Lee, *Government by Pen: Scotland under James VI and I* (Urbana, Ill, 1980), ch. 3, 'Dunbar in Power: the Triumph of the Bishops', ch. 4, 'The Dunfermline Administration'.

28 The master of Elphinstone was forced out of the treasurership in 1601 to make way for Dunbar. After this, there was only a half-hearted and abortive attempt by Spottiswoode to unseat Dunfermline in 1606. The secretary, Lord Balmerino, was disgraced in 1609, but this was less because of faction than because the king needed a scapegoat in a complicated dispute with the pope.

29 Work had been continuous since at least 1614; G Donaldson, *The Making of the Scottish Prayer Book of 1637* (Edinburgh, 1954), pp. 31–5. Cf. 'A Scottish liturgy of the reign of James VI', in G. Donaldson (ed.), in *Scottish History Society Miscellany*, x (Scottish History Society, 1965).

30 P. H. R. Mackay, 'The reception given to the five articles of Perth', *Records of the Scottish Church History Society*, xix (1977).

31 Kellie to Mar, 26 Aug 1624, HMC, *Report on the Manuscripts of the earl of Mar & Kellie preserved at Alloa House* (London, 1904–30), ii, p. 210.

32 Melrose to Mar, 10 Apr. 1622, ed. M. Lee, *Scottish Historical Review*, lviii (1979); on Mar in 1612, see Viscount Fenton to Mar, 24 Oct. 1612, HMC, *Mar & Kellie*, ii, 43–4.

33 J. Goodare, 'The Scottish parliament of 1621', *Historical Journal*, xxxviii (1995), 43–5.

34 *RPC*, 2nd series, i, 1–3. He died on 27 Mar.

35 Rothes to Ancram, 14 Apr. 1625, *Correspondence of Sir Robert Kerr, First Earl of Ancram, and his Son, William, Third Earl of Lothian, 1616–1649*, 2 vols, ed. D. Laing (Bannatyne Club, 1875), I, 35–8.

36 *RPC*, xiii, pp. lxiii-lxv, 559–63.

37 Essential reading here is M Lee, *The Road to Revolution: Scotland under Charles I, 1625–1637* (Urbana, Ill, 1985), ch. 1: 'The end of the Jacobean system'. But whether the regime of Melrose, Mar and Chancellor Hay amounted to a distinctive 'system' is questionable.

38 Supplication of 1634, in W. C. Dickinson *et al* (eds), *A Source Book of Scottish History*, 3 vols, (2nd edn, Edinburgh, 1961), iii, pp. 79–82.

39 Melrose to James, 26 July 1621, in J. Maidment (ed.), *State Papers and Miscellaneous Correspondence of Thomas Earl of Melrose* (Abbotsford Club, 1837), ii, pp. 411–12.

40 The debate provoked by P. Zagorin, *The Court and the Country: the Beginnings of the English Revolution* (London, 1969), is reviewed by D. D. Brautigam, '*The Court and the Country* revisited', in B. Y. Kunze and D. D. Brautigam (eds), *Court, Country and Culture* (Rochester, NY, 1992).

41 Lee, *Government by Pen*, pp. 208–9.

42 J. Wormald, 'James VI and I: two kings or one?', *History*, lxviii (1983).

Constitutional Revolution, Party and Faction in the Scottish Parliaments of Charles I

J Scally 1996 *in* C Jones (ed.), *The Scots and Parliament*, Edinburgh (Edinburgh University Press), 54–73.

In the last few months of 1649, Sir James Balfour of Denmylne, Lord Lyon King at Arms to Charles I, recorded in a tortuous sentence the refusal of John, Earl of Crawford-Lindsay, recently deposed Lord Treasurer of Scotland, to acknowledge that the last full parliamentary session in the reign of Charles I was illegal:[1]

> My Lord wes ever contentit to give the churche all reasonable satisfaction, bot to declare that sessione of parliament quherby the engagement for the King's liberatione against the perfidious hereticks and faithbreake[r]s of English, wes unlawfull, being commandit by parliament, and him to acknouledge the last sessione of parliament, quho had no uther warrant for their meitting, bot the indiction of that wich they disannulled; that he wold not doe one aney tearmes, for if he should so doe, then he behoved to ratiffie that sessione of parliament, that had quyte altered the government established by the former sessione of parliament, quherin were above 65 of the nobility, and in this, not above 3.

Crawford-Lindsay's refusal to subscribe to the illegality of the Engagement Parliament of 1648 rested upon the fact that the nobility were not adequately represented at the rump session which followed it and declared the Engagement Parliament illegal. Without the presence of the noble estate in adequate numbers, the authority of parliament was severely diminished.

Crawford-Lindsay was one of the leading Covenanters throughout the 1640s along with Archibald, first Marquess of Argyll, John, first Earl of Loudoun, John, sixth Earl of Cassillis, James, second Lord Balmerino, Robert, second Lord Burleigh, and Sir Archibald Johnston of Wariston. He was also the brother-in-law of James, third Marquess and first Duke of Hamilton, who, along with Hamilton's brother, William, first Earl of Lanark, Secretary of Scotland, was the architect of the Engagement of 1647–8. At the height of the Engagement preparations, Crawford-Lindsay, with Lanark as his second, had been involved in a duel with Argyll, the chief opponent of the Engagement.[2] The Earl of Crawford-Lindsay's behaviour at the end of the Parliaments of Charles I encapsulates the central theme of this essay: that despite a rebellion against the King's authority in 1638, despite a constitutional revolution focused in Parliament between 1639 and 1641, despite a war against the King between 1643 and 1646, and despite a war to save the King in 1648, the operation of politics, particularly in Parliament, followed an established pattern based on the social hierarchy.

II

Of course, certain groups enjoyed a higher profile than hitherto, notably the barons in parliament, who replaced the clerical estate in 1640 and had their voting power doubled,[3] but their political role, whilst greatly enhanced, did not lead to a breakdown in traditional political relationships based on the landed and social hierarchy. In fact the barons were an integral part of the landed hierarchy being, like the higher nobility (or peerage), tenants-in-chief of the Crown and the elected representatives of the shires.[4] Even during the most vociferous phase of the Covenanting period between 1644 and 1646 their traditional identity changed little – they were described in the sederunt roll as the 'Commissionaris for the Barronies', occasionally as the 'Commissionaris for the Shyres', and were referred to in the Parliamentary Registers not as the gentry, nor the shire commissioners, but as the 'Barons' with all the associations with the noble estate that this implies.[5] Behind the scenes, the barons and burgesses packed the numerous committees of Parliament during the 1640s and shouldered the bureaucratic workload of that tumultuous decade. But, although impressive in numbers, they did not occupy the political cockpit during this period. Moreover, they did not seek to overturn, or in most cases to challenge, the political hierarchy. Commissioners for the barons such as Sir Archibald Johnston of Wariston and Sir Andrew Fletcher of Innerpeffer were important spokesmen both for their estate and on the floor of the House, but they were always in the shadow of their political superiors and collaborators, Archibald, Marquess of Argyll, and James, Duke of Hamilton, respectively.

It is within this context that the politics of party and faction determined how individuals behaved in Parliament – and it was these labels which were used by contemporaries to describe political groups. In the years 1647 and 1648, for example, Robert Baillie, although often bewildered by the machinations of 'our great men' in the Committee of Estates and Parliament over how to respond to the treatment of the King in England, described political alignments in terms of 'party' and 'faction'.[6] As with most political labels[7], they carried with them derogatory connotations, especially 'faction', which, in the hands of hostile commentators, often denoted a group intent on undermining the body politic to gain an advantage.[8] However, a more striking feature of the use of these contemporary labels was the naming of a party or faction after its leader, in particular the two dominant figures in parliamentary politics of this period, Archibald, eighth Earl and first Marquess of Argyll, and James, third Marquess and first Duke of Hamilton. And this was a telling indicator of the hierarchical nature of Scottish parliamentary politics in the reign of Charles I.

Patterns of allegiance to a parliamentary party were complex, and difficult to recover with any certainty given the absence of parliamentary division lists, records of debates or diarists' scribblings, though Henry Guthry's observation on the reasons for following Hamilton's Engagement in 1648, albeit from a hostile source, are revealing: 'so absolute was duke Hamilton's power, that he could carry what he pleased, many adhering to him upon interest of blood and friendship; and others conceiving him to be for the king'.[9] It was the mixture of traditional kin and blood ties harnessed to a national issue, in the above case the fate of the King, that defined parties in the Scottish Parliaments of the 1640s. Indeed the regular sitting of either Parliaments, Conventions of Estates or Committees of Estates throughout the decade 1639–49 permitted the establishment of loose parties, with a committed core, and led by a noble magnate, which articulated a policy on national issues such as the constitutional settlement of 1639–41, the Solemn League and Covenant of 1643–4 and the Engagement of 1647–8.[10]

III

Traditionally, Scottish parliaments were both infrequent and short-lived, the exception being the period 1639–51 when Parliament or one of its mutated forms – a Convention or Committee of Estates – was regularly in place in Edinburgh.[11] Yet the overarching characteristic that defined the Scottish Parliament before 1640 was not that it had three estates,[12] nor that it was unicameral, but that on convening it promptly surrendered its legislative and deliberative function to a committee, the Lords of the Articles.[13] The procedure for choosing members of the Articles, and the number of them, changed over time until a precedent was set in the early seventeenth century whereby the nobles chose eight of the clergy, the clergy chose eight nobles, and then these two estates jointly elected eight each from the Commissioners for the barons and burghs. Finally the King or his Commissioner, elected eight officers of state to complete the membership of the Articles.[14] At the Coronation Parliament of Charles I in 1633 this was all done by the nobles, clergy and the King away from the chamber.[15] Immediately upon the announcement of the membership of the Articles, the remainder of the Estates dispersed and left the Committee to deliberate and frame legislation. Following the Articles' deliberations, the whole Parliament was re-convened and passed all of the legislation in a single day – as was the custom.[16]

As an institution then, the Scottish Parliament was neither over-sophisticated nor could it be described as a forum for continuous debate in the unicameral chamber, since on convening it passed that function to the Lords of the Articles. Its spasmodic and short meetings in the sixteenth and seventeenth centuries militated against the constitutional and procedural development of parliament. Yet even with these flaws it was one of the few national institutions, in a society dominated by provincial magnates and the Crown, capable of bringing together the political nation under one roof. After the departure of King James VI and I in 1603 and the subsequent dispersal of the Scottish court, the status of Parliament as a national institution was correspondingly enhanced.

IV

Charles I has passed into history as a monarch with a devotion to episcopacy and a detestation of Parliaments. In England, from 1629 to 1640, he famously ruled without Parliament and ended up fighting against the Long Parliament (which the Scottish Covenanters forced him to call in November 1640) for the next eight years. In Scotland he called a Coronation Parliament in 1633, after eight years of delays and excuses, and forced through his own legislative programme whilst punishing even the most innocuous opposition.[17] Six years later, when the Covenanters' resistance to his civil and ecclesiastical policy enjoyed the support of most of the country, Charles allowed a Parliament to assemble only to avoid the complete breakdown of his authority – and to allow him time to raise forces in England and Ireland for an ambitious, and ultimately futile, assault on his Scottish kingdom.[18] As in Scotland, the English Parliament became the hub of resistance to the King during the 1640s. In both instances the political nation chose Parliament as the forum for opposition to the King and the institution through which settlement was to be validated – although both institutions would have to be reformed first in strikingly similar ways.[19]

That the Covenanters intended to use the Scottish Parliament as the platform for their resistance to the absentee rule of Charles I explains why changes to Parliament were so high on their agenda. The initial aim was to transfer the personnel of the Tables, the unofficial and illegal, executive of the Covenanters, into a reformed Parliament.[20] The 1633 Parliament had demonstrated that it, through the operation of the Lords of the Articles, was a mere rubber stamp for royal legislation. The Covenanters recognised that bishops were the agents of the despised religious changes and, just as importantly, had aspirations in civil spheres which encroached upon the nobility's traditional interests.[21] Finally, it was essential to separate the civil and ecclesiastical functions of the state with Parliament and Privy Council on one side and General Assembly and ecclesiastical courts on the other.[22]

Since episcopacy had been abolished at the Glasgow Assembly in 1638 (re-confirmed in the Edinburgh Assembly in August 1639), there was an immediate problem of a missing estate in the Parliament of August–November 1639.[23] As it turned out, the barons, as Commissioners of the Shires, eased themselves into the former Episcopal estate, and so lay interest benefited at the expense of clerics. Nonetheless, it was also resolved temporarily, and after considerable protest, to allow John, first Earl of Traquair, Lord Treasurer and the King's Commissioner in parliament, in the name of the Crown, to assume the role that the bishops had had in the election of the Committee of the Articles.[24] Such a measure was only allowed in this session, as the majority, led by Argyll, believed that each Estate should be allowed to choose their own representatives on the Articles.[25] Traquair's problems, however, were exacerbated by the want of the Parliamentary Registers which undoubtedly favoured the innovators.[26] Moreover, the central role of the Earl of Argyll in orchestrating the elections to the Articles was underlined by the King's Commissioner in his report back to court.[27]

Yet it was not until the next session of Parliament the following year that far reaching constitutional change was introduced by the hitherto cautious Covenanters, under the guidance of the Earls of Argyll, Rothes, Montrose, Eglinton, Cassillis, Lothian and Lords Lindsay, Balmerino and Burleigh. This time Parliament met from 2 to 11 June in defiance of the Crown's proclamation to extend the previous prorogation and with no King's Commissioner present.[28] Throughout the session it was iterated that the King had failed to appear personally or to send a Commissioner whilst at the same time mobilising his other two kingdoms (England and Ireland) to invade Scotland, an action tantamount, in effect, to abandoning his duties to his native kingdom.[29] So the threat of impending invasion and the alienation of the supreme magistrate ushered in radical constitutional change in Parliament. Immediately on convening, and 'by his Ma[jes]ties speciall indictione and authoritie', a president of Parliament was elected to replace the King's Commissioner. The next priority was to underline that the new composition of the three estates represented 'a compleit and perfyte Parliament':[30]

And ordeanes all Parliamentis heireftir to be constitute and to consist onlie in all tyme comeing of the Noblemen Barronis and Burgess as the memberis and thrie estates of parliament. And reschindis and annullis all former laws and actis of Parliament mad[e] in favouris of whatsoever Beshopis Archbeshopis Abbotis Pryoris or other prelates or churchmen whatsoever for thair ryding sitting or vo[i]ceing in Parliament.

After prohibiting 'all personis whatsomevir to call in questione the authoritie of this present Parliament . . . under pain of treason', a raft of some 60 acts were introduced that formed the core of the constitutional revolution.[31] All acts of the Glasgow and Edinburgh Assemblies were ratified including subscription of the National Covenant as a test for civil and ecclesiastical office. A Triennial Act ensured that a Parliament would be called at least every three years. Proxies were disallowed and noblemen who did not own land in Scotland were no longer allowed to sit.

As for the overmighty Committee of Articles, it was stated on 6 June that 'all subsequent parliamentis may according to the importance of effaires for the tyme either choose or not choose severall Committies for Articles as they shall thinke expedient'. It was emphasised that the Committees, if chosen, were to prepare articles which they received from the Estates, and then return them to the chamber, where they would be debated and the estates would 'ordeene suche of the saidis articles as they find to desserve consideration to be formed and past as articles to be voyted in plaine p[ar]liament'. Finally, and most importantly, it was stressed:[32]

That the rest of the estates by and beside these of the severall Comitties of the Articles shall be holdine continowally to sit for receiving advysing and discussing of all articles propositions overtures and materes [that] shall be presented to them fro[m] the begining of the Parlia[men]t to the cloosure thereof.

So with the Articles cut down to size, legislative power shifted into the chamber and Parliament became a debating, consultative and legislative body.[33] The demise of the old Lords of the Articles spawned a committee system in which various committees, rather than one all-powerful Committee of Articles,[34] considered items and dutifully reported back to the chamber.[35] A Committee of Estates was also invested with full parliamentary power and usually sat in the interval between parliaments, at least during the three kingdom crisis.[36]

In 1640 the Covenanters justified their constitutional agenda in *A True Representation of the Proceedings of the Kingdom of Scotland* in which it was stated that 'Parliament is the onely lawfull mean to remeid[y] our evils, remove distractions, and settle a solide and perfect peace.'[37] Most of the Covenanter fire was aimed at the bishops who had 'usurped to be the Kirk, and did in name of the Kirk represent the third estate', and it was argued that at the Glasgow Assembly in 1638 'both' of these functions were 'renounced and condemned' by the Kirk.[38] It was also claimed that bishops were responsible for the recent excesses of the Lords of the Articles. Historically the Articles, since King David II (1329–1371), had not always been used but when they were:[39]

> the nomination and election of them, was ever with the common consent and advice of the whole parliament, till the Parliament in *anno* 1617. That the Bishops took upon them to remove out of plaine Parliament, to the Inner-house, and choysed some out of the Noblemen, & the Noblemen them, and they two choysed the Commissioners to be on articles of Shires and Burroughs, which as it was against the first institution, & form of election of al preceeding articles, introduced by & with prelates: So do it fall & ought to be removed with them.

The Articles, it was argued, were never intended to have 'a boundlesse and illimited power' and were designed to be 'onely preparative, and no wayes determinative'.[40]

The changes of 1639–40 transformed parliamentary procedure but were largely prepared beforehand by the Covenanter leaders and received a fairly easy passage in the invasion-threatened 11-day session of 1640.[41]

V

By the parliamentary session of 1641 (15 July–17 November), however, the Covenanters were less united and focused than they had been in previous sessions. The repellent Prayer Book had been withdrawn, bishops were gone and the threat of war had receded. A Parliament sat at Westminster, the Scottish and English armies were on the point of disbandment, the peace treaty of London was being brought from England to be signed in parliament and the King had decided to attend the session in Edinburgh.[42] In addition, James, fifth Earl of Montrose's Cumbernauld Band of August 1640 – an anti-Argyll polemic rather than a coherent political agenda – signalled a split in the Covenanter ranks when it was revealed in November 1640.[43] It was apparently a reaction to the alleged treason spoken by the Earl of

Argyll, the leader of the Covenanting Movement, in June 1640, in which he confirmed that a king could be deposed if found guilty of certain crimes.[44] The Band proved to be a damp squib, but it did lead to the formation of another party headed by Montrose at the end of the year (with Lord Napier, Sir George Stirling of Keir and Sir Archibald Stewart of Blackhall) who established links at court with the Earl of Traquair, now exiled Lord Treasurer, and James, fourth Duke of Lennox, gentleman of the King's Bedchamber and the King's cousin, and offered to serve Charles in Scotland if religion and liberties were secured by the King in Parliament.[45] It was also rumoured that Montrose intended to accuse (presumably of treason) the Marquess of Hamilton, the King's Court adviser on Scottish affairs,[46] and the Earl of Argyll, 'in the face of Parliament'.[47]

Charles therefore had the bones of a royalist, or anti-Campbell/Hamilton, party prior to his trip to Scotland, a group with connexions at court, a charismatic, though politically naïve, leader in Montrose, and a moderate, and able, polemicist in Lord Napier.[48] Still, some of their potential was lost from June onwards following the forced retirement of Traquair from court and the imprisonment of the Montrose group in Edinburgh.[49] On the other side, Hamilton's proximity to the Scottish Crown – next in line after the royal Stewarts – added a further dimension to the Argyll/Hamilton friendship, fuelled over the summer visit not only by the memory of Argyll's talk of deposing the King but by negotiations for a marriage between Argyll's son and Hamilton's eldest daughter in the second half of the year.[50]

The political situation in Scotland was therefore highly combustible, quite apart from the difficult parliamentary negotiations over the Scottish settlement that was ostensibly the purpose of the royal visit.[51] Charles's main aim when he arrived in Edinburgh on 14 August was to settle Scotland, dissolve the Parliament and return to England and do the same. Instead, when he left on 17 November, the Covenanters under Argyll and Hamilton had virtually been handed control of the country and the Irish rebellion, which began on 22 October, gave the English parliament a new *raison d'être*.

The full Parliament had been sitting at Edinburgh since 15 July preparing business for the King's arrival.[52] On 19 July, in the final phase of reform which had begun in 1639, new orders for the Parliament were introduced. In 1632 preparations had commenced to construct a new building to house Parliament and the Convention of Estates, Court of Session and Privy Council. Although the building was first occupied in August 1639, it was not finally completed until 1640–41.[53] The new Hall of Parliament, which was to be the official meeting place of the Estates until 1707, was 120 feet long, 50 feet wide, and 40 feet high, with a hammerbeam roof of Danish oak by John Scott.[54] Stimulated more by the acquisition of a new building than by revolutionary fervour, it was decided to consider new orders for conduct, protocol and attendance in Parliament.[55] The interior walls of the new chamber were 'to be hung and the claith of state put up'. Each member was allocated a seat which was left vacant in their absence, fines were imposed for non-attendance,[56] 24 hours was allowed for each estate to consider propositions, prayers were to be said at the beginning and end of each day, all dialogue was to be directed through the

President, and swords only were to be worn by Members in the chamber. Thus the acquisition of a new building provided another opportunity to enhance the status of Parliament and to further formalise its procedures.

Charles came to Parliament at 11 a.m. on 17 August with due ceremony: Hamilton bore the crown, Argyll the sceptre and the Earl of Sutherland the sword.[57] The Treaty of London was ratified nine days later, but the other vexed issues of the Incendiaries, the Montrose group and the appointment of officers of state dragged on to the beginning of October.[58] Charles eventually agreed to appoint officers of state, judges and councillors with the advice and approval of Parliament on 16 September which signalled the start of a bruising contest largely with Charles nominating candidates and the Earl of Argyll's circle (Cassillis, Balmerino, Burleigh, Lindsay, Loudoun, Glencairn and Wariston), in alliance with Hamilton, rejecting them; and marked by particularly acrimonious exchanges over the appointment of a Chancellor and Treasurer.[59] As Robert Baillie succinctly put it, 'upon these jarres whole moneths were mispent'.[60]

Argyll and Hamilton constituted the most powerful force in the parliamentary negotiations, especially since Montrose languished in the castle.[61] If Argyll's growing dominance and alleged talk of deposing the King in 1640 had split the Covenanter movement, Hamilton's alliance with Argyll in 1641 enraged royalists in Scotland. This was reflected in the vengeful atmosphere against the two noblemen that developed towards late September.[62] From this familiar miasma around the King came the conspiracy to remove Hamilton and Argyll known as the Incident.[63] The plot was essentially a *coup d'état*, probably sanctioned by the King, to remove the dominant Argyll/Hamilton axis from Parliament and replace it with a ragbag of royalist anti-Campbell opportunists headed by the Earls of Montrose and Crawford, Will Murray of the Bedchamber, some officers from the recently disbanded Scottish army, and an outer circle, or alternative parliamentary party, containing the Earls of Home, Roxburghe, Airth, Mar, Lords Gray, Ogilvy, Kilpont (or Kinpont), Ker, Almond and, lastly, William Drummond.[64] It was also an attempt to overawe the Parliament by a show of force dressed up as a legal process.[65] And significantly it was Parliament, ably controlled in the absence of Argyll and Hamilton by the Chancellor John Campbell, Lord Loudoun, the President of Parliament Lord Balmerino, the Earl of Lauderdale (a Hamiltonian), Lord Lindsay (Hamilton's brother-in-law), and Archibald Johnston of Wariston, who took it as a severe infringement of parliamentary privilege that some of its Members had to flee for their lives from the capital.[66] Equally it was only under the protection of Parliament that Argyll, Hamilton and the Earl of Lanark, Secretary for Scotland (and Hamilton's brother), agreed to return to Edinburgh.[67] By gambling so much on the plot, its failure meant the loss of much of the King's credibility and power in Scotland.[68] Unwittingly, by engaging in a trial of strength with his newly reformed Scottish Parliament, Charles had greatly enhanced its status as an effective buffer against a bullying Crown. As so often happened, Charles's actions produced an effect that was far worse than the situation that had caused him to act in the first place – now Parliament controlled the executive and the judiciary. Parliament was dissolved on

16 November and next day Charles departed from Edinburgh leaving the government of Scotland to the Argyll party of the Covenanters (Loudoun, Balmerino, Cassillis, Eglinton, Burleigh, Crawford-Lindsay, Lothian, Glencairn and Wariston) for the next six years – it would not be until 1647 that a party, ironically led by Hamilton, would take control of parliament in the King's interest.

VI

The only hiccup in the Argyll Covenanters' unhampered control of the reformed Parliament and Convention of Estates between 1641 and 1646 was the limp attempt by a faction led by Hamilton (Lanark, Lauderdale, Southesk, Roxburgh, Annandale, Callendar and Dunfermline) in the summer of 1643 to spoil the negotiations between the Scottish and English parliaments for the Solemn League and Covenant – a military treaty to ensure the English Parliament defeated Charles in England and a coalition for mainland religious uniformity, Presbyterian of course, to satisfy the Scots.[69] The split between Argyll and Hamilton that led to the latter heading a rival faction against Argyll's dominant party was occasioned by the single issue of whether the Scots should intervene in the Civil War in England, and it was this clash that dominated the period from late 1642 down to the meeting of the Convention of Estates on 22 June 1643.[70] Argyll's supporters eventually gained the initiative through skilful exploitation of fears of papists in arms in England, the consequent threat to domestic religion and liberty and the omnipresent dangers in Ireland.[71] On the other hand, Hamilton's delicate, perhaps over-cautious, policy of Scottish non-alignment in the English Civil War, peppered by assurances that the gains of 1638–41 were safe in Charles's hands, was dealt a serious blow in early June by revelations of Catholic plots to effect a royalist rising in Scotland.[72] To many, it was further proof that the papist, with a letter of approval from the King, was on the march in the three kingdoms. Consequently, Hamilton's and Lanark's vocal support for the King's many assurances that religion and liberties were secure rang hollow on the eve of the Convention of Estates.[73]

With the Anti-Solemn Leaguers softened up beforehand, the Convention of Estates was a less even contest than it might have been.[74] Yet it was still the case, as it had been since at least the beginning of the year, that members had initially to fall in behind either Hamilton or Argyll. At the first meeting, the King's letter was read out restricting the Convention to discussions of how to maintain the Scots army in Ireland and how to get repayment of the Brotherly Assistance from the English Parliament. Above all, the Convention was not to 'medle with the affaires of England'.[75] The profile of the Convention was clearly shown on 24 June by the membership of the committee to draw up an act of constitution defining the Convention's powers.[76] In short the committee would decide whether the Convention should obey the King's restrictions or not. The membership of the committee showed that Hamilton had most of the nobility behind him, but Argyll carried more support in the other two estates, the barons and the burgesses.[77] Thus, on 26 June, the committee concluded that the Convention had power 'to treat, consult and determine in all matters that shall be proposed unto them'.[78] This effectively handed control of the Convention to Argyll and from that day Hamilton never returned to the Chamber.[79] Yet this meant that the King did not have his most effective politician in the House, leaving his potential supporters leaderless. By trying to restrict the Convention's remit so absolutely Hamilton, and Charles, had foolishly manoeuvred themselves into a corner and out of the Parliament House. The Convention of Estates sat on without Hamilton and the other royalists who had chosen not to participate. In early August, the long-awaited Commissioners from the English Parliament arrived requesting 'mutuall defence against the papists and prelaticall factioun and their adherents in both kingdoms'.[80] In just over a week, the Solemn League and Covenant was drawn up,[81] and in January 1644 another Covenanted army marched into England, as it had done in 1640, to tilt the balance, once more, away from the King.[82]

Meanwhile, Charles's imprisonment of Hamilton in England at the end of 1643 on allegations of treason brought by the Montrose group ensured that any parliamentary faction capable of mobilising moderate Covenanter opinion in favour of the King would be leaderless.[83] Instead Charles opted for the extra-parliamentary guerrilla tactics of Montrose, which enjoyed initial spectacular successes before inevitable defeat at Philiphaugh in September 1645.[84] Until the King's arrival at Newcastle in May 1646 under the 'protection' of the Scottish army, and Hamilton's release from prison in April, parliamentary politics in Scotland was dominated by Argyll's party. Given that, the first five sessions of the first Triennial Parliament (4 June 1644–4 February 1646) were largely occupied with prosecuting the war in England, quelling the rebellion in Ireland and organising the campaigns against Montrose in Scotland.[85]

VII

The sixth session of the First Triennial Parliament which assembled at Edinburgh on 3 November 1646 signalled the beginning of a sea-change in Parliament. The thorny problem of what to do with an uncovenanted King who had been defeated in England and was now at Newcastle with the Scottish army was the key political issue, and this was counterpointed by the steady collapse of the military and religious alliance between the Parliaments of England and Scotland. Although unwilling to sign the Covenant or accept the Newcastle Propositions, Charles generated considerable support in Scotland by throwing himself on the mercy of his native subjects, and, moreover, as the survival of Secretary Lanark's letter-book shows, dispensing numerous gifts to a great number of the parliamentary élite assembled in Edinburgh, many of whom travelled south to kiss the King's hand.[86]

Significant too, was the arrival of the Duke of Hamilton back onto the political scene, for he was a totem of moderate Covenanter opinion which had lacked a leader since 1643 against Argyll, Cassillis, Balmerino, Wariston and the other committed Solemn Leaguers. Not only that, the duke could, in the changed political circumstances of 1646–48, rely on a potent inner circle of family collaborators including

Secretary Lanark, Lord Treasurer Crawford-Lindsay, the Earls of Glencairn and Haddington, the Laird of Bargany, Sir John Hamilton of Orbiston, Justice Clerk, Sir James Lockhart of Lee, and Sir John Hamilton of Beil. Yet for all that, Hamilton was reluctant to champion the King's case in Parliament. He had already been imprisoned in 1643 for failing to hold an untenable position for the Crown, and was unwilling to do so again. To secure Hamilton's support in Parliament Charles had to accept the Covenant, otherwise the King's position in Scotland was futile.[87] It was a political necessity, not a religious one, that Charles accepted the Covenant. Not only Hamilton, but other Covenanters such as Crawford-Lindsay, Loudoun, Lauderdale, Lanark and Glencairn believed this too. From his experiences between 1638 and 1642 Hamilton also knew that Charles only made concessions when he was pressed extremely hard to do so.[88] When one applies these factors to the Hamilton party's position between 1646 and the signing of the Engagement in December 1647, then their policy becomes more coherent. Neither royalists nor hard-line Covenanters, and true to the traditions and ambiguities of the National Covenant, they are better described as the Hamilton party or the Hamilton faction.[89]

The sea-change in the Parliament of 3 November 1646 was reflected in the membership of the main parliamentary committee, the committee for the burdens and pressures of the kingdom in which the Hamilton party balanced the Argyll party.[90] The two main issues of the moment were discussed by the committee: what to do with the King and with the Scots army in England. However, with the King refusing to concede ground at Newcastle and dabbling in his usual intrigues, Hamilton's party were both unwilling and unable to press a royalist case without the required concessions from Charles.[91] It was in this spirit of despondency that Hamilton and his supporters viewed the surrender of the King to the English Commissioners at the beginning of 1647 on payment of £200,000, half of the agreed sum owed to the Scots by the English Parliament.[92] Even worse, Charles was handed over before the Parliament received an answer to their request that any decision on the King's future should be decided by the two kingdoms.[93]

A sentimental attachment to the King of Scotland, and a sense of shame that they had sold him to a pack of sectaries in England, was enough to alter the complexion of parliament in Hamilton's favour.[94] On 11 March it was decided to send the Earl of Lauderdale, a Hamiltonian, to England with new instructions for himself and for the commissioners in London which illustrated a softening of the Scottish Parliament's stance not only towards the King, but to former incendiaries such as the Earl of Traquair, and supporters of the Earl of Montrose like Lord Ogilvy.[95] In particular, the instructions stated that Charles might only have to accept the Covenant as a law, but not subscribe it himself.[96] In this mood the Parliament was dissolved on 27 March 1647, after appointing a Committee of Estates to sit in the interval before the first session of the Second Triennial Parliament due to assemble in March 1648.[97]

The membership of the Committee of Estates illustrated once again that the balance of power was still on a knife-edge, divided between Argyll and Hamilton.[98] Two issues separated the protagonists during the lifetime of the Committee: first how to respond to the deteriorating situation in England, especially after the King was seized by the English New Model army on 4 June, and secondly, what to do with the Scots army under Argyll which was campaigning in the West. On the first issue, Hamilton's supporters publicly encouraged the belief that the King was in imminent danger from the English sectarian army whilst privately hoping that Charles's deteriorating situation in England would force him to make the appropriate concessions to the Scots that would allow them to invade on his behalf. On the other side, Argyll's party at heart felt the King's unreliability disqualified him from being offered military assistance in England. The second issue, that of the Scottish army, was a critical element to both political factions. The restructuring of the Scottish army that left Newcastle at the beginning of 1647 had favoured Argyll since the commanders were loyal to him. Hamilton, therefore, throughout most of the year of the Committee of Estates (March 1647–March 1648) pressed for the army to be disbanded, and until that was achieved argued against aiding the King. Hamilton nearly achieved his aim on 8 September, but at another 'frequent' meeting of the Committee on 15 October Argyll managed by a single vote to have the army kept intact until the meeting of the Parliament in March.[99]

Meanwhile, on 17 and 18 August, following the return of Argyll from campaigning in the west, the Committee of Estates framed new instructions for the Commissioners in London, including a request that the King be allowed to go to the capital to receive further propositions. In addition, and most importantly, two more commissioners, the Earls of Lanark and Loudoun, were to go south.[100] The two were representative of both leading parties: Lanark for his brother Hamilton, and Loudoun for his kinsman Argyll. Yet on balance this was a victory for Hamilton, since Loudoun was neither as hard-line as Argyll, nor was he as opposed to aiding the King. Even more significant, however, Loudoun was to concern himself with matters relating to the English Parliament while Lanark was to concentrate on matters relating to the King.[101] Evidence also suggests that the Hamiltons were already involved in secret negotiations with the King through Lauderdale and Robin Leslie, a servant who had been in Hamilton's circle since at least 1630.[102]

What all this eventually led to, amidst a flurry of peace proposals from the English army and the English Parliament, intensified by rumours that plans were aloft 'to destroy his Ma[jes]ties person', was the signing of the Engagement on 26 December 1647 between the Scottish Commissioners and the King.[103] The Engagement stated that Charles would establish presbyterian church government in England for a trial period of three years, the Solemn League and Covenant would be confirmed in the English Parliament but universal subscription would not be pressed, and finally moves would be made for economic union and, if possible, 'a complete union of the kingdoms' according to the designs of James VI and I.[104] News of the Engagement was initially very well received in the Committee of Estates and after a detailed report by Loudoun and Lauderdale on 10 February the Commissioners' proceedings were approved.[105] However, the Commission of the Kirk was split over the deal, but eventually came out against the Engagement when it became apparent that Hamilton, not Argyll, was the driving force behind it.[106]

The final contest between Hamilton and Argyll, the two main political figures in Scottish politics throughout the decade from 1639, took place in the first session of the second Triennial Parliament, the last full session of a Parliament in the reign of Charles I. The profile of the so-called Engagement Parliament which sat down on 2 March 1648 is best described by Argyll's supporter, Robert Baillie, in his wry summary:[107]

> Never so many noblemen present in any of our Parliaments; near fyftie Earls and Lords. Among whom were found about eight or nyne for our way; Argyle, Eglintone, Cassillis, Louthian, Arbuthnot, Torpichen, Rosse, Balmerino, Cowper, Burleigh, and sometimes the Chancellour and Balcarras. All the rest, with more than the halfe of the barrons, and almost the halfe of the burgesses, especiallie the greater tounes, Edinburgh, Perth, Dundee, Aberdeen, St Andrews, Linlithgow, ran in a string after the Duke of Hamilton's vote.

As had become the custom since the demise of the Lords of the Articles, a committee was established to consider the principal issues that concerned the Parliament, appropriately named in this instance the 'Committee for Dangeris, Remedies and Dewties'.[108] The committee's remit was to discuss the Engagement agreed with the King and how it should be put into effect, though this was couched in more emotive language of 'the dangeris iminent to Religion The Covenant The Kingis Ma[jes]tie Monarchicall government and the thrie kingdomes'.[109] However what was new, and echoed back to the overarching role of the old Lords of the Articles, was the granting of new powers to the committee on 17 March to operate unilaterally in matters concerning the safety of the kingdom.[110] In an atmosphere of increasing violence which had led to a series of duels involving, most notably, Argyll and Crawford-Lindsay, and Eglinton and Glencairn, Argyll immediately protested at the committee's new powers and when his protest was denied he walked out of Parliament with about 47 of his supporters, including the Earls of Cassillis, Eglinton, Lothian, Lords Balmerino, Burleigh, Coupar, Arbuthnot and Torphichen, as well as the Lairds of Wariston, Scotiscraig and Humbie and George Porterfield, burgess of Glasgow, and John Short, burgess of Stirling.[111]

Although Argyll and the others were called back and took their seats, the support for the Engagement was now overwhelming and Parliament occupied itself with choosing commanders and mobilising the country for an invasion, whilst simultaneously canvassing assistance from sympathizers in Ireland and England.[112] The Engagement Parliament was finally dissolved on 11 June, and, as had been the custom for most of the 1640s, a Committee of Estates was appointed to sit in the interval before the convening of the second session of the second Triennial Parliament. By the time Parliament sat down again on 4 January 1649, Hamilton's army had been ignominiously defeated at Preston, and Argyll, with the assistance of Cromwell, had taken control of Parliament just in time to preside over the chaos caused by the execution in London of King Charles I of Scotland on 30 January.[113]

Never in the history of the Scottish Parliament has there been a series of rollercoaster events such as those in the reign of Charles I. Seven years late, he presided over his Coronation Parliament in 1633 with a rod of iron, only to have it turned against him by the Parliament of 1639–41 which initiated a constitutional trans-formation that allowed it to govern Scotland with an agenda fashioned first by Argyll's political party, then by Hamilton's party in 1647–48. In the crucial period between 1639 and 1641 Parliament, housed in a magnificent new building, became a consultative and legislative body freed from the control of the all-powerful Lords of the Articles. As an institution Parliament was robust enough to act as an effective buffer against an aggressive Crown in 1641, as well as mobilising the country for war between 1643 and 1646, and in 1648. Perhaps the triumph of the Covenanting period was the creation of a Parliament capable of doing this.

In terms of personnel, Parliament also experienced considerable change. The clerical estate was outlawed in 1639, and the estate was occupied by the barons of the shires. In the period 1639–51 the barons played an important, though not the leading, role in Parliament. Together with the burgess estate, the barons largely accepted the hierarchical nature of Scottish politics in Parliament, a pattern in which the nobility were the natural leaders of political parties and factions. Although the political landscape in Parliament had altered dramatically during the reign of Charles I, the nature of political relationships had not changed correspondingly. For the decade immediately following Charles's death it would temporarily be a different story.

NOTES

1 *The Historical Works of Sir James Balfour of Denmylne and Kinnaird* (4 vols, Edinburgh, 1824) [hereafter Balfour, *Works*], III, 435. The second session of the second Triennial Parliament commenced on 4 Jan. 1649, and Charles I was executed on the 30th of the month while the session was in progress. It appears that about 14 to 16 of the nobility attended the first day of Parliament on 4 Jan. See, *The Acts of the Parliaments of Scotland* (12 vols, Edinburgh 1884) [hereafter *APS*]; VI, II, 124–56; Balfour, *Works*, III, 373; *The Memoirs of Henry Guthry, late bishop of Dunkeld* (2nd edn, Glasgow, 1747), pp. 301–302.

2 Balfour, *Works*, III, 395–6. When the parties convened at Musselburgh Links for the duel, Argyll refused to fight.

3 Barons were the elected representatives of the shires. Traditionally each shire had a single vote in Parliament even though they were entitled to send two representatives. But in 1640 the two barons who represented a shire were given a vote each, which effectively doubled the voting power of the estate. See, D. Stevenson, *The Government of Scotland under the Covenanters, 1637–1651* (Edinburgh, 1982), p. xxiii.

4 The nobles, higher nobility or peerage were tenants in chief along with the lesser or small barons, but they had long been divided; the former attended parliament by personal right, the latter by election. The most accurate assessment of this group is provided by James VI who, in *Basilikon Doron*, observed 'the small barronis are but ane inferioure pairt of the nobillite & of thaire estait', *The Basilikon Doron of James VI*, ed. J. Craigie (2 vols, Edinburgh, 1944), I, 88–9; see also, J Wormald, 'Lords and Lairds in Fifteenth-

century Scotland: Nobles and Gentry?', *Gentry and Lesser Nobility in late Medieval Europe*, ed M. Jones (Gloucester, 1986), p. 181; A. Grant, 'The Development of the Scottish Peerage', *Scottish Historical Review*, LVII, (1978), 1–27 *passim*.

5 For 1640–41 see for example, *APS*, V, 258–261, 279, 312, 384. For 1644–46 see *APS*, VI, I, 60–61, 71, 83–4, 93–4, 95–6, 284, 429, 440–1, 474–5, 612–13. In the roll of the Convention of Estates on 25 Jan 1644, the nobility and barons are listed together, with the 'burgess' [sic] listed below, *APS*, V, I, 73. For 1646–48, see Scottish RO, PA 7/24, f 200r; PA 11/5, ff 3–218; PA 11/6, f 1r-v. The term 'Commissionaris for the Barronis' was first used in July 1593, see *APS*, IV, 6–7.

6 *The Letters and Journals of Robert Baillie*, ed. D. Laing, (3 vols, Edinburgh, 1841–2) [hereafter Baillie, *Letters and Journals*], III, 18, 20, 34, 35, 38. See also, Guthry, *Memoirs*, pp. 262–5; P. Gordon, *A Short Abridgement of Britane's Distemper*, ed. J. Dunn (Spalding Club, Aberdeen, 1844), pp 206, 223. For the earlier 1640s, cf. J. Gordon, *History of Scots Affairs, 1637–1641* (3 vols, Spalding Club, 1841), III, 78, 133; Gordon, *Britane's Distemper*, p. 146. In 1643 Baillie talks of 'faction' and Gilbert Burnet recorded the contemporary labels, 'Argyle's party' and 'Hamilton party', Baillie, *Letters and Journals*, II, 59; G. Burnet, *The Memoirs of the Lives and Actions of James and William Dukes of Hamilton* (Oxford, 1673), p. 262. See also, *The Diplomatic Correspondence of Jean De Montereul and the Brothers De Bellievre, French Ambassadors in England and Scotland, 1645–1648*, ed. J. G. Fotheringham (2 vols, Edinburgh, 1898–9), *passim*. Charles I also viewed parliamentary factions in Scotland in the same way, see below.

7 A. I. MacInnes, 'The First Scottish Tories?', *Scottish Historical Review*, LXVII (1988), 56–66.

8 See, for example, Baillie's venomous description of the Independents in England, Baillie, *Letters and Journals*, III, 26–31. See also Guthry, *Memoirs*, p. 263.

9 Guthry, *Memoirs*, p. 262.

10 At least two streams are evident in recent writing on the nature of the political nation in Scotland 1560–1637; the first, championed by Maurice Lee jr argues for a conservative and declining nobility engaging with an innovative Crown allied to a rising middling sort, *John Maitland of Thirlestane and the Foundation of Stewart Despotism* (Princeton, 1959) and *idem, Government by Pen, Scotland under James VI and I* (Urbana, 1980). This view has also been influential in J. M. Goodare, 'Parliament and Society in Scotland, 1560–1603' (2 vols, University of Edinburgh PhD, 1989); *idem*, 'The Nobility and the Absolutist State in Scotland, 1584–1638', *History*, LXXVIII (1993), 161–82. The second stream, of a powerful nobility working with a robust Crown, can be recovered from J. Wormald, 'Bloodfeud, Kindred and Government in Early Modern Scotland' *Past and Present*, No. 87 (1980); *idem, Court, Kirk and Community* (London, 1981), pp. 151–2, 157; K. M. Brown, *Bloodfeud in Scotland, 1573–1625* (Edinburgh, 1986), *idem, Kingdom or Province? Scotland and the Regal Union, 1603–1715* (1993), pp. 33–51, esp. pp. 42–5. For the 1640s, the key role of the gentry in Parliament – a Scottish Commons, in fact – is powerfully argued in J. R. Young, 'The Scottish Parliament, 1639–1661: A Political and Constitutional Analysis' (3 vols, University of Glasgow PhD, 1993); A I Macinnes, *Charles I and the Making of the Covenanting Movement, 1625–1641* (Edinburgh, 1991); *idem*, 'Early Modern Scotland: The Current State of Play', *Scottish Historical Review*, LXXIII (1995), 37–40, 42. This article argues for a continuation of elements of the second stream into the parliamentary politics of the 1640s.

11 K. M. Brown, *Kingdom or Province*, pp. 13–14; D. Stevenson, *The Government of Scotland under the Covenanters, 1637–1651* (Edinburgh, 1982), Appendices, pp. 174–98; Young, 'The Scottish Parliament, 1639–1661', *passim*; Goodare, 'Parliament and Society in Scotland 1560–1603'; R. S. Rait, *The Parliaments of Scotland* (Glasgow, 1924); C. S. Terry, *The Scottish Parliament: Its Constitution and Procedure, 1603–1707* (Glasgow, 1905).

12 It was accepted *de facto* by some contemporaries that with the division of the lords temporal or nobles into higher nobility, or peerage and lesser barons there were unofficially four estates in Parliament, see Stevenson, *Government under the Covenanters*, pp. xxii-xxiii.

13 The historical context of the Lords of the Articles is best described in *APS*, I, 15–18.

14 The numbers varied between six and ten for each Estate and Officers of State, with an average of eight. See, for example, *APS*, IV, 194, 261, 280, 365–6, 413, 466–7, 526–7, 594–5; V, 9; Rait, *Parliaments*, pp. 7–8; Terry, *Parliament 1603–1707*, pp. 103–20. In 1606 there was a debate whether new Lords of Articles should be elected at the start of each session of Parliament or, as was the case, at the beginning of each Parliament, see *APS*, IV, 279–80.

15 *APS*, V, 9. According to the Covenanters in 1640, the retiring away from the chamber was introduced along with the bishops in the Parliament of 1617, see below. But it is hard to tell from *APS* since on some occasions the registers recorded that 'Eodem die domini electi ad articulos', *APS*, IV, 467 (1612), 526 (1617), 594 (1621). At other times the Registers state only 'Domini electi ad articulos', *APS*, III, 4 (1567), 195 (1581), 290 (1584). However, in 1592 it was stated 'the haill estaittis of parliament cheisit [. . .] derwttn to be lordis of the articles', *APS*, III, 530, and in 1604 'the q'lk day the haill estaittis of parliament [sic] cheisit the lordis underwrittin to be upoun the articlis', *APS*, IV, 260. In 1639, the Earl of Argyll questioned the method of election away from the chamber, *APS*, V, 252–3.

16 *APS*, IV, 467, 527, 595; *APS*, V, 11.

17 Macinnes, *Covenanting Movement*, pp. 86–9; P Donald, *An Uncounselled King: Charles I and the Scottish Troubles, 1637–1641* (Cambridge, 1990), pp. 29–32.

18 J. J. Scally, 'The Political Career of James, Third Marquis and First Duke of Hamilton (1606–1649) to 1643' (University of Cambridge PhD, 1992), pp. 214–62.

19 The most important of the reforms to the Scottish Parliament – Triennial Parliaments, parliamentary approval of the appointment of officers of state – quickly became demands in the English Parliament, cf C Russell, *The Causes of the English Civil War* (Oxford, 1990), pp. 27–8.

20 For the composition and political role of the Tables, see Macinnes, *Covenanting Movement*, pp. 166–8; Stevenson, *Government under the Covenanters*, pp. xv-xvi; J. K. Hewison, *The Covenanters* (2 vols, Glasgow, 1913), I, 256, 264.

21 Scally, 'Hamilton', pp. 209–10.

22 The division is clearly stated in *APS*, V, 260. See also, Scally, 'Hamilton', pp. 214–97.

23 *APS*, V, 251–8.

24 *Ibid.*, pp. 252–3; Traquair MSS, (Maxwell-Stuart, Traquair House, Innerleithen), 28/iii/41 (21 Aug 1639); 43 *passim*.

25 Traquair MSS, 28/iii/41 (21 August 1639).

26 *Ibid.*

27 *Ibid.*, Traquair to Charles I, 30 Aug 1639.

28 Parliament had reluctantly agreed to a prorogation in the last session, and when the King attempted to prorogue Parliament again they decided to sit on the day appointed, 2 June 1640. See *APS*, V, 258–9; Traquair MSS, 28/iii/43 (1–5 Nov. 1639).
29 *APS*, V, 259, 261.
30 *Ibid.*, p 260. The two main acts that the Covenanters rescinded were: Act, 15 Ja, VI c 235, concerning the Kirk, particularly prelates representing the third estate; Act 18 Ja, VI c 2, for the restitution of the estate of bishops.
31 *APS*, V, 258–300. Of the 60 items of legislation, about 50 were public acts that formed the core of the constitutional revolution. Thirty-nine of the most important of these were published. The public acts printed in the reign of Charles I are bound together in a volume in the National Library of Scotland, shelfmark Nha L92 (1–8).
32 *APS*, V, 279.
33 Parliament exercised greater power during the incompetent and absentee reign of David II (1329–71), and took on the executive role, see *APS*, I, 15, 73–6.
34 It became a regular feature that at the beginning of a session a powerful committee (variously called, *inter alia*, the Committee for 'Dispatches', or 'for Burdens and Pressures' or 'Dangers, Remedies and Duties') composed of leading party élites would be established to consider key issues, then report back to Parliament, cf *APS*, VI, I, 287, 477–8; VI, II, 10, 13 and below.
35 The Scottish parliamentary committees of the period, and much more besides, are listed and thoroughly analysed in Young, 'The Scottish Parliament, 1639–1661', *passim*. Dr Young's work on the Scottish Parliament is to be published by John Donald in 1996.
36 The Committee of Estates was often further divided with some members staying in Edinburgh, some travelling with the Covenanting Army, and other members chosen as Commissioners to attend the English Parliament in London.
37 *A True Representation of the Proceedings of the Kingdom of Scotland since the Late Pacification: By the Estates of the Kingdome* ([Edinburgh], 1640), p. 13.
38 *Ibid.*, p. 11.
39 *Ibid.*, p. 20.
40 *Ibid.*, p. 21.
41 At the beginning of the session in June 1640, a Committee of the Articles in the old style was chosen with four of each estate; it was not until a week into the session and after 'diverse questions [had] arisen, that the Covenanters fully reformed the Articles, see *APS*, V, 262, 278–9.
42 C. Russell, *The Fall of the British Monarchies 1637–1642* (Oxford, 1991), pp. 303–29; Donald, *Unconselled King*, pp. 259–319; Scally, 'Hamilton', pp. 298–323.
43 It was signed by 17 lords including Marischal, Montrose, Wigton, Kinghorne, Home, Athol, Mar, Perth, Seaforth, Almond and Johnstone, as well as Carnegy, master of Lour, see M. Napier, *Memorials of Montrose and His Times* (2 vols, Maitland Club, Edinburgh, 1848–51), I, 254–5.
44 Tollemache MSS. (Sir Lyonel Tollemache, Buckminster Park, nr Grantham, Lincs), 3748 (deposition of Walter Stewart, 5 June 1641); Traquair MSS, 28/iii/20, information against Argyll and Rothes [n. d.]; Scottish R O, GD 406/1/1382 Loudoun to Hamilton, 13 July 1641.
45 Tollemache MSS, 3748, deposition of Walter Stewart, 5 June 1641. See also, Russell, *Fall of the British Monarchies*, pp. 311–15; Donald, *Uncounselled King*, pp 292–5; Stevenson, *Scottish Revolution*, pp. 224–7.
46 Hamilton had been drifting away from the King since the summer of 1639, and his

deepening friendship with Argyll over the spring/summer of 1641 was another visible sign of this, see Scally, 'Hamilton', pp. 263–307.

47 Baillie, *Letters and Journals*, I, 391. Montrose, by focusing his fury on the two most able politicians of the 1640s, seems at least this once to have caught the measure of the King's dilemma.

48 For Napier, see Stevenson, *Scottish Revolution*, pp. 225–7; and *idem*, 'The "Letter on Sovereign Power" and the Influence of Jean Bodin on Political Thought in Scotland', *Scottish Historical Review*, LXI (1982), 25–43.

49 Stevenson, *Scottish Revolution*, p. 228.

50 HMC, *Hamilton, MSS*, p. 55 (item 117), contract of marriage [n. d.]; National Register of Archives (Scotland), No. 1209, Argyll Muniments, p. 31 (bundle 61), antenuptial contract of marriage, 10 Jan., 22 Apr., 1642.

51 Russell, *Fall of the British Monarchies*, Chapter 8, *passim*. See also Stevenson, *Scottish Revolution*, pp. 233–42; Donald, *Uncounselled King*, pp. 299–319; S. R. Gardiner, *History of England, 1603–42* (10 vols, 1883–4), X, 3–80.

52 The Parliament had been prorogued a number of times, see *The Diary of Sir Thomas Hope of Craighall, 1634–45*, ed. T. Thomson (Bannatyne Club, Edinburgh, 1843), p 148; Scottish R O, GD 406/1/1386, Loudoun and Dunfermline to Charles I, 16 July 1641. Apart from framing the orders of the House, most of the time was spent preparing evidence against the Incendiaries (Traquair, Sir John Hay, Sir Robert Spottiswood, Walter Balcanquhal and the Bishop of Ross) and the Montrose group or the Plotters (Montrose, Napier, Keir and Blackhall), cf. Traquair MSS, 37/18, 11/47.

53 R. K. Hannay and G. P. H. Watson, 'The Building of the Parliament House', *Book of the Old Edinburgh Club*, XIII, (1924), 1–78, esp. pp. 76–7. Sir Thomas Hope recorded in his diary that the session beginning in Aug. 1639 sat in the new Parliament House, Thomson (ed.), *Diary of Sir Thomas Hope*, p. 105.

54 J. Gifford *et al*, *Edinburgh* (1984), pp 119–23; Hannay and Watson, 'The Building of the Parliament House', pp. 1–6, 17–58.

55 *APS*, V, 313–14.

56 Fines for non-attendance per day reflected the social position of each estate: noblemen, 18 shillings, barons, 12 shillings, and burgesses, 6 shillings, see *ibid.*, 314.

57 Nat. Lib. Scotland, Adv. MS 33.7.7, p. 44.

58 *APS*, V, 342–344; Russell, *Fall of the British Monarchies*, pp 321–2; Stevenson, *Scottish Revolution*, p. 235.

59 The Covenanter nominees were Argyll for Chancellor and Loudoun for Treasurer. Charles put forward Morton for Chancellor and Loudoun for Treasurer, but Argyll vigorously opposed Morton even though he was his father-in-law. Then Charles proposed Loudoun as Chancellor and Almond as Treasurer, but Almond was rejected. Loudoun was eventually appointed chancellor at the end of September.

60 Baillie, *Letters and Journals*, I, 391. Appointment of officers of state was a very important issue, see Scottish R O, GD 406/1/1396, [Privy Council] to Charles I, 24 July 1641.

61 Bodl. Lib., MS Carte I, ff 456–66, esp ff 465–6, Sir Patrick Wemyss to Ormond, [early Oct] 1641; Scottish R O, GD 406/1/1430, Henry Percy to Hamilton, 20 Sept [1641]; *The Nicholas Papers: Correspondence of Sir Edward Nicholas, 1641–1652*, ed. G. F. Warner (4 vols, Camden Soc., new ser. XL, L, LVII, 3rd ser. XXXI, 1886–1920), I, 12–13, Vane to Nicholas, 17 Aug 1641; Earl of Clarendon, *History of the Rebellion and Civil Wars in England*, ed. W. D. Macray (6 vols, Oxford, 1888) [hereafter Clarendon, *History of the*

Rebellion], I, 389 n; Stevenson, *Scottish Revolution*, p 237; Donald, *Uncounselled King*, pp. 310–11.

62 On 29 September a drunken Lord Ker, son of the Earl of Roxburgh, had sent the Earl of Crawford with a message challenging Hamilton to a duel, see Baillie, *Letters and Journals*, I, 391; HMC, *Salisbury MSS*, XXII, 368; Bodl. Lib., MS Carte 1, ff. 465–6, Sir Patrick Wemyss to Ormond, [early Oct] 1641; HMC, *4th Report*, p. 167, Will Murray's deposition, 25 Oct 1641; Clarendon, *History of the Rebellion*, I, 389 n.

63 For a full examination of the Incident, see Scally, 'Hamilton', pp. 307–14; and Charles's affection for plots, see C. Russell, 'The first Army Plot of 1641', *Unrevolutionary England, 1603–1642* (1990), pp. 281–302.

64 HMC, *4th Report*, pp. 163–70, especially p. 167.

65 The day after the plot was revealed, Charles went to parliament escorted by an armed force, amongst whom were many of the men who had been implicated in the conspiracy, see Scottish R O, GD 406/1/1440, relation of the Incident by Earl of Lanark.

66 *APS*, V, 373–5, 378; Scottish R O, GD 406/1/1542/1–2, draft addresses to Parliament; GD 406/M1/284, [copies] Order of Parliament, President of Parliament (Balmerino) to Hamilton, Argyll and Lanark, Charles I to Hamilton, Argyll and Lanark, 1 Nov 1641; GD 406/1/1449, Loudoun to Hamilton, 1 Nov 1641. For Baillie's account of the Incident see, *Letters and Journals*, I, pp. 391–5. For Montrose's supplication to Parliament, see Scottish R O, GD 406/M1/284.

67 *APS*, V, 373–5, 378.

68 Charles tried something similar in England in January of the following year with his attempt to arrest some of his adversaries in the English Parliament on a charge of high treason, see *L J*, IV, 500–1; Gardiner, *England*, X, 135–142; Russell, *Fall of the British Monarchies*, pp. 447–53; A. J. Fletcher, *The Outbreak of the English Civil War* (1981), pp. 180–4.

69 Scally, 'Hamilton', pp. 328–38.

70 Ibid., pp. 329–31; *The Register of the Privy Council of Scotland, 1625–1660, 2nd Series* (8 vols, Edinburgh 1899–1908) [hereafter *RPCS, 2nd Ser*], *1638–43*, pp. 359–404; Scottish R O, GD 406/1/1692/1–3; Traquair MSS, 14/26; Baillie, *Letters and Journals*, II, 57–64. Before the Convention met, without the King's permission, Hamilton and Argyll had slogged it out in the Privy Council.

71 Burnet, *Lives of the Dukes of Hamilton*, p. 280, Councillors and Conservators to Charles I, 2 May 1643; *RPCS 2nd Ser, 1638–43*, pp. 429–34.

72 The Earl of Antrim, the Catholic Earl of Nithsdale and Lord Aboyne, the Earl of Huntly's son, were the main protagonists though Henrietta Maria, Huntly and Montrose were also involved, *RPCS, 2nd Ser, 1638–43*, pp. 436–8; Baillie, *Letters and Journals*, II, pp. 72–5; Stevenson, *Scottish Revolution*, pp. 270–5. For a full account of Antrim's career see, J. H. Ohlmeyer, *Civil War and Restoration in the Three Stuart Kingdoms: The Career of Randall MacDonnell, Marquis of Antrim, 1609–83* (Cambridge, 1993).

73 Just before the Convention, the English Parliament requested that the Earls of Morton, Roxburgh, Annandale, Kinnoul, Lanark and Carnwath be charged as Incendiaries. See *RPCS 2nd Ser, 1638–43*, pp. 450–2; Baillie, *Letters and Journals*, II, pp. 77–8.

74 The Covenanters' request that the King call a Parliament was refused, and the First Triennial Parliament was not due to assemble until June 1644, see Scally, 'Hamilton', pp pp. 330–1.

75 Baillie, *Letters and Journals*, II, 76–77; Traquair MSS, 14/26, 'Relation Concerning sume passagis of business in Scotland'.

76 Stevenson, *Scottish Revolution*, pp. 276–8.
77 *APS*, VI, 5–6; Stevenson, *Scottish Revolution*, p 277. The committee was made up of eight from each estate and the nobles voted for Hamilton, Argyll, Morton, Roxburgh, Lauderdale, Southesk, Lanark, Callendar and Balmerino.
78 *APS*, VI, I, 6.
79 Baillie, *Letters and Journals*, II, p. 77.
80 The English commissioners were the Earl of Rutland, Sir William Armyn, Sir Henry Vane the younger, Thomas Hatcher and Henry Darley, see *APS*, VI, I, pp. 23–4. They were accompanied by two English ministers, Stephen Marshall and Philip Nye.
81 *Ibid*, pp. 6–23, 23–43. The Covenant is at pp. 41–3. Both sides got what they wanted; the English their military alliance and the Scots their religious coalition.
82 *Ibid.*, pp. 43–59; Traquair MSS, 14/26, 'Relation Concerning sume passagis of business in Scotland'. For Baillie's version, see *Letters and Journals*, II, pp. 76–101. For a detailed narrative, cf Stevenson, *Scottish Revolution*, pp 284–91; G. Donaldson, *Scotland: James V–James VII* (Edinburgh, 1987), pp. 329–33.
83 Scally, 'Hamilton', pp. 334, 340. Montrose, Nithsdale, Aboyne, in alliance with Queen Henrietta Maria, were the authors of Hamilton's fall.
84 Montrose was eventually defeated by David Leslie at Philiphaugh in Sept. 1645. Before being defeated Montrose, uncharacteristically, in his capacity as Lieutenant Governor of Scotland had summoned a Parliament on 20 Oct 1645, see Donaldson, *Scotland*, p. 334.
85 *APS*, VI, I, 95–611.
86 Tollemache MSS, 3750, ff. 5v-40r. Charles's bounty caused consternation in the Committee of Estates who tried to limit it to those recommended by Parliament, see Scottish R O, GD 406/1/1965, 18 May 1646. For Charles's answer, see *ibid.*, 2027.
87 The correspondence between Hamilton in Edinburgh and Sir Robert Moray at Newcastle shows that both men felt the King's position in Scotland was hopeless unless he accepted the Covenant and Presbyterianism in some form, see, for example, Scottish R O, GD 406/1/2099, 2102, 2105, 2106, 2108; *The Hamilton Papers*, ed. S. R. Gardiner (Camden Soc, new series, XXVII, 1880), pp. 106–47.
88 Scally, 'Hamilton', pp. 214–98.
89 In 1646 Charles I distinguished '4 factions' in Scotland, 'Mountroses, the Neutralls, the Hamiltons, and the Campbells', see *Charles I in 1646: Letters of King Charles I to Queen Henrietta Maria*, ed. J. Bruce (Camden Soc., old series, LXIII, 1856), pp. 48–9.
90 This committee was a variation on the Committee of Dispatches which considered the most pressing issues confronting Parliament. There were ten from each Estate on the committee. The nobles were split thus, with Hamilton, Lanark, Glencairn, Roxburgh, Tullibardine, and possibly Findlater; and on the other side Argyll, Marshall, Cassillis and Balmerino, cf. *APS*, VI, I, 616. The Earl of Loudoun, Chancellor, and the Earl of Crawford-Lindsay, President of Parliament, were voted supernumeries and both were slowly moving towards Hamilton's party.
91 Scottish R O, GD 406/1/2102, 2106, 2108, 2109. Charles's public position can be recovered from the Moray/Hamilton correspondence cited above, whilst his covert thoughts are evident in his correspondence with the Queen, see Bruce (ed.), *Charles I in 1646, passim*, especially pp. 24–5, 27.
92 Guthry's claim, even if it is true, that Fletcher of Innerpeffer, one of the Shire Commissioners, had twice in Nov 1646 offered the support of the barons should Hamilton declare for the King must be viewed in the light of Hamilton's views on Charles's intransigence and, moreover, Guthry's dislike of Hamilton which went back at least to

1638, see Guthry, *Memoirs*, pp. 234–6. Guthry did concede that Hamilton and Lanark, with the Earls of Kinghorne and Tullibardine, Lords Spynie and Elibank, as well as eight commissioners from the barons and burghs, voted against leaving the King at Newcastle, *ibid.*, p. 237. The agreed sum to be paid was £400,000; half was to be paid before the Scots army withdrew, see D. Stevenson, *Revolution and Counter-Revolution in Scotland, 1644–1651* (1977), p. 73.

93 *APS*, VI, I, 659.

94 However, Argyll had managed to force through the disbandment of the Army that had been in England, leaving only a new model force under David Leslie to clear the Highlands of rebels, see Stevenson, *Revolution and Counter-Revolution*, pp. 82–3.

95 *APS*, VI, I, 764–6.

96 Instruction 2, 'that his Matie may sweare and subscryve the solemne League and covenant at least give his consent that it may be confirmed as a law'. *APS*, VI, i, 764.

97 *Ibid.*, pp. 766–8, 856.

98 The committee consisted of 60 from the three estates (21 nobles, 19 barons, and 20 burgesses) with about ten supernumeraries including Lord General Leven, Chancellor Loudoun, the Lord Treasurer and President of Parliament Crawford-Lindsay, as well as the Scottish Commissioners in England, see Scottish R O, PA 11/5, ff. 3r–5v. Curiously, Argyll is not included in the list of nobles, but took the oath after the powers of the committee was read out, and appears in the subsequent attendance lists, see, PA 11/5, ff. 5v, 7r–21v. The Hamiltons apparently believed they had more than half of the committee on their side, see Fotheringham (ed.), *Diplomatic Correspondence of Jean De Montereul*, II, 70–1.

99 Scottish R O, PA 11/5, ff. 92r–v, 93r–4v, 112r, 118v, 119r–20r (15 Oct.), 131v–4r. A Frequent meeting of the committee was one which most of the members attended; certainly one where heads of the main political factions were present.

100 *Ibid.*, ff. 59v–60v, 61r, 71v–72v, 74v–75r, 75v. The Independents in the House of Commons objected to Lanark's appointment as a commissioner, but he was defended by Sir Henry Vane the elder, Hamilton's old friend, see Scottish R O, GD 406/1/2254, Lauderdale to Lanark, 14 Sept. [1647].

101 Scottish R O, PA 11/5, f 76r, Committee of Estates to Commissioners in London, 21 Aug 1647; *ibid.*, ff . 77v, 97r, 107r, 109r–v.

102 Scottish R O, GD 406/1/2246, Robin Leslie to [Lanark], 25 July [1647]; Will Murray to Hamilton, 5 Mar 1627/8.

103 *Ibid.*, 9773, [drafts of letters] Lanark to Charles I, 22 Nov to 13 Dec 1647. These letters show that Lanark was inching towards an agreement, yet concerning the Covenant he reminded Charles that he was wrong to believe thet 'Scotland would be engaged at an easier rate'. See also, Scottish R O, PA 11/5, ff. 107v–8r.

104 S. R. Gardiner, *Constitutional Documents, 1625–1660* (Oxford, 1899), pp. 347–53, esp. p. 351.

105 Scottish R O, PA 11/5, ff. 199v (21 Jan. 1648), 209v–10v, 212v.

106 *Ibid.* f 216r (25 Feb 1648); Scottish R O, GD 406/1/2377; Baillie, *Letters and Journals*, III.

107 Baillie, *Letters and Journals*, III, p. 35. Fifty-six nobles are recorded in the sederunt for 2 Mar., see *APS*, VI, ii, 3–4. Argyll's party, normally so adept at mobilising the barons of the shires, appears to have suffered as a result of 'double-elections' whereby of the two barons sent, one supported Hamilton, the other Argyll, see Guthry, *Memoirs*, p. 259.

108 *APS*, VI, ii, 10.

109 *Ibid.* There were six of each Estate on the Committee plus Loudoun as supernumerary; Argyll and Wariston were members but were hopelessly outnumbered by the supporters of Hamilton and Callander.
110 Initially this concerned the immediate securing of Berwick and Carlisle, see *APS*, VI, ii, 13.
111 Guthry, *Memoirs*, pp. 262–4; Baillie, *Letters and Journals*, III, 37–8; *APS*, VI, ii, 13.
112 *APS*, VI, ii, 23–124; Scottish R O, PA 11/6, ff 1–47; Baillie, *Letters and Journals*, III, 37–55; Guthry, *Memoirs*, pp. 263–301.
113 *APS*, VI, ii, 124–316.

The Reluctant Revolutionaries: Scotland in 1688

IB Cowan 1989 *in* E Cruickshanks (ed.), *By Force or By Default? The Revolution of 1688–89*, Edinburgh (John Donald), 65–81.

The antecedents to the Glorious Revolution in England found few if any parallels in Scotland despite the similarity of the policies pursued by James VII in his northern kingdom. Even the birth of his son 'the Prince Royal and Stewart of Scotland' on 10 June 1688, which precipitated the succession crisis in England and led to the invitation to William of Orange to intervene by restraining, if not necessarily displacing, the king occasioned little interest north of the Border.[1] Willliam's proclamation addressed to the Scots which echoed the corresponding English version issued on 10 October stressing the unconstitutional nature of James's rule and the threat of Catholicism but silent on other ecclesiastical issues, fell on equally deaf ears.[2] Even the news of the outbreak of the revolution in England occasioned by William's landing at Torbay on 5 November brought little initial reaction among the Scots and if a number of anti-catholic riots characterised early December, only the flight of James on 23 December brought the Revolution in Scotland closer to fruition.[3]

The Scottish reluctance to rebel stemmed from a variety of reasons both political and ecclesiastical. In political terms James appeared to be impregnable and indeed enjoyed more widespread support than his brother before him. Much of this stemmed from James's inherent knowledge of the Scottish political situation which he had viewed at first-hand during his stay in Scotland as royal commissioner to parliament at the height of the Exclusion crisis which attempted to preclude his succession to the throne of England.[4] Even in this emergency, royal authority in Scotland was largely unquestioned for although there may have been mutterings in private, few, other than extreme presbyterians, publicly questioned the validity of the appointment of James duke of York as commissioner in a court in which, by an act of 1609, no catholic might be a member.[5] The passage of the Succession Act securing the right of hereditary succession and the Test Act requiring office holders to swear adherence to the protestant faith as expressed in the Scots Confession of 1560 meant various problems were soon to arise for the Confession (which contained statements totally at variance with the substance of the Test) uncompromisingly defined Christ Jesus as 'the only heid of his kirk' and further declared that the sovereign was only to be obeyed in matters 'not repugning to the worde of

God'.[6] Not only was the recognition of the king's supremacy inconsistent with the Scots Confession, but the Test Act taken in conjunction with the earlier act of succession implied that James as a future catholic sovereign would become supreme governor of the protestant church. As Lord Belhaven astutely remarked, the Test Act was 'a very good act for securing our religion from one another . . . but not an act to secure our religion against a Popish or fanatical successor to the crown'.[7] Conveyed to Edinburgh castle for his pertinent remark and accused of treason, he was released only after a formal apology.[8]

The latent religious opposition to an otherwise obsequious parliament in 1681 should have alerted the duke that it was possible to put too great a strain on the obedience of the Scottish Estates. The loyalty of his Council, however, may have blinded him to this possibility for in May 1682, on his return to England after advising the Council to suppress rebellious persons and protect the orthodox clergy, the Council for its part praised the duke for 'the excellent patterns of government which wee have had from yow and for the great proffes of your kindnes to us upon all occasions'.[9] Moreover, James's first parliament after his accession to the throne, elected under the conditions prescribed and meeting during the excitement of Archibald Campbell, ninth earl of Argyll's anti-catholic rebellion in Scotland and of the duke of Monmouth's similarly motivated rising in England, was to prove exceedingly loyal despite fears to the contrary, when James warned his commissioner Queensberry 'to suffer nothing to pass to the prejudice of the Roman Catholics more than was already'.[10] Despite rumours of the king's intentions on religious issues, members of parliament evinced the most exemplary obedience, initially pledging their lives and fortunes to 'assist, support, defend and mentain king James the Seventh'.[11] In further token of their loyalty they ordered that 'all of this Nation, betuixt sixty and sixteen, armed and provyded according to their abilities, shall be in readiness for his Majesties service, where and oft as it shall be his royal pleasure to require them'.[12] As a more immediate sign of dutiful obedience parliament then proceeded to grant the excise duty to the crown for all time.[13]

Encouraged by this submissiveness and the ease with which the earl of Argyll's rebellion 'For God and Religion, against Poperie, Tyrannie, Arbitrary Government and Errestianisme' had been crushed, the king pressed on with his plans to promote Catholicism by proceeding to announce the conversion of his subservient councillors, the pliant lord chancellor, James Drummond, fourth earl of Perth and of the two secretaries of state, the mischief-making John Drummond, first earl of Melfort (Perth's brother) and Alexander Stewart, fifth earl of Moray, who was rewarded by being chosen to replace the protestant William Douglas, first earl of Queensberry as commissioner in the new session of parliament in 1686.[14]

The state of euphoria which his previous successes had engendered led James to press on with his plans to benefit further his co-religionists with the recommendation to the Estates that 'others our innocent subjects, those of the Roman Catholick religion' might 'have the protections of our lawes and that security under our government which others of our subjects have, not suffering them to lye under obligations which their religion can not admitt of'.[15] Realising that some inducement might be required to achieve this goal, James also prudently announced that the opening of free trade with England would be 'oure particular care'. Even then parliament's reply was not enthusiastic, promising only to take the king's recommendations into 'serious and dutiful consideration' and with 'tendernes to their persones', it promised to 'go as great lengths therein as our conscience will allow'.[16]

Interpreting this answer in the spirit in which it had been given, the king's ministers tried to overawe this apparently intractable parliament into submission. Members of parliament who held commissions were ordered to attend to the duties of their posts, but they offered instead to tender their resignations.[17] Others who held offices under the crown were dismissed, while burgess members were threatened with an investigation into their qualifications as resident traders.[18] Attempts were made to persuade opponents to absent themselves and numerous pamphlets in favour of toleration were circulated.[19] All this was unavailing for, although the act narrowly survived its passage through the Committee of the Articles and parliament was kept in session until the middle of June 'to weary out the poorer sort, who had exhausted both their money and credit', parliament had eventually to be prorogued to prevent defeat.[20] 'The finger of God,' it was asserted by one contemporary, 'was much to be seen in the steadfastness of this Parliament, who had not one great man in publict place to oune them: and it behooved to be from some hyer principle that Noblemen, Gentlemen, Bishops and others cheerfully laid doune their places, rather than violat their consciences'.[21] The Tory parliament of James VII had shown for the first time since 1660 that there was a limit to the arbitrary power of the crown. Yet in the overthrowal of James VII, parliament was to play no part and the actions which it had taken in 1686 had no direct results. In the eyes of James and his councillors parliament's action only confirmed the view expressed in 1674 by John Maitland, second earl and duke of Lauderdale, that 'Scots parliaments are . . . useless at the best' and endorsed his conclusion of 1663 'that this kingdome returne to the good old forme of government by his Majesties privie councell'.[22] James after venting his spleen on Queensberry by removing him from the presidency of the council, decided to follow Lauderdale's advice with the added precaution of restructuring the Council's membership; a task made somewhat easier by granting new members dispensation from the Test and informing them that he had suspended the operation of the penal laws against catholics.[23] The effectiveness of the purge was also reinforced by a further edict which forbade municipal corporations to elect new town councils and soon afterwards provosts were nominated whom he authorised to choose magistrates and councillors.[24] This step was accompanied by the dissolution of parliament, for the king intended to summon another, in which he might rely upon support from the burgesses.[25]

James's belief in his rectitude and in his own abilities was unshakeable. His experience of Scottish affairs which might have proved an asset remained unutilised and advice from others was unwelcome. His belief in toleration appears to have been genuine, but this naïve assumption that others would share this feeling reveals how poor a politician he was. These weaknesses were not lost, however, on other Scottish politicians, many of whom would have agreed with the judgement that James had 'nather great conduct, nor a deep reach in affairs, but was a silly man', and in this belief they hoped to exploit these traits to their own advantage.[26] In consequence, James was open to manipulation by a series of politicians whose advice to him was seldom disinterested. On a few basic issues he could not be moved, but otherwise he could be manipulated and this factor served not only to create an instability in Scottish politics, but also to keep unscrupulous politicians loyal to his cause in the hope that political influence could either be retained or hopefully obtained at the expense of others. Thus, Melfort and Perth, two unprincipled careerists who encouraged James in his most extreme policies, urging him along on the claim that he was an absolute monarch, not only strove to ingratiate themselves with the king, but also worked relentlessly to undermine the influence of Queensberry whom James in deference to their wishes dismissed in 1686 after an unremitting campaign against him.[27]

John Campbell, first earl of Breadalbane, an intelligent but wary politician on the other hand, avoided this fate by supporting toleration in the 1686 parliament.[28] Success was, however, sometimes short-lived and the rise of George Gordon, first duke of Gordon was equally effectively blocked by the jealousy of Perth and Melfort. They too, like their royal master who suppressed his deep distrust of Scottish presbyterians when he imposed toleration in 1687, overlooked their hatred of presbyterianism to collaborate in James's policies. At least, they hoped by so doing to gain concessions for their co-religionists.[29] Others who served the king including Breadalbane, John Mackenzie, master of Tarbat and Sir John Dalrymple had no excuse other than rank opportunism.[30] Through such sycophants James ruled Scotland by means of an exceptionally unrepresentative government fittingly described as 'a strange mixture of rogues and converts to Roman Catholicism'.[31] If other politicians who were effectively barred from power by such a coalition might have been expected to resist the king's policies, it is clear that the hope of supplanting one or other of the councillors kept many equally unscrupulous rivals ostensibly loyal to the crown, while others who may have contemplated rebellion may have remembered the fate of Argyll and those whose opposition had ended in exile in Holland. Even the knowledge that William of Orange had landed at Torbay brought no immediate reaction from politicians who wished to assure their own positions before committing themselves to a new master.

For the same reason established churchmen were equally unwilling to shed the status which they had already enjoyed lest their privileged position be hazarded, and in the case of the presbyterians until further concessions were on offer. In this respect the catholic faction had much to lose and little to gain; certainly the Scottish catholics to whom James had shown singular favour were unlikely to assume the role of prospective revolutionaries and were instead committed to the support of a king who had steadfastly supported his co-religionists. Unfortunately for James, Catholicism in Scotland was in a much weaker state than he had estimated. All in all there were perhaps only about two thousand catholics between the Moray Firth and the Solway, many of these concentrated in Dumfries-shire and in the highland areas of Aberdeen and Banff in north-east Scotland.[32] Many more, it was claimed, existed in the Highlands and Islands, but estimates sent in 1681 to the Congregation of Propaganda in Rome claiming some twelve thousand adherents in these parts are extremely unreliable, the correct figure being close to four thousand.[33] James VII's attempts to augment their numbers, however, were none too successful. Admittedly in many parts both catholics and protestants had only a superficial foothold but if the populace in some of these regions showed a greater proclivity for Catholicism than Protestantism it was an advantage which could not be readily exploited by the handful of priests who served the area.

The aftermath of the Popish Plot made this task even more difficult, the mission in the central and west Highlands and the Isles for a time being reduced to two priests.[34] However, with the encouragement of James and assisted with a royal grant of two hundred pounds the mission increased its strength to twelve.[35] In the new climate, some waverers who headed traditionally Catholic clans – Alasdair Macdonald of Glengarry and Coll Macdonald of Keppoch – for example, were induced to embrace Catholicism.[36] Clan influence possibly swayed these conversions which did not carry much personal conviction, but others were apparently prompted by a greater zeal for the faith. By 1685 Kenneth Mackenzie, fourth earl of Seaforth had not only converted, but also influenced his younger brothers John Mackenzie of Assynt and Alexander to do likewise.[37] Sir John Maclean, sent at the king's insistence for education in France in 1688 converted at the Scots College in Paris, and thereafter remained committed, as did most other converts, to the Catholic and Jacobite cause.[38] Other conversions, however, were motivated neither by clan interest nor by personal conviction but appear to have stemmed from purely self-interest. Archibald Campbell, Lord Lorne, for instance, embraced Catholicism in the unrealistic hope that he would regain the Argyll estates.[39] The conversion of the master of Tarbat who hoped to gain Lewis from Mackenzie of Seaforth was not only in vain, but ill-timed, taking place in November 1688.[40] As has been observed, the cynical assumptions these conversions revealed was the belief 'that James would reverse his most important policies to please a convert or sacrifice the previous convert to the more recent'.[41]

Certainly in attempting to build up a power base on the strength of conversions, James proved singularly inconsistent. Some early converts obtained their anticipated rewards but even old established catholic families could not be certain of royal favour. The duke of Gordon obtained the governorship of Edinburgh castle in 1685, but had to wait another eight months before gaining a place in the Council and Treasury, and rose no further largely at the instigation of Perth and Melfort, who, despite their own conversions, bitterly opposed their fellow catholics.[42] Divisions of this kind did little to create a united catholic front which might have protected the king's interests north of the Border.

In other circumstances, such protection might have been more readily obtained from the established episcopal church, but here too while revolution was not on the agenda, criticism of the king's policies was at times very much to the fore. Nevertheless, the established church had become so dependent upon the state that although signs of opposition appeared over the Test act of 1681, the threat posed by the eventual succession of a catholic king was accepted by most members of the established church. Nevertheless ministers who had loyally supported the episcopal regime throughout all its previous difficulties found James's Catholicism a bitter pill to swallow. The ultra-conservative synod of Aberdeen was constrained to issue an explanation of the meaning of the Test Act after ministers had stated their objections to it. Among other features this apologia reserved for the establishment intrinsic spiritual power, permitted meetings for church discipline and for the protection of Protestantism and admitted the possibility of the alteration of church government when not accomplished by arms of sedition.[43] A similar declaration was issued by the synod of Dunkeld and in the face of such protests the Council was constrained to issue their own interpretation of the Test on 3 November 1681.[44] It explained that ministers who took the Test need not swear to every proposition or clause contained in the Confession of Faith 'but only to the true protestant religion founded on the word of God . . . as it is opposit to poperie and phanatisisme'.[45] This concession which was in itself inconsistent with the declaration in the Test that it was to be taken 'in the plain genuine sense and meaning of the words, without any equivocation, mental reservation, or any manner of evasion whatsoever', had also been accompanied by the threat that those who deviated in the terminology of the oath should be 'esteemed persons disaffected to the protestant religion, and to his majesty's government'.[46]

No number of explanations and concessions could persuade some of the validity of the Test Act. Among the ministers who refused the Test, the most notable was Laurence Charteris, professor of Divinity at Edinburgh university, and his example was followed by a considerable number of ministers who were consequently deprived.[47] Just how many deprivations took place is questionable as estimates have varied between thirty and eighty.[48] Some clue to the actual number may be found, however, in the fact that many of these deprived were from the Lothians and that John Paterson, bishop of Edinburgh, stated in February 1683 that there were more recusants in the two contiguous presbyteries of Dalkeith and Haddington than in all the rest of Scotland.[49] At least seventeen ministers were ousted in these two presbyteries and, if accurate, this would favour the lesser of the two estimates, but a figure of thirty or so deprivations is probably a conservative assessment. The final count may have been nearer fifty, of whom about twenty followed the example of Gilbert Burnet, later bishop of Salisbury, and entered the Church of England, an action which has never been fully investigated.[50] Whatever the total number, the church once more had been purged of dissidents and emerged more strongly committed to the establishment and the dictates of the crown.

The church's unswerving loyalty was dutifully transferred to James VII in 1685 and thereafter continued unimpaired despite the king's overt Catholicism. Indeed it appears that some episcopal ministers were even prepared to cast a blind eye at missionary activity by catholic priests in areas which had traditionally favoured that faith.[51] Catholic conversions among the magnates were met with an equally discreet silence and more positively by an injunction to the clergy not to preach on the subject of conversions, a reference in one sermon by an incumbent to 'fallen stars among us and yet they keipt their station' bringing swift retribution.[52] Even bishops were not immune from censure or even dismissal as was initially demonstrated when episcopal opposition arose during the crown's attempts to press for toleration in the 1686 parliament in which the bishop of Dunkeld imprudently stated 'old constitutions are, for their salubrity compared to old-lived men, and not rashly to be altered'; an allusion in the eyes of the chancellor to the antiquity of the laws against popery.[53] For his temerity the bishop was deprived of his see; a fate which the bishop of Ross narrowly escaped after preaching a sermon 'which scandalized the Papists extremely'.[54] To avoid further controversy, Robert Douglas the bishop of Dunblane was also forbidden to preach 'because he would not give assurance to forbear the preaching against Popery, nor show his papers'.[55] Even these salutary reminders of royal authority were insufficient to silence opposition: as in early 1687 Archbishop Alexander Cairncross of Glasgow was also deposed for allowing anti-catholic sermons to go unpunished.[56] This action, far from provoking further opposition not only acted as a warning to other clergy that further criticism might prove unwise, but also as a salutary reminder that the security of the church lay with the crown, without whose protection rival factions might triumph. The possibility of a meaningful catholic resurgence was, however, slight in comparison to that of a presbyterian revival.

For the presbyterians, revolution was not a new phenomenon as the struggle against royal authority had lasted for much of the seventeenth century. In the struggle against Charles I they had initially shared a common cause with the English parliamentarians, but had latterly fought for both Charles and his son against the Cromwellians, only to suffer conquest and military occupation. The Restoration brought independence to the Scots but little comfort to the presbyterians who found themselves yet again ranged against a state which had reimposed an episcopal establishment upon those who had favoured a presbyterian solution. In consequence, by 1663 almost one third of the ministry had either elected to leave the church or had been deprived for their failure to conform to an edict commanding ministers presented to their charges since 1649 to receive presentation from their former patrons and collation from their bishops.[57]

Some of the ousted ministers thereafter held meetings or conventicles while many of their parishioners followed their example and withdrew from their parish churches; an action which inevitably provoked government reprisals. This in turn culminated in two armed rebellions, one in 1666 – the Pentland Rising, and another and more serious outbreak in 1679 which ended in the defeat of the conventicling army at Bothwell Bridge by a government army commanded by the Duke of Monmouth. Between these two incidents, a policy of offering Indulgence to non-conformists had met with only partial success and had created a rift between those able to accept some measure of state control and those who were not willing to accede to such a compromise. These differences came to a head before the battle of Bothwell Bridge in a series of declarations and counter-declarations which were to be crucial for both presbyterians and the covenanting cause.[58] One faction which was essentially clerical in its leadership, in a declaration affixed to the mercat cross of Hamilton reaffirmed the defensive nature of the rising which they averred had been occasioned by the woeful state of the land and church through the brutal execution of the laws and refusal of redress from the authorities.[59] In stressing the subjects' allegiance to the magistrates, their maintenance of the king's authority, and in their desire for a free parliament and a free General Assembly they accepted a degree of compromise and developed an appeal to presbyterianism at large which placed them nearer the Indulged than the extremists which they were destined to fight beside. Their opponents on the other hand railed against all the defectors and encroachments upon the prerogatives of Jesus Christ and stressed in their declarations their abhorrence of the Indulgences and the Indulged. A king who had broken the covenant, altered the polity of the church and waged war against the godly was equally to be distrusted.[60]

Defeat at Bothwell Bridge brought these differences to a head with the extremists – the Cameronians, led by their minister Richard Cameron declaring war upon the king and the state in a series of declarations, while the moderate presbyterians, dispirited and powerless in defeat, faced continued persecution aimed at harrying their adherents back into the ranks of the established church. This policy, accompanied by the systematic withdrawal of licences granted under earlier Indulgences (including those given under a short-lived Indulgence of 1681 as a momentary attempt at conciliation following Bothwell Bridge) left the presbyterians seriously weakened, although in practice reunited with those who sought a measure of support from the state.[61] In the early 1680s concessions of this sort must have seemed a remote possibility and with the advent in 1683 of James Renwick as a preacher to the Cameronians; an event described by the moderate presbyterians as the 'great cause and occasion of all the troubles of the country', their cause declined further as persecution began to have its desired effect and dissidents reluctantly returned to the established church. The prospect of a united church at that point seemed attainable.[62]

That this in the end proved not to be so owed less to the Cameronians than to the folly of James VII who, in his desire to aid his co-religionists, was forced to include quakers and presbyterians in his concessions. If in the first Indulgence of February 1687, presbyterians were discriminated against, this was more than rectified in a second Indulgence issued in July in which all restrictions, with the exception of those against field conventicles, were lifted and leave was granted to all subjects 'to meet and serve God after their own way and manner, be it in private houses, chapels or places purposely hired or built for that use'.[63] The effect was immediate. Ministers and others released from prison were joined by exiled ministers from Holland. Many of them met in Edinburgh on 20 July and on the following day penned an address of thanks to the king. This gratitude influenced presbyterian attitudes to their catholic sovereign; further armed conflict was far from their mind; reliance on royal favour rather than revolution against royal authority was their immediate preoccupation.[64] Plans were drawn up for implementing the Indulgence and establishing of an embryonic presbyterian structure. The bitter infighting which had characterised the reception of the earlier Indulgences had all but disappeared and co-operation was henceforward to be the keynote. Presbyteries were to be established and meetings of these courts were to be convened at least once a month at which ministers were to seek advice and submit themselves to the discipline of their fellow ministers.[65] The setting up of meeting houses was also to be a co-operative venture since it was conceded that 'it cannot be expected, that there can be as many meeting houses as parishes'.[66] Provision was also made for encouraging students, licensing them and ordaining them to congregations.[67] In practice, the presbyterians set about re-erecting the body of their church in so far as this could be accomplished within the terms of the privileges conceded to them.

The gratitude shown to James by the presbyterians was not shared by the extreme Cameronians. Leaderless since the death of Richard Cameron in a skirmish and the subsequent execution of their sole remaining minister, Donald Cargill, in 1681, they had been led since 1683 by their minister James Renwick who viewed the Toleration Act as an erastian breach of Covenant and refused to accept its concessions or its terms. A *Testimony against Toleration* was transmitted to a meeting of ministers in January 1688 and the tradition of conventicling was commended by Renwick and his followers who even ventured to hold such gatherings in the vicinity of Edinburgh.[68] After one such meeting Renwick was apprehended on 1 February and after examination declared an irreconcilable opponent of the king. This position was maintained at his trial seven days later and made sentence of death inevitable. Thereafter, intensive efforts were made even by his prosecutors to gain some acknowledgement of the king's authority which might be used to mitigate the sentence. It was all to no avail, but if radical conventiclers could still expect such a fate, the ecclesiastical climate was already undergoing change. The shadow of religious rebellion had been dispelled by the Indulgences and the compromising attitude of the presbyterian ministers who were even willing to pray for a catholic king in order to retain their new-found privileges.[69] In isolation the Cameronians were revealed as a small insignificant sect who, despite their spirited and sonorous declarations had no longer the ability or the resources for initiating, far less sustaining, war against the state, either to gain their objectives or to express their disapproval of James's catholicising policies. The open disapproval of the Cameronians coupled with the failure of the established church to accept their principles could not in themselves have been expected to initiate Revolution and even at this juncture decisive action by the Council might have contained the situation, but before the king's departure panic had replaced wise counsel.

On 10 December the chancellor, the earl of Perth, spurning the security of Edinburgh castle, fled to castle Drummond, leaving the Council who thereafter added several members to their secret committee, to their own devices.[70] That evening a mob sacked the abbey of Holyrood, the nave of which served as a catholic chapel royal, looted the Jesuits' quarters and schools and desecrated the tombs of Scottish kings.[71] Two days later the Council, meeting under Atholl's presidency, commissioned Breadalbane to explain the riot to James who, it was hoped, could be persuaded to abandon his pro-catholic policies and entrust the conduct of Scottish affairs, under the guidance of William of Orange, to traditional Scottish leaders.[72]

The king's flight ended such hopes and revealed the venality and self-interest of many of the councillors who, as unrest swept the country, accepted a change of sovereign without any undue concern.

Mob rule, encouraged by the absence of standing forces which had been called south in anticipation of the expected invasion, rather than constitutional reform at first prevailed. Following the riot in Edinburgh, covenanting presbyterians seized the opportunity to rabble curates of the established church who before ejection from their manses and livings were forced to surrender their church keys and communion plate after being stripped of their clerical apparel; a process frequently accompanied by physical violence.[73] To much of this the Council was oblivious, its members intent only on protecting their own interests. Even the retention of Edinburgh castle by the catholic Duke of Gordon remained unchallenged on account of the bitter rivalry between Atholl and Queensberry who might have regained custody but for Atholl's intervention.[74] The departure of most of the councillors for London where office under the new regime could alone be secured, left Scotland in chaos with a privy council bereft of authority and largely ungoverned for almost three months.[75]

During this period, support for James wavered further. His ill-judged policies, his flight to France and the consequent declaration in the English Bill of Rights that he had thereby abdicated the throne allowed presbyterian politicians such as John Cunningham, tenth earl of Glencairn, William, eighteenth earl of Crawford and Sir James Montgomerie of Skelmorlie, an influence which they might have been otherwise denied.[76] A return to normality was not easily achieved for although the Council as early as 24 December had urged William to call a free parliament, this plea had to be reiterated formally in early January 1689 when a meeting of Scots notables asked William to summon a convention, but it was not until 14 March that such a meeting took place.[77]

Although attempts had been made by the presbyterians to influence the composition of the convention, Jacobites were almost as numerous at its commencement as their opponents. However, whereas the opposition were single-minded in their resolve to dispose of James, his supporters through lack of direction and leadership were uncertain as to their best course of action. Waverers and place-seekers abounded, the narrowness of the gap between the contending parties being initially apparent in the close contest for the presidency of the assembly between William Douglas, third duke of Hamilton, representing the Williamites and John Murray, second earl of Atholl for the Jacobites, the former only narrowly winning the day.[78] Although important this result was not decisive, that moment being reserved for the reading on 16 March of letters from the rivals for the crown. That of William was a model of diplomacy, safeguarding the protestant faith, but making no firm pronouncement on the future form of church government. James's letter, on the other hand, threatened all who forsook their natural allegiance; a loyalty which many believed could encompass papal as well as royal authority. Even James's most loyal supporters were disheartened and many, including Atholl left the convention which was subsequently dominated by William's supporters.[79]

Thereafter events moved with an ever-quickening pace. On 4 April, it was resolved that James had not abdicated, but had rather forfeited the throne through his misdemeanours; A Claim of Right which laid down fundamental constitutional principles and condemned prelacy as 'a great and insupportable grievance and trouble to the nation' was accepted on 11 April and was followed by the proclamation of William and Mary as joint sovereigns.[80] Two days later the passage of the Articles of Grievances reinforced the ecclesiastical and constitutional ideals of the Revolution settlement in their reaffirmation of the rejection of episcopacy and their specific condemnation of the Committee of the Articles.[81] On 11 May, William and Mary accepted the crown of Scotland, apparently (though this was questioned) on the terms already outlined.[82] A basis of the Revolution settlement had been determined by this date. Only the Jacobite rising led by viscount Dundee which, despite victory at Killiecrankie on 27 July 1689, was halted by the death of its leader and the subsequent defence of Dunkeld on 17–18 August, delayed the final constitutional and ecclesiastical settlement until 1690.[83]

A revolution which had such inauspicious beginnings was to prove to be a major turning point in the political and ecclesiastical governance of Scotland. It is undeniable, however, that the Scots who so enthusiastically embraced such principles in the course of 1689–90 had at the onset been very reluctant revolutionaries.

NOTES

1 *The Register of the Privy Council of Scotland* [*Reg Privy Council*], ed. J. H. Burton and others (Edinburgh, 1877), 3rd series, xiii, p xlvii; *Historical Notices of Scottish Affairs, Selected from the manuscripts of Sir John Lauder of Fountainhall, bart., one of the senators of the College of Justice* [Fountainhall *Historical Notices*], ed. D. Laing, 2 vols (Bannatyne Club, 1848), ii, 896–7. Fountainhall records that although the court of session sat during November 1688, yet by the Prince of Orange's arrival in England, no business was done, save on a few bills (Fountainhall, *Historical Notices*, ii, 884).

2 R. Wodrow, *The History of the Sufferings of the Church of Scotland from the Restoration to the Revolution*, 2 vols, [Edinburgh, 1721–2] cited hereafter in the later edition ed. R. Burns, 4 vols (Glasgow, 1828–30), iv, pp. 470–2.

3 D. Burnet, *Siege of Edinburgh Castle, MDCLXXXIX*. Presented by Robert Bell (Bannatyne Club, 1828), 13; G. Donaldson, *Scotland: James V–James VII*, The Edinburgh History of Scotland, 4 vols, (Edinburgh, 1969), 384.

4 W. Ferguson, *Scotland's Relations with England: A survey to 1707* (Edinburgh, 1977), pp. 158–61; Paul Hopkins, *Glencoe and the End of the Highland War* (Edinburgh 1986), pp. 68–71, 83–8.

5 James, duke of York arrived in Scotland in November 1679 (*Reg Privy Council*, 3rd series, vi, 331, 344) and left in February 1680 (ibid., vi, 392–3). He returned to Scotland in November 1680 (*Reg. Privy Council*, 3rd series, vi, 565–8) and became royal commissioner in July 1681 (*The Acts of the Parliaments of Scotland* [*Acts Parl. Scot.*] eds T. Thomson and C. Innes (Edinburgh, 1814–75), vi, p. 406); *Reg. Privy Council*, 3rd series, vii, 148; he finally departed on 6 March 1682 (Fountainhall, *Historical Notices*, i, 349).

6 *Acts Parl. Scot.*, ii, 530–532; *ibid.*, iii, 14, 23, 36; viii, 238, c2; 243, c6; *The Works of John Knox*; collected and edited by David Laing, 6 vols (Bannatyne Club, 1846–64), ii, 108–12.

7 Fountainhall, *Historical Notices*, 307.

8 *Ibid.*, 307–8; *Acts Parl. Scot.*, viii, 242.

9 *Reg Privy Council*, 3rd series, vii, 373.

10 Fountainhall, *Historical Notices*, 677.

11 *Acts Parl. Scot.*, viii, 459–60.

12 *Ibid.*, viii, 459–60.

13 *Ibid.*, viii, 460.

14 Fountainhall, *Historical Notices*, 715–18.

15 *Acts Parl. Scot.*, viii, 579–81.

16 *Ibid.*

17 Fountainhall, *Historical Notices*, ii, 723–34.

18 *Ibid.*, ii, 723, 734–5.

19 Fountainhall, *Historical Notices*, ii, 726–35.

20 *Ibid.*, 735–6; *Reports of the Royal Commission on Historical Manuscripts* [*Hist MSS Comm*] (London, 1870–): *MSS of the Earl of Mar and Kellie* (1904), 216–19.

21 Fountainhall, *Historical Notices*, ii, 737.

22 *The Lauderdale Papers*, ed O Airy, 3 vols (Camden Society, 1884–5), i, p. 172; iii, p. 36.

23 Fountainhall, *Historical Notices*, ii, pp. 740–1, 748, 750–1.

24 *Ibid.*, ii, pp. 750–7.

25 *Ibid.*, p. 745.

26 *Ibid.*, i, p. 327.

27 'Duke Queensberry was an atheist in religion, a villain in friendship, a knave in business and a traitor in his carriage to him' [James] (Melfort to the duke of Hamilton, 3 December 1685) *HMC* 11th Rep. App. VI, 171); Fountainhall, *Historical Notices,* ii, pp. 675, 740.

28 Hopkins, *Glencoe*, p. 104.

29 Fountainhall, *Historical Notices*, ii, pp. 13, 794, 822; Burnet, *The Siege of Edinburgh Castle*, pp. 5–6; Hopkins, *Glencoe*, pp. 107–8.

30 Donaldson, *Scotland: James V–James VII*, p. 383; Fountainhall, *Historical Notices*, ii, pp. 733, 736, 772, 783.

31 B. Lenman, *The Jacobite Risings in Britain 1689–1746* (London, 1980), pp. 28–9.

32 M. Dilworth, 'The Scottish Mission in 1688–1689' in *Innes Review*, xx (1969), 70–5.

33 A. Bellsheim, *Geschichte der Katholischen Kirche in Schottland*, 2 vols, (Mainz, 1883); English trans with additions by Hunter Blair, 4 vols (Edinburgh 1887–90), iv., 128; P. Anson, *Underground Catholicism in Scotland* (Montrose, 1970), p. 76; D. Maclean, 'Roman Catholicism in Scotland in the Reign of Charles II' in *Records of the Scottish Church History Society*, iii (1929), pp. 48–50.

34 A. MacWilliam, 'A Highland Mission: Strathglass, 1671–1777', in *Innes Review*, xxiv (1973), 82–4, provides evidence for the number of priests at work in the Highlands and Islands in this period.

35 *CSP Dom.*, 1689–90, 383; W. Forbes-Leith, *Memoirs of Scottish Catholics during the XVIIth and XVIIIth Centuries*, 2 vols (London, 1909), ii, pp. 148–9.

36 Paul Hopkins, *Glencoe*, 105–6.

37 Fountainhall, *Historical Notices*, ii, 759; Hopkins, *Glencoe*, p. 106.

38 *Ibid.*, 106; *Reg Privy Council* 3rd series, xiii, p. xlvii.

39 Hopkins, *Glencoe*, p. 106, citing *The Lockhart Papers*, ed. A. Aufrere, 2 vols (London, 1817), i, p. 63.

40 Hopkins, *Glencoe,* p. 106.

41 *Ibid.*, p. 106.
42 Fountainhall, *Historical Notices*, ii, pp. 713, 759, 762.
43 Wodrow, *History*, pp. 304–6, 308.
44 *Ibid.*, iii, pp. 308–9.
45 *Ibid.*, iii, p. 309.
46 *Acts Parl. Scot.*, viii, 245.
47 Wodrow, *History*, iii, 310; G. Burnet, *History of My Own Time*, ed. O. Airey, 2 vols (London, 1897–1900), iii, pp. 318–19.
48 Ferguson, *Anglo-Scottish Relations*, p. 60; Wodrow, *History*, iii, p. 310; I. B. Cowan, *The Scottish Covenanters, 1660–1688* (London, 1976), p. 109.
49 *Ibid.*, p. 109.
50 Hew Scott, *Fasti ecclesiae Scoticanae. The Succession of ministers in the parish churches of Scotland from the reformation, 1560 to the present time*, revised edition, 8 vols (1915–50), pp. 305, 307, 310, 312, 316, 318, 333, 344, 348, 353, 357, 363, 372, 389, 393, 397, 399.
51 Hopkins, *Glencoe*, p. 105, 117n, 147.
52 Fountainhall, *Historical Notices*, ii 670–1, 708–9, 717; *Historical observes of memorable occurrents in church and state from October 1680 to April 1686. By Sir John Lauder ot Fountainhal*, ed. A. Urquhart and D. Laing (Bannatyne Club, 1840), p. 243.
53 Fountainhall, *Historical Notices*, ii, 722.
54 *Ibid.*, ii, pp. 726, 728.
55 *Ibid.*, ii, p 735.
56 *Ibid.*, ii, pp. 775–6.
57 Cowan, *The Scottish Covenanters, 1660–1688*, pp. 50–55.
58 *Ibid.*, pp. 82–102.
59 Wodrow, *History*, iii, pp. 94–5; Wodrow avers that this declaration was published and printed at Glasgow, but J. King Hewison, *The Covenanters*, 2 vols (Glasgow, 1913), ii, p. 308, claims that it was first affixed to the mercat cross at Hamilton and subsequently printed in Glasgow.
60 Wodrow, *History*, iii, pp. 66–7.
61 The Queensferry Paper, 1680 (Wodrow, *History*, ii, Appendix, p. xlvi); Sanquhar Declaration, 1680 (*ibid.*, ii, Appendix p. xlvii); *Reg Privy Council*, 3rd series, vi, 265.
62 A Shields, *The Life and Death of . . . J Renwick*, (Edinburgh, 1724), pp. 52–3.
63 Wodrow, *History*, ii, Appendix cxxix; crf *Reg. privy Council*, 3rd series, xiii, 123–4; Wodrow, *History*, ii, Appendix cxxxiv; cf. *Reg. Privy Council*, 3rd series, xiii, 156–8.
64 Wodrow, *History*, iv, p. 428.
65 *Ibid.*, iv, pp. 431–3.
66 *Ibid.*, iv, p. 432.
67 *Ibid.*, iv, p. 432.
68 King Hewison, *The Covenanters*, ii, p. 506.
69 Wodrow, *History*, iv, pp. 431–3.
70 *Ibid.*, iv, 473; Burnet, *The Siege of Edinburgh Castle*, pp. 16–17.
71 *Ibid.*, 17–19; Wodrow, *History*, iv, 472–4; *Memoirs touching the Revolution in Scotland, MDCLXXXVIII–MDCX*, Colin Earl of Balcarres, ed Lord Lindsay (Bannatyne Club, 1841), pp. 38–43.
72 *Reg Privy Council*, 3rd series, xiii, p xiii; Hopkins, *Glencoe*, p. 120.
73 King Hewison, *The Covenanters*, ii, p. 518.

74 *An Account of the Proceedings of the Estates in Scotland*, ed. E. W. M. Balfour-Melville, 2 vols (Scottish History Society, 1955), i, pp. 1–15, 27, 32–3, 56–7, 105, 110, 125–6, 128–30; Hopkins, *Glencoe*, pp. 120–1.

75 Fountainhall, *Historical Notices*, ii, 884; *Extracts from the Records of Edinburgh, 1681 to 1689*, ed. M. Wood and Helen Armet (Edinburgh, 1954), pp. 256–8, 263–4; Hopkins, *Glencoe*, p. 121 (Edinburgh, 1968), pp. 1–2.

76 W. Ferguson, *Scotland, 1689 to the Present, The Edinburgh History of Scotland*, 4 vols (Edinburgh, 1968), pp. 1–2.

77 W. Fraser, *The Melvilles Earls of Melville and the Leslies Earls of Leven*, 3 vols (Edinburgh, 1890), iii, 193; Balfour-Melville, *Proceedings of the Estates in Scotland*, i, p. 1.

78 *Ibid.*, i, 1; W. Ferguson, *Scotland, 1689 to the Present*, pp. 2–3.

79 Balfour-Melville, *Proceedings of the Estates*, i, 4–5, 33, 47; *Acts Parl. Scot.*, ix, 9, 10n.

80 Balfour-Melville, *Proceedings of the Estates*, i, 25–6; *Acts Parl. Scot.*, ix, 37–41.

81 *Ibid.*, ix, 45.

82 *Facsimiles of the National Manuscripts of Scotland* (London, 1867–71), iii, no. cvii.

83 *Reg Privy Council*, 3rd series, xiii, 565–6; *ibid.*, xiv, 82–4, 125–6; Balfour-Melville, *Proceedings of the Estates*, pp. 183, 185–7, 220–5.

Scottish Cultural Change 1660–1710 and the Union of 1707

RL Emerson 1995 in J Robertson (ed.), *A Union for Empire: Political Thought and the British Union of 1707*, Cambridge (Cambridge University Press), 121–44.

I

Seventeenth-century Scotland has been described as a backward land made dull and benighted by repressive Calvinists and politically turbulent by ministers and a greedy aristocracy. Those who wish to see it in these ways can and easily do find evidence of even greater savagery beyond the Highland Line. But Scotland was not alone in being backward, uncouth and even savage in the seventeenth century. Descriptions of France show as great a range of manners, intellectual attainments and cultivation and an even more complex linguistic situation than obtained in Scotland. No one who has read much about the Thirty Years War thinks even Highlanders were unduly savage. And there was another Scotland, albeit small, whose members belonged and knew they belonged to a European world of learning and civility. This was a thin slice of the Scottish social elite and one constantly attenuated by emigration. Nevertheless, its members were influential, reasonably well educated and articulate and interesting. They shared the culture of Europeans, read the same books, and confronted many of the same problems. In doing so, they also increasingly shared a common culture with the English. How these Scots thought and felt bears upon the Union of 1707 which was in part made feasible by the convergence of ideas and feelings in both Scots and Englishmen.

II

One area in which such convergence was notable was religion, which in both countries and throughout Europe was still deeply politicised. Scots as well as English participated in the great religious debates about the nature of the church and its relation to societies and states. Both kingdoms saw the Whigs triumph politically in 1688–9. Protestant Europe applauded as Calvinist political theory was transformed into Whiggery of various sorts. Both Scots and Englishmen argued vociferously at Dort, at Westminster and in books often printed in Holland and read in France about the mysteries of their religion and the terms in which these could be discussed.

As they did so, the epistemological and metaphysical commitments of Boyle, Tillotson or Locke tended to converge with those of Bayle and Desmaizeau – all were read in Scotland. Calvinist scepticism about human nature was related to the careful qualifications given to knowledge claims by Bayle, Locke and Newton whose world, like Calvin's, was designed by and was known to point toward an unfathomable Creator. Rational theologies were possible as the *virtuosi* of all nations agreed by the 1690s. By 1700 religions and philosophical controversy in both countries had prepared Scots for the rapid assimilation of the views of Newton and Locke who entered Scottish classrooms between *c.* 1690 and 1715. In moral theology similar trends had also been at work. English Puritans such as Richard Baxter had come in roundabout ways to emphasise works as the Anglicans always had. But so too had the Scottish divines for whom 1688–9 opened the way to power in the colleges and Kirk. In both England and Scotland the bases of morality had shifted somewhat from the Two Tables of the Law to reason, conscience and the passions. As that happened, moralists had again to examine Calvinist activism. This had traditionally seen naturally social beings cherishing and regulating their societies for the glory of God and the improvement of man's fallen estate. By 1700 this meant not only the maintenance of liberty but the pursuit and use of science and state power to effect improvements.

As the religious situation in both England and Scotland cooled and moderated, it also produced more Vicars of Bray and more cynics and sceptics. In the last generation of the seventeenth century such figures abounded at the court in London and in city taverns frequented by the likes of Dryden, Charles Blount or John Toland, who also had been a student at Glasgow and Edinburgh. English sceptics, deists and atheists found Scottish counterparts in Sir Robert Sibbald, Thomas Halyburton, Archibald Pitcairne, MD and Thomas Aikenhead. Sibbald's doubts led him to Episcopacy *via* Catholicism. Halyburton's were resolved through prayer and determined efforts to believe; they led to the St Andrews divinity chair. Pitcairne, a reputed deist, attended episcopal services. Aikenhead's atheism, however, ended at the Grassmarket scaffold in Edinburgh in January 1697. The presence of such men amongst the Scottish elite in the 1690s shows how much Scotland had changed since 1660 when its saints were driven from power. It should come as no surprise that by the 1680s Scots were reading Father Richard Simon or ten years later worrying about deists. Their reading habits had changed remarkably since 1660. To understand that shift one must look briefly at what had gone on in the universities.[1]

III

Throughout the seventeenth century, Scots students, like those elsewhere, got a good deal of Latin, Greek and religion. Aristotle's metaphysics, logic, ethics and physics bulked large in the syllabus until *c.* 1680. In this respect Scots most resembled the Dutch: 'The theses for disputation at Leiden, for example, are very similar to the Scottish graduation theses, while most of the authorities whose works were debated are the same as those quoted by the Scottish university teachers.' By the 1670s or

1680s the logic and metaphysics dictates of the Scottish regents often had references to modern philosophers including Bacon, Descartes and the Port Royal Fathers.[2] Aristotelian moral philosophy had been enriched by the moral theology and casuistry of Puritan divines, by the works of some Cambridge Platonists, such as Henry More whose *Enchiridion ethicum* was sometimes read, and by the 1680s, by some of the natural lawyers – Grotius, Cumberland and Pufendorf. Until c. 1660 the natural science of the Scots was largely based on Aristotle's *Physics* taught with some modern criticisms. Between *c.* 1660 and 1700 this was radically changed. Copernican cosmology and the new astronomy appeared in the 1660s. 'The sudden appearance of the mechanistic philosophy of Descartes and Boyle about 1670 in theses from St Andrews, Aberdeen and Edinburgh, marked a break with the old tradition, and favoured the espousal of Descartes' vortex theory.' By 1700 'scientific teaching in the Scottish universities was thoroughly up to date and probably as good as was to be found anywhere in Europe'.[3] By then, when Scots graduated they were likely to know something about Copernicus, Kepler, Brahe and even Newton; about Galileo, Toricelli, Borelli; about van Guericke, Huygens, Leeuwenhoeck, Gassendi, Mersenne and Mariotte; and about various French and Dutch textbook writers like Jacques Rohault and Jean LeClerc. The story was much the same in all the colleges save Glasgow which was slower to adopt the new science.[4] Even there by 1691 a professorship of mathematics had been created and the College had begun to look more modern and less poor. Change in the colleges was real and important but we do not yet know exactly how and when it came and who brought it about.

Innovators in Scottish thought at the mid-century everywhere included men from both the Presbyterian and Episcopalian wings of Scottish Christianity, from the king's friends and from his foes. At Glasgow the faculty between 1640 and 1670 included at one time or another James Dalrymple (1619–1695), later 1st Viscount Stair, George Sinclair (?–1696 or 1699) and Gilbert Burnet (1643–1715), later Bishop of Salisbury. Sinclair was a mathematician, engineer and experimentalist best known for his defence of the belief in witchcraft. *Satan's Invisible World Discovered* (1685) was in part an attempt to justify the witch-hunting activities of his relatives, in part his attempt to be a Scottish Glanvill proving empirically the existence of a spirit world. Sinclair was a Presbyterian outed from his Glasgow regency in 1666. He was readmitted in 1689 after the Glorious Revolution. Stair began as a Covenanter, soldiered between 1639 and 1641 and then served Glasgow as a regent for six years. After a year of private study, the one-time infantry captain 'passed advocate' in 1648 and thereafter was active as a lawyer, judge and politician who served Cromwell, Monck, Charles II and eventually James VII and William and Mary. He is best known for his *Institutions of the Laws of Scotland* (1681); Stair also published other legal and political works and a treatise on natural philosophy. He trimmed with each regime and ministry but always managed to retain the respect of most Presbyterians throughout the grim years of the 1660s, 1670s and 1680s. Burnet too was a trimmer but he was much more. An able theologian, something of a philosopher, an early member of the Royal Society of London and a good historian, he was also a fair-minded and astute politician. All three men were remarkable and all three produced works in more than one field. Dalrymple and Sinclair were educated in Scotland; Burnet studied in Cambridge, Oxford, London, Amsterdam and Paris before teaching at Glasgow. All three were later abroad, two certainly as political refugees, which was probably Sinclair's status too when he visited Holland in 1681.

What was true in Glasgow was equally so in Edinburgh. There during the 1650s the teachers included Robert Leighton (1611–1684), sometimes called the Scottish Pascal, Thomas Crawford (c. 1620–62), and John Wishart. Leighton impressed upon his students a relatively tolerant view of things rooted not only in the love of God and men but also in the limited capacity of men to know anything by natural means. Crawford taught mathematics but is also remarkable for having written a *History of the University of Edinburgh from 1580 to 1646* (published in 1808), a work indicative of an increasing concern in Scotland both with antiquities and history and with the old theme of vindicating the honour of the kingdom.[5] Wishart was an Aristotelian who by the 1670s was prelecting on Descartes and mentioning or alluding to the optical theories of Sir Isaac Newton.[6] When Sir Robert Sibbald (1641–1723) looked back at Edinburgh University in the late 1650s he remembered Leighton with fondness and respect but mentioned learning modern philosophy from the works of two of Galileo's correspondents and defenders, Sir Kenelm Digby (1603–65) and Thomas White (1593–1676), two English Catholic philosophers who then worked abroad in France and Spain. That his experience in a Presbyterian college was not unique is suggested by what little is known about the extra-curricular reading of other Edinburgh students.[7]

At St Andrews there was probably no brilliant teacher at the mid-century save Samuel Rutherford (1600–61). There was, however, by 1668 a regius chair of mathematics filled by the first of a long line of academic Gregories.

In Aberdeen things were different. The King's College Principal during the 1650s was John Row (1598–1672), the author of a Hebrew grammar and dictionary and the continuer of his father's *History of the Kirk of Scotland 1558–1637*. At the Restoration he was sacked and succeeded by Alexander Middleton who by the 1680s was known to members of the Oxford Philosophical Society as a *virtuoso*. By that time King's had others who had contacts with English *virtuosi*. Among them were Henry Scougal (1650–78), the Principal's son George Middleton (1645–1726), and James Garden (1647–1726) whose brother George (1649–1733) sold the College a telescope in 1712.[8] Throughout the century, King's possessed an instrument collection.[9] Earlier George Gordon, 1st Earl of Aberdeen (1637–1720), had taught at King's before leaving to make a career as a lawyer, judge and statesman too tolerant to serve King James VII. At neighbouring Marischal College the Principal during the 1650s, William Moir (c. 1600–after 1661), also held the chair of mathematics. Moir published on mathematics and mechanics. In 1661 he was replaced as Principal by James Leslie, MD, a physician educated on the continent. His place as mathematics professor was taken by Duncan Liddell (1667–?) who had 'taught Geometry, navigation, and Gunnery, for several years in London'.[10] At both Aberdeen colleges the tolerant views of the 'Aberdeen Doctors' continued to be discussed and, after 1660, were again promoted as was somewhat later the mystical piety exemplified in Henry Scougal's *The Life of God in The Soul of Man* (1677).[11]

In all the colleges during the 1650s and 1660s, Scots students were kept abreast of currents of thought and discussion elsewhere. Moreover, English political and religious discussions were hardly irrelevant to Scots ruled first by their own covenanting 'Saints' and then by Cromwell's Major-Generals. Cromwellian government had also been stimulating in other ways. Sectarian and Quaker views circulated within the kingdom and unorthodox Calvinist ideas were uttered in the schools. Historians, antiquaries and lawyers were stimulated to think and write as they reflected upon the Union which had been forced upon them. Englishmen more determined to rule in the Highlands than Scots had ever been were also more successful. Even medical men found some stimulus in the works of men such as Richard Wiseman. Scots might have found the English obnoxious but contact with them was not wholly useless. It taught some Scots one thing, some another; others it provoked to defences of their nation's honour and to attempts to recover and write a more adequate natural and civil history of the Kingdom, a project which had already engaged Drummond of Hawthornden and Sir James Balfour of Denmiln.[12] Finally, that period was in an odd way to be repeated *c.* 1685–1707 when again uncertainties about the church, state and universities revived old arguments which the prospects of war and disorder made urgent.

IV

Outside the colleges there are other clear indicators (*pace* Trevor-Roper[13]) that during these years Scots did not remain excluded from important currents of European thought. A sampling of the published matriculation list for Leyden[14] shows a continuous increase in the numbers of Scottish students from 1640–50 into the 1690s with numbers increasing again after 1710. Leyden figures may understate the number of those going abroad from Scotland before 1650. Other universities were more distinguished, better and more orthodox. What these figures also suggest is that warfare and unrest in Scotland and on the continent had as much to do with student numbers as ideology and ties to England. Be that as it may, by the 1680s there was clearly in Scotland a 'critical mass' of foreign-educated Scots who could respond to calls to imitate or emulate what they had seen abroad.[15] Those calls were increasingly made by Scots concerned with economic improvements but also by intellectuals and professionals.

Between the late 1660s and 1700 the Scots copied others in many fields. They produced a more powerful parliament, mercantilist legislation, banking and colonising schemes. They strengthened professional bodies for lawyers, physicians, and surgeons; created the Order of the Thistle (1687–8) and clubs and societies such as the Royal Company of Archers (1676)[16] or Dr Sibbald's antiquarian and natural history societies (1680–?1703). Even the universities in the 1680s and 1690s began to be reformed in ways which would keep students at home by giving them what they could have found abroad – polite education in the classics and history, training in law and medicine and in the disciplines ancillary to those fields. Most of these initiatives were related to the political needs of the Stuart kings or the Whigs after 1689–90. They were mostly imitative of developments elsewhere and indicated that by the 1680s many Scots were familiar with foreign institutions and ideas and were prepared to copy them. They had adopted new attitudes toward knowledge and its uses and were seeking ways to institutionalise and perpetuate their new outlook on knowledge, themselves and their country. Important to that transition were not only those who studied abroad but those who left Scotland for long periods to work in other lands but who did not sever their ties with Scotland.

Scots abroad included some who held important or interesting intellectual posts. Scottish science might have looked considerably different if men such as John Wedderburn (1583–c. 1654), an early defender of Galileo, had found places at home rather than in Padua and Moravia.[17] Similar cases could be made using others whose careers were mostly made outside Scotland, for example Robert Morrison (1620–83), professor of botany at Oxford, or Ninian Campbell who was for some time professor of rhetoric at Saumur. Others like Duncan Liddell (1561–1613) who founded the mathematics chair at Marischal College, to which he also left his instrument collection, returned only after years abroad. With him or with a political exile like Thomas Forbes, MD, who had taught philosophy and medicine at Pisa between 1659 and 1662, came new ideas which would eventually influence Scottish university teaching. The Reformation had not kept these men out of Catholic Europe, which like the Protestant states also welcomed Scottish soldiers. Gordon Donaldson has estimated the numbers of Scottish mercenaries as peaking between 1600 and 1620 at over 10,000 in the Baltic region alone.[18] In the 1630s the French also had about 10,000 Scottish troops. The officers among these men were often educated and cultivated and would have been another source of intellectual change in Scotland. Moreover these men, in the mid seventeenth century, were often exiles who when they returned came back to status and power. There could not have been many among them as brilliant as Sir Robert Moray (1608–73) but he is unlikely to have been unique.

Sir Robert Murray was an extraordinary mercenary soldier who left Britain for France in the 1640s. Before he did so he had probably been connected with others seeking esoteric wisdom in the masonic lodge of Edinburgh. In Europe Sir Robert had contacts with a surprising number of intellectuals. They ranged from the Jesuit polymath Athanasius Kircher to the Huguenot ministers Jean Daillé, Charles Derlincourt and Raymond Gaches; from the French academician Christian Huygens to the Anglo-Irish projector Sir William Petty. Even before he became a Fellow of the Royal Society of London, Moray's correspondence came from European capitals, the Caribbean, North America, Africa and the East Indies. When he was sent to Scotland to rule it for Lauderdale in 1663 he found it a dull place with few interested in the subjects which excited him – natural history, chemistry, mechanics and improvements based on new knowledge.[19] But 'few' at least implies that some, such as the apothecary Matthew Mackaile, the mathematician and astronomer James Gregory and Andrew Balfour, MD, were interested.

Perhaps the best evidence of how much Scottish opinion was to shift in the later seventeenth century is provided by what is known of private libraries and Scottish publishing. These show Scots to have been anything but isolated. They followed European and English debates on issues which were perplexing to men everywhere. Medical men, divines and lawyers clearly situated themselves in a European cultural world to which by the 1680s they also sought to contribute. How they oriented themselves at the Restoration may be seen in two libraries gathered before 1685, those of Thomas Kincaid Sr (1620–91) and Robert Leighton (1611–84).

Kincaid was an Edinburgh surgeon whose career began in the late 1630s. He was notable enough to win appointment as a regimental surgeon to a regiment which marched south into England in 1644. After the civil wars, Kincaid settled into a civilian practice as a surgeon-apothecary. He died in 1691 leaving a valuable library of which his son Thomas gave 228 books (titles) to the Edinburgh Incorporation of Chirurgeons in 1709.[20] These volumes provide clues to what a medical man in the mid-seventeenth century knew and whence his information came.[21]

Kincaid's books (41 folios, 48 quartos, 97 octavos and 42 duodecimos) mostly dated from the period 1630 to 1670, the years in which most of the volumes must also have been purchased. The latest work was issued in 1685 and only a handful of his books were published after 1674. Most deal with modern medicine, anatomy, surgery, botany, chemistry and pharmacy. If his whole library was given,[22] then Kincaid had relatively few volumes dealing with magic, alchemy, astrology or the ancients, no incunables and only forty-one volumes (19 per cent) published during the sixteenth century. Those were mostly classical texts or landmark works such as those by Fallopius, Paracelsius or Libavius. This was clearly the working library of an up-to-date general practitioner. While we can only speculate about where he purchased his books, we know where they were published. The largest number were printed in Holland; Germany and France ranked second and third. These were also his most modern books. Those from Italy tended to pre-date 1620. The collection is surprisingly lacking in works of general natural philosophy and contains gaps which are puzzling. There are few volumes by famous seventeenth-century physicians and surgeons whose reputations came from particular studies and practice rather than teaching. It is also curious that Kincaid lacked the works of Harvey and Richard Wiseman even though he may have known the latter. Despite these peculiarities, this collection is interesting. Those using it would have found works by Cartesians, iatro-mechanists, iatro-chemists, books by medical 'positivists' like Sylvius (but not Sydenham) and eclectic synthesisers 'who tried to harmonize neo-Galenic doctrine and Paracelsian chemistry'.[23] When these books were purchased they had related Mr Kincaid to a very European medical world, one in which there were no certainties but controversy and disputes over methods, facts, remedies and the basic processes by which life was sustained. He was open to debates whose participants came from everywhere in Europe: Uppsalla and Salerno, London and Riga and many places in between. Kincaid may have made only one trip outside Scotland – to England – but he was certainly part of a European medical world throughout his career. This was a world where Scots would not figure as innovators until the 1680s and 1690s. Those who did so then had generally read more iatro-mechanists than iatro-chemists.[24] In short, they had changed with the times.

TABLE 5.1. *The library of Thomas Kincaid, senior surgeon-apothecary of Edinburgh: place of publication of books by number and per cent*

PLACE	NUMBER	PER CENT
Holland	73	32
Germany	49	21
France	42	18
Switzerland	23	10
England	14	6
Italy	11	5
Spanish Netherlands	4	2
Scotland	2	1
Denmark	1	0.66
Poland	1	0.66
Sweden	1	0.66
Unknown	6	3
Total	227	100

Another indicator of what moved Scots can be found in the gift of 1390 volumes made by Archbishop Robert Leighton (1611–84) to the clergy of the diocese of Dunblane. This was a library oriented toward classics, divinity and philosophy, but one which did not exclude science and medicine. Leighton owned a lot of classical and scholastic philosophy, much divinity but also works by Bacon, the Fathers of Port Royal, the Cambridge Platonists, Hobbes' *Leviathan* and works against it, many of the great natural lawyers, Samuel Rutherford's *Lex Rex* and a great deal of Anglican divinity, much of which was tinged with the irenical spirit for which Jeremy Taylor was famous. Leighton had some history books and late in life clearly bought latitudinarian works. Books of mystical piety were, however, about as numerous as these and came from Catholic as well as Protestant pens. Leighton's views were shaped in England where he grew up, in France where he travelled, but also at Edinburgh where he studied. His books seem to reflect a taste and an outlook fixed by the 1660s to which Puritans, Covenanters, Catholics and Anglicans had contributed.[25]

Scottish intellectuals born in the 1630s and 1640s continued to depend upon English and continental thinkers for new ideas but their libraries suggest that they also had deeper interests in novel philosophical ideas.

Sir Robert Sibbald left a collection of over 4,000 volumes of which perhaps 75 per cent were in Latin.[26] About 20–30 per cent of his books were published in the sixteenth century with a somewhat smaller number purchased in his old age during the eighteenth century. The remaining 60–70 per cent were issued in the seventeenth century, generally in its second half. He had a good collection of the classics, a little scholastic philosophy and theology but a distribution of modern volumes which one would expect from a *virtuoso*. History, antiquities, natural history, natural philosophy, the various sciences, medicine, the improving and scientific literature of the time were all well represented as was modern literature. Among the modern philosophers one notes Bacon, Descartes, the Port Royal Fathers, Kenelm Digby, Thomas White, Athanasius Kircher, Goerge Sinclair and his opponent, James Gregory, but also a host of men who belonged to the Royal Society of London or to some comparable foreign body. Here *virtuosi* and natural theologians such as Walter Charleton, John Ray, Edward Lhuyd, Francis Willughby, Nehemiah Grew, Robert Hooke, John Woodward, Hans Sloane, Edmund Halley and William Whiston (but not Newton) gave a distinctly modern and scientific flavour to his list of the erudite. Sibbald had formed and sold an earlier collection of books so this one may not wholly reflect his earlier taste. Surviving manuscripts suggest that in only one respect might the earlier collection have been much different. He probably had had more works written by sixteenth-century Scots.

Sir James Lauder of Fountainhall (1646–1722) also left a particularly good indicator of what a genteel Scots lawyer was likely to buy and read during the period 1667–79. In those years Lauder bought or was presented with about 500 volumes. He recorded the titles or subject of 478 of these which are distributed into categories in table 5.2.[27] This table separates his earlier purchases (1667–75), made when he was a student and establishing a law practice, from the later ones of a rising young advocate (1675–9). Again, what is most significant about Lauder's list is its modernity. While he was not much interested in science and natural philosophy, he owned works by John Dee, Bacon, Hobbes, Boyle, Glanvill and Stillingfleet. This suggests at least a slight interest in epistemology and mitigated scepticism, an interest also supported by his ownership of the principal works of Gassendi. He possessed few books on mathematics and the sciences but among them were three on hydrostatics and a mathematics text by John Wallis. He bought volumes by Augustine and Aquinas and read Thomas à Kempis, but his taste in divinity ran more toward the works of Jean Daillé, Hugo Grotius, Jeremy Taylor, Richard Baxter, Edward Stillingfleet, Gilbert Burnet, and John Tillotson, all forerunners or sources of the Scottish Moderates. Lauder was a latitudinarian who cared little about the forms of Kirk government. His law books included editions of Grotius and other natural lawyers, but most of them seem technical and not oriented toward political theory. *Belles lettres* are represented not only by the ancients but by such moderns as Shakespeare, Milton, Dryden, Shadwell, Settle, Wycherly, Behn, Sir George Mackenzie, Sir William Temple and a few other poets and playwrights. Like other Scots, he also enjoyed the old works of 'Blind Harry' and Sir David Lindsay. Lauder had a fondness for history. In an assortment of volumes written by Polydore Vergil, Holinshed, Sir Richard Baker, Francis Bacon, Lord Herbert of Cherbury, William Camden, John Rushworth and modern memorialists of the reigns of James VI and Charles I he could follow the course of English history. His collection of French historians was not quite so good but he presumably knew a good deal about France from *c.* 1480 to his own time. Scottish history was represented by Knox,

Leslie, Buchanan and a few other writers, but we know that he hoped it would improve since he was one of several lawyers to give Sir Robert Sibbald 'Ane Account of Manuscript Histories' then held in private hands.[28] Perhaps equally good guides to his outlook are books difficult to categorise such as more's *Utopia*, Burton's *Anatomy of Melancholie* and Montaigne's *Essays*. He also liked joke books and owned at least five.

TABLE 5.2 *The libraries of James Lauder of Fountainhall, and John Spotiswoode of that ilk*

	LAUDER OF FOUNTAINHALL		SPOTISWOODE	
Category of book	Purchased 1667 to June 1675 (%)	Purchased 1675 to 1679 (%)	1667– 1679 (%)	(%)
Theology, sermons	21 (11)	79 (27)	100 (21)	37 (19)*
Natural philosophy and astronomy	3 (2)	1	4 (1)	7 (4)
Mathematics	1 (1)	4 (1)	5 (1)	1 (1)
Medicine	4 (2)	1	5 (1)	2 (1)
Military and naval	1 (1)	2 (1)	3 (1)	1 (1)
Geography	3 (2)		3 (1)	2 (1)
History	19 (10)	24 (8)	43 (9)	13 (7)
Biography	1 (1)	7 (2)	3 (2)	
Moral philosophy and manners	18 (10)	20 (7)	38 (8)	7 (4)
Law	35 (19)	61 (21)	96 (20)	84 (44)
Acts etc	13 (9)	2 (1)	15 (3)	
Political theory and pamphlets	23 (12)	6 (2)	9 (6)	8 (4)
Heraldry	1 (1)		1	
Reference books	1 (1)		1	
Texts	4 (2)	5 (2)	9 (2)	
Language books	2 (1)	5 (2)	7 (1)	6 (3)
Classics	7 (4)	15 (5)	22 (5)	8 (4)
Essays and romances		2 (1)	2	4 (2)
Plays	11 (6)	9 (3)	20 (4)	
Poetry and songs	9 (5)	8 (3)	17 (4)	10 (5)
News	3 (2)	5 (2)	8 (2)	
Miscellaneous	8 (4)	35 (12)	44 (9)	
Improvements	1 (1)			1 (1)
University materials				
Unknown	3 (2)	4 (1)	7 (1)	
Totals	188 (100)	290 (100)	478 (100)	191 (100)

* Percentages in this column are based on a total which excludes acts, proclamations, etc.

Fountainhall's library by 1680 is a good guide to the taste of those who projected the Advocates' Library in July of that year. Foremost among these men was George (later Sir George) Mackenzie of Rosehaugh (1636–1690). Mackenzie was prolific. His works include a book on rhetoric and eloquence, poetry, a novel, history, legal compilations and commentaries, political pamphlets, a study of heraldry, and even a treatise on natural philosophy. All these made him welcome amongst the London wits and, after his retirement (really exile) from Scotland in 1689, in Oxford where he became a member of the Philosophical Society. The Library which he promoted and justified had from its inception a broad definition of what lawyers needed to read and know. This of course gave primacy to books on the law, but it also found plenty of room for the 'three branches of learning [which] are the handmaidens of Jurisprudence, namely, History, Criticism and Rhetoric' not only in the ancient but in the modern worlds. [29] Mackenzie had somewhat earlier noted that '[b]eing bred to the law . . . requires a whole Man and his whole Age'. 'The knowledge of the Law is not easy and . . . none should pretend to it, but such as have illuminated their excellent natural Parts with laborious learning, and have polish'd that Learning by long Experience.'[30] Within a few years the Library was purchasing in a wide range of fields which included philosophy and natural history. Setting up such a library institutionalised a conception of learning which made lawyers *virtuosi*. It also gave Scotland a model of what polite and useful learning was. That was carried into the eighteenth century and promoted by extra-mural law teachers in Edinburgh such as John Spotiswoode (1666–1728), and it undoubtedly helped to push the colleges toward reforms which allowed them to serve the needs of the upper-class boys who attended them but expected to go on to study medicine or law in Holland or France where this polite mode of education was already in place. This programme of modernisation and reform received political support in the 1680s from men in the entourage of James, Duke of Albany (James VII).[31]

It was not only lawyers and physicians who prized innovation. The Reverend William Carstares (1649–1715), a Calvinist plotter from the 1680s who became chaplain to William III and Principal of Edinburgh University (1703–15), also left a library of some interest. It had a great deal of divinity but one might not have expected so much church history. Carstares had a personal interest in this topic and seems to have possessed numerous books on the ancient churches and on the spread of Christianity. Among those books is found Richard Simon's *Critical History of the New Testament*. All this was supplemented by ancient and modern historians ranging from Livy and Polybius to Samuel Pufendorf, Louis de Maimbourg, Bishop Bossuet and William Nicolson, whose *Scots Historical Library* (1702) had been produced with the help of Edinburgh antiquaries. Carstares had known many of the English latitudinarians and he owned their works. His collection of Boyle Lectures was complete to 1714; he also possessed other works by Newtonians such as James Keill.[32] After he came to Edinburgh as Principal of its university in 1703, its standard of teaching improved and ecclesiastical history was added to the complement of chairs. He probably also tried to found a civil history chair. When one was created in 1717 it went to a member of his family.[33]

The library lists of two men much younger than Sibbald and Carstares survive to show that by the early eighteenth century Scottish tastes were becoming more catholic and current – those of John Spotiswoode and Charles Erskine (1680–1763). Spotiswoode's library is that of an erudite *virtuoso*; Erskine's is that of an enlightened gentleman. In those descriptions is symbolised the transformation of the Scottish intelligentsia between *c.* 1690 and 1730.

Spotiswoode[34] was a lawyer educated in Edinburgh and Leyden who for many years taught law extra-murally in Edinburgh but never gained the university chair he sought. He was polymathic in his interests and reading and encouraged his students to make grammar, rhetoric, logic, history and philology their especial studies.[35] This did not mean a neglect of philosophy, science, mathematics, modern literature or of the law which required all the other sciences in the successful scholar and practitioner.[36] The spur to the efforts to master all these was in part the patriotic determination to improve, modernise and make respectable his own kingdom which seemed so negligible in the republic of letters. He was full of projects to effect the changes which seemed to be required in Scotland.[37] Like others of his time, his allegiances were complex. He seems to have sympathised with the Stuart cause but he chose his 'spiritual guide[s]' from amongst the evangelical clerics of Edinburgh, although those might not have approved his reading in the mystical divinity of the French.[38]

The catalogue of Spotiswoode's books made in 1728 listed 2,982 titles of which some were collections containing several items.[39] Of these titles 401 were folios, 741 quartos and the rest (1840) octavos and duodecimos. A sampling of his collection suggests that it was distributed as shown in Table 5.3

The number of Latin volumes in his library might suggest that Spotiswoode was a late humanist of sorts. He can more fairly be described as a *virtuoso* whose interests were serious and professional. Latin places him not among philologists and humanists but among scholars of every sort. Secondly, one is struck by the range of the man's interests. He possessed some of the early Fathers of the Church but also religious works by Cicero, Erasmus, Luther, Calvin, Guillaume Viret, Theodore Beza, Joseph Hall, Moïse Amyrault and a collection of modern free thinkers which included Richard Simon, Charles Blount, John Toland and other English deists. Those who wrote against the deists were represented by Robert Burton, Richard Baxter, Edward Stillingfleet, John Tillotson and Charles Leslie. His philosophers included Plato, Aristotle, Epicurus, Cicero, Augustine, Duns Scotus and Thomas Aquinas. Other traditions among the moderns were represented by Montaigne, Charron and Naudé; Silhon and Gassendi; Descartes and Malebranche; Bacon, Boyle and Fellows of the Royal Society; Chillingworth, Stillingfleet and Tillotson; Henry More, Cudworth and other Cambridge Platonists. There were, surprisingly, no volumes by Locke or Newton. All of the great natural lawyers were there but so too were Machiavelli, Hobbes, Harrington and Andrew Fletcher of Saltoun. Spotiswoode possessed the works of Buchanan and continental *monarchomachi.* His natural philosophy shelves were loaded with physico-theological books by Ray, Grew, Charlton, Boyle and some of the Boyle lecturers. Spotiswoode also had many works on astronomy, dialling, physics, chemistry and pure mathematics. Here Archimedes, Galileo, Boyle, Huygens, Mariotte and Swammerdam rubbed shoulders with LeMort, Rohault, Lemery, Steno and an impressive collection of mathematical writers which included Barrow, Steven, various of the Gregories and some ancients. This lawyer owned enough medical works to have taught himself to practise. They included some anatomical books, systematic works by Sanctorius, Senert, Hoffman, Wecker and Borelli; Sydenham and even recent texts on midwifery by Mauriceau and Glisson. Harvey jostled Scots writers on fevers and medical Newtonians associated with Archibald Pitcairne. Modern botany books included ones by Robert Morrison and James Sutherland, both Scots; he had many more on pharmacy and chemistry. Spotiswoode also possessed a considerable collection of works on fortification and other military and naval topics. He had, in effect, complete histories of Greece, Rome, France, England and Scotland with many miscellaneous volumes on special topics and peoples. In the works of Bodin, Bayle and a few other moderns, he possessed works on historical method and the purposes to be realized by antiquaries and historians such as he and his friends aspired to be. His interests were catholic but he had also bought many Scottish authors.

TABLE 5.3 *The library of John Spotiswoode, 1728*

Books printed in	1400s		1500s		1600s		1700s	
	–		17%		78%		4%	
Books in	Latin	French	English	Italian	Dutch	Greek	Hebrew	
	67%	12%	13%	3%	2%			
	folio		quarto		8 & 12		Totals	
Books by subject:*	No	%	No	%	No	%	No	%
Religion	9	14	12	20	16	24	37	19
Philosophy	1	2	4	7	4	6	9	4
Law	42	65	16	27	26	39	84	44
Politics	1	2	5	8	2	3	8	4
Science and technology	–	–	5	8	–	–	5	3
Mathematics	–	–	–	–	1	2	1	1
Medicine	1	2	1	2	–	–	2	1
Military and naval	1	2	–	–	–	–	1	1
Classics	2	3	2	3	4	6	8	4
Languages	–	–	2	3	4	6	6	3
Belles letters	4	6	6	10	4	6	14	7
Trade and geography	–	–	2	3	1	2	3	2
History	4	6	6	9	4	6	13	7
Others								
Totals	65	100	60	100	66	100	191	100

* This sample of 191 titles probably understates his interests in mathematics, sciences (especially chemistry), medicine and military matters.

Charles Erskine (1680–1763) was educated at Edinburgh, Utrecht and Leyden (1708) and had in 1699 sought a St Andrews regency. [40] He served as an Edinburgh regent from 1701 to 1707 and then until 1734 held the largely sinecure post of Professor of Public Law. Erskine qualified as an advocate in 1711 and thereafter was active as a lawyer, MP, Solicitor-General, Lord Advocate and judge in the Courts of Session and Justiciary. He was connected politically with his kinsman John Erskine, the 10th Earl of Mar, and from *c.* 1726 on with the Argathelian interest which looked after him very well.[41] He was clearly a bookish man with a library of 1,361 volumes catalogued principally in 1731 but with additions still being made to it until 1762.[42] It was much like Spotiswoode's but there were also clear signs of change. Of 68 quartos sampled (he had 470) half were written in English and the other half in Italian (29, 43 per cent), French 3, 4 per cent) and Spanish (2, 3 per cent). His shelves, predictably, had far more editions printed after 1680 and the earliest of his books were almost all works standard for lawyers. He read a lot of history and *belles lettres*, was interested in the deistic controversy and certainly kept up his philosophy, including natural philosophy or science.[43] He possessed editions of Locke, Newton, Colin MacLaurin, Lord Shaftesbury, Francis Hutcheson, Duncan Forbes, David Hume, Lord Kames and some FRS's while continental philosophy was represented by Charron, Descartes, Pascal, Malebranche, père Buffier, the abbé Pluche and Mandeville. Erskine bought works on Scottish history including those by Thomas Innes and William Robertson. His books are those of a man who started out an *erudite* and *virtuoso* but ended up as an enlightened and polite member of the fashionable Edinburgh clubs to which Hume and his friends also belonged.

What these libraries show is that by 1707 the outlook of well-educated Scots had much in common with their counterparts elsewhere, especially those in England. This was particularly true of medical men, lawyers, educators, some soldiers and almost certainly of those who sought to make careers which depended on English patronage. Even the ministers were not as inward looking as is sometimes assumed. This is also borne out by what Scots published in the latter seventeenth century.

Most of what Scottish printers produced is contained in Harry G. Aldis's *A List of Books Printed in Scotland Before 1700* (Edinburgh, 1904, 2nd edn, 1970).[44] From 1650 to 1699 the total number of imprints counted is only 3,901 of which 36 per cent were produced in the 1690s and 64 per cent in the last two decades of the period. From 1630 to 1680 the Scottish printers had produced on average 46 titles each year with highs coming in 1638 (55 imprints), 1643 (69), 1660 (138) and 1679 (71) for political and economic reasons. A sustained but uneven rise in publications began only after 1677. The Restoration appears not to have had any immediately stirring effect upon Scottish thinkers but it did change the political and religious orientation of local publications. It also introduced more news and publications which foreshadowed secularisation. Between 1660 and 1689 there was clearly a new category for Scottish printers which we might anachronistically and euphemistically call 'science'. Many almanacs were produced by Scots. Works on mathematics and natural philosophy by George Sinclair, James Corss (Corse or Cross), James and David Gregorie, Matthew Mackaile, Sir Robert Sibbald, James Sutherland, William Saunders and James Paterson had appeared before 1689 as had a few medical items. These were novel publications and probably more numerous than works of Scottish Latinity or translations from Latin or Greek into English. Scots published classical authors as well as works written by Erasmus, Castellio, and Buchanan, while *The*

Westminster Confession and portions of the Bible were put into Latin for school-boys. So much for Scottish humanism in the local press![45] There were other signs of encroaching modernity in the various items by Francis Bacon, Robert Boyle and some of the Latitudinarian divines; certainly Richard Simon's *Opuscula critica adversus Isaacus Vossium* (1685) belongs here. Most years saw books or pamphlets against Quakers and Covenanters and numerous political polemics, proclamations and news items. Bits of Dryden, Settle and other English poets had appeared but Scots probably preferred and bought more copies of the poems of Sir David Lindsay, 'Blind Harry', John Barbour and Robert Henryson or of 'The Flyting of Polwart and Montgomery' and 'the Salms [*sic*] newly translated'. Judged by these lists the average Scottish mind by 1688 had not shifted over much but it had evinced some interest in science and modern literature and it had been forced to hear Episcopalian and Royalist, even Romanist arguments after a steady diet of Presbyterian views from the 1630s until 1660. If there was a Royalist Enlightenment beginning *c.* 1680, only one of its exponents, Sir George Mackenzie, bulked large in this index. He was the most frequently published Scottish writer and published at least twenty-one items between 1660 and 1689. A change in this pattern came in 1688–9 with the Revolution.

In those years there was an outpouring of printed matter double that of most of the decade's earlier years. Once again the political-religious pendulum swung back to the Presbyterians and the royalist press at Holyrood House, like the 'college' there, disappeared.[46] *Salus populi suprema lex* could again be printed and Sir James Steuart, its author, like many other exiles could come home again.

The 1690s saw other signs of change. Deism which had been noticed earlier found a local martyr in Thomas Aikenhead, a student executed for blasphemy in Edinburgh in 1697.[47] Behind his death there was a certain amount of local printed discussion of deism. Edmund Hickeringill's *The Ceremony-Monger* had been printed in 1689, a year after Dryden's *Hind and the Panther* which had argued for the need of an infallible teaching church just as his earlier poem, *Religio laici* (1682) had justified the rational theology of latitudinarian divines. A number of other titles refer to deism in 1695 and, a year after Aikenhead's death, Charles Leslie's *Short and Easie Method with the Deists* (1698) was printed in Edinburgh. Sir William Anstruther's essays against 'atheists' appeared three years later. By then Scots had also had a taste of the controversies in England over the nature of the church and the state's right to alter its established position and privileges. By the 1690s the Scots were also discussing their economic life and how it might be improved. That too was a new topic for their printers.[48] Equally furious, if not more numerous, were medical publications in which Newtonian and Jacobite physicians attacked and ridiculed others who were Whigs but perhaps less medically up-to-date. The nosology, causes, prognoses and treatments of fevers would concern Edinburgh physicians for 100 years.[49] So too would agriculture which also figures in the titles of the 1690s.[50] Some antiquarian and historical titles also show a broadened interest in the Scottish past. That this had a modern counterpart is indicated by an attempt to print in Edinburgh the *Bibliotheca Universalis* (1688) and the *History of the Works of the Learned* (1699). Law theses were now being

TABLE 5.4 *Scottish imprints: the Aldis List (1970)*

Category	1660s No.	%	1670s No.	%	1680s No.	%	1690s No.	%	Totals No.	%
Sermons	14	3 /4*	10	2/3	21	2/3	33	2/3	78	2/3
Religious works	59	11/15	139	28/40	156	14/22	162	12/17	516	15/21
Moral philosophy	12	2/3	2	-/1	3		3		20	1/1
Law			2	-/1	16	1 /2	62	4/6	80	2/3
Law cases	2	-/1	8	2/2	41	4/6	39	3/4	90	
Acts, proclamations, etc	141	27/-	158	31/-	394	36/-	427	31/-	1120	32/-
Politics and polemics	66	12/17	38	8/11	168	15/24	74	5/8	346	10/14
Political economy			3	1/1	8	1/1	24	2/2	35	1/1
Natural history and philosophy	1		1		3		6	-/1	11	
Mathematics	2	-/1		1/1	8	1/1	4		14	
Astronomy	1				1		1		3	
Almanacs	12	2/3	15	3/4	38	3/5	36	3/4	101	3/4
Technology, military, naval	1				2		3		6	
Medicine and pharmacy	7	1/2	1		2		22	2/2	32	1/1
Surgery and anatomy			1				1		6	
Botany					2		4		6	
Chemistry	2	-/1	1		2				5	
Zoology							1		1	
Improvements							49	4/5	49	1 /2
Agriculture							2		2	
Metaphysics										
Logic and philosophy of mind					3		1		4	
Rhetoric and criticism	7	1/2	3	1/1	1		5	-/1	16	-/1
Poetry and song	25	5/6	31	6/9	46	4/6	51	4/5	153	4/6
Plays	1				1				2	
Tales, novels, essays	6	1/2	1		3		6	-/1	16	-/1
Geography			1		10	1/1	6	-/1	17	-/1
History and antiquities	8	1 /2	4	1/1	8	1/1	8	-/1	28	1/1
Biography	1				7	1/1	7	-/1	15	-/1
Education					2		4		6	
Periodicals and news	112	21/29	20	4/6	84	8/12	213	15/22	429	12/18
Dictionaries	1		1		3		3		8	
Grammars	9	2/2	14	3 /4	7	1/1	17	1 /2	47	1 /2
Classics	7		12	2/3	2		9	1/1	30	1/1
Textbooks	5	1/1	10	2/3	2		12	1/1	29	1/1
University materials	16	3 /4	17	3/5	27	2/4	32	2/3	92	
Miscellaneous	10	2/3	5	1/1	22	2/3	44	3/5	81	2/3
Unknown	3	1/1	5	1/1	13	1 /2	25	2/3	46	1 /2
Total Imprints	531	100	503	100	1106	100	1399	100	3539	100
Imprints excluding Acts, etc.	390	100	345	100	712	100	972	100	2419	100

*The 'numerator' is the percentage of total imprints; the 'denominator' is the percentage of imprints excluding Acts, etc.

regularly printed and more theses were coming from university regents now teaching more modern topics. These books, mostly printed in Edinburgh, contain few real novelties but they clearly show that Scots were aware of and now themselves contributing to discussions which would be formative of the Scottish, even the European Enlightenment.

By the early 1700s both the lists of books in private libraries and the titles of Scottish imprints suggest that significant shifts had come in Scottish thinking. Scots were interested in a wider range of things and they were clearly trying harder to participate in the republic of letters. They were also far better prepared to do so than they had been for a very long time. But that only means that more of them were thinking like men in England, France, Holland and Germany. The patterns of cultural unity and convergence were not only British but also European.

This convergence of outlook among Scots and Englishmen may have been a precondition for the Union of 1707; certainly it helped to make union a success. But there was something else which marked the attitudes of many Scots in the latter seventeenth century. That was a new confidence that they could emulate as well as imitate others. It is evident in the projects of Sir Robert Sibbald and his friends but it is equally apparent in the patriotic and improving works of many others. The Union of 1707 was aided by this change of spirit. Without it, interest in improvements and the confidence that Scots could equal or outstrip the English would have been lacking and the Union would have been like earlier ones an unwelcome exercise of force or royal power.

NOTES

1 I have addressed some of these issues elsewhere: R. L. Emerson, 'Calvinism in the Scottish Enlightenment', in Joachim Schwend, Susanne Hagemann, Hermann Völkel (eds), *Literatur in Kontext – Literature in Context: Festshcrift für Horst W. Drescher* (Frankfurt-on-Main, 1992), pp. 19–28; R. L. Emerson, 'Science and moral philosophy in the Scottish Enlightenment', in M A Stewart (ed), *Studies in the Philosophy of the Scottish Enlightenment* (Oxford, 1990), pp. 11–36; R. L. Emerson, 'The religions, the secular and the worldly: Scotland 1680–1800', in James E Crimmins (ed.), *Religion, Secularization and Political Thought: Thomas Hobbes to J. S. Mill* (London, 1989), pp 68–89; R L Emerson, 'Science and the origins and concerns of the Scottish Enlightenment', *History of Science*, 26 (1988), pp. 333–66. See also: David C. Lachman, *The Marrow Controversy 1718–1723* (Edinburgh, 1988); Eric G. Forbes, 'Philosophy and science teaching in the seventeenth century', in Gordon Donaldson (ed.), *Four Centuries: Edinburgh University Life 1583–1983* (Edinburgh, 1983); Gordon Marshall, *Presbyteries and Profits: Calvinism and the Development of Capitalism in Scotland, 1560–1707* (Oxford, 1980), especially pp. 65–112; Brian G. Armstrong, *Calvinism and the Amyraut Heresy* (Madison, 1969); H. R. McAdoo, *The Structure of Caroline Moral Theology* (London, 1949).

2 Forbes, 'Philosophy and science teaching', pp. 28–37, 28, 31. See also Norman Fiering, *Moral Philosophy at Seventeenth-Century Harvard* (Chapel Hill, 1981).

3 Forbes, 'Philosophy and science teaching', p. 35.

4 J. D. Mackie, *The University of Glasgow 1451–1951* (Glasgow, 1954), pp. 144–5.

5 Sir Robert Sibbald, MD, studied mathematics with Crawford and noted of Leighton, then Principal, that he 'had excellent discourses to us in the Common Hall, sometymes in latine, sometymes in English, which, with the blessing of God upon y^m, gave me strong inclinations to a serious and good lyfe. I shunned the plays and divertisements the other students followed, and reach much in my study, for which my fellowes gave me the name of Diogenes in Dolio'. *The Memoirs of Sir Robert Sibbald (1641–1722)*, ed. Francis P. Hett (London, 1932), pp. 54–5. Later in life Sibbald became a patriotic antiquary and, like Leighton, a seeker whose religious career led him from Presbyterianism to Episcopacy, to Rome and finally again to the Scottish Episcopal Church to which he remained loyal after 1689. Crawford seems to have discussed some natural historical topics with his students; Sir Robert Sibbald, 'Ane Essay Relating to the Natural History of Scotland', Advocates MSS, National Library of Scotland, MS 33.5.19, pp. 59, 212.

6 Forbes, 'Philosophy and science teaching', p. 34.

7 Jonquil Bevan, 'Seventeenth-century students and their books', in Donaldson (ed.), *Edinburgh University Life 1583–1983*, pp. 16–27.

8 Curricular change at Aberdeen has been most recently discussed by P. B. Wood, *The Aberdeen Enlightenment: The Arts Curriculum in the Aberdeen Universities 1717–1800*, (Aberdeen, 1993), ch 1.

9 Emerson, 'Natural philosophy and the problem of the Scottish Enlightenment', *Studies on Vaire and the eighteenth century*, 242 (1986), pp. 243–91, 258, 268.

10 *Officers and Graduate of University & King's College, Aberdeen MVD-MDCCCLX* (1495–1860), ed. Peter John Anderson (Aberdeen, New Spalding Club, 1893), *passim*; *Fasti academiae Mariscallanae Aberdonensis*, 3 vols, ed. P. J. Anderson (Aberdeen, New Spalding Club, 1889–1898), *passim*; the quote is from p. 53.

11 W. G. Sinclair Snow, *The Times, Life and Thought of Patrick Forbes, Bishop of Aberdeen, 1618–1635* (London, 1952), pp 142–78; G. D .Henderson, *Mystics of the North-East* (Aberdeen, Spalding Club, 1934), pp. 1–70.

12 Sir James Balfour of Denmylne, *The Historical Work of*, ed. James Hais (Edinburgh, 1824), pp. x-xxiv; Gordon Donaldson, ' A Lang pedigree', *Scottish Historical Review*, 65 (1986), 1–16.

13 Hugh Trevor-Roper, 'The Scottish Enlightenment', in *Studies on Voltaire*, 58 (1967), 1,935–58; 'The Scottish Enlightenment', *Blackwood's Magazine*, 322 (1977), 371–88.

14 For Scots abroad in foreign universities see: John Durkan, 'The French connection in the sixteenth and seventeenth Centuries', in T. C. Smout (ed.), *Scotland and Europe 1200–1850* (Edinburgh, 1986), pp. 19–44; Paul Nève, 'Disputations of Scots students attending universities in the northern Netherlands', in W. M. Gordon and T. D. Fergus (eds), *Legal history in the Making: Proceedings of the Ninth British Legal History Conference, Glasgow 1989* (London and Rio Grande, 1991), pp. 95–108, especially pp. 96–9; Edward Peacock, *Index to English Speaking Students who have Graduated* [read: *matriculated*] *at Leyden University* (London, Index Society, 1883).

15 27 per cent of the Leyden men 1580–1749 had matriculated by 1680. Others had doubtless attended classes without matriculating.

16 Hugh Ouston, 'York in Edinburgh: James VII and the patronage of learning in Scotland, 1679–1688), in J. Dwyer, R. A. Mason, A. Murdoch (eds), *New Perspectives on the Politics and Culture of Early Modern Scotland* (Edinburgh, n.d. [1982]), pp. 133–55.

17 I thank Paul Wood for this information.

18 Gordon Donaldson, *The Scots Overseas* (London, 1966), pp. 30–1.

19 Alexander Robertson, *The Life of Sir Robert Moray . . . 1609–1673* (London, 1922); David Stevenson, *The Origins of Free Masonry. Scotland's Century, 1590–1710* (Cambridge, 1988), ch. 3.

20 *List of Fellows of the Royal College of Surgeons of Edinburgh* (Edinburgh, 1874). Andrew Cunningham, 'The medical professions and pattern of medical care: the case of Edinburgh, *c.* 1670–*c.* 1700', in Wolfgang Eckart and Johanna Geyer-Kordesch (eds), *Heilberufe und Kranke im 17 und 18 Jahrhundert* (Munster, *Munstersche Beitrage zur Geschichte und Theorie der Midizin*, 18, 1982), 9–28, 20; John D. Comrie, *History of Scottish Medicine*, 2 vols (London, Wellcome Historical Medical Museum, 1932), I, pp. 231, 246; Minute books of the Royal College of Surgeons of Edinburgh, College Library, IV, p. 18.

21 I am grateful to Dr Rosalie Stott for having made available to me this library list with her annotations. She is presently writing an extended analysis of this collection.

22 It is likely that Kincaid's son Thomas retained a portion of his father's books.

23 Lester King, *The Road to Medical Enlightenment, 1650–1695* (New York, 1970), p. 94; and King, *The Philosophy of Medicine: The Early Eighteenth Century* (Cambridge and London, 1978), p. 82.

24 Lester King dates the division between the schools to *c.* 1675, in *Philosophy of Medicine*, p. 98; see also Antonia J. Bunch, *Hospital and Medical Libraries in Scotland* (Glasgow, 1975).

25 D. Butler, *The Life and Letters of Robert Leighton* (London, 1903), pp. 590–2.

26 'Bibliotheca Sibbaldiana . . . with A curious Collection of historical and other Manuscripts', Sibbald MSS, Library of the Royal College of Physicians, Edinburgh. Bunch, *Hospital and Medical Libraries*, pp. 18–19, gives a rough subject catalogue of the library worked out from the published catalogue of 1722.

27 *Journals of Sir John Lauder, Lord Fountainhall*, ed. Donald Crawford (Edinburgh, Scottish History Society, 1st series 36, 1900), pp 283–99; see also Thomas I. Rae, 'The origins of the Advocates' Library' in Patrick Cadell and Ann Matheson (eds), *For The Encouragement of Learning: Scotland's National Library 1689–1989* (Edinburgh, HMSO, 1989), pp. 1–22, 13–14. Crawford reproduced the list of purchases made between 1667 and 1679. In addition to these, Lauder had earlier acquired 536 books many of whose titles are noted in the *Journals*. My total for his purchases 1667–1679 differs from Rae's (456 titles) probably because where Lauder gave no title but listed the topic of a book I have counted it in the appropriate category.

28 *Remains of Sir Robert Sibblad, Knt, MD, Containing His Autobiography . . . and an Account of his MSS* (Edinburgh, 1837), p. 4.

29 'Sir George Mackenzie's speech', trans. James H Loudon in J[ohn] W. Cairns and A. M. Cain (eds), *Oratio Inauguralis in Aperienda Jurisconsultorum Bibliotheca: Sir George Mackenzie*, (Edinburgh, 1989), p. 73.

30 John Cairns, 'Sir George Mackenzie, the Faculty of Advocates, & The Advocates Library', in *Oratio*, pp. 18–35, 26.

31 Ouston, 'York in Edinburgh', pp. 133–55.

32 I have not found a complete catalogue of this library but my comments are supported by 'The correspondence of Andrew and William Dunlop 1715–1720', preserved at Glasgow University Library, MS Gen 83. The Dunlops were his nephews.

33 Alan Dunlop, *William Carstares and the Kirk by Law Established* (Edinburgh, 1967), p. 105, n. 2; D. B. Horn, 'The University of Edinburgh and the teaching of history'. *University of Edinburgh Journal*, 17 (1953–4), pp. 161–76, especially p. 161. The first

professor of Ecclesiastical History, John Cuming of Relugas (*c.* 1641–1714) was interested in Scottish antiquities and may have belonged to the antiquarian club existing in Edinburgh for some time after 1702, *Early Letters of Robert Wodrow 1698–1709*, ed. L. W. Sharp, Scottish History Society, 3rd series, 23 (Edinburgh, 1937), pp. 191, 261–2. Cumin's successor was Carstares's nephew, William Dunlop. Charles Mackie, the first professor of civil history, was Carstares's nephew by marriage.

34 John Cairns, 'John Spotiswoode, Professor of Law: A Preliminary Sketch', *The Stair Society Miscellany Three*, XXXIX (Edinburgh, 1992), pp. 131–59; see also, Cairns, 'Rhetoric, language and Roman Law: legal education and improvement in eighteenth-century Scotland', *Law and History Review*, 9 (1991), 31–58.

35 Spotiswoode MSS, NLS MS 2934.

36 Spotiswoode MSS, NLS MS 658, John Spotiswoode, *A Discourse Shewing the Necessary Qualifications of a Student of the Laws and What is Propos'd in the Colleges of Law, History & Philology, Establish'd at Edinburgh*, (Edinburgh, 1704).

37 NLS MS 2934 ff 92, 105, 108, 121, 123–4; 125–6; 137. Elsewhere Spotiswoode made proposals for studies of Scottish coins, weights and measures, great men, topography and history. He possessed an outlook much like Sir Robert Sibbald's. See R. L. Emerson, 'Sir Robert Sibbald, Kt, The Royal Society of Scotland and the origins of the Scottish Enlightenment', *Annals of Science*, 45 (1988), 41–72. Spotiswoode's name clearly belongs on the list given there on p 71.

38 NLS MS 658, ff 18–20.

39 'A Catalogue of Curious and Valuable Books, Being the Library of Mr John Spotiswoode' (Edinburgh, 1728); NLS MS Bc 5 1(1).

40 St Andrews University Minutes, 10 June 1699, St Andrews Muniment Room.

41 John Stuart Shaw, *The Management of Scottish Society 1707–1764* (Edinburgh, 1983), pp. 49, 68–81 *passim*; *The History of Parliament, The House of Commons 1715–1754*, 3 vols, ed. Romney Sedgwick (New York, 1970), I, pp. 420–1.

42 'Tinwald Library', Erskine-Murray MSS, NLS MS 3283.

43 One of Erskine's colleagues at Edinburgh University, Robert Steuart (1675–1747), professor of natural philosophy, left a remarkable memorial in the form of 'the Physiological Library'. This has been analysed by Michael Barfoot: 'Hume and the culture of science in the early eighteenth century', in Stewart (ed.), *Studies in the Philosophy of the Scottish Enlightenment*, pp. 152–60.

44 I have used the second edition prepared by the National Library of Scotland (Edinburgh, 1970). My categorisation of books listed by Aldis is rough: one cannot always judge a book by its title.

45 This is not of course the whole story, since I have not touched upon works printed outside Scotland. For a partial list of these, see J. F. Kellar Johnstone and A Webster Robertson, *Bibliographia Aberdonensis . . . 1641–1700*, 2 vols (Aberdeen, 3rd Spalding Club, 1930). Their entries often show Scots intellectually active and important in English and continental contexts.

46 The Duke of York set up a Catholic school within the precincts of Holyrood Palace; his printer working within the same bounds was James Watson.

47 Michael Hunter, 'Aikenhead the Atheist: the context and consequences of articulate irreligion in the late seventeenth century', in Michael Hunter and David Wootton (eds), *Atheism from the Reformation to the Enlightenment* (Oxford, 1992), pp. 221–54.

48 These debates are noticed in William Ferguson, *Scotland's Relations with England: A Survey to 1707* (Edinburgh, 1977), pp. 180–253, *passim*.

49 Andrew Cunningham, 'Sydenham *versus* Newton: the Edinburgh fever dispute of the 1690s between Andrew Brown and Archibald Pitcairne', *Medical History,* Supplement 1 (1981), 71–98; Cunningham also believes the Edinburgh medical community was restructured in the period 1670–1700; see: Cunningham, 'The medical professions'.

50 Ian Whyte, *Agriculture and Society in Seventeenth-Century Scotland* (Edinburgh, 1979), pp. 252–5.

Clans of the Highlands and Islands: 1610 Onwards

Extracted from A MacKillop 2001 *in* M Lynch (ed.), *The Oxford Companion to Scottish History*, Oxford (Oxford University Press), 95–6.

Within Scottish history clanship and kinship tend to be very closely identified, indeed, often seen as one and the same. Yet it is far more accurate to say that one, kinship, formed a component part of a wider social system, namely, clanship. That the word clan is derived from the Gaelic *clann* (children) underlines kinship's central place within clanship as a whole. Its importance cannot be better exemplified than by the way each clan was conceptualized as a *siol*; that is, as the seed, or direct blood descendants, of a powerful and prestigious founder whose historic exploits and status justified and confirmed the position of each clan group. Thus, for example, the MacLeods of Dunvegan were distinguished from the MacLeods of Lewis in that the former saw themselves as *siol Tormod* (the seed of Norman) and the latter as *siol Torquil* (the seed of Torquil). Yet the belief that every member of an entire clan was the direct kin of such a founder was not the exclusive or even predominant mechanism for expressing the organizing principle of kinship.

Of equal importance with this collective sense of kinship was the person of the chief and his immediate family. Thus it was that each chief's patronymic was that of the original clan founder: hence the head of the Campbells of Argyll was known as *MacCailein Mor* (the son of big Colin). It is important to stress that, at the start of the 17th century at least, any potential incompatibility between a collective sense of kinship and this notion of the *ceanncinnidh* (chief) was more apparent than real. At this time, the chief was still seen in many respects as the trustee, or protector, of his clan's *duthchas*; that is their heritage, or more specifically, their prescriptive access to and possession of certain, specific lands. Traditionally, this notion of *duthchas* has been taken to mean that the clan, because they were all either distantly or closely related kin, somehow held the land in common – that a clan's territory did not belong to the chief but rather to the *siol* as a whole. Yet care is needed when making such an argument. First, the notion of a clan all being related to each other did not necessarily find tangible, day-to-day expression on the ground: indeed, in a sense, kinship worked against this notion of a common collective descent. Instead, the use of patronymics – that is stressing one's father, grandfather, etc. – was as likely as the notion of calling oneself by a collective clan name. Second, concepts of kinship served more as a broad, overarching theme rather than a specific claim to actual descent, or to specific farms of lands. Thus, bonds of manrent and bonds of friendship tied obviously non-related kin groups into a wider military, political, and land/food resource sharing alliance of clanship. The small sept of the MacMartins of Letterfinlay who, for example, were allied closely with the Camerons of Locheil, might conceive of themselves as distinct within their own lands, but also saw themselves as Camerons if operating elsewhere outside Lochaber.

These forms of local association reveal that, while clearly central, kinship was but one element within what was a multifaceted form of social organization. For example, while the concept of *duthchas* might well entrench a belief in a collective right to the resources of the land, the crown envisaged the chief as the sole owner of his territories – his *oighreach* – a function that simultaneously made him accountable for those populations that lived upon it. Thus, in the early 17th century, the crown reissued charters of ownership to chiefs in an effort to imbue elites with a sense of legal responsibility. In other words, while the traditional perception is that clanship perpetrated violence and disorder, in an official sense it was seen as an organizing mechanism for local legal arrangements. It was in fact clan gentry acting as arbitration panels that often thrashed out issues of property theft and compensation in the localities: indeed, it was precisely because it actively sought to co-opt the legal authority of the gentry that the Commission for Securing the Peace, instituted in 1682, was so successful. In a more extreme form, commissions of fire and sword were simply orders from the privy council sanctioning the use of one clan to carry out de facto policing upon another. Part of the problem with clanship's historical image is that it is the official view from the centre, from Edinburgh and London, which has predominated. Of course it was certainly the case that during the 16th century clanship could spawn significant levels of violence. However, from the early years of the 17th century, two central features of clan violence are worthy of note. First, incidents of large-scale feud were in steep decline, largely because the military aspects of clanship had suffered considerable erosion. Indeed, the last private feud fought occurred in 1688, and was fought between the MacDonalds of Keppoch and the Mackintoshes over lands in the Braes of Lochaber. Similarly a survey from 1705 of the Grant estate in Eastern Inverness-shire reveals that of over 600 men, a mere 12 per cent were armed with a sword and a gun. A second important dimension to clan violence was that, increasingly, it occurred because the political centre was willing to back one side or the other. Campaigns of Alasdair MacColla against the Campbells of Argyll in the mid-1640s were in some fundamental respects a traditional feud legitimized by Scottish national politics. However, as the century wore on, clans simply would not commit themselves to violence without the crown's official sanction. Thus, Lachlan Mackintosh, chief of Clan Chattan, only moved against Keppoch in 1688 because the crown was prepared, not only to recognize the validity of his claim, but also to actively intervene on his behalf by supplying troops to augment his levies.

Ultimately, however, it was nothing as dramatic as military violence, either between different clans or by the crown, which led to the demise of kinship and clanship. Instead, clanship was in a sense hollowed out by processes whereby commercial productivity and profitability replaced kinship as the means of organizing relations between Highland elites and their clansmen. The same criteria now also governed the leasing of land to clansmen, even if they were of the same kindred. The early decades of the 17th century had witnessed a growth in black cattle droving from the region. The devastation of the Wars of the Covenant and the indebtedness that it had spawned ensured the Restoration period witnesses sustained development in this economic activity. Subsequent profits ensured that the concept of *duthchas* was undermined in practice, if not yet in appearance, by the tendency for clan chiefs to mortgage clan lands in return for credit. These wadset arrangements bestowed on the creditor effective property rights until the original loan was repaid. However, kinship and commercialism should not be seen as automatically incompatible. As specialists in the droving trade, for example, most of the new wadsetters were in fact clan gentry and kinsmen of the chief. Likewise, even as late as the 1770s, the fact that MacLeod of Dunvegan managed his debt in such a way as to ensure that his main creditors were kinsmen, rather than banking institutions, was a vital component in staving off the family's bankruptcy.

Nonetheless the decades from the 1660s to the early 1700s also witnessed more fundamental alterations in clan society. Tacks, or leases, which had once run for up to 90 years or even several lifetimes, were now restricted by chiefs to a period of nineteen years or less. In effect, the chief no longer saw land in terms of *duthchas*, as a resource for the maintenance of his kinsman – real and fictive – but rather in terms of his *oighreach* – his territory or property. The result was that the social and economic position of the tacksman was undermined – above all as chiefs sought to access the differential between what subtenants paid to their tacksmen and what the latter then paid to their chief. That these leading tenants had formed the vital link between the chief and the mass of his clan, as well as providing much of the managerial and agricultural expertise that had marshalled and dispensed food resources on the ground, was now increasingly irrelevant.

Clan Support for the House of Stuart

AI Macinnes 1996 *in* PGB McNeill and HL MacQueen (eds), *Atlas of Scottish History to 1707* Edinburgh (The Scottish Medievalists and the Department of Geography, University of Edinburgh), 148–50.

The clans – the Gaelic-speaking, patriarchal amalgams of kinship, local association and feudal deference – were the bedrock of both the Royalist campaigns of 1644–47 and the first Jacobite rising of 1689–90. The persistence of hosting and the ready mobilisation of the clans by passing round the fiery cross meant a lower threshold in the Highlands than the Lowlands for the resort to arms. The militarism of the clans can be overplayed, however. The resolution of territorial disputes by the wholesale recourse of clans to arms was becoming less of an occasional practice, more of a rarity in the course of the seventeenth century. Technological change meant that it was becoming no longer fashionable to take arms off trees. The chiefs and leading gentry of the clans were increasingly reluctant to meet the expense of providing guns. The professional backbone to the Royalist and Jacobite campaigns was formed by Irish troops. Three regiments served under James Graham, marquis of Montrose during the civil war, and John Graham, viscount Dundee from 1689. The 'Highland charge' deployed successfully on both campaigns was probably introduced to Scotland by Montrose's major-general, Alasdair MacColla, who can be said to have imported from Ulster in the summer of 1644 a tactic for irregular infantry which was designed to suit highland terrain, the technology clans could afford and the effectiveness of the sword and targe in close-quarters after the discharge of firearms.

In terms of strategy, clan support for the house of Stuart was most effective in the pursuit of guerrilla warfare. After joining forces in August 1644, Montrose and MacColla commenced a twelve-month campaign of continuous movement running up a series of six bloody victories that culminated in the defeat of the Covenanting forces at Kilsyth. Each victory attracted increased support from the clans. However, the military success of guerrilla warfare was not converted into political achievement, notably the capture of leading towns, the key to control in the Lowlands. Within a month of parting from MacColla and the western clans, Montrose's fortunes went into rapid decline. From his defeat at Philiphaugh in September 1645, until his departure into exile twelve months later, Montrose was a spent force in Scotland. Although he was eventually forced to retire to Ireland by July 1647, MacColla fared relatively better on the western seaboard where his continued pursuit of guerrilla warfare was distinctly less naïve and more constructive. Other than the MacDonalds of Sleat who preferred to remain neutral rather than accept his leadership, MacColla's affiliations to the lineal descendants of the Lords of the Isles created a ready reservoir of support. Unrivalled charisma based on his personal valour in battle and the fact that he was not required to lay siege to large towns enabled MacColla to occupy Kintyre and Islay and thus maintain, for eighteen months, a Royalist bridgehead with Ireland. Nor did the successful pursuit of guerrilla warfare prove politically remunerative during the first Jacobite rising. Dundee's stunning victory at Killiecrankie in July 1689 was neutralised by his death in the course of battle. The burgeoning clan support occasioned by his personal charisma and his inspired generalship was soon dissipated by insipid and inept leadership from his officers with the Irish forces who assumed command but failed to make a military breakthrough either into the central Lowlands or areas of Jacobite affinity in the north-east. Admittedly, the Stuart cause was not helped by the fluctuating nature of clan support during the Jacobite rising as during the civil war. While undoubtedly influenced by their desire to return home with booty, this fluctuating support was attributable more to the clans' reluctance to disrupt the agrarian cycle of sowing and harvesting and, above all, to their aversion to prolonged absence from their patrimonies which sustained campaigning left exposed to the ravages of cateran bands or reprisals by political opponents. For although around 5,000 clansmen were mobilised during the civil war and again for the Jacobite rising, the 47 foremost clans were never united in their support for the Stewarts albeit over 60% of the clans actively supported or shifted their support in favour of the royal house on both occasions.

Clan support for the house of Stuart as hereditary rulers of Scotland was based primarily on the projection of traditional values of clanship onto the national political stage. As the chiefs were the protectors of the clan patrimonies, so were the Stuarts trustees for Scotland. At the same time, clan support for Charles I during the civil war was essentially reactionary. The 21 clans who declared unequivocally for the Royalist cause were fighting less in favour of that absentee monarch than against the Covenanting movement which was making unprecedented demands for ideological, financial and military commitment. More especially the clans were reacting against powerful nobles whose public espousal of the Covenanting cause masked the private pursuit of territorial ambitions. Thus, the Mackays took up the Royalist mantle to defend their patrimony of Strathnaver against the acquisitive overtures of John Gordon, earl of Sutherland. The most acquisitive influence, however, was undoubtedly that of the Clan Campbell, the main beneficiaries of the expropriation of MacDonalds from Kintyre, Islay, Jura and Ardnamurchan since the outset of the seventeenth century. Having been evicted by Campbells from Colonsay in 1639, the determination of MacColla to perpetuate the feud under the Royalist mantle was endorsed by the Irish regiments under his command which were recruited almost exclusively from among his kinsmen on the Ulster estates of Randal MacDonnell, earl of Antrim, whose own territorial ambitions on the western seaboard had encouraged Campbell forces enlisted in the Covenanting army despatched to Ireland in 1642 to wreak havoc on the isle of Rathlin and the glens of Antrim. The deliberate but wanton ravaging of Argyll and northern Perthshire during the winters of 1644 and 1645 persuaded six clans hitherto contained within the territorial spheres of Campbell influence to cut loose in support of the Royalist cause albeit the two most prominent, the Lamonts and MacDougalls, were subsequently massacred for their temerity to switch sides and plunder Campbell estates. The polarizing impact of the Campbells was not confined to the western seaboard since their chief, Archibald, marquis of Argyle, in the four years prior to the outbreak of the civil war, had utilised military commissions not only to harry suspect Royalists in Atholl, braes of Angus, Braemar and Deeside, but also to push his territorial claims over Badenoch and Lochaber. Because their chief was in the tutelage of the marquis, Camerons of Lochiel who held their lands of the house of Argyle, maintained a prudent neutrality throughout the civil war. Conversely, aversion to the hitherto pervasive influence of the Royalist magnate, George Gordon, marquis of Huntly, in the central Highlands, persuaded the Frasers and originally the Grants to declare for the Covenanters and for the Mackintoshes, but not all of the Clan Chattan to remain neutral. The willingness of the Royalist commanders to despoil territories of clans reluctant to join their cause convinced the Grants of the expediency of switching sides. The MacLeods of Dunvegan and the Sinclairs limited their support for the Covenanting movement to the protection of their clan patrimonies. Torn between the defence of their clan patrimonies and the political ambitioning of their vacillating chief, George, second earl of Seaforth, the MacKenzies, together with their allies, the MacRaes and MacLeods of Assynt, demonstrated an unparalleled lack of touch in switching adversely whenever Royalist or Covenanting forces enjoyed ascendancy.

While the Campbells and the other clans who campaigned offensively for the Covenanting Movement were in broad sympathy with Presbyterianism, the militant Catholicism of the Irish forces, while espoused by MacColla and the leading branches of the Clan Donald, was certainly not shared by the majority of the Royalist clans. However, religion was a principal factor influencing clans to come out for the first Jacobite rising. The sporadic inroads of Catholic missions served to solidify the opposition of former Royalist clans to the disposition of James VII. More significant in attracting support from hitherto neutral clans and in persuading Covenanting clans to adopt a neutral standpoint was the spread of episcopalianism during the Restoration era, which not only provided a religious complement to the hierarchical nature of clanship, but inculcated a spirit of obedience and submission to royal authority throughout Gaeldom. Accordingly, the replacement of James VII by William of Orange was interpreted as a breach of patriarchal duty by Gaelic poets for whom the sundering of genealogical continuity imperilled the lawful exercise of government which, in turn, subverted the maintenance of a just political order. Far from being tyrannical or oppressive, James VII had won a favourable press from the clans. When duke of York, he had instituted the commission for pacifying the Highlands in 1682 which, for the next three years, had sought the co-operation of chiefs and leading gentry in maintaining law and order. This commission represented a brief, but welcome, respite from the grasping and intimidatory policies of successive regimes in the Restoration era which had sought to tarnish the Highlands as an area of endemic lawlessness in order to maintain a standing army and facilitate the collection of onerous taxes. Moreover, James had proved notably responsive in redressing the acquisitiveness of the house of Argyle. Although the marquis had been executed in 1661, when his son Archibald was restored as ninth earl two years later, he embarked upon a credit squeeze that revived his father's policy of forcing heavily indebted chiefs and leading gentry to accept the feudal superiority of their house. By exploiting the legal technicalities of public and private indebtedness, Argyle even had chiefs and leading gentry of the Macleans of Duart expropriated from Tiree, Mull and Morven by 1679. Six years later, when the ninth earl rebelled against the accession of James VII who had engineered his forfeiture in 1681, over 4,000 clansmen under the command of John Murray, marquis of Atholl, drawn from clans throughout Gaeldom, but predominantly from the victims of Argyle's acquisitiveness, systematically ravaged mid-Argyll, Cowal and Kintyre. This 'Atholl Raid' gave a foretaste of the simple antipathy to the restoration of the house of Argyle at the Revolution. Clans within Campbell spheres of influence who had switched their allegiance in the course of the civil war declared openly for James VII in 1689. Only the MacAllisters declared for the Whigs, as earlier for the Covenanters, before switching sides.

The 27 clans that declared unequivocally for the Jacobite cause demonstrated not just an increased willingness to support the royal house at the outset of campaigning, but also masked a pronounced movement of 10 clans in favour of James VII with a loss of 4 former supporters of Charles I. The only Royalist clan actually to declare for the Whigs were the Mackays, principally because one of their leading gentry, major-general Hugh Macrae of Scourbie, commanded William of Orange's forces in Scotland. Although the MacDonnells of Antrim opted to concentrate their political energies on Irish affairs, a small contingent from the Isle of Rathlin served with the Kintyre clan fighting for James VII. Of the 25 clans who maintained the same political standpoint towards the house of Stuart, 17 loyal to Charles I remained loyal to James VII, albeit the MacDonalds of Keppoch remained apart from the main contingent of Jacobite forces, being more committed to plunder than military campaigning. The Mackintoshes, against whom they fought the last clan battle at Mulroy on the braes of Lochaber in August 1688, were the only clan to remain neutral during the Jacobite rising as during the civil war. No more than 3 clans committed to the Covenanting cause sided with William of Orange, albeit 12 actually fought exclusively for the former and 8 for the latter. The most notable loss arose from the breaking of ranks within the Clan Campbell. Not only did clansmen in territories appropriated by the Campbells in the course of the seventeenth century fail to adhere to the Whig cause, but the principal cadet, John Campbell of Glenorchy, recently ennobled as the earl of Breadalbane, affirmed his political independence of the house of Argyle by remaining neutral. That family solidarity was less pronounced during the first Jacobite rising than during the civil war was borne out by the split allegiance of Grants and the Atholl Men. Whereas the majority of Grants in Strathspey followed their chief in declaring for William of

Orange, the Grants of Ballindalloch consistently adhered to the Jacobite cause while the Grants in Glenmoriston and Glenurquhart, after an intimidatory measure of persuasion from neighbours, switched in favour of James VII. Although the marquis distanced himself from commitment to either cause, a small contingent of Atholl Men supported the Whigs at the instigation of his eldest son, Lord Murray; but the majority switched to Jacobitism in the aftermath of Killiecrankie under the leadership of his second son, Lord James. While the extension of civil war between as well as among the clans was the most innovatory feature of the first Jacobite rising, the MacKenzies and their associates were again afflicted by inept leadership. Although Jacobite in sympathy they were neutral by default because Kenneth, fourth earl of Seaforth, dallied with James VII on his hapless Irish venture. When Seaforth belatedly returned to rally his clansmen in the spring of 1690, the discredit of the Irish officers commanding the Jacobite clans was all but complete. It is important to stress, in conclusion, that the clans were contained rather than defeated in the course of the first Jacobite rising. That the Whig government should instigate the massacre of MacDonalds of Glencoe in February 1692, because of the technical default of their aged chief in making timely acceptance of its offer of indemnity, served to consolidate support among the clans for the exiled house of Stuart.

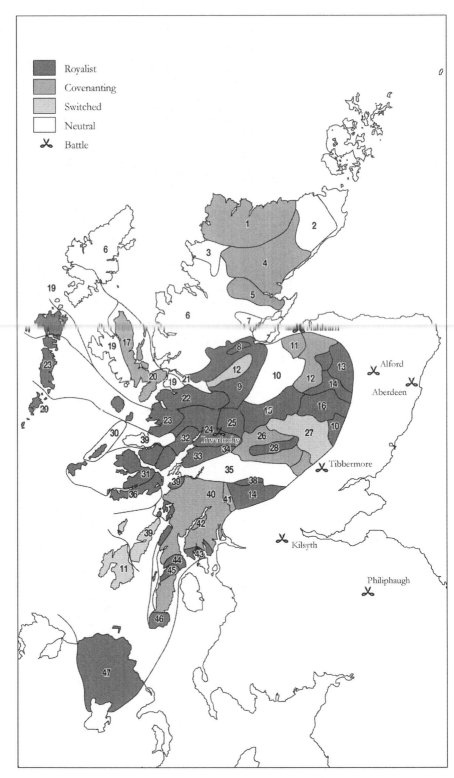

Map 1   Covenanter Clans

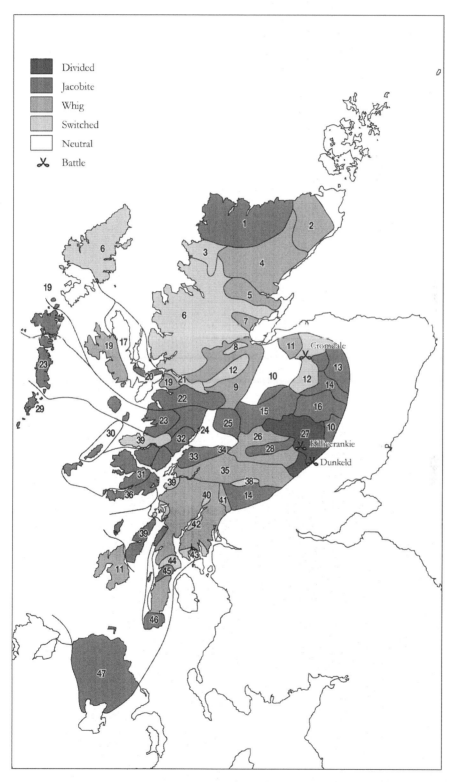

Map 2   Jacobite Clans

KEY TO MAPS 1 AND 2

1 Mackays (Strathnaver)
2 Sinclairs (Caithness)
3 Macleods of Assynt
4 Sutherland Men (Gordons & Gunns)
5 Rosses (Easter Ross/Dornoch Firth)
6 Mackenzies (Ross & Lewis)
7 Munros (Easter Ross, Cromarty Firth)
8 Chisholms (Strathglass)
9 Frasers (Strathconon, Strathfarrar & Stratherrick)
10 Mackintoshes & Clan Chattan (Strathnairn, Strathdearn & the Braes of Angus)
11 Campbells of Cawdor (& Islay)
12 Grants (Glenmoriston, Glenurquhart & Speyside including Ballindalloch)
13 Gordons (Glenlivet & Strathdon)
14 MacGregors (Strathavon, Deeside with Stewarts, & the Trossachs)
15 Macphersons (Badenoch)
16 Farquharsons (Braemar)
17 MacDonalds of Sleat (with Trotternish & North Uist)
18 Macleods of Raasay
19 Macleods of Dunvegan (with Harris & Glenelg)
20 Mackinnons (Strathswordale)
21 MacRaes (Kintail)
22 MacDonalds of Glengarry (with Knoydart & North Morar)
23 MacDonalds of Clanranald (Moidart, Arisaig, South Morar, Small Isles, Benbecula & South Uist)
24 Cameron (Lochaber & Sunart)
25 MacDonalds of Keppoch (Braes of Lochaber)
26 Menzies (Lochtayside)
27 Atholl Men (Stewarts, Murrays, & Fergussons)
28 Robertsons (Rannoch)
29 MacNeills of Barra
30 Macleans of Coll (and Muck)
31 Macleans of Duart (with Tiree & Morvern)
32 Macleans of Ardgour
33 Stewarts of Appin
34 MacDonalds of Glencoe
35 Campbells of Glenorchy (Lorne & Breadalbane)
36 Maclaines of Lochbuie
37 MacDougalls (Dunnolly, Firth of Lorne and Craignish)
38 MacNabs (Glendochart)
39 Campbells of Argyle (with Kintyre, Colonsay, Jura & Ardnamurchan)
40 MacNaughtons (Glenaray, Glenshirra & Glenfyne)
41 Macfarlanes (Arrochar and Glenfalloch)
42 Maclachlans (Strathlachlan & Glendaruel)
43 Lamont (Kyles of Bute & Cowal)
44 MacAllisters (Tarbert & Knapdale)
45 MacDonalds of Largie
46 MacNeills of Gigha and Taynish (& Mull of Kintyre with MacDonalds of Sanda)
47 MacDonnells of Antrim (including the Rathlin Isles)

Calvinism and the Gaidhealtachd in Scotland

J Dawson 1994 in A Pettegree, A Duke and G Lewis (eds), *Calvinism in Europe 1540–1620*, Cambridge (Cambridge University Press), 231–53.

In the early modern period Scotland was divided by language into two separate regions. The Gaidhealtachd, the Gaelic-speaking area, had receded during the later middle ages. By the start of the sixteenth century, except for a pocket in the south-west of Scotland, it was largely confined to the region beyond the Highland Fault Line covering the Highlands and the Western isles. In the Lowlands, Scots was spoken and was the language of the Court, its government and administration. This linguistic divide reflected a growing polarisation between distinct Highland and Lowland cultures. An increasingly hostile view of Gaelic society developed in Scotland from the later sixteenth century. This process was accelerated by the union of the crowns of Scotland, England and Ireland in 1603 and the subsequent removal of the Court to London. In the new British state the Gaelic language in both its Irish and its Scottish homelands would be subjected to the cultural imperialism of the dominant Anglo-Scots vernacular.[1]

The existence of two distinct languages and cultures in Scotland faced the new Protestant Kirk with a problem. In common with other European Protestants, the Kirk was committed to abandoning the Latin of the Catholic church and using the local vernacular. But Scots and Gaelic were not simply two dialects; they were separate languages with completely different linguistic roots. The Kirk had to cope with two vernaculars and, of even greater importance, two diverging cultures and societies. Misunderstandings could easily arise, as in 1624 when some Lowland ministers instructed their clerical brethren from the Highlands to stop attending presbytery meetings in 'unsemly habits'. The Lowlanders, who had been carrying out a visitation of the presbytery of Inverness, were shocked by the sight of ministers dressed in bonnets and plaids.[2] To Lowland eyes they must have appeared to be barbaric men who did not belong in the Scottish Kirk at all. Although the Gaelic clergy looked completely alien to their Lowland counterparts, they were wearing the normal dress of a Highlander. These ministers were good Calvinists but they were also good Gaels. They had evolved a distinctively Gaelic form of Calvinism by taking the ideas and institutions of the Kirk and fitting them into a Highland context.

The characteristic feature of the type of Calvinism found in Scotland's Gaelic-speaking areas was the willingness to adopt set forms and practices and adapt them to suit the local situation. This was demonstrated in the adoption of the traditional methods and personnel of the 'Gaelic learned orders' to communicate the Protestant message and spread it throughout the Highlands and Islands. It can also be viewed in the flexible approach to the institutional structures of the Scottish Kirk which strove for maximum effectiveness on minimal resources. In these ways the Gaelic clergy had the self-confidence and assurance both to fit Calvinism into their own culture and to change that culture to accommodate the new demands of the Protestant message.

The creation of a Gaelic Calvinism in the first century of the Scottish Reformation has gone largely unnoticed. As in the case of the Lowland attitude towards clerical tartan, appearances can be deceptive. It was perfectly true that the kind of reformation achieved by the Scottish Kirk in the Lowlands between 1560 and 1660 was not replicated in the Highlands and Islands. However, this did not mean that James VI was correct when he asserted that his Gaelic subjects were 'wilde savages voide of Godis fear and out obedience'.[3]

I

The strong Protestantism which spread into the Highlands and Islands between 1560 and 1660 was of a very different nature to that practised in the Lowlands of Scotland. It was a Gaelic version of Calvinism not only in the sense that it employed the Gaelic language in its worship but also because it had been adapted to fit Gaelic society and culture. In early modern Scotland the Gaelic language itself took two different forms: Scottish Vernacular and Classical Common Gaelic. The literary language of Classical Common Gaelic was shared with Gaelic Ireland and was the vehicle for the high culture of a single pan-Gaelic world. Traditional learning in law, medicine and literature was composed and then transmitted in this common tongue. In particular, it was the language of the professional poets with their complex and rigid rules of composition and versification. This literary tradition was transmitted in manuscript form using the specialist corra-litir script by the Gaelic learned orders.[4]

By the sixteenth century Classical Common Gaelic survived in both manuscript and oral form. Its orthography and typography remained in an experimental state and it had not yet made the transition to a printed language with the consequent standardising effect. The classical language was not in everyday use but was primarily employed by an elite to perform certain specific tasks.

It is a matter of learned debate precisely how much the common people understood of the compositions in Classical Common Gaelic. Over time the spoken language in Scotland had diverged from the more archaic literary language and was also moving away from the corresponding Irish vernacular. In the sixteenth and seventeenth centuries Scottish Vernacular Gaelic was becoming more self-confident and developing its own freer forms of poetry. However, Classical Common Gaelic remained the prime vehicle for literary culture.[5]

To some extent the products of this literary culture needed to be interpreted to make them fully comprehensible in the vernacular of the day. The Gaelic learned orders, and to a lesser extent the aristocracy, acted as bridges between the two forms of the language. This was made much easier because of the great emphasis upon the oral performance and transmission of the literary culture and produced what Professor Thomson has styled 'the culture of oral literacy'.[6] The normal skills acquired by a member of the learned orders made them the natural interpreters into the vernacular.

The Gaelic learned orders, with their carefully graded hierarchies, provided the professional skills for the rest of their society in the fields of literature, music, law, medicine and some of the specialist crafts such as armourer. They were drawn from hereditary families who were given special status and privileges within Gaelic society. The orders placed great emphasis upon oral transmission and memorisation. These skills were taught by the tradition-bearers in the long and extremely rigorous training of the special schools, most of which were located in Ireland. The professional poets learned to compose their poems entirely in the mind, working out the complicated metrical structures whilst, it is claimed, they were lying on their backs in a darkened hut with a boulder on their chests. They also developed literary skills but these were regarded as subordinate to the traditional methods of non-literate learning.[7]

The setting for the oral transmission of this literary culture in Classical Common Gaelic was provided by the regional courts of the major magnates of Gaelic Scotland. As well as acting as patrons to the learned orders, the Gaelic chiefs and their households were conversant with the literary culture and language of the orders. Some, such as the first earl of Argyll and his countess, were themselves able to compose poems in the special metres.[8]

During the later medieval period both the learned orders and that native aristocracy had employed their communication skills to increase contact with the rest of Scotland and Europe. They had provided the linguistic and cultural links between vernacular Gaelic and Latin and Scots, the languages of the church, international scholarship, government, law and administration. The contributors to the Book of the Dean of Lismore demonstrated that they were literate in three languages, Gaelic, Scots and Latin and moved easily between the three cultural worlds. Located in the communications corridor between Perthshire and Argyll which linked the east and west of Scotland, these men were fully in touch with the developments in Lowland Scotland and the rest of Europe.[9]

By the time of the Reformation both the learned orders and the aristocracy had considerable experience as the key points of contact between the relatively enclosed world of the Gaidhealtachd and the wider world of European culture. The members of the orders, in particular, had developed the fascinating combination of skills as literate tri-lingual scholars and as oral transmitters. It was this unique expertise which was to prove of crucial importance to the spread of Protestantism in the Gaidhealtachd.

A direct translation of the Protestant message from Scots into Gaelic was not possible because neither Scottish Vernacular nor Classical Common Gaelic were ideally suited to act as the sole medium of transmission. In order to convey new theological and philosophical concepts in a manner which could be readily understood by non-literate Gaels, different aspects of the two varieties of Gaelic needed to be combined. A printed, literary language had to be linked to a totally comprehensible vernacular and transmitted to a predominantly non-literate population. This required complete familiarity with both varieties of Gaelic and of the Scots and Latin of the Calvinist texts. The learned orders and the aristocracy possessed the necessary expertise to translate Calvinism properly and comfortably into the Gaelic language.

This oral literate culture made it possible for the Protestant message to be disseminated through the traditional channels of communication within Gaelic society. The Protestant faith was novel and it challenged many of the old ways of life and thought but it could become the basis for a new set of traditions which would themselves harness older concepts and be handed down in the established way. This was clearly recognised by John Carswell, the most important champion of the Reformed faith in the early years of the Reformation.

Carswell provided the perfect example of a man who combined the skills of the learned orders with those of the conventional university training of a late medieval cleric. It is not known whether Carswell, like some of his contemporaries, acquired his Protestant convictions whilst studying at St Andrews University. By 1560, the time of the Scottish Reformation, Carswell had become the clerical leader of the campaign to evangelise the Western Highlands. He was made superintendent of Argyll in the new Kirk and also held the office of bishop of the Isles until his death in 1572. [10] He was the head of a group of Protestant ministers based in Argyll which was fully supported by the large and extremely powerful Clan Campbell led by the Calvinist fifth earl of Argyll, who was Carswell's personal patron. This backing gave that group the self-confidence to develop their own brand of Calvinism.[11]

The confidence and clarity of vision of the Argyll Protestants can be seen in Carswell's greatest achievement, his translation of the Book of Common Order, the 'Foirm na n-Urrnuidheadh', published in Edinburgh in 1567.[12] Carswell saw this liturgical translation as part of a wider programme which would have included the Scriptures if he had had the opportunity to complete them. He wanted to provide a new corpus of Protestant material to replace Catholic doctrine and ideas in Gaelic culture.

Although he wished to change the subject matter taught by the learned orders, Carswell did not want to alter the traditional methods of transmission. In the Introduction to his 'Foirm', he berated the professional poets who preferred to 'maintain and improve vain hurtful lying worldly tales composed about . . . the sons of Milesius and about the heroes and Fionn mac Cumhaill and his warriors', instead of teaching the Word of God. Carswell was not attacking the poets themselves but wanted them to employ Biblical stories in their poetry instead of the ancient epics. He wanted them to stop praising the warrior honour code of pre-Christian Ireland and start writing about religious values and virtues.[13]

Carswell had clearly encountered some opposition in the 1560s from professional poets within Gaelic society and certain families such as the MacMhuirichs, the learned orders of South Uist. Despite his modest disclaimers, Carswell had some professional training in the composition of classical poetry and made every effort to ensure that his 'Foirm' would reach the exacting literary standards which would satisfy some of his critics. The 'Foirm' was the first book ever printed in Gaelic and was a landmark of literary prose in Classical Common Gaelic. The very fact that Carswell was able to undertake the translation and to employ words and concepts which would be acceptable and comprehensible in a certain sector of Highland society, suggest that he was working within a milieu which was already familiar with the language of Gaelic Protestantism.[14]

Through his work as a translator and as a superintendent, Carswell sought to capture the expertise of other members of the learned orders for the Protestant cause. In the medieval period one major section of the Gaelic orders had pursued their careers within the church. They had taken clerical orders and held benefices or acted as notaries. During the first century of the Reformation, most of these professional clerics remained at their posts and provided the personnel for the new Kirk in the Highlands.[15] The MacPhails of Muckairn were one well-documented family who provided a succession of Protestant ministers to carry on the clerical tradition of their Catholic ancestors.[16] The familiar names of the clerical families such as the Omeys, the MacLachlans, the MacEwans, the MacKinnons and the MacQueens, reappear in an early seventeenth-century list of ministers serving in the church in the Islands.[17] A generation later the detailed records for the Synod of Argyll show that the majority of the ministers who attended the synod came from the families of the old learned orders with a few more recently established clerical dynasties, particularly the specialised cadet branches of leading clans such as the Campbells, Macgregors and the MacLeans, providing nearly all of the rest.[18] Serving the church was exclusively a family affair in the Highlands and Islands until the severe dislocation caused in 1690 by the Presbyterian/Episcopalian split after the Glorious Revolution.[19]

The importance of gaining this professional clerical group and turning it into the spearhead of the Reformation in the Highlands cannot be overestimated. These men provided the personnel to staff the Kirk and the expertise to mediate the Protestant message to the rest of Gaelic society and to give Calvinism its Gaelic voice and dress. The policy of translation employed by the Gaelic scholars demonstrated that they sought something more than the transference of the Scots version of Calvinism into another tongue. They were consciously striving to create their own brand of the Reformed faith. Carswell used the Book of Common Order promulgated by the Scottish General Assembly but also returned to the original Latin version of the 'Form of Prayers' (1556) of the English-speaking congregation of Geneva, on which it was based. He was prepared to make major textual changes when he deemed them necessary. He included an entirely new blessing for a boat with set responses, which was of obvious relevance to the seafaring society of the Highlands and Islands. He also created a new Catechism which, while based on Calvin's Little Catechism, was a free adaptation designed to suit his needs.[20] Following the same pattern the later Gaelic translators of the Bible and the longer

Catechisms went directly to the texts in Latin or the Biblical languages rather than working from the Scottish versions.[21]

The culture of oral literacy helps to explain why the delay in securing a printed Gaelic Bible did not prevent the spread of Protestantism within the Gaidhealtachd. Although Biblical translation was part of Carswell's original plan, the complete Bible in Scottish Gaelic was not produced until 1801 though a Classical Gaelic version had been available a century earlier and a New Testament from 1603 in Classical Gaelic and one in Vernacular Scottish Gaelic by 1767.[22]

Evidence from elsewhere in Europe would suggest that without a printed vernacular Bible the spread of Protestantism would be seriously inhibited. However, in the Highlands, despite the lack of a Scottish Gaelic Bible the Biblical message was conveyed to the people. Rob Donn, the non-literate poet, who was active in the first half of the eighteenth century before there was a printed version in the Scottish vernacular, possessed a profound knowledge of the Bible. His poetry was full of allusions to Biblical characters and stories and he employed the main tenets of Reformed theology without difficulty. He could have achieved this easy familiarity with Scripture only through listening to the local minister.[23]

Rob Donn and many others before him would have attended weekly worship which started with the reader's service. This was an hour-long reading of the Bible which the Reader would translate directly from the English printed version in his hand.[24] Further instruction would be given in the exegetical sermon which followed. There were numerous personal translations of parts of the Bible which had been made by the ministers in their sermon preparation. In 1657 a search was made for 'sundrie parcels translated allreadie' by the ministers of the Synod of Argyll to provide the basis for their proposed translation of the Scriptures.[25] The advantage of these informal systems of translation was that the Biblical content could be conveyed in the vernacular and even in the particular local dialect so that it was completely comprehensible to the listeners. When Dr Samuel Johnson was travelling in the Hebrides in 1773 he was informed by Mr MacLean, a minister in Coll, that even though there was a printed New Testament in Scottish Vernacular the minister still preferred to use his own translation as he could then adapt the language to local needs.[26]

This highlights the problem which an earlier translation would have encountered. Until the 1653 translation of the Shorter Catechism the other religious literature, such as Carswell's liturgy and Calvin's Catechism, had been rendered into Classical Common Gaelic. A printed version of the Bible in this literary language needed some interpretation to be entirely comprehensible to the ordinary people. A similar problem arose over the typography and orthography of the Classical Gaelic Bible. Before it could be circulated in Scotland it had to be reprinted in Roman type and the language modified to suit Scottish requirements. When these technical problems were combined with the much lower levels of literacy in the Highlands, the delays over the production of a vernacular Bible became more explicable. It must be stressed that the absence of such a Bible in the first century after the Reformation did not cripple the evangelical effort.[27]

In addition to teaching them the Biblical narrative, the Calvinist ministers had two further methods of conveying their Protestant message. The first and most important was the sermon. In 1583 when he was rigorously examined by the Presbytery of Stirling, John Campbell, bishop of the Isles, could prove that he had preached regularly at Iona and Ardchattan. He had stopped preaching only when he had travelled into the Lowlands. The Presbytery, who also insisted upon a trial sermon, were satisfied with the doctrine of the sermon but felt that he had not sufficiently opened up the sense and meaning of the text. Campbell accepted the criticism, apologising for having to rush his sermon preparation on that particular occasion as he had to go to Glasgow to reconcile two of his friends who had been feuding.[28]

By the middle of the seventeenth century two sermons and two lectures every Sunday were regarded as normal. The Presbytery of Skye was severely rebuked by the Synod of Argyll for providing preaching only once on the Lord's Day.[29] In a 'mixed' parish with both Highlanders and Lowlanders the minister was expected to preach one diet (a sermon and lecture) in Gaelic and the other in Scots. This burden was sufficiently onerous for Donald McCloy the old minister at Kilmodan (Cowal) to resign his charge because he was unable to preach twice 'for want of breath to make out ane hours speaking'.[30]

In 1623 the Irish Franciscan friars, who had been sent to recover the Highlands for Catholicism, were in no doubt that Protestant preaching was the major obstacle to the success of their mission. They dismissed the significance of the communion services remarking, somewhat surprisingly, that it was the same as the mass anyway so not doing as much harm as the sermons! The friars felt that they needed to be able to refute the arguments which were presented by the Protestant preachers. To do this they requested formal permission from their superiors to listen to the morning sermons incognito so that they could produce counter arguments in the afternoon.[31]

The primacy of preaching within the Highland Kirk was demonstrated by the system of priorities for a vacant parish. The minister with his sermons came to the parish but the parishioners had to travel to the nearest minister themselves for the services of baptism and marriage. In fact the excellent cover provided by the preachers in one vacant parish was given as the main reason why the parishioners were so slow to fill the vacancy.[32]

As well as the formal sermons on the Lord's Day and during the week in those places where there were mid-week services, there were the 'exercises' of the presbytery and synod. These were primarily in-service training for the clergy but the lay elders who also attended these meetings of the higher church courts would have heard a sermon or lecture a day from the participating ministers. At these occasions 'expectant' or prospective ministers gave trial sermons. The Synod of Argyll was particularly diligent in testing preaching ability in Gaelic as well as knowledge of the Biblical languages and Reformed doctrine. In the more linguistically mixed area under the jurisdiction of the Synod of Moray ministers who could preach only in English were permitted to remain in post. In the Western Highlands the synod of Argyll was considerably tougher and told the extremely competent

James Garner who had no Gaelic to resign his 'Highland' parish in Kintyre and move to a 'Lowland' one.[33]

Alongside the sermon the other major method of introducing Calvinist tenets into Gaelic society was through the Catechism. In an oral culture learning by rote was the normal manner in which knowledge was acquired and stored in the memory. In 1567 Carswell had included his own version of Calvin's Catechism in the 'Foirm'. This was followed by the translation at the start of the seventeenth century of Calvin's catechism which was printed c. 1630. The two initial catechisms were composed in Classical Common Gaelic but in 1653 the Shorter Catechism was translated by a team of ministers into Scottish Vernacular. It was so popular that within six years it had to be reprinted. A shorter and simpler version with only twenty or thirty questions for use by the very young and the very old was planned but not completed.[34]

Every Sunday the minister was expected to explain two of the questions from the Catechism during the lecture immediately after the sermon. Just before the blessing two different members of the congregation were called upon to repeat two of the questions. These exercises were in addition to the weekly catechising which the minister was expected to undertake in some part of his parish and to the religious instruction he provided on his domestic visits.[35] The careful exposition of the Classical Common Gaelic phrases of the catechism by the minister helped this Calvinist text to become the 'theological classical poetry' of the early modern period in the Highlands. A skilful minister could explain the words and concepts in his sermons and play 'tunes' with them in the same way as the professional poets had manipulated the traditional metres and images in their compositions.[36]

Within the Highlands and Islands boys were used to teach the catechism to individual households. In return for their board and lodging and some help from the church's poor box, the boys stayed with a household until all its members had mastered their catechism by heart. A rather more ambitious scheme, also using poor boys, was tried which attempted to teach more people to read in English so that they could read the Scriptures directly themselves. Not surprisingly in view of the complexities of the task, this was less successful. Knowledge of the catechism was required by parishioners before they could avail themselves of any of the services offered by the Kirk, whether communion, baptism or marriage. Anyone who refused to learn the catechism by heart or at least to 'use diligence' to memorise it was to be cited before their presbytery.[37]

The singing of metrical psalms was one method employed by Calvinist communities throughout Europe to spread the Protestant message among the non-literate. Translating the psalms into Gaelic presented a whole range of technical problems. Neither the musical tradition nor the normal forms of versification in Gaelic culture fitted the requirement of regularly stressed syllables necessary for the metrical psalms. Although the first fifty psalms in Gaelic, the 'Caogad', were produced in 1659 the complete Psalm Book did not appear until 1694.[38] With little popular poetry in Gaelic surviving from the Reformation period, it is difficult to know whether many Protestant poems and songs were composed or used. Several of the exponents of the emerging vernacular poetry were clergymen, such as Hector MacLean of Coll (An Cleirach Beag), John Stewart of Appin and MacCulloch of Park. They did employ religious themes in their work as did the poets the MacMhurchaidhs, the father and son who were Mackenzies of Achilty. Where clear doctrinal viewpoints emerged in this poetry, they were Protestant and sometimes recognisably Calvinist.[39]

The Gaelic ministers used the conventional Protestant tools of the Biblical narrative, explained and reinforced by the sermon and catechism, to evangelise the Highlands and Islands of Scotland. They were far more effective in spreading Calvinism through a remote rural area than their struggling counterparts in comparable regions of Europe.[40] They were able to utilise to the full the existing culture of oral literacy. Although there was a linguistic barrier between Classical Common Gaelic and Scottish Vernacular, this did not produce a horizontal split between elite and popular cultures. The traditional role of the learned orders in bridging the language-gap was taken over by the Gaelic ministers. This ensured that, despite the lack of printed material in Gaelic, Calvinist precepts could be brought to the non-literate in forms which they could understand.

II

Traditional communication skills were the key element in the spread of Calvinism within the Gaidhealtachd, but the formal framework of the Kirk was also important. It was one of the few institutions which functioned properly in both the Highlands and Lowlands of Scotland. In theory it was organised in exactly the same way in both regions. However, there were three main practical problems in extending the tight Lowland organisation to the Highlands and Islands. Within the Highland region itself, with the minor exceptions of Inveraray and later Stornoway and Campbeltown, there were no urban centres.[41] The small, 'frontier' burghs on the eastern fringe of the Highlands, such as Inverness, Chanonry or Dingwall, could provide a meeting place for the church courts but they were not large enough to act as a religious powerhouse for their rural hinterlands, as some burghs had done in the Lowlands.

By far the greatest obstacle was the parish structure itself which the Kirk had inherited from its medieval predecessor. This legacy combined the old problem of size with a new Protestant difficulty over accessibility. The parishes within the Gaidhealtachd were very large, some of them stretching twenty miles across. In addition to the geographical extent and inhospitable terrain of the parishes, many of the church buildings in the Highlands were placed in peculiarly difficult locations. They had been built on the holy sites associated with the intrepid Celtic church saints who had preferred isolation to comfort. Frequently the saints had chosen small islands off the coast or in the middle of a loch to withdraw from the world. In the medieval period the location of these churches did not present too many problems because they were primarily used for special religious festivals or as pilgrimage centres.

The Reformation brought about an even more dramatic change to the pattern of worship within the Highlands than elsewhere in Scotland. Under the Protestant regime all parishioners were expected to attend worship at their parish church every Sunday. For the first time this created serious difficulties within the Highlands and Islands over access to those buildings which were in such awkward locations. The necessity of ferrying the whole congregation to Inishail church, on an island at the top of Loch Awe, for a set time every Sunday morning, brought severe logistical complications. This situation left regular worship open to disruption by the weather or occasionally by human agency. In the middle of a dispute about a new church at Appin, the ferryman simply refused to carry the minister across the narrow stretch of water from the island of Lismore and so no services could take place in Appin.[42]

The obvious solution of building new churches in suitable locations was not possible because of the immense cost. Sufficient resources were not found for the Highlands and Islands until the 'parliamentary' churches of the early nineteenth century and the massive church-building programme undertaken after the Disruption of 1843. There were ambitious plans in the seventeenth century for a complete rationalisation of the existing parish system. Some useful adjustments to parish boundaries were made but only a handful of new churches were built.[43] As a cheaper compromise other buildings were used for worship. There was a 'preaching-house' at Campbeltown in Kintyre in addition to the parish church. Some of the medieval chapels were also utilised and this became the source of a dispute in Mull.[44]

Many religious services were held in the open air, just as local courts continued to be convened outside on traditional sites, such as moot hills. It would have been natural to gather in the open to listen to a preacher in the warmer summer months, when so much of Highland life was lived out of doors or in the temporary shelters of the shielings in the summer pastures. Even when there was a local church close by as at Kilmalieu, the people of Inveraray came to the Parson's Pulpit under a rock on the banks of Loch Fyne to hear Ninian MacVicar.[45]

When viewed from the outside or through the eyes of contemporary Lowlanders the huge parishes and the paucity of churches and clergy appeared to leave the Highlands and Islands very badly provided and almost incapable of producing a truly reformed community. Although the difficulties could not be entirely overcome, they could be circumvented. In the Lowlands the organisation and efficiency of the Kirk were regarded as essential to the creation of the godly society. In the less formal society of Gaelic Scotland the structures of the church were not given such a prominent place. The difference in attitude can be seen in the modification of the parish ministry to suit the conditions of the Highlands and Islands.

Although the Highlands and Islands had exactly the same set of institutions, they did not operate in the same way as those in the Lowlands. The ministers were still called to particular charges and their main task was to serve their parishes. To a far greater extent than in the Lowlands, a Highland minister was an itinerant, working as a member of a team moving on circuit through his district.[46] The clergy had to travel to different locations within their parishes which could be uncomfortably large and preach by turn in each district. The parish at Inveraray (Kilmalieu), which covered a relatively small area, had four named preaching stations.[47] In addition the ministers shared the burden of preaching in those parishes which were vacant. Every opportunity was used to increase the number of sermons and to turn any journey into a preaching tour. One minister from Arran was instructed to stop and preach both on his outward and on his return journeys to the presbytery. Special efforts were made by the clergy to provide extra sermons at the fishing grounds for the seasonal influx of fishing folk. These itinerant practices reflected the peripatetic nature of Gaelic society and had similarities to the traditional bardic circuits.[48]

The parish was not treated as the primary unit of organisation within the Highlands and Islands because it did not correspond to the social, political or geographical divisions with the Gaidhealtachd. The ministers were forced to work together in a team at the district level. This usually corresponded with the presbytery but, as in the division of the presbytery of Lorn, were sometimes smaller areas which made greater geographical sense.[49] Particularly in the remoter areas where, if the local clan chief were uncooperative, the kirk session was weak or non-existent, cases of church discipline tended to be passed up to the presbytery or even the synod. These higher courts were constantly trying to tighten the institutional structure and chivvied recalcitrant kirk sessions or presbyteries, inspecting their books and demanding improvements. But they did realise the practical limitations imposed upon them by the communications system of the Highlands. As the ruling elders who attended the Synod of Argyll complained, no-one else in Scotland had to travel so far or so long to attend meetings. As a consequence the number of meetings was reduced, particularly for the winter months, and a more lenient standard of attendance enforced on those who came from the Isles.[50] It was remarkable that both the clergy and the eldership were prepared to spend so much time and effort travelling to ensure that the presbyteries and synods functioned as efficiently as they did. The Gaelic ministers wanted to retain the institutional framework of the Scottish Presbyterian system, though they were quite prepared to modify it to suit the practicalities of their region.

III

The long-term success of Protestantism and its ability to put down roots depended upon the conversion of the Gaelic aristocracy. The dominant position of the chiefs and their massive influence within the kin-based society of Gaelic Scotland was recognised by the Protestant ministers. Throughout the first century of the Reformation the clergy looked to the lay magnates for support. In return they praised their aristocratic patrons almost as fulsomely as the professional poets. They were far more willing than their Lowland counterparts to give a dominant role in the running of church affairs to such 'godly nobles'. This appreciation of the importance of the regional princes was clearly set out by Carswell in his Epistle addressed to his own patron, the fifth earl of Argyll. He compared the Campbell chief to the kings of the Old Testament such as David and Hezekiah who had brought the true religion into their territories and had destroyed idolatry.[51]

Such praise for the nobility reflected the social and political realities of Gaelic Scotland where even royal authority was exclusively exercised through the regional magnates. Protestantism would not have made any real impact without the support of the earls of Argyll and their Campbell kin. Clan Campbell was the most powerful kin group in the Western Highlands and the earl of Argyll's influence extended over the whole region. Throughout the early modern period the Campbells remained totally committed to the Calvinist and later Covenanting Kirks. In the northern Highlands Protestantism was encouraged by the earls of Seaforth with their MacKenzies. In addition, the Kirk could rely upon the active cooperation of many of the lesser kindreds, such as the Rosses of Balnagown and the Munros of Fowlis in the north and the MacLeans of Duart and MacLeods of Harris and Skye in the Western Isles.[52]

In its crudest form the support of the powerful Gaelic chiefs gave the Kirk access to military muscle and enabled it to coerce its enemies. In 1562 the fifth earl of Argyll had travelled through the south-western Highlands 'destroying idolatry' and 'cleansing' the churches. Carswell praised his patron and chief as a great protector of ministers in those difficult and dangerous early days of the Reformation.[53] The legal authority of the chiefs, who held extensive heritable jurisdictions and gave the law to the Highlands, was also employed to reinforce church discipline through civil penalties imposed in their courts.

More important than coercion was the example which a Protestant chief set for his kin, friends and allies. In matters of religion, as in war and peace, it was assumed that clansmen would normally follow their chief's lead. An interesting exception to this occurred in Clan Campbell when the seventh earl was converted to Roman Catholicism. He was virtually disowned by his strongly Protestant clan and the leadership passed to the earl's son, the future covenanter marquis of Argyll.[54] Alliances between Protestant kin groups were frequently consolidated by marriage ties or by fostering children from other clans. In the strongly Protestant atmosphere of the fifth earl of Argyll's household, his foster son, Lachlan MacLean of Duart, the future chief of the main branch of the MacLeans, became a convinced Protestant.[55] In the Gaidhealtachd, as elsewhere in Europe, women also had an important part to play in the spread of Protestantism. The network of Perthshire chiefs who were prepared to give military support to the Protestant lords of the Congregation in 1559–60 were all linked by marriage alliances to women from Protestant families. One of those women, Katherine Ruthven, the sister of Patrick, Lord Ruthven and the wife of Colin Campbell of Glenorchy, was a close friend of John Carswell.[56]

The Franciscan friars of Antrim knew to their cost the great importance of the local chief and the extent of Protestant success in winning over the native aristocracy in the Highlands and Islands of Scotland. During the first half of the seventeenth century they had embarked upon a series of evangelising missions to Gaelic Scotland. They were under no illusions about the difficulty of their task. Despite the advantage of being native Gaelic speakers who, unlike any Lowland Scottish missionary, could fit easily into Scottish Highland society they still had to operate under cover. One priest assumed the identity of a Gaelic poet to explain his presence and journey throughout the region. In this disguise he penetrated a chief's household and attempted to convert the chief. This ploy achieved one notable success when Campbell of Cawdor was converted to Roman Catholicism.[57]

In their reports to Rome the missionaries explained that it was impossible to establish a permanent base in Scotland because they were always operating in hostile, Protestant territory. Although they had the support of a few Catholic chiefs, the friars were constantly on the move and frequently had to escape from danger by sailing back to northern Ireland. The mission achieved its greatest success in the southern Hebrides because it was assisted by the Catholicism of the major proprietors, the MacNeills and the Macdonalds of Clanranald, who held the Uists and Barra.[58]

Much of Protestant activity was also focused upon the chief's court or household which provided the key point of contact between Gaelic society and the outside world. Here, new ideas, people and habits were first encountered and, from this secure bastion, spread out into the rest of Gaelic society. This process can be seen at work in the changes in personnel and ideology which transformed the household of the Campbells of Glenorchy when Grey Colin and his son Black Duncan ruled Breadalbane.[59]

In Gaelic society a regional magnate maintained a large retinue and moved with it throughout his 'country'. His peripatetic court would lodge with his clansmen and tenants consuming the rents in kind. On these periodic progresses the chief would bring his Protestantism along with his household.[60] The religious component of the visit would include Protestant services conducted either by the local minister or the chaplain who accompanied the chief. More informally there would be Bible readings at the end of the meal before the guests had left the table.[61] As lavish hospitality for large numbers of guests was regarded as one of the most important attributes of a good chief, these readings would reach many of the people in the area. In these settings the Protestantism of the elite could spread naturally throughout society.

In the early years of the Reformation the chief's visit to the remoter regions of the Highlands and Islands might provide the first encounter with the new religious ideas. This would offer an opportunity to experience Protestant worship and hear sermons and Scriptural readings within the chief's household. It would also be the occasion for settling the new religion into the locality. In this way the normal chief's circuit through his territories could easily assume the attributes of an ecclesiastical visitation. This happened in 1574 when Colin, sixth earl of Argyll, ensured that all the churches were properly 'planted' in his region and each was supplied with either a minister or a reader supported by an adequate stipend. All the parishes visited on the progress possessed and were using for worship and discipline copies of Carswell's 'Foirm'.[62]

If regular attendance at church can provide a reliable guide, Protestantism was spread from the chief and his household to large sections of the population in the Highlands. Some unexpected evidence for church attendance can be found in the account of a vicious feud. The MacLeods of the Waternish peninsula on Skye were all in a building at Trumpan which they used for worship though their parish church was several miles away at Kilmuir, Dunvegan. One Sunday the Macdonalds of Uist sailed across the Little Minch and, knowing that the whole community was at worship and there would be no lookouts, were able to sneak up and lock the door of the building. In revenge for the previous massacre of their clansmen on Eigg, the Macdonalds then set fire to the thatched roof killing everyone inside except one girl who raised the alarm.[63] In 1603 the same fate is alleged to have befallen the congregation of the church in Kilchrist, Easter Ross when the Glengarry Macdonalds burnt the building.[64]

The new Protestant requirement that the whole parish attend worship at a set time each week left that community vulnerable to its enemies. The Sunday service provided all too tempting an opportunity if those enemies were intending to massacre the entire population including the women and children rather than fight a clan battle between the two groups of warriors. An effective defence was made more difficult by the practice of not carrying weapons into the church buildings. One Protestant clan, the Macfarlanes of Arrochar, who feared a Sunday attack, left a few men with all the weapons on guard watching the 'String Road', the route to the church at Luss, whilst the rest of the clan listened to the Calvinist sermon.[65] This unexpected hazard for those clans who fully embraced Calvinism does provide the historian with some indications of church attendance!

IV

The willingness of the Gaelic clergy and aristocracy to mould Calvinism and Presbyterian structures to fit their own culture was most strikingly displayed in their acceptance of certain aspects of local belief, which other Calvinist ministers found it all too easy to condemn. Unlike their Lowland brethren, the Gaelic clergy did not regard all forms of witchcraft as inherently evil. During the scares which afflicted the rest of Scotland in the sixteenth and seventeenth centuries there was no witch-hunting in the Highlands. [66] The Gaelic language had a rich vocabulary to distinguish the different varieties of supernatural activity and the particular contexts in which they were employed. This enabled the Gaelic clergy to be much more discerning and to condemn black magic and sorcery but tolerate other supernatural beliefs. In particular they made a sharp distinction between witchcraft and the hereditary gift (or curse) of second sight.[67]

The tradition of the seer was an integral part of Highland life.[68] The Gaelic clergy saw no reason to condemn it nor to associate it in any way with the Devil. They regarded the foretellings as a natural phenomenon and linked them with some of the forms of prophecy found in the Old Testament. Ninian MacVicar, the minister at Inveraray, was renowned for his prophecies including the accurate prediction of the circumstances of his own death by drowning.[69] The Gaelic clergy took a similar relaxed attitude towards the fairy culture of Gaeldom.[70] Within the Highlands and Islands belief in the fairies had remained distinct from the world of Catholic saints and miracles. The clergy could therefore accept the fairies and yet attack all those practices associated with Catholic worship and reverence for the saints.[71]

The willingness of the Gaelic ministers to judge for themselves what they felt to be appropriate within their own culture was demonstrated by their attitude towards the rituals of death. This was an area of immense significance within Gaelic society where the bonds of blood and kin were seen to embrace all generations whether living or dead. It was important to be buried with one's kin in the clan burial ground even if this were not the local parish church. This frequently involved carrying the coffin considerable distances along one of the network of coffin routes to bring it to the right graveyard.[72] Most of the customs associated with these large funeral processions and the wakes which preceded them had not been explicitly connected with Catholic worship. They could be left intact by the Protestant Gaelic ministers who, at the same time, had no compunction about changing the funeral service itself. The one element of the funeral rituals which the Protestant clergy did try to suppress was the 'corronach' or wailing by the mourning women. This practice was thought to be 'unseemly to be used in any true Christian kirk, where there is preaching and true profession of the comfortable resurrection of the dead'. It was recommended that the local minister explain why it should not be used when he preached or taught the catechism. Those subsequently offending were to be punished.[73]

In the sixteenth and seventeenth centuries the Gaelic ministers demonstrated remarkable assurance in their willingness to accept Calvinism whilst adapting its structures to suit their own cultural heritage. They seemed confident that they could be true to both aspects of their identity as learned Gaels and Calvinist ministers. In the same way the Gaelic magnates who became Protestant saw no major conflict between this and their traditional role as clan chiefs. But it became increasingly difficult to live successfully in the two worlds of the Highlands and the Lowlands and this put a tremendous strain upon Gaelic Calvinism.

The Scottish Kirk, dominated by Lowland preconceptions, found it almost impossible to recognise the merits of the adaptations which the Gaelic ministers had made. It interpreted the religious situation in the Gaidhealtachd as a failure to implement the full presbyterian system and so strove to extend the Lowland model to the Highlands and Islands. In particular, the use of the Gaelic language as the main medium for the Protestant faith was viewed with increasing suspicion. It was felt that in Scotland 'true' religion and 'civilised' behaviour could be found only in an Anglo-Scottish cultural setting. The whole of Gaelic society, its language and culture were steadily eroded by the unrelenting pressures towards uniformity and centralisation placed upon it by the British state. Together Kirk and state ensured that, although some aspects did survive into the eighteenth century, in its early modern form, Gaelic Calvinism was a relatively short-lived plant.

In the century after the Scottish Reformation, men such as John Carswell had been able to create a Calvinist church in one of the most unpromising environments in Europe. By exploiting the unusually strong culture of oral literacy, they produced a rural Calvinism which worked. Their success provides a healthy reminder that Calvinism could flourish in communities with the scattered settlement patterns of upland pastoral areas. It also demonstrates that it was possible for Calvinism to survive with little help from the printing press and without a popular literate culture based on the printed word. The partial assimilation of Calvinism to Gaelic culture achieved in the Scottish Gaidhealtachd can help to provide an explanation for Calvinism's overall success within Europe. The evidence from this peripheral and unusual region points to the flexibility of the Calvinist movement during the early modern period. It suggests that Calvinism was able to adapt to the various indigenous cultures of Europe whilst retaining a sufficiently coherent core for it to remain a recognisable international movement. Despite the ridicule of their Lowland contemporaries and the neglect of historians, the Highland ministers in their bonnets and plaids had no doubts about their own double identity. They were both good Gaels and members of the brotherhood of international Calvinism.

NOTES

1 C. J. Withers, *Gaelic in Scotland, 1698–1981* (Edinburgh, 1984); *Gaelic Scotland* (London, 1988).

2 *Extracts from the Records of the Synod of Moray*, ed. W. M. Cramond (Elgin, 1906), p. 7.

3 James VI's Instructions to the Commission to Improve the Isles, 8 December 1608, in *Collectanea de Rebus Albanicis* (Iona Club, 1847), p 115.

4 D. S. Thomson, *Introduction to Gaelic Poetry* (Edinburgh, 1990 edn), ch. 1; R. Black, 'The Gaelic Manuscripts of Scotland', in *Gaelic and Scotland*, ed. W. Gillies (Edinburgh, 1989), pp. 146–74.

5 Thomson, *Introduction*, ch. 3.

6 Ibid., p. 99.; J. Bannerman, 'Literacy in the Highlands', in *The Renaissance and Reformation in Scotland*, ed. I. B. Cowan and D. Shaw (Edinburgh, 1983), pp. 214–35.

7 D. S. Thomson, 'The Gaelic Learned Orders and Literati in Medieval Scotland', *Scottish Studies*, 12 (1968), 57–78.

8 W. Gillies, 'Courtly and Satiric Poems in the Book of the Dean of Lismore', *Scottish Studies*, 21 (1977), 35–53.

9 D. E. Meek, 'The Scots-Gaelic Scribes of Late Medieval Perthshire: An Overview of the Orthography and Contents of the Book of the Dean of Lismore', in *Bryght Lanternis*, ed. J. D. Maclure and M. Spiller (Aberdeen, 1989), pp. 387–404.

10 D. E. Meek and J. Kirk, 'John Carswell', revised version in J. Kirk, *Patterns of Reform* (Edinburgh, 1989), pp. 280–304.

11 J. Dawson, 'Clan Campbell and the Scottish Reformation', unpublished paper given to the Scottish Reformation Conference, 1990.

12 *John Carswell's Foirm na n-Urrnuidheadh*, ed. R. L. Thomson (Scottish Gaelic Text Society, XI, Edinburgh, 1970).

13 *Foirm*, pp. 179–80.

14 I am grateful to Dr Meek for this observation.

15 *Originales Parochiales Scoticae*, ed. C. Innes (Edinburgh, 1854); *Records of the Dioceses of Argyll and the Isles, 1560–1860*, ed. J. B. Craven (Kirkwall, 1907); *Fasti Ecclesiae Scoticanae*, ed. D. E. R. Watt (Scottish Record Society, Edinburgh, 1969); C. Haws, *Scottish Parish Clergy at the Reformation* (Scottish Record Society, Edinburgh, 1972); Kirk, *Patterns*, pp. 285–6.

16 J. Bannerman, *The Beatons* (Edinburgh, 1986), pp. 150–1.

17 Report of the diocese of the Isles, 1626 in *Collecteana*, pp 122–5; J. Bannerman, 'The MacLachlans of Kilbride', *Scottish Studies*, 21 (1977), 5, 12.

18 *Minutes of the Synod of Argyll, 1639–61* (2 vols, Scottish History Society, 3rd ser. 37 & 38, 1943–4).

19 J. Macinnes, *The Evangelical Movement in the Highlands of Scotland* (Aberdeen, 1951). For the post-1690 difficulties see W. Ferguson, 'The Problems of the Established Church in the West Highlands and Islands in the Eighteenth Century', *Records of the Scottish Church History Society*, 17 (1969–72), 15–31.

20 *Foirm*, pp. lxxv-vi.

21 *Adtimchiol an Chreidimh: The Gaelic Version of John Calvin's Catechismus Ecclesiae Genevensis*, ed. R. L. Thomson (Scottish Gaelic Text Society, Edinburgh, 1962), p. xvi.

22 D. E. Meek, 'The Gaelic Bible', in *The Bible in Scottish Life and Literature*, ed. D. F. Wright (Edinburgh, 1988), pp. 9–23; 'Language and Style in the Scottish Gaelic Bible, (1767–1807), *Scottish Language*, 9 (1990), pp. 1–16.

23 T. McCaughey, 'Protestantism and Scottish Highland Culture', in *An Introduction to Celtic Christianity*, ed. J. P. Mackey (Edinburgh, 1989), pp. 180–1.

24 J Macinner, 'The Christian Church', in *The Hub of the Highlands: The Book of Inverness and District* (Edinburgh, 1975), p. 159.

25 *Synod of Argyll*, II, p. 146.

26 *The Companion to Gaelic Scotland*, ed. D. S. Thomson (Oxford, 1983), p. 23.

27 Meek, 'Gaelic Bible', and 'Gaidhlig is Gaylick anns na Meadhon Aoisean', in *Gaelic and Scotland*, pp. 131–45 (English abstract pp. 233–5); C. J. Withers 'The Highland Parishes in 1698', *Scottish Studies*, 24 (1980), 63–88. Similar problems arose later in Ireland, N. O'Ciosain, 'Printed Popular Literacy in Irish, 1750–1850: Presence and Absence', in *The Origins of Popular Literacy in Ireland*, eds M. Daly and D. Dickson (Dublin, 1990), 45–57. I am grateful to Dr Houston for drawing this article to my attention.

28 *Stirling Presbytery Records*, ed. J. Kirk (Scottish History Society, XIX, 1981), pp. 79–80, 82–4, 103–4, 146–9, 164–6.

29 *Synod of Argyll*, II, pp. 103, 119.

30 *Ibid.*, I, pp. 147–8, 207.

31 *Irish Franciscan Mission to Scotland, 1619–46*, ed. C. Giblin (Dublin, 1964) pp. 30, 69.

32 *Synod of Argyll*, I, p. 210; II, pp. 52–3, 101, 129–30.

33 *Ibid.*, I, p 6; II, pp. 94, 135, 212–13.

34 *Ibid.*, II, pp. viii-ix, 131.

35 *Ibid.*, II, pp. 40–1, 55, 103.

36 I am grateful to Dr Meek for this observation.

37 *Synod of Argyll*, I, pp. 192–4; II, pp. 35, 40–1, 84–5.

38 *The Gaelic Psalms, 1694*, ed. D. C. MacTavish (Lochgilphead, 1934).

39 Thomson, *Introduction*, pp. 107–39; McCaughey, 'Protestantism', pp. 182–3.

40 For example in the Netherlands, A. Duke 'The Reformation of the Backwoods', in *Reformation and Revolt in the Low Countries* (London, 1990), pp. 227–68. Nearer to home, there was also the important contrast with the situation in Gaelic Ireland, which had an almost identical culture to the Scottish Gaidhealtachd but where neither the Gaelic learned orders nor the native aristocracy were favourable to Calvinism. The type of Protestantism which flourished in Ireland was associated with the English Conquest and was extremely hostile to Gaelic language and culture. After the Ulster Plantation, it was reinforced by the radical elements of Scottish Lowland Calvinism, see A. Ford, *The Protestant Reformation in Ireland* (Frankfurt-am-Main, 1987).

41 These were burghs in the legal sense of having a formal charter and being permitted to trade, but they remained small communities with only Inveraray developing into a proper communications centre.

42 J. Dawson, 'The Origin of "The Road to the Isles": Trade, Communications and Campbell Power in Early Modern Scotland', in *People and Power in Scotland: Essays in Honour of T. C. Smout* (Edinburgh, 1992), pp 74–103.

43 *Synod of Argyll*, I, pp. 49–59, 227–54; II, pp. 68–73.

44 *Ibid.*, II, p 72; *Collecteana*, pp. 126–7.

45 *Records of Argyll*, ed. Lord Archibald Campbell (Edinburgh, 1885), pp 50–1. I am grateful to the late Mr Mackechnie of Bridge of Douglas (Argyll) for sharing his great knowledge of Inveraray and its environs with me.

46 Cf. similar practices in the nineteenth century, D. E. Meek, 'Dugald Sinclair: The Life and Work of a Highland Itinerant Missionary', *Scottish Studies*, 30 (1991), 59–91.

47 *Records of Argyll*, 50.

48 *Synod of Argyll*, I, pp 91–2; II, pp 145–6, 156.

49 A. E. Anderson, 'Notes from the Presbytery Records of Lorne', *Transactions of the Gaelic Society of Inverness*, 36 (1931–3), 112–38.

50 *Synod of Argyll*, I, pp 5, 27, 73, 172.

51 *Foirm*, pp. 173–9.

52 Macinnes, *Evangelical Movement*, ch 1.

53 *Foirm*, pp. 176–7.

54 E. J. Cowan, 'Fishers in Drumlie Waters: Clanship and Campbell Expansion in the Time of Gilleasbuig Grumach', *Transactions of the Gaelic Society of Inverness*, 54 (1984–6), 269–312.

55 N. Maclean-Bristol, 'The Macleans from 1560–1707', in *The Seventeenth Century in the Highlands* (Inverness Field Club, 1986), p. 79.

56 J. Dawson, 'The Ties That Bind: Clan Campbell and Marriage Alliances', unpublished papers given to the Conference of Scottish Medievalists, 1990. Letters from John Carswell to Katherine Ruthven, Scottish Record Office, GD 112/39 at 8/15 and 11/3.

57 Giblin, *Irish Franciscan Mission*, pp. 26, 53–4.

58 *Ibid.*, pp. 33, 51, 55, 59, 106, 108, 174, 178.

59 G. Macgregor, 'The Macgregors' (unpublished PhD thesis, University of Edinburgh, 1989).

60 J. Dawson, 'The Fifth Earl of Argyle, Gaelic Lordship and Political Power in Sixteenth-Century Scotland', *Scottish Historical Review*, 67 (1988), 1–27.

61 Description of the household of Sir Lachlan MacLean of Duart (d. 1648) in poem cited in Thomson, *Introduction*, p. 132.

62 *Calendar of State Papers Relating to Scotland*, eds J. Bain *et al.* (Edinburgh, 1898–1969), V, p 34.

63 This incident is known as the Battle of the Spoiling of the Dyke after the subsequent mass burial when the MacLeods caught up with the MacDonalds and killed them, C. Bingham, *Beyond the Highland Line* (London, 1991), p. 107.

64 By tradition this massacre was the setting for the clan piobaireachd, Cill Chriosd or Glengarry's March, I. F. Grant and H. Cheape, *Periods of Highland History* (London, 1987), p. 115. However, a case for dismissing the whole tale has been made, D. J. Macdonald, *Clan Donald* (Edinburgh, 1978), pp. 340–1.

65 *The Dewar Manuscript*, ed. J. Mackechnie (1964), pp. 107f.

66 C. Larner, *Enemies of God: The Witch-hunt in Scotland* (Edinburgh, 1981).

67 J. G. Campbell, *Witchcraft in the Highlands* (Wakefield, 1974 edn); evidence concerning the use of witchcraft at the end of the sixteenth century came to light during the investigations over the murder of Campbell of Cawdor, *Highland Papers*, ed. J. Macphail (Scottish History Society), I, pp. 165–9; see also, W .Matheson, 'The Historical Coinneach Odhar and Some Prophecies Attributed to Him', *Transactions of the Gaelic Society of Inverness*, 46 (1969–70), pp. 66–88.

68 *The Seer in Celtic and Other Traditions*, ed. H. E. Davidson (Edinburgh, 1989).

69 *Records of Argyll*, p. 53.

70 The learned Episcopalian minister, Robert Kirk of Aberfoyle, as well as his work as a biblical translator and advocate of the Gaelic language, collected the fairy lore and wrote his account in *The Secret Commonwealth of Elves, Faunes and Fairies* (1691); D. Maclean, 'The Life and Literary Labours of the Rev. Robert Kirk of Aberfoyle', *Transactions of the Gaelic Society of Inverness*, 31 (1922–4), pp. 328–66.

71 For example *Synod of Argyll*, I, p. 67. For a wide-ranging discussion of the relationship between Christianity, Celtic culture and the supernatural see, J. P. Mackey, 'Magic and Celtic Primal Religion', *Zeitschrift für Celtische Philologie*, 45 (1992), 66–83.

72 Dawson, 'Road to the Isles'.

73 *Synod of Argyll*, I, p. 61; II, p. 175.

General Alexander Leslie, the Scottish Covenanters and the Riksråd Debates, 1638–1640

Extracted from A Grosjean 2000 *in* AI Macinnes, T Riis and FG Pedersen (eds) *Ships Guns and Bibles in the North Sea and the Baltic States, c.*1350–1700, East Linton (Tuckwell Press), 115–38.

The extent of Sweden's involvement in domestic Scottish politics from 1638 to 1640 is unprecedented in the history of Scottish–Swedish relations. When King Charles I's proposed policies threatened the Scottish nation to a degree they could not accept, war in Scotland became inevitable in 1638.[1] Extraordinary debates followed in the Swedish state council (hereafter Riksråd) meetings during that period concerning the radical missions of two Scottish envoys, General Alexander Leslie and Colonel John Cochrane. While explaining their intellectual and military opposition to Charles' reforms, these Scots not only requested foreign military aid but also presented a definition of their national identity as separate from the multi-kingdom Stuart domain. These debates are integral to explaining Scotland's wider European role in the seventeenth century.[2]

The Leslie Connection

Alexander Leslie's successes as a Covenanting general owed much to his Swedish experiences and contacts. By 1638 Leslie's Swedish service had spanned thirty years, during which time he had become a loyal and trusted servant of the Swedish Crown. For personal reasons he became keen to return to Scotland from October 1637 onwards, and certainly by 1st January 1638 he left Stralsund, bound for his native country.[3] He therefore was probably in Scotland before or at the time of signing the Covenant on February 28. Once in Scotland Leslie remained in contact with the Swedish Chancellor, Axel Oxenstierna, as the first surviving letter dated June 1638 refers to a previous letter explaining his two-month delay in Edinburgh. Leslie detailed the relations between the Scots and Charles I, including the threatened excommunication of the Episcopalian clergy, and he clearly stated that the two causes of conflict in Scotland were religion and national liberty. A copy of the National Covenant was also included.[4] This letter was read out in the Riksråd meeting on 28 June and the issues of national and religious freedoms in Scotland came to be repeatedly debated in the Riksråd.[5]

Leslie left for Sweden at the end of July, before the Glasgow Assembly had been held where the Covenanting movement was confirmed as the leading political power in Scotland.[6] At this time the Swedish State Marshall, Jacob de la Gardie, told the Riksråd of Leslie's desire for a swift decommissioning from Swedish service as, in order to undertake military service in Scotland, he had to return before Charles I's proposed naval blockade of the Scottish coast was implemented.[7] Within a week the Chancellor not only agreed to Leslie's request for release but more importantly his request for artillery.[8] Oxenstierna advised that the artillery should follow Leslie as though it were an advance on his salary, as it would not do for Sweden to be seen to be subverting Charles I's authority. Despite concerns for Sweden's relations with Charles, Oxenstierna's immediate reaction unquestioningly respected Leslie's requests for support. However, losing a field marshal like Alexander Leslie would not have been a welcome option for the Swedes at this point, and so the Riksråd resolved to debate the issue of Leslie's release with Oxenstierna.

A discussion lasting two weeks followed, with the most intensive debates on 9 and 10 August, about the release of Leslie from Swedish service. First they pondered Leslie's written submissions. They felt that his request for decommissioning could not be refused on the grounds of his lengthy and faithful service and that he was well-liked. From the beginning the personal friendship between the Swedes and Leslie was highlighted. The Riksråd understood that it was *solus amor patriae*, the love of his country alone without hope of reward for his actions, which forced his decision. The Riksråd conceded that Leslie also had other concerns in Scotland, having placed all his earnings from Swedish service into land there, and that his son had married into the nobility there.[9] It was also remarked that if Leslie were to be refused he would only become an unwilling servant of the Swedish Crown. As for Leslie's military responsibilities, it was agreed that these could be taken over by the competent General Johan Banér, for as long as Leslie was absent. Leslie was prepared to take a temporary leave if the Swedes could not let him go permanently, but he vigorously argued that it was imperative that he return to Scotland in order to defend it.[10]

The Riksråd was very aware that by supporting Leslie it ran the risk of offending Charles I and being seen as the fomenter of the civil unrest in Scotland. Releasing Leslie from Swedish service before his return to Scotland was integral to minimising the impression that Sweden condoned the use of arms against Charles I. However the anti-Stuart risk was deemed to be worth the potential benefits, particularly given the suspected pro-Danish attitude in the Stuart court. If Charles gained the upper hand in Scotland some of the Riksråd felt that he would become an enemy of Sweden. Thus the Scots were considered important allies for Sweden should they enter war with England. The release of these Scottish officers was seen by the Swedes to be more important than retaining them unwillingly in service. As for the weapons Leslie requested, the Riksråd argued that these could be provided under the pretext of reward for lengthy service.[11]

The next day the Riksråd summoned Leslie to address them personally. He reassured the Swedes that as soon as Scotland was at peace he would return to serve the Swedish Crown. This had the desired effect and the councillors granted his requests in honour of the respect Leslie showed for his native land. The artillery supplies Leslie requested would be provided privately by a merchant who would obtain them from the Crown. Not only would he receive 2000 muskets, but also copper could be supplied for crafting weapons in Scotland, which the Swedes hoped to get in return. The Swedish military council authorised the delivery of 200 muskets with accompanying pieces through the Scottish merchant in Stockholm, James Maclean, for Leslie's use. The rest would be arranged through his nephew John Maclean at Göteborg.[12] When Leslie took his final leave of the Swedish government on 22 August he thanked the Riksråd for all its affection and reiterated his promises of a swift return to Swedish service.[13]

Although no battles took place, the Covenanters ultimately forced Charles I into a truce at Berwick and in September 1639 Queen Kristina of Sweden apparently commended Charles I on making peace with his subjects.[14] Charles I suffered defeat at the hands of the Covenanters due to their superior numbers, organisation and strategy developed in Swedish service in the first Bishops' War. He was determined to re-assert his authority, which led to preparations for a second war during the early months of 1640. These preparations were evident on the Continent, as Christian IV of Denmark noted the arrival in Glückstadt in early 1640 of Scottish colonels and captains who had been in Swedish service in Germany.[15] In November 1639 Leslie informed Oxenstierna of the latest Scottish developments. The Scots continued to demand 'la continuation de restablissment de la religion et de la liberté du royaume par des synodes libres de l'église générale et parlement de l'estat' [the continuation of the restoration of the religion and liberty of the kingdom by free general assemblies and parliaments]. Leslie continued that although Charles had initially agreed to some of the Scots' demands, he had been dissuaded again by his religious advisors. Leslie stated that it was the repeated postponement of parliament and Charles' refusal to see the Scottish commissioners which had forced the issue. It was 'la liberté fondamentale' [fundamental liberty] and 'la préservation de leur liberté' [the preservation of their liberty] which fueled the Scots who now believed that

> . . . les prélats et papists d'Angleterre seront cause que le Roy nous attaque encore avec ses armées tant par terre que par mere. Cela fait que tout coeur loyal soit froisse de voir un Roy bouder contre son ancien et native royaume par les boutfeues de Rome. Cela anime l'esprit de chaque bon compatriot et enflamme les coeurs de chaque bon crestien pour mettre et sacrificier leur biens et leur vies pour la defence de leur religion et liberté selon le solennel pact qu'ils ont faict avec Dieu, lequel a esté approuvé et signé à la dernier assemblé par le deputé du Roy.[16]

> [the English bishops and papists were the reason for the king's attack on us again, with his armies by sea and by land. Thus any loyal person would be upset

to see a king turned against his ancient and native kingdom by the troublemakers of Rome. It provokes the spirit of each good compatriot and inflames the hearts of every good Christian to give up and sacrifice their goods and lives to defend their religion and freedom according to the Covenant they made with God which was approved and subscribe at the last general assembly by the king's commissioner.]

At a committee meeting of the Short Parliament in April 1640 it was noted how the Covenanters were still able to access supplies from Sweden: 'The Scotts are able to draw in the Goth and Vandalls and other great Armies; and when the Swedes are quiett for ought I know they may offer them the Crowne of England.'[17] This was just the time the Covenanters were organising foreign missions. Leslie was re-appointed to command the Covenanters' army for the Second Bishops' War and the army was an estimated 16,000 men 'with expert captains and commanders'.[18] More military supplies would be needed for this campaign and so a new Covenanting mission to Sweden was undertaken.[19]

Cochrane as a Covenanter envoy

Colonel John Cochrane, a veteran of both the Danish and Swedish armies, was chosen to represent the Covenanter committees on an official embassy to seek foreign aid and various Scottish Covenanting nobles signed his travel pass to Scandinavia in April 1640.[20] New diplomatic missions for foreign support were authorised as the Covenanters knew that the peace Charles I had offered them was only temporary.[21]

Chancellor Axel Oxenstierna informed the Riksråd on 8 July 1640 of Colonel Cochrane's arrival as a representative of the 'Directors of the Scottish league', the Swedish term for the Committee of Estates in Scotland.[22] Cochrane had several letters of accreditation, one for Queen Kristina, and two for Axel Oxenstierna. Of the two letters for Oxenstierna, one came from the Covenanters and the other from Alexander Leslie. Once again, albeit indirectly, Leslie engaged himself in a Covenanting mission to Sweden, more than just a familiar contact to lend credence to Colonel Cochrane's presence and requests, rather as a trusted guarantor.

Cochrane soon gained an audience with the Riksråd in the name of the directors of the Scottish people.[23] Although he apologised on behalf of the Scots for not having informed the Riksråd of their domestic situation earlier, this was a formality as Oxenstierna was *au fait* with events in Scotland through his private correspondence with Leslie. Cochrane explained that the escalation of the discord had been caused by two issues. The first of these was that Stuart policy would re-introduce Catholicism in Scotland by the enforcement of new religious practices and offices. The Scots feared that the likes of a Spanish inquisition was close at hand.[24]

The second concern was that the polity of Scotland was being altered: their laws and freedoms were being removed and the kingdom was being reduced into a province.[25] Cochrane related how the Scottish Estates had united in opposition to this: the leaders were prepared to upset all that was dear to them in the name of God and Scotland. Cochrane reiterated that the Scottish Estates had not wanted to impose on the Swedish Crown, particularly in view of the great friendship and benevolence the Swedish monarchy had already shown Scotland.[26]

Chancellor Oxenstierna accepted Cochrane's mission on behalf of the Riksråd. He too hoped for successful maintenance of the sixty-year relationship between Sweden and Scotland, particularly through the continued service of Scotsmen to the Crown.[27] He felt that this situation between the king in England and the Scottish nation was regrettable and Sweden should try to rectify it, although the form of support Sweden could take required much consideration, and would therefore be dealt with later. Before Cochrane left the Riksråd he emphasised that the Covenanters sought neither soldiers nor money, as both of these Scotland had in supply, but some ships with the relevant munitions. These were to be borrowed and returned when no longer needed.[28]

Although Oxenstierna urged impartiality in this development at the start of the closed Riksråd discussion, he also stated that nothing would be more dangerous than that the now united Scottish nation should be oppressed into a state of confusion.[29] This was a sentiment he claimed to have shared with Leslie when he was still in the country. Oxenstierna believed that Charles I could settle the dispute by curtailing the influence of his clerics, applying moderation in his reforms and compromising a little. Charles might even gain English support against Scotland.[30] Oxenstierna decided to persuade Cochrane privately that immediate and especially hostile action was not prudent, but that selling ships and munitions was feasible.

It was not until 18 July that Oxenstierna revealed a private discussion he had undertaken with Cochrane. The Swedes had received information that the Scottish dispute was resolving itself and they did not know how to proceed. Despite this, Queen Kristina's affection for and desire to support the Scottish nation had been passed on.[31] Cochrane denied that any amelioration between the Covenanters and Charles I had occurred, and emphasised that Charles I's decision to attack Scotland, once made, would unfold quickly. This uncertainty as to the extent of hostilities between Charles and the Scots persisted throughout much of the debate.[32] Cochrane reminded Oxenstierna of the Scottish enthusiasm for Swedish military service and pointed out that it was Scotland's close relations with Sweden that had provided the Covenanting army with its officers.[33] Oxenstierna's reservations concerned placing Sweden in a compromising position between Charles I and the Scottish nation, and playing judge in a situation in which no other nation was involved. In addition, Sweden was at war and on uneasy terms with her neighbours.[34] Cochrane said that the Covenanters understood this, but if the English gained the upper hand over Scotland even Sweden would suffer for it. They only requested munitions which were in very short supply in Scotland, with hardly enough to see them in the field, let alone for defence at sea or in garrisons.[35]

Oxenstierna presented the Riksråd with two items to decide: whether to undertake any action or not, and if so, what form that action would take and how to do it inconspicuously. Admiral Clas Flemming suggested the use of Scottish merchants in Gothenburg again, who were not only capable and trustworthy, but would get the best price for the weapons being sold to the Covenanters.[36]

Oxenstierna placed the Scottish developments into a wider European context. The Scots wanted to strengthen their long-lasting alliance with France, which Charles I would take any opportunity to destroy. Oxenstierna described how war in Scotland would just be the first flame of a North Sea fire, which would engulf all neighbouring lands. This would draw strong naval powers like Spain and Denmark–Norway into the quarrel between Charles and the Scots.[37] Oxenstierna used the example of Holland to explain himself: had Spain successfully suppressed the Dutch republic in her rebellion, all the neighbouring countries would have been forced into action to safeguard their own nations.[38]

Cochrane was still waiting on a reply almost two weeks later when the Riksråd debated the Scottish issue again.[39] Oxenstierna maintained caution as it was still not certain which way the situation would develop. The Riksråd believed that should the war actually erupt, it would be an unfair one for Scotland with the smaller population.[40] When the Riksråd became split in its support for Scotland, Oxenstierna departed from his neutral stance and put paid to any anti-Covenanting element present. He explained that either one tolerated civil unrest or one supported tyranny and general confusion, offering a clear insight into his personal view of Charles' actions.

Oxenstierna then delivered a brief history of the political changes in Scotland which had led to the Covenanting movement. Once Charles I had removed all apparatus of law from Scotland into England, leaving only the Privy Council, and even this only in name, all decisions were taken in England by the House of Lords, whose membership was by birthright only, and included clergy. Despite this and the placement of an archbishop as Chancellor, opposition to royal authority only began when the question of religion was broached, leading to the National Covenant. Oxenstierna believed that people in this situation could not be persuaded to remain quiet and obedient.[41]

Finally, and most importantly, Oxenstierna made a comparison to Sweden's own history by stating that if the Swedes under Engelbrekt and King Gustav I Vasa had not taken hold of their own situation they would still be under Denmark's yoke, just like Norway.[42] Oxenstierna had the Riksråd convinced, and it was resolved to aid the Scottish nation with military supplies again through the Scottish merchants in Gothenburg and Stockholm.

In mid-August Cochrane informed Oxenstierna that the Covenanting army had marched into England and the ships, weapons and copper he had requested were required.[43] The Riksråd again discussed how England, and especially Charles I, had always been against the Swedes in their efforts in the Thirty Years' War, particularly by blocking the recruitment of Scottish soldiers, let alone whole regiments. The Scots on the contrary had been in the Swedish Crown's service for many years, and even at the present time the finest gentlemen were to be found in the Swedish army. By helping Scotland now the Scots would be obliged to supply soldiers in the future.[44]

Although there is a hole in the parchment at the point where the Riksråd specified what Cochrane should receive in terms of Swedish military support, and the name of the merchant involved is also lost, he was most likely either James or John Maclean, as with Leslie's mission. There is another good reason to assume that it was John Maclean: in April 1639, Axel Oxenstierna made a personal visit to Gothenburg on official business and he met Maclean at his home. Bearing in mind that it was Oxenstierna who had most of the personal contact with Alexander Leslie, the Swedish chancellor was well placed to discuss Scottish developments with Maclean.[45] Cochrane's mission had been a success and he was to receive the items on behalf of the Scottish nation.[46] In addition, the Swedes agreed to provide ships to transport the goods for the Scots at great risk to themselves.

Shortly thereafter five Swedish ships sailed from Gothenburg to Stockholm and returned through the Sound to the United Provinces, and although the Riksråd records indicate a connection with Cochrane's mission the original text is illegible.[47] The ships were used to transport the munitions and copper requested from Stockholm to Holland, from where they were further despatched to Scotland. In October the admiral reported that the five ships had safely come through the Sound without incident, and pointed out that this had never been achieved before.[48] Whether by coincidence, rather unlikely given Christian IV's relationship with Charles, or by collusion remains unclear.[49]

Scots in Sweden and the Riksråd

The previous sections have shown that the personal relationship between Axel Oxenstierna and Alexander Leslie practically guaranteed Swedish support for the Scottish Covenanters on two separate occasions. However, Oxenstierna was not the only ally the Scots had within the Swedish government and military élite. By 1638 the Scottish assimilation into Swedish society was extensive. Scots had not only become burgesses from the first decades of the seventeenth century, but had been ennobled in Sweden since 1625, and had married into the highest levels of Swedish society since they had started emigrating and/or taking service there.

The Swedish navy played a crucial role in support for the Covenanters and there again there were already extensive Scottish influences present.[50] Two Scottish admirals were serving at the time: Simon Stewart and John Clerk. Stewart was a lieutenant admiral and had been ennobled in 1634, giving him recourse to influence the nobility. John Clerk was possibly the most important of the Scots connected to the navy. He entered Swedish service in 1606 and was engaged as a Stockholm 'holm' admiral by 1630. Thus, at the peak of Covenanting activity the Scots had two fellow nationals in considerable positions of authority regarding the Stockholm fleet. Even John's son Richard, who was married to Lunetta Macklier, the daughter of John Maclean of Gothenburg, was also in the navy at this point. Another Scot, Carl Netherwood, although born in Sweden, served the Swedish councillor and admiral Carl Gyllenhielm at this period. As for Maclean himself, the merchant who undertook the weapons shipping for the Covenanters, he had long been established in Gothenburg and had been a town councillor there since 1632. Another Scottish town councillor in Sweden was Anders Boij who served in Stockholm from 1632 onwards.[51] The importance here is the length of time these Scots had already been in Sweden to enable close relations through every level of society there.

Scottish influences could also be exerted at court level and within governing circles. Queen Kristina's personal physician was a Scot, Dr James Robertson, who had been ennobled in 1635 for both medical and diplomatic services. Irrespective of what his personal politics were, he was in an ideal position to provide the queen with information about Scotland and Scottish society, which would have filtered through to the Riksråd through Oxenstierna. Additionally, the queen's chief Lady in Waiting was married to a Scot, Alexander Irvine. There were also other Scotsmen who had been ennobled in Sweden before or at the time of the Covenanting movement: John Burdon, James Forbes, John Ramsay, and James Spens junior.[52] The scope for potential pro-Covenanting influence was thus already extensive in Sweden, even without the missions of specific Scottish envoys.

The significant presence of Swedish-born Scots, and their interest in Scottish affairs cannot be dismissed simply because their parents had emigrated. The brothers Anders and David Stuart, served at the Vasa court from Gustav II Adolf's time onward and were some of the earliest Scots to be ennobled in Sweden in 1625. The brothers Mattias and Arvid Forbes, although born in Finland, were ennobled in 1638 and thus were two further sources for pro-Scottish influences. Vilhelm Spens, another one of James Spens' sons, was also ennobled and present at the 1638 and 1640 Swedish parliamentary sessions.

Given the additional pressure the Scots officers, merchants, nobles and local government officers could exert on their friends in power a secondary aspect to the Covenanting diplomacy becomes clear. Neither Leslie nor Cochrane were acting in a void when they presented their missions to the Swedish Riksråd.

Conclusion

During the Bishops' Wars private Scottish–Swedish relations took priority over Sweden's official contacts with the Stuart monarchy. Charles I's lack of effective and efficient military support to Sweden during her nineteen-year campaign in Germany was never forgiven by the Swedes. When the crunch came, both in 1638 and 1640 the Swedish Riksråd had little difficulty or doubt about supporting the 'Scottish nation' against the Stuart king.

The Riksråd debates reveal that the revolution in Scotland would have been almost impossible to achieve without the co-operation of the Swedes in three vital ways. Firstly, Sweden, through Chancellor Oxenstierna, was the first foreign state to recognise the Covenant and as such paved the way for later developments, such as recognition by the Danes.[53] Secondly, the Swedish armies were prepared to release many of their trusted and experienced high-ranking officers to return to Scotland. The greatest Swedish aid came in the form of returning officers, highly experienced in recruiting, organisational, tactical and technological innovations of war to create the most formidable army in the three Stuart kingdoms.[54] Thirdly, Sweden twice provided the Covenanters with weapons, ships and other military supplies.

NOTES

1 Events were set in motion which would at their very conclusion lead to Charles I's execution. For a more in-depth analysis of the Covenanting movement see D. Stevenson, 'The financing of the cause of the Covenants, 1638–1651' in *Scottish Historical Review*, vol. li, 2, no.152, (1972). D. Stevenson, *Scottish Covenanters and Irish Confederates*, (Belfast, 1981); M. Lee jnr, *The Road to Revolution: Scotland under Charles I 1625–37* (Illinois, 1985); D. Stevenson, *The Covenanters, the National Covenant and Scotland*, (Edinburgh, 1988); J. Morrill (ed.) *The Scottish National Covenant in its British context 1638–51*, (Edinburgh, 1990) ; A.I. Macinnes, 'Covenanting, revolution and municipal enterprise' in J. Wormald, (ed.) *Scotland Revisited* (London, 1991); A.I. Macinnes, *Charles I and the making of the Covenanting movement 1625–1641*, (Edinburgh, 1991).

2 The view that Scotland had no foreign policies of her own after regal union in 1603 has already been refuted in this volume and elsewhere. See the preceding chapter by Steve Murdoch. For a fuller discussion see also S. Murdoch, 'Scotland, Denmark-Norway and the House of Stuart 1603–1660, a diplomatic and military analysis' (unpublished PhD, University of Aberdeen, 1998).

3 1 June 1638, *Rikskansleren Axel Oxenstiernas Skrifter och Brefvexling* (hereafter *RAOSB*), (15 vols., Stockholm, 1888–1977), vol. ix, pp. 480–1. The letters of Johan Banér to Axel Oxenstierna from 29 October, 4 November 1637 and 1 January 1638 in *RAOSB*, vol. vii, pp. 460, 467, 487–8. See also 19 February and 16 April 1638, *CSPV*, vol. xxiv, p. 373 and p. 398. Macinnes noted that Leslie was attending the Marquis of Hamilton at Dalkeith in July 1638 in *Charles I*, p. 191. For a copy of the Scottish National Covenant see *The Constitutional Documents of the Puritan Revolution 1625–1660*, ed S.R. Gardiner, (Oxford, 1899), pp. 124–34.

4 1 June 1638, 'Exemplar illius confessionis et foederis, cui subscripserunt omnes regni incolae praeterquam papistae et Regis officiari", in *RAOSB*, vol. ix, pp. 480–1.

5 28 June 1638, *SRP*, vol. vii, p. 252. 'de motibus Scoticis . . . religionem et libertatem patriae'.

6 Macinnes, *Charles I*, p. 189.

7 28 July 1638, *SRP*, vol. vii, p. 272.

8 2 August 1638, *SRP*, vol. vii, p. 274.

9 Alexander Leslie junior was married to Margaret Leslie, daughter of John, Fifth Earl of Rothes, see *The Scots Peerage*, eds. Sir James Balfour Paul and R. Douglas (9 vols., Edinburgh, 1904–1914), vol. v, p. 378.

10 9 August 1638, *SRP*, vol. vii, p. 276. When Leslie's words are quoted Charles is referred to as the King in Britain, and not England.

11 *Ibid.*, pp. 276–7.

12 10 August 1638, *SRP*, vol. vii, pp. 278–9. These Macleans were known in Sweden as 'Macklier' or 'Mackler'. Relying on the Macleans was no new method for dealing with Scots and supplies. Already in 1635, the clergyman Eleazer Borthwick obtained his wages through James Maclean for negotiating on behalf of the Marquis of Hamilton and Charles I with the Riksråd. See 8 August 1635, *SRP*, vol. v, p. 127.

13 22 August 1638, SRP, vol. vii, p. 289. There is a copy of Queen Kristina's letter of decommission for Field Marshall Leslie dated 14 August 1638, SRO GD 26/section 13/ G/322.

14 These reports may have originated with Roe as a face-saving ploy on behalf of Charles, see 20 June 1639, John Coke to Thomas Roe, PRO SP81/47 f. 85 and 6 September 1639, Thomas Roe to unknown, PRO SP 81/48 f. 12.

15 *Kong Christian den Fjerdes egenhændige Breve*, (hereafter *KCFB*) eds. C.F.Bricka and J.A. Fridericia *et al.* (8 vols., Copenhagen, 1878–1947), vol. iv, p. 300. Although Christian notes that 'all' the colonels and captains were present, this seems highly unlikely given the number of officers who had already returned to Scotland. It is probable that the colonels and captains noted were General James King, Colonel Francis Ruthven, Lieutenant-Colonels James King, John Leslie, and H. Gladstone, and Captain William Ogilvie who had signed a certificate of weapons being transported to England from Hamburg in June 1639, see PRO SP 81/47, f. 102.

16 Riksarkivet, Sweden (hereafer Ra. Sv.), Brev till Axel Oxenstierna, Leslie to Oxenstierna, 18 November 1639. See also *RAOSB*, vol. ix, pp. 483–5.

17 *Proceedings of the Short Parliament*, eds. E.S. Cope and W.H. Coates, Camden 4th series, vol. 19, (London, 1977), p. 77.

18 Spalding, *History and troubles*, vol. i, pp. 195, 214.

19 8 July 1640, *SRP*, vol. viii, p. 97.

20 See Rigsarkivet, Denmark foreign chancellery section (hereafter Da. Ra.,TKUA) Skotland A II 4, f.79a 14/24 of April 1640. These included Argyll and Montrose, who continued to play significant roles in Scandinavian relations and later became enemies.

21 However approaching Sweden was no longer a straightforward issue for some Covenanters, who viewed Lutheranism as another form of Catholicism as it retained bishops in its religious hierarchy: 'the assistance of Lutherans, let be of Papists, at this tyme, was, to our divines, a leaning to the rotten reed of Egypt', Laing, *Baillie's Letters*, vol. i, p. 191. Despite this, French support was also being sought from Cardinal Richelieu, see Stevenson, *Scottish Covenanters and Irish Confederates*, p. 91.

22 8 July 1640, *SRP*, vol. viii, p. 93.

23 *Ibid.*: 'nomine Directorum gentis Scoticae'.

24 *Ibid.*, p. 97. 'Religionen och gudztiensten bliffver med några nya och papistiske stadgar förvänd; them påtränges emot deres kyrkiordning ovanlige officia, och alt dirigeres där hän, att man befruchter ther inthet bätre än thet hade sig med inquisitione Hispanica'.

25 *Ibid.*, p. 97: 'regnum bliffver redigerat in formam provinciae'.

26 Cochrane flattered the Riksråd by saying that the Scots feared that Sweden would feel obliged to defend them, in view of the Swedish practice of defending those in need, and then Cochrane continued that the Scots were seeking help from a country to whom they were already in debt and would remain in eternal service and gratitude, 8 July 1640, *SRP*, vol. viii, p. 97.

27 *Ibid.*, p.98. 'Och såsom den Skottske nationen haffver nu ifrån een rund tijd, vid pas 60 åhr, hafft stoore kundskaper och umgenge med oss, och en god deel af bemälte Skotske nation bevijst vår framfarne Konungar och Chronan berömelige tienster, att och för denne skull dess lycha och välstånd haffver icke mindre varit oss önskelig än den Skotske nationen sielffver'.

28 9 July 1640, *SRP*, vol. viii, p. 99.

29 *Ibid.*, p. 99: 'inthet är farligare och meera att befruchta, [än] att Skottske nationen, som nu henger tillsamman, bliffver förträn[g]t och således ligger alt omkull'.

30 *Ibid.*, p. 99: "Om Konungen i Engelland [. . .] vinna till sig the Engellska och exaggerera difficulteeterne i Skottland, skulle han snart venda thetta spelet effter sin begäran".

31 18 July 1640, *SRP*, vol. viii, pp. 118–9.

32 *Ibid.*, pp.118–19. See also 27 July 1640, *SRP*, vol. viii, p.158.

33 18 July 1640, *SRP*, vol. viii, p.119.

34 *Ibid.*, p.119.

35 *Ibid.*, p.120.

36 *Ibid.*, p.120. James Maclean had already been of service in 1635, when the cleric Eleazer Borthwick was negotiating on behalf of Hamilton and Charles I with the Riksråd. Borthwick obtained his wages through Macklier, 8 August 1635, *SRP*, vol.v, p.127.

37 'Kan nu eder Konung [Charles I] inthet med eder [the Scots] förlijkas, så drages Konungen af Spagnen och Danemark uti spelet med', *ibid.*, p. 120.

38 18 July 1638, *SRP*, vol.viii, p.120. Again, see 27 July 1640, *SRP*, vol.viii, p.158 for a reiteration of these fears.

39 27 July 1640, *SRP*, vol.viii, p.158.

40 27 July 1640, *SRP*, vol.viii, p.159.

41 *Ibid.*, p.159. 'nekar man, att subditi uti sådana fall inthet må tala, så bijfaller man och indrager een tyrannidem in rempublicam et rerum omnium confusionem'.

42 27 July 1640, *SRP*, vol.viii, p.160. 'hade icke våre förfäder fattat een god resolution under Engelbrecht och gamble Konung Gustav, vij hade i thenne dag legat under Danmark med samma condition som Norrige'.

43 18 August 1640, *SRP*, vol. viii, p.217.

44 *Ibid.*, p.217.

45 H. Almqvist, *Göteborgs Historia, grundläggningen och de första hundra åren* (2 vols., Göteborg, 1929–1935),vol. i, p. 348.

46 18 August 1640, *SRP*, vol. viii, p.217. Colonel John Cochrane received a gold chain of 200 kronor and 300 kronor in cash to cover his expenses during his stay in Stockholm. This was the norm for official envoys and proves that the Swedes had accepted the legitimacy of Cochrane's mission. See 28 August 1640, *SRP*, vol. viii, p. 243.

47 The commander of the fleet was probably holm major Richard Clerck who is listed as commmanding a fleet on a 'business' journey to Amsterdam in 1640, see A. Zettersten, *Svenska Flottans Historia 1635–1680* (Norrtelje, 1903), pp. 598–9. See also 8 September, *SRP*, vol. viii, p. 262. This explains previous assumptions that the Covenanters received all their supplies from Holland. See for example Furgol, *Regimental History*, p. 3 and E. Furgol, 'Scotland turned Sweden: the Scottish Covenanters and the military revolution', *National Covenant*, ed. Morrill, p. 137.

48 They were vulnerable to Danish confiscation in the Sound, as was a frequent occurrence at the time. See 29 August and 22 October 1640, *SRP*, vol. viii, p. 245 and p. 299.

49 See S. Murdoch, 'Scotland, Denmark-Norway and the Bishops' Wars, 1638–1640', *The Awkward Neighbour*, eds. A.I. Macinnes and J. Ohlmeyer (Forthcoming 1999).

50 For a fuller discussion of Scots in the Swedish navy see A. Grosjean, 'Scottish-Scandinavian Seventeenth Century Naval Links: a case study for the SSNE database', *Northern Studies*, vol. 32 (1997).

51 Both these men later became ennobled, and Anders Boij even took part in several parliamentary sessions.

52 See *Scotland, Scandinavia and Northern Europe 1580–1707* (hereafter SSNE) database, on the internet at www.abdn.ac.uk/history/datasets/ssne for further information on these men.

53 See 10 November 1640, Christian IV to the Scottish Estates, Dk. Ra. TKUA Skotland, A I 4. f/79b.

54 As Furgol pointed out, 32 out of every Covenanting army regiment's 70 officers needed to be experienced and trained officers, see 'Scotland turned Sweden', p. 136.

The Scottish Parliament and European Diplomacy 1641–1647: The Palatine, the Dutch Republic and Sweden

Extracted from JR Young 2001 *in* S Murdoch (ed.), *Scotland and the Thirty Years' War, 1618–1648*, Leiden (Brill), 77–106.

THE DUTCH REPUBLIC AND THE MISSION OF THOMAS CUNNINGHAM

Having established the alliance with England through the Solemn League and Covenant, the Scottish leadership turned their focus back to continental Europe. Important steps were taken in 1644 to promote closer diplomatic contacts with the States General of the United Provinces. These had important implications for the extension of the Solemn League and Covenant to the Dutch Republic, but the Committee of Estates appointed in June 1640 had also been involved in attempts to create a tripartite confederation involving the States General of the United Provinces and the Scottish and English Parliaments.[1] Such a confederation would have left Scotland in direct conflict with the Spanish Habsburgs through this association. The scheme never came to fruition and events became complicated through increasing tension between King and Parliament in England, the marriage of the king's eldest daughter Mary to William, son of Frederick Henry, Prince of Orange and the support of Frederick William for the Royalist cause over the Parliamentarian one. This, in turn, aggravated the Calvinist republicans in the Dutch Republic.[2] Nevertheless, the important point here is that at the time of the Anglo-Scottish treaty negotiations the Covenanters were not 'exclusively concerned with a bipartisan approach to internationalism' but had their eye firmly on continental politics as well, despite the consequences involved in confederating with a polity in open arms against Spain.[3]

The Dutch connection resurrected itself in 1644 in light of recent British developments, however. The Scottish commissioners in London informed the army section of the 1643 Committee of Estates on 22 February of developments with the English Parliament. The Committee of both Houses had informed the commissioners that they wanted some 'fitt man' to be sent to Holland to join with Mr Matthew Strickland, the English agent there, for 'the joynt transaction of all busines there in the name of both kingdomes'.[4] The committee and the army were also asked to think of appropriate people who could be employed to go into Sweden, or Switzerland and deal with other Protestant princes and states.[5] By 1 March it had been decided that one Thomas Cunningham was the appropriate man to fulfil this task, the Scottish commissioners had already met with him by this date and Cunningham had been told to proceed to the committee with the army for further instructions. Correspondence personally signed by Argyll stated that Cunningham was indeed 'a fitting person to be employed from us for agenting our effares in Holland'.[6] Cunningham had been involved in shipping military supplies to the Covenanters in 1639 and in March 1644 was instructed by Argyll as part of the army section of the Committee of Estates to buy 20,000 weight of gunpowder.[7] By April Matthew Strickland was becoming 'very anxious' that Cunningham should be employed as a 'joynt agent' and Cunningham was sent north to Edinburgh for the reconvening of the 1644 Convention so that 'he may be so employed if it is thought fit'.[8] It was not until 10 May 1644 that the Committee of Estates in Edinburgh appointed Cunningham as Commissioner and Ordinary Agent in the Netherlands. Two months later Cunningham's appointment as Conservator of the Scottish Staple at Campvere was reconfirmed.[9]

Cunningham received 10 sets of instructions from the Committee to complement his commission of appointment. These make it clear that Strickland and Cunningham were to operate as an Anglo Scottish diplomatic duo acting in the interests of the kingdoms of England and Scotland. Cunningham was directly answerable to the Committee of Both Kingdoms, 'whose instructions and directions' he was to 'punctually observe'.[10] Nevertheless, he was to report back to the Committee of Estates on a monthly basis. Crucially, the instructions issued by the Committee of Estates (personally signed by Chancellor Loudoun) also make it clear that the struggle in the British Isles was perceived as a religious struggle and a war of religion – part of the general conflict which had started in Bohemia. As part of his remit, Cunningham was required to acquaint himself with 'the preachers of Gods word in these countreys and labour to procure their zealous concurrence to stirre up the people to a right understanding and sense of our condition'.[11] The Cunningham mission was therefore not restricted to issues of high diplomacy and material agreements. Rather, it was perceived to be an exercise in Calvinist empathy for a European Protestant cause against a perceived common enemy. Of crucial significance here is the fact that Cunningham was instructed to secure the agreement of these preachers 'to joyne with us in the Covenant and really assist this cause wherein the glorie of God and propagation of his gospell are so much interested'.[12] The desired religious objective was the extension of the Solemn League and Covenant to the Dutch Republic. This provides a crucial insight into the expansionist ideology of the leaders of the Covenanting movement in 1643–44, men, such as Sir Archibald Johnston of Wariston, who had been responsible for securing Covenanting entry into the English Civil War. Presbyterianism was to be imposed on the two other kingdoms of the British archipelago in terms of a British religious settlement. The Solemn League and Covenant was also to be extended to the Dutch Republic along the lines of a defence league for European Protestantism. Scottish Calvinism had fundamentally accepted the canons of the 1619 Synod of Dort as 'the definable standards of Protestantism'.[13] The key role played by Chancellor Loudoun in Covenanting diplomacy is confirmed by his signing of Cunningham's commission and instructions.[14]

Cunningham was to make the Dutch aware of the 'treacherous and bloodie attempts and conspiracies of the enemies of God who were never more uncessantly working' for the 'subversion of the true religion'.[15] Having achieved this via Cunningham, the Committee of Estates in Edinburgh was therefore confident that 'such kingdoms and states as professe the same that they will not only joyne with the kingdoms of Scotland, England and Ireland in this Solemne League and Covenant for opposing poperie and prelacie and establishing the true religion'.[16] This was not only to apply to the Dutch, but Cunningham's instructions indicate that the Dutch were to play a pivotal role for the wider European dimension. The Committee of Estates therefore hoped that the Dutch would join the Solemn League and Covenant, and also 'invite all other Christian princes to doe the lyke'.[17] The presence of Chancellor Loudoun and Lauderdale as the leading Covenanters present at the diet of the Committee of Estates of 10 May is particularly revealing, especially given the fact that Loudoun was in touch with Axel Oxenstierna and was aware of the fact that a Swedish agent was being sent to Scotland (see below). Put quite simply, Loudoun and Lauderdale appear to have sanctioned the extension of the Solemn League and Covenant on a European basis.

Protestant empathy also transcended issues of high diplomacy and politics. Cunningham was to secure further supplies and aid from the Dutch to 'continue their begune charitie for the distressed *British* in Ireland, and Scots army who are hazarding their lyves for defence of the true Protestant religion'.[18] Ireland, therefore, represented to the Scots, a religious zone of conflict for the European Protestant cause – an extension of the continental wars – and the Dutch would hopefully contribute to this cause just as 'the Pope, Spanjard and other popish powers are in supplying the rebells and assisting them in their bloodie designes'.[19] Yet again, another reference to the wars of the three kingdoms being part of the Europe-wide religious struggle in the minds of the Scottish leadership.

Evidence has survived of a speech Cunningham gave to the States of Holland and Westfriesland which had been given with Strickland's approval. He reported the contents back to Scotland in March 1645 adding that he had been 'sufficiently assured (by continuall testimonies upon all occasions) of their reall affection and exemplary respect towards the Parliamentary cause of both nations'. Accordingly, Cunningham and Strickland had agreed that it was a 'very seasonable opportunity for my publique reception in that venerable and (of all the United Provinces) most considerably interested assembly'. Extracts from Cunningham's speech confirm his earlier instructions regarding the extension of the Solemn League and Covenant to the Dutch. In tenor with those instructions, Cunningham had emphasised that it was now 'fitt and necessary' as well as 'beneficial and expedient' for '*all Protestant Potentates and Republicques to enter or joyne in the same or suchlyke Solemn Covenant with the kingdomes of Great Brittaine, and so go on unanimouslie against the common enemy'*. The response of the Estates of Holland and Westfriesland to this demand of Protestant expansionism, however, was lukewarm. The Estates certainly reaffirmed their desire to preserve the true Christian Protestant religion, but essentially they were adopting a neutral and non-interventionist position concerning the conflict between 'his Majestie of Great Brittaine and his subjects of England and Scotland'. From the beginning of the British Troubles, the Estates argued, they 'have been moved and inflammed by a fervent zeale that they might bring water to quensh the kindled fyre and help to settle the unhappy differences'.

Both the substance of the instructions issued by the Committee of Estates on 10 May 1644 and his speech to the States of Holland and Westfriesland would appear to confirm the fears of Queen Henrietta Maria over Protestant objectives towards Catholicism on a European basis. Early in 1644, Giovanni Battista Nani, the Venetian Ambassador in France, had noted the proactive attempts of Henrietta Maria to prevent an offensive and defensive alliance between the Swedes and the *English* Parliament. According to Nani, Henrietta Maria represented 'the matter as one of importance, involving the most far reaching consequences, as this would be a *realisation of the design conceived a long while ago by the Protestants to form an alliance between all those who are antagonistic to the Catholic faith, to conquer it and ruin it from its foundations'.*[20] Nani's observations of the wider strategic implications of such an alliance were particularly perceptive from his commentary position in 1644. It was in French interests to oppose such an alliance, not only from the parochial stance of French interests per se, but also in terms of the wider 'general interest' due to the fact that 'an alliance of this sort cannot fail to be suspect, since *there is no doubt but that they will invite Holland to come into this alliance treaty'.*[21]

THE SCOTTISH PARLIAMENT AND CONFEDERATION WITH SWEDEN

By the time the Scottish Parliament convened on 4 June 1644, Covenanting diplomacy had not only taken on a British agenda, but was also seeking to extend the Solemn League and Covenant to other Protestant princes and states. In accordance with closing legislation of the 1641 Parliament, the first session of the First Triennial Parliament convened in Edinburgh on 4 June 1644. Parliament sat until 29 July 1644 and as part of its proceedings, it dealt with proposals for a confederation between Scotland and Sweden – another country actively fighting the Habsburgs.[22] Covenanting diplomacy was therefore simultaneously concerned with a British agenda in tandem with policy options towards the Dutch and the Swedes.

The Committee for Both Kingdoms was empowered to negotiate with foreign states as part of its remit. On 5 March the committee had decided that 'Foreign Affairs' were to be dealt with each Thursday on a weekly basis and that this was to include Sweden.[23] On the same day, the Scottish commissioners in London informed the Committee of Estates in Edinburgh of one 'Du Gar: come from Sweden' seeking 20 or 30 ships and that representatives be sent from both kingdoms to Sweden. The commissioners also noted that the Swedes 'are willing to enter in a strict league with both kingdomes, and to give what conditions they shalbee pleased to demand'.[24]

Four days later on 9 March the committee decided that 'the business of the Swedish agent be taken into consideration',[25] and by 4 April the Committee for Both Kingdoms had now decided that 'there be some persons in the nature of Agents from both kingdoms sent with all speed to the Swedes with instructions to maintain a good correspondence with the Crown, and such as may be an occasion of nearer alliance with the same'.[26] Sir Henry Vane had been instructed to inform the House of Commons of this decision, although the correspondence of Hugh Mowatt, one of the Swedish agents in England, of January 1645 indicates a personality clash between the two men and Mowatt perceived Vane to be recalcitrant to his cause.[27] The Scottish commissioners at this diet of 4 April, and at earlier meetings at which Swedish affairs were briefly mentioned, were Lord Maitland, Sir Archibald Johnston of Wariston and Robert Barclay.[28] Anglo-Scottish diplomatic correspondence sent from Westminster on 1 May 1645 to the king advocating a pro-Swedish and anti-Danish stance concerning the Scandinavian conflict was also signed by Lauderdale (the former Lord Maitland), Chancellor Loudoun, Johnston of Wariston, Hugh Kennedy and Robert Barclay. The commissioners were particularly concerned that Christian IV of Denmark-Norway should not transport any forces to intervene in the British troubles. In terms of commercial policy, it was the 'joynt desire and expectation' of the commissioners that the 'Liberation' and 'imunity from the Danish Exactions' and 'rigid Impositions, be comon to the *British*, with the Swedish merchants'.[29] Mowatt's correspondence with Queen Kristina in April 1645 also noted the enthusiasm of the Scottish commissioners to his mission, especially Chancellor Loudoun and Lauderdale.[30]

As Alexia Grosjean has shown, Du Gar (De Geer) was in London by March 1644, and the representatives of the Scottish and English Parliaments were aware that the Swedes sought a confederal alliance. The Swedish Riksråd had instructed Mowatt, a Scotsman employed in the service of the Swedish crown and the Swedish representative in the Dutch Republic, to raise a levy of 2,000–3,000 £ Scots as part of the anticipated military action against Denmark-Norway.[31] Mowatt was to be the more senior of the two Swedish representatives.[32] Oxenstierna had already informed Loudoun to expect Mowatt's arrival and had also briefed Loudoun on the nature of the current tension with Denmark-Norway.[33]

Three days after the opening of Parliament, Robert Baillie, the Covenanting minister of Kilwinning in Ayrshire and one of the ministers of the Church of Scotland's delegation sent to the Westminster Assembly of Divines, noted that 'The Swedds has sent agents for a strict league with us'.[34] Towards the end of June Parliament was dealing with issues of Swedish diplomacy more directly and initiating parliamentary structures to deal with these issues and it would appear that Mowatt was in Edinburgh by this stage. On 25 June in Parliament a session committee was appointed with a membership of two representatives from each of the three estates. Chancellor Loudoun and the Earl of Lauderdale represented the nobility, Sir Archibald Johnston of Wariston and Sir Charles Erskine of Cambuskenneth represented the shires, whilst Sir John Smith (Edinburgh) and Patrick Leslie (Aberdeen) represented the burghs. This session committee had three main tasks to fulfil. Firstly, the committee was personally to receive Hugh Mowatt as the Queen of Sweden's agent. Secondly, the committee was also to receive Mowatt's letters and thirdly the committee was then to report back to the House.[35] Issues of Swedish diplomacy would appear to have been discussed over a two-day period and on 26 June a letter from the Queen Kristina to the Scottish Parliament was read out to the assembled House. Her letter consisted of four main propositions or 'heades'.

The first 'head' contained an answer to correspondence sent to her by Charles I and the Scottish Parliament in 1641 concerning the delay of ending any league with the Emperor of Germany 'in preiudice of religione and the Palatins house'.[36] The second point provided an explanation of the 'trew cause' of the current war between Sweden and Denmark and the attempt of Christian IV to oppress her subjects and allies with tolls 'more by quadruple then euer by him heirtofor exacted'.[37] The third 'head' indicated that the Swedish Queen sought a 'league of perpetuall amitey with this kingdome' and the levies of more men in Scotland, if they could be spared.[38] The fourth and final 'head' requested that Hugh Mowatt should be treated with faith and credit as her servant 'to thesse thinges he should proposse in her name'.[39] The response of the House was to appoint a further session committee of five members of each estate to hear Mowatt's instructions and then report back to the House.[40] It is clear that this committee was to liaise directly with Mowatt in tandem with Chancellor Loudoun.

Loudoun reported back to the House on 9 July and explained the position taken by the session committee in response to the Queen of Sweden's demands. Accordingly, he explained that the committee had perceived these demands to be threefold. Firstly, the willingness of the Swedish crown's amity with the Scots and that the Swedish queen would 'hartily enter in leauge and associatione with ws of Scotland and England, offensiue and defensiue, if so wee wer pleassed therwith'.[41] The second demand envisaged a mediatory role for the Scottish Parliament in Swedish-Danish relations. This focused on the regional conflict over the extortionate levels of tolls being charged by Christian IV of Denmark. Hence the Swedish Queen sought that 'wee wold endeuor to free ourselues from the tyranney of the King of Demarkes insupportable tolles' and that she would never agree with him on this issue unless the Scots were 'lykwayes comprehendit within that accord'.[42] In order to pursue this issue further, Kristina wanted the Scots to send 'some persone weill instructed for the bussines forsaid'.[43] The third demand, as explained by Loudoun, focused more directly on the Mowatt mission. Essentially, Kristina was advocating that the Covenanters should also be mediators in Anglo-Swedish relations. Hence Mowatt was to proceed to England after his business in Scotland had been concluded and Kristina and her council were keen that 'the staittes of Scotland wold be mediators betuix her and England, and moue them to accept of her and her realmes to enter in that mutuall league with Brittane for defence of religione'.[44]

The Loudoun–Oxenstierna axis was further consolidated in the aftermath of the 1644 Parliament. Loudoun's correspondence to Oxenstierna clearly indicates that the Swedish Chancellor was being briefed on and was fully aware of proceedings in the Scottish Parliament relating to Swedish–Danish hostilities. Thus, Loudoun informed Oxenstierna that 'I did signifie to the estats of the parl't of this kingdome who were then sitting and did appoynt some of there number with me to reseave the Queen of Sueden's Letter, Which I did present in plaine parl't and did my with my beste Endevors secound the desyre thereof, To w'ch the parl't hes returned there anwser whereof this inclosed is the Copie'.[45] Therefore it would appear that the session committees established in the 1644 Parliament to consider Queen Kristina's letter were formed directly on the initiative of Chancellor Loudoun, but were also undoubtedly sanctioned by the Covenanting leadership.

Loudoun's briefing to Oxenstierna went on to inform him of wider British developments and Loudoun explained how he would be shortly leaving for England to 'treat in a joynt Committee of both kingdoms at London for establishing of Religion and removeing of the deplorable differences and distractions betuixt the kings ma[jes]tie and his subjects. That we may injoy a happie peace at home and be the more helpful to the Christian Churches and such kingdomes and Common-wealthes as ar in league and freindship with us'.[46] The prospect of a closer alliance between Scotland and Sweden was also commented on by Loudoun, who informed Oxenstierna that 'The motion of a neerer alliance and league betuixt this kingdome and Sueden is acknawledged as a reall and sure testimonie of trew respect and freindship'.[47] However, any such alliance would have to be taken along British lines following the Solemn League and Covenant and the Committee of Both Kingdoms; 'the neer conjunctions and obliga'ones betuixt us and o'r brethern of England (with whom wee ar laitlie entered in a solemne league and Covenant) Is such as we cannot give a positive answer to that proposition Till Both nations Joyntlie'.[48] Despite these formal jurisdictional restrictions, Loudoun promised that he would 'contribut my best assistance that it may have such assistance as may testifie the good will and affection this nation hes of Strengthining and increasing the ancient friendship and alliance betuixt this kingdome and the kingdome of Sweden'.[49] By August 1644 Scottish parliamentary representatives were instructing their diplomatic commis-sioners to secure the support of the English Parliament for an Anglo-Scottish parliamentary alliance with Sweden.[50] The Earl of Leven was also in contact with Oxenstierna briefing him on British affairs.[51]

Mowatt arrived in London in December 1644 seeking permission to secure a levy of 5,000 Scottish troops and the hiring of 24 warships. In return for this he was empowered to offer a defensive and offensive alliance with Parliament against any third party with whom they were hostile, and that would have included both Denmark-Norway and the Habsburg empire. Mowatt's proposal was therefore remitted to the Committee for Both Kingdoms, but it proved difficult to proceed on the negotiating front due to the outbreak of the Royalist rebellion in Scotland led by the Marquis of Montrose.[52] As events unfolded in the mid-1640s, the Mowatt mission became increasingly focused on the English Parliament. Scottish influence, in the context of British diplomacy through Anglo-Scottish parliamentary co-operation and consensus became increasingly marginalised. This can be attributed to a variety of complex reasons. The Committee for Both Kingdoms was a 'British' institution in name only. As the civil war progressed in England, the military successes of the New Model Army reduced the relative appeal of the Covenanting armed forces (whose reputation had been severely tarnished by the successes of Montrose and MacColla in Scotland anyway). In turn, this tended to reduce the relative political importance of the Covenanting diplomatic representatives in England. Despite the fact that a letter jointly signed by Scottish and English representatives was sent to Queen Kristina in May 1645 explaining the delay in proceeding with her propositions of 1644, correspondence from Mowatt which reached Sweden in July 1645 tended to stress an Anglo-Swedish agreement at the expense of the Scots.[53] Alexia Grosjean's doctoral thesis has established the nature of the debates which took place internally within Sweden over a 'British' policy during this period. Thus, by October 1645 Queen Kristina was moving towards a more specific English sphere of interest and acting on the advice of Oxenstierna that Swedish envoys should be sent to England, Mowatt's diplomatic orders were redefined to deal primarily with the English Parliament. Prior to this development, the Swedes had also been concerned about the strategic and diplomatic implications of a British confederation and were worried that it could lead to a 'mutual defensive' alliance between Denmark-Norway and the Dutch to counteract naval co-operation between England and Sweden.[54]

In January 1645, with Mowatt pursuing his mission in England, Agostini, the Venetian Ambassador in England, noted that Mowatt was trying to prevent French aid for the Royalist cause of Charles I. Mowatt was therefore offering Swedish assistance if the French 'or any other foreigners invade the country' and he assured the English parliamentarians, according to Agostini, that 'all Swedes will take the covenant with the English'.[55] However, as the year went on Mowatt's letters back to Sweden displayed a growing irritation not only of the inertia which he believed developments were proceeding on the part of his superiors *vis-à-vis* a British confederation, but also of his belief that he was being neglected, out of favour and left to fend for himself with severe implications for his own financial welfare.[56] In terms of wider diplomacy, he had also become increasingly concerned at Danish attempts to aid the Royalist cause in England, French diplomatic interference in British affairs to obstruct Mowatt's mission[57] and a belief among the Scottish and English Parliamentarians that the Swedish desire for a confederation had waned following the conclusion of a Swedish-Danish peace.[58]

As late as 1646, however, the Scottish Estates were still keen on a Swedish alliance, as was reflected in draft correspondence to the Swedish *Riksråd*, but no agreement could be reached with the English Parliament.[59] Even at this juncture, then, the Covenanters pursued a British approach, in line with the Anglo-Scottish parliamentary alliance and a unilateral Scottish-Swedish confederation was not envisaged. Anglo-Scottish parliamentary correspondence to Queen Kristina from this period reflects the desire of the parliamentary commissioners to enter into a 'strict Allyance' and 'Confederacie'.[60] This had been put on hold by Kristina until a peace treaty had been secured between Charles I and the English and Scottish Parliaments. The correspondence was signed by the Earl of Manchester, temporary Speaker of the House of Lords, William Lenthall, Speaker of the House of

Commons, and Lauderdale, 'in name of the Commissioners of the Parliament of Scotland'.[61] Kristina was given an update of British affairs and the reluctance of Charles I to agree to peace propositions. She offered to mediate in the British peace process and she was assured by the parliamentary triumvirate that their main objective was a 'safe' and 'well grounded Peace' with Charles I. Yet even at this stage Manchester, Lenthall and Lauderdale informed Kristina that they were still willing to embrace the 'Confederacy' and 'Union' previously proposed via Mowatt and that they were willing to do so once a peace had been secured with the king.[62]

But the terrain of English politics was to change with the rise of an aggressive English Independent faction (which sought an *English* solution to the Irish problem, exclusive of the Scots).[63] The marriage of the Anglo-Scottish parliamentary alliance headed for divorce with the Covenanting sale of the king in the aftermath of the First Civil War in England, the withdrawal of the Covenanting armed forces and the king left abandoned to the English Parliament. Divorce was to lead to a full breach with the signing of the 'Engagement' Treaty of December 1647 between Charles I, who had escaped from the custody of the English army to the Isle of Wight, and Covenanting nobles who had been closely involved in Covenanting diplomacy in British and European terms, namely Chancellor Loudoun and the Earl of Lauderdale. The Earl of Lanark was also involved in the agreement and his brother, the Marquis of Hamilton, was now in the process of gaining the upper-hand in Scotland in terms of a the political revival for the king's cause.

NOTES

1 Edinburgh University Library, Dc.4.16, Transactions of the Committee of Estates of Scotland, August 1640–June 1641, folio 93. See J.R. Young, *The Scottish Parliament 1639–1661: A Political and Constitutional Analysis* (Edinburgh, 1996), pp. 28–9.

2 S.R. Gardiner, *History of England from the Accession of James I to the Outbreak of the Civil War 1603–1642*, 10 vols (London, 1884) IX, 244–5, 257–8, 288–9; *Journals of the House of Lords*, 4, 1628–1642, pp. 176, 178, 180; E.N. Williams, *The Penguin Dictionary of English and European History 1485–1789* (Harmondsworth, 1980) pp. 160–1, 457.

3 A.I. Macinnes, 'The Scottish Constitution, 1638–51: The Rise and Fall of Oligarchic Centralism', in *The Scottish National Covenant in its British Context*, ed. J. Morrill (Edinburgh, 1990) pp. 131–2, footnote 49.

4 *The Journal of Thomas Cunningham of Campvere*, ed. E.J. Courthope (Edinburgh, 1928), p. 5.

5 *Ibid.*

6 *Ibid.*, p. 14.

7 A. Grosjean, 'Scots and the Swedish State: Diplomacy, Military Service and Ennoblement 1611–1660', unpublished PhD (Aberdeen, 1998) 182–3; *The Journal of Thomas Cunningham of Campvere*, p. 251.

8 *Ibid.*, 16. The 1644 Convention did not sit on a continuous basis and it met over four distinct blocks; 3–11 January, 25 January–2 February, 10–16 April and 25 May–3 June (Young, *The Scottish Parliament*, p. 83).

9 *The Journal of Thomas Cunningham of Campvere*, pp. 82–83; *Correspondence of the Scots Commissioners in London 1644–1646* (Edinburgh, 1917), p. 7. The 1644 Convention was not in session at this point and the Edinburgh section of the Committee of Estates sat from 2 December until 31 May, essentially having a managerial role over the Convention's proceedings (Young, *The Scottish Parliament*, pp. 72, 83). The original manuscript commission is listed in NAS PA 11/1, Register of the Committee of Estates, 28 August 1643–31 May 1644, ff. 220–1.

10 *Ibid.*, pp. 85–8.

11 *Ibid.*

12 *Ibid.*

13 A.I. Macinnes, *Charles I and the Making of the Covenanting Movement* (Edinburgh, 1991), p. 27.

14 NAS PA 11/1 Register of the Committee of Estates, 28 August 1643–31 May 1644, folio 219.

15 *Ibid.*

16 *Ibid.*

17 *Ibid.*

18 *Ibid.*

19 *Ibid.*

20 *Calendar of State Papers and Manuscripts relating to English affairs, existing in the archives and collections of Venice and in other libraries of Northern Italy* [CSPV] (London, 1924–7), 1643–47, p. 168.

21 *Ibid.*

22 Young, *The Scottish Parliament*, pp. 90–112.

23 *Calendar of State Papers Domestic, Charles I*, 1644, p. 34.

24 *Correspondence of the Scots Commissioners*, 9.

25 *Ibid.*, p. 44.

26 *Ibid.*, p. 95.

27 Swedish Riksarkivet [Sv. Ra.], Stockholm, AOSB SER B. E583, Mowatt to Oxenstierna, London, 31 January 1645.

28 *Correspondence of the Scots Commissioners*, pp. 34, 44.

29 Sv. Ra. Anglica 521.

30 Sv. Ra. AOSB SER B. E583, Mowatt to Queen Kristina, 12 April 1645.

31 Grosjean, 'Scots and the Swedish State', pp. 193–5. See also S. Murdoch, 'Scotland, Denmark-Norway and the House of Stuart 1603–1660 a diplomatic and military analysis', unpublished PhD (Aberdeen, 1998) pp. 150–1.

32 Grosjean, 'Scots and the Swedish State', p. 195.

33 Loudoun and Rowallan Deeds, the archives of the Marquis of Bute, Dumfries House, Loudoun Deeds Bundle 1/1, in large green suitcase containing contents of two boxes; docketed 'Chan'r of Suedens l're to the L. Chan. of Scotland'. Chancellor of Sweden to the Chancellor of Scotland, Holland, 26 March 1644. I am grateful for this reference originally from Allan Macinnes and passed on to me by Alexia Grosjean.

34 R. Baillie, *Letters and Journals, 1637–1662*, 3 vols (Edinburgh, 1841–2), II, p. 191.

35 J. Balfour, *Historical Works*, 4 vols (Edinburgh, 1824–5), II, p. 194.

36 *Ibid.*, p. 195.

37 *Ibid.*

38 *Ibid.*

39 *Ibid.* Her letter was also subscribed by Chancellor Oxenstierna.

40 *APS*, VI, i, p. 141.
41 Balfour, *Historical Works*, II, p. 209.
42 *Ibid.*
43 *Ibid.*, p. 210.
44 *Ibid.*
45 Loudoun and Rowallan Deeds, the archives of the Marquis of Bute, Dumfries House, Loudoun Deeds, Bundle 2/2, in large green suitcase containing two boxes docketed: 'draught of a letter to the Chancellor of Sweden', n.d.
46 *Ibid.*
47 *Ibid.*
48 *Ibid.*
49 *Ibid.*
50 Grosjean, 'Scots and the Swedish State', 196.
51 Sv. Ra. AOSB SER B. E583, Mowatt to Oxenstierna, 4 August 1645.
52 Grosjean, 'Scots and the Swedish State', p. 196.
53 Grosjean, 'Scots and the Swedish State', p. 197.
54 Grosjean, 'Scots and the Swedish State', pp. 197–201.
55 *CSPV*, 1643–1647, p. 171.
56 Sv. Ra. AOSB SER B. E583 Mowatt to Oxenstierna, 4 August 1645, 20 August 1645, 13 September 1645, 27 September 1645, 14 November 1645, 28 November 1645.
57 For the craftiness of French diplomacy during this period, as well as earlier destabilising French influences, see the *Montereul Correspondence 1645–1648*, two volumes, ed. J. G. Fotheringam (Edinburgh, 1898–99).
58 *Ibid.*
59 Grosjean, 'Scots and the Swedish State', p. 200.
60 Sv. Ra. Anglica p. 521.
61 *Ibid.*
62 *Ibid.*
63 See, for example, J. Adamson, 'Strafford's ghost: the British context of Viscount Lisle's lieutenancy of Ireland', in *Ireland from Independence to Occupation*, ed. J.H. Ohlmeyer (Cambridge, 1995) pp. 128–59.

Whatever Happened to the Medieval Burgh? Some Guidelines for Sixteenth- and Seventeenth-century Historians

M Lynch 1984 *in Scottish Economic and Social History*, 4, 5–20.

It was probably to be expected that most of the articles published in this journal would be concerned with the social and economic history of Scotland in the modern period; no article in the first three volumes has attempted to penetrate further back than 1750. In a recently published set of essays on Scottish urban history the period before 1600 was left to historical geographers – with mixed results.[1] 1660 has for some time been the virtual frontier of Scottish economic and social history. The most important contributions to our knowledge of the seventeenth century have come in Dr Devine's analyses of the increasingly ambitious Scottish merchant community after 1660 and Dr Whyte's remarkably detailed study of rural society, which, again, detects a change of gear in the Restoration period.[2] The main focus of these studies has been forwards – to try to link and refine the ambiguities, undercover patterns of investment and false starts in the later seventeenth-century economy that prepared the way for the undoubted change which took place in the following century. The bridge with the past – the preceding century and a half – has yet to be built. This is the case with both urban and rural history. The ramifications of Dr Sanderson's pioneering work on sixteenth-century rural society have yet to be fully felt in the century which followed; there is still a gulf to be bridged between the new found security of tenure which she describes[3] and Dr Whyte's picture of restless but limited change.

The gap is all the wider for the post-1660 urban historian, who is admittedly largely forced back on his own resources. It is not surprising that Dr Devine is more concerned with tackling the problem of placing the burghs more accurately in the changing later seventeenth-century economy than with tracing the changes in the burghs themselves through the void of urban history which exists earlier in the century. The problem of change has become more fashionable for the later seventeenth-century historian than the problem of continuity. Attention has, as a result, tended to focus on the 'pre-industrial town',[4] in which interest concentrates on the rapid abandonment at some point in the later seventeenth or the eighteenth century of the restrictive features in the institutions and structure of the medieval burgh. The 'early-modern town', which implies an examination of how those institutions and structure were subjected to increasing strain in the sixteenth and early seventeenth centuries,[5] has scarcely reached the currency of Scottish historiography.

Yet it is clear enough that historians of early modern Scotland now have at the forefront of their concerns a desire to define more closely the various aspects of the transition of the Scottish economy and society which was palpably under way by 1600, if not before. The two most recent textbooks to cover sixteenth-century Scotland both have important implications within them for the period beyond the point at which they close. Dr Wormald, while admitting that there was still 'more conservatism than innovation' in the economy maintains that there was, nonetheless, enough innovation within it 'to make the late sixteenth century notably different from the past'. Although Professor Duncan admitted that the rising expectations of the burghs and the growing complexity of the social structure within them still had the status of 'unresolved historical problems', he gave clear warning that these questions should 'not be avoided by anyone who would study seventeenth-century Scotland'.[6] The medieval burgh is too easily tossed into the dustbin of history after 1660 when it has suffered serious neglect in the preceding century or so.

The 'problem of the early modern town' in Scotland has been caused by a combination of simple neglect and the working assumptions of historians rather than a lack of evidence. It has been suggested, in one of the most illuminating works on English urban history written in recent years, that

> The real break for the urban historian comes with the change not in the substance but in the materials of history, with the beginning of any considerable – and surviving – town archive. That beginning transforms the study of urban history by making it possible to ask and answer many more questions.[7]

The same historian turned, as a result, to the fifteenth century. In Scotland the urban historian would usually have to turn to the sixteenth century rather than the fifteenth to find new and substantial burgh archives but by then it is quite normal to find some combination of council minute books, burgh court books, accounts of town treasurers or deans of guild, burgh registers of deeds or notarial protocol books, stent rolls and even, on occasion, a muster roll. Yet, sadly, not many extra questions have been asked of this range of new evidence and fewer still have been satisfactorily answered. With the early burgh, where documentary evidence has long since been taken to its cultivation limits, historians have been forced either to turn to other disciplines such as archaeology for advice or to ask new questions of limited evidence. Thus Professor Duncan has transformed our understanding of the twelfth-century burgh by rigorously applying to it the notion of the market.[8] The same has yet to be done for the sixteenth- or early seventeenth-century burgh. A beginning has been made with the painstaking study of the Dumfriesshire testaments recorded between 1600 and 1665, which revealed, rather surprisingly, that farmers tended to turn to fellow-farmers rather than to burgh merchants for loans of money. Dumfries merchants had a number of personal connections with Edinburgh and it may be that the admission of apprentices and burgesses from rural areas, which was becoming increasingly obvious in many burghs, served as an indirect stimulus to internal trade by adding to the range of personal contacts of the merchant community.[9] Until the market economy has been more fully explored generalizations about the relations between royal burghs and burghs of barony or between overseas and internal trade and the alleged transformation which overtook both in the 1670s lack a longer-term historical perspective.

The market economy is only one of a number of fundamental questions which have still to be asked of the Scottish early modern town. Four others readily come to mind and there may well be more. What was the effect, for instance, on the structure of burgh society of the doubling or more of population in many royal burghs in the course of the sixteenth century? It is a question which has, of course, been asked of Glasgow in the seventeenth century[10] but it may have wider application if transposed a century forward. Precise figures are, of course, difficult to come by. There are some for Edinburgh, which was credited with having 400 houses or thereabouts in 1400. In 1592 a kirk session counted 2,239 households and by 1635 there were 3,901.[11] The increase in population was dramatic enough to force the kirk session to consider splitting the centuries-old single parish of St Giles into eight model parishes with approximately a thousand examinable persons in each.

TABLE I: *Edinburgh*

QUARTER	PARISHES	HOUSEHOLDS	EXAMINABLE PERSONS
SE	South 1	253	971
	South 2	282	1027
SW	South 3	293	1053
	South 4	297	976
NW	North 1	280	956
	North 2	240	982
NE	North 3	299	1040
	North 4	295	995
	Total	2239	8000

The historic identity of medieval burgh and parish could not survive population increase on this scale. In most other burghs demographic guesswork would, of course, be much less certain before the late seventeenth century. Yet the question posed is not one of precise population statistics. It is rather what happened to the medieval burgh – its institutions, social structure and working habits – when it was subjected to the pace and pressure of population increase on this scale?

Another question to be asked concerns the effect on burgh society of the dramatic and sustained upward movement of prices in this period. The exact dimensions of price inflation may be in doubt, but whether one thinks in terms of a fourfold increase in general prices between 1550 and 1625 or a tenfold increase in grain prices in the century after 1535[12] the point at issue is the effects of these pressures rather than their precise proportions. Because, as Professor Lythe pointed out, there was not a single correlation between wages and prices, some groups within burgh society fared distinctly better than others. The top-grade craftsman probably kept pace with price inflation whereas the unskilled or unfree fell badly behind.[13] The relative fortunes of larger and smaller merchants remain largely unknown but were probably just as starkly divergent.[14] Were these different movements in the economic fortunes of the various groups within burgh society without social or political consequences? The question is all the more important to ask because price inflation was coupled, as never before, with significant population increase.

The political and religious upheavals of the sixteenth century were inextricably linked with the burghs. They were the growth points of the reformed church after 1560. Yet the burghs were not always capable, so the most recent study of the Reformation has argued, of taking their own decisions; it was the local lairds or nobles who usually took the lead in fostering Protestantism and burghs took their cue accordingly.[15] Power in the localities rested with the natural leaders of local society – the nobles and their networks of kin – and it was they rather than the crown who provided much of the stability in an unstable century. Yet by the personal reign of James VI royal government was coming to take a fresh and increasingly direct interest in the affairs of the local communities.[16] This fundamental revision of the shifting nature of power in early modern Scotland calls for an equally fundamental review of the position of the burghs. Two questions seem to arise from it. How were the traditional notions of independence and privilege which lay at the root of the thinking of royal burghs affected by the interest increasingly taken in their affairs, particularly in the fifteenth century, by local nobles and lairds and how were those same burghs affected by the intervention of the crown in the localities late in the next century?

The burghs had begun their formal existence in the twelfth century as distinctive creations of the crown. Yet they had come within a relatively short space of time to work within a remarkably loose set of reins for a feudal realm.[17] The relations between royal burghs and feudal kingship had been redrafted in the course of the fourteenth century as a more precise financial arrangement had been arrived at, partly through the setting of burgh lands in feu farms. A combination of factors, not least the large-scale redistribution of noble lands and titles in the 1450s, had encouraged a drift of many burghs into the patronage networks of nobles or lairds. Aberdeen, for example, had chosen to enter into a bond of manrent with the earl of Huntly in 1463. This tendency may have been both more complex and more uneasy than hitherto suspected. By the early sixteenth century Aberdeen had on its own council the clients not only of the Gordons of Huntly but also those of a string of other nobles including the earls of Errol and Buchan.[18] Throughout the sixteenth century a potentially abrasive set of relationships existed between the Gordons, their client family in Aberdeen, the Menzies, and the burgh itself.[19]

The burghs had thus for centuries drifted in and out of the direct province and concerns of the crown. It is possible, as a result, for a recently completed thesis on Dundee spanning the years 1443–1610, to talk of the 'recurrent isolation' of a major burgh from national politics.[20] It is an argument which is, however, increasingly difficult to apply to Dundee and the bulk of the royal burghs by the third or fourth quarters of the sixteenth century. Just as the nobles were pulled, often reluctantly, into the limelight of national politics as a result of the Reformation crisis of 1559–60,[21] so were many of the burghs. It had become fairly common by the early sixteenth century for the crown or faction in control at court to place its own nominee as provost in some burghs. In the Reformation crisis the court had displaced whole town councils in Edinburgh, Perth and Jedburgh and during the 1560s Queen Mary had made a number of attempts to nominate office-holders to the Edinburgh council. By the 1580s whole town councils were purged or placed in Edinburgh at the behest of the shifting groups within the court and even, in 1584, the whole kirk session. Edinburgh was, as a capital, particularly vulnerable to political interference of this kind. Yet it was in this period not so much the exception as the testing ground for an increasingly aggressive interventionist policy on the part of the crown. In the later 1580s a succession of royal nominees, including the earls of Athol and Montrose, were imposed as provost of Perth to counter the traditional local power of the earl of Gowrie. Two different factions followed their respective masters in and out of power. The bizarre events which followed the abortive Gowrie conspiracy of 1600, when a large proportion of Perth's burgesses were interrogated as to their political loyalties, was the climax of a political battle which had been going on for fifteen years.[22] Perth's town council had become the focus of a struggle between two factions, perhaps best described as court and country parties. The later sixteenth century witnessed the return, in a number of different ways, of the royal burghs to the national stage and their closer involvement with central government.

The re-emergence of the burghs and their reappraisal by the crown was part of a more general shift in the relations between government and the localities. The single most important factor in this new relationship which jolted 'people in the localities . . . out of their relative isolation' was, so it has been argued, the new incidence from the 1580s onwards of regular national taxation.[23] Taxation was, it might well be deduced, the key factor in bringing the burghs once again into a closer relationship with the crown. Yet its effects did not stop there. Taxation also jolted the internal structure of burgh society. A good deal of use has been made of the various lists of the assessments made on each burgh for national taxation in the sixteenth and seventeenth centuries. These lists have been used by a number of historians to show how one burgh or another moved up or down the ranking list in terms of the percentage of national taxation it paid. Little has been done, however, to analyse the shifts which took place *within* individual burghs in the course of the sixteenth and seventeenth centuries to meet this new and ever-growing burden of taxation.

The best-documented example is again that of Edinburgh, where the increasing weight of taxation during the regency of Mary of Guise had resulted in measures being taken as early as the 1550s to spread its burden. Sons of merchant burgesses were drawn into the net before they had gained burgess-ship. Considerable opposition had resulted in the scheme being abandoned as 'a novelty' in 1557. Yet in 1584 it was reintroduced 'in respect of the alteration of the time and great charges daily falling upon the town, intolerable to a few number'.[24] This is an early example of a new strain on the old notion of the burgess community. Whole new classes of inhabitants were being brought within the tax threshold for the first time. The numbers of those who were individually assessed for taxation rose in Edinburgh from about 400 (allowing for exemptions) in 1565 to 527 in 1581 – an increase of almost a third.[25] The phenomenon which most clearly distinguishes the characteristically medieval burgh of the late fifteenth century from the early modern town emerging by the late sixteenth century was the size of its taxable population.

A third question needs to be added to the customary two asked by the burgh historian of this period. It is not enough to ask how many burgesses there were and what proportion of them were admitted to the merchant guildry. Also necessary, not least because it vitally affects the first two questions, is the question, what was the size and distribution of the burgh's taxable population? It is likely that the precise answer will vary significantly from burgh to burgh. Historians have perhaps become over-conscious of the pitfalls and deficiencies in using the evidence of tax or stent rolls. They are not reliable indicators of town population or, indeed, of the relative populations of different towns or relative movements of populations.[26] Yet they might be worked more intensively to compare in different towns what they were intended to reveal – the tax-paying sector of the burgh community. The possible results of such an exercise have been demonstrated by Dr Devine, using poll tax records of the 1690s, in his comparison of the pyramids of wealth in Aberdeen and Edinburgh.[27] Much the same comparison could be effected a full century earlier by a comparison of stent rolls. There is a regular series of rolls for Edinburgh from 1581 and for Aberdeen from 1592. An initial survey of this evidence has shown an appreciable difference in the upper layers of the social structure of the two burghs. 1,245 Edinburgh inhabitants paid tax in 1583, 506 in Aberdeen in 1592, but the two pyramids were quite differently shaped.

TABLE 2

	EDINBURGH (1583)	ABERDEEN[28] (1592)
Percentage of taxation paid by top 10%	56%	30%
Percentage of taxation paid by top 20%	71%	49%
Percentage of taxpayers paying half of all taxation	8%	21%

The comparison, however preliminary, highlights the fact that significant differences in social structure existed between one large burgh and another behind the façade of their similar constitutions. A number of stent rolls of this period also exist for some smaller burghs, which might be used in a similar way.

What steps were taken to accommodate burgh government to more regular taxation? In Edinburgh the most significant of the changes in the make-up of the taxable population came as a result of the revision of the burgh's constitution in the decreet-arbitral of 1583 – a constitution which was quickly copied by Aberdeen in its Common Indenture of 1587 and subsequently by a number of other burghs. The significance of the Edinburgh decreet has habitually been taken to be the increase it made in the number of craftsmen who sat on the town council; six craft deacons joined the two existing craft councillors. It was, however, equally significant that the decreet altered the status of craftsmen as taxpayers. The crafts had until then been assessed corporately and paid a fixed proportion – set at a quarter – of all burgh taxation. From 1583 craftsmen were assessed individually, like all other taxpayers, and the rising status of some of them was clearly revealed. The proportion paid by the burgh establishment – the top 125 or 10% of taxpayers – remained virtually the same: it had been 55% in 1565 and was 56% in the first tax levied after the decreet. But the establishment now included fifteen craftsmen within it. The assessment on some crafts went up dramatically: the goldsmiths found that they together paid three times as much in tax after 1583 as before; the tailors paid two and a half times as much. If craftsmen were forcing their way into more positions of power, they had to pay a price for it.[29]

What now seems necessary in the study of urban history of the sixteenth and early seventeenth century is to try and bring to bear on the burghs what have emerged in a number of recent general works as the central questions in Scottish history of the period. The five major problems have been identified here as the market economy; population increase; price inflation; politics and patronage, both of crown and nobles; and the effect of the ever-growing burden of taxation. What is above all necessary is that urban historians try to consider the *combined* impact of those problems.[30] These five problems will not apply everywhere with the same force or in the same combination. Yet they do, woven together, form the backcloth against which urban history in this period was shaped and provide much of the answer to the question of what happened to the medieval burgh.

It is important to ask new questions of the evidence; perhaps just as important is to re-examine the older questions. The study of urban history is largely a matter of evaluating the balance between change and continuity. It is unfortunate that to many historians the key element of change in Scottish urban history of the fifteenth and sixteenth centuries has been taken to be the emergence of a new and serious friction within the burgh community – a struggle between merchants and craftsmen, which seemingly gained a momentum of its own and dwarfed other concerns. The argument has been put thus:

> It is very plain that the fifteenth century witnessed great tensions within the burghs and important changes between the exponents of these two principal economic functions . . . Legislation, especially the act of 1469, established very

clearly a sharp differentiation between merchant and craft functions, and ensured for the merchants something approaching a monopoly of government within the royal burghs.[31]

The same study, to be fair, went on to make a number of reservations: it admitted that the effects of this stream of legislation on burghs in the reign of James III – 1467 c 2, 1469 c 5, 1474 c 12, 1487 c 13 – may have been patchy. The act of 1469 was not enforced in Peebles until 1504.[32] It and the act of 1474, it might be added, were not enforced in Aberdeen until the 1590s and only then after the intervention of the privy council. It is possible to extend the list of qualifications and reservations considerably further. It seems difficult to talk of a general conflict between merchants and craftsmen when there seems to be no evidence for it in certain burghs, especially smaller ones, like Dunfermline. It is rather difficult to think of a general pattern of conflict between two groups when the precise answer to the question of who comprised one of those groups varies from burgh to burgh. A maltman, for instance, was a craftsman in Dundee and Perth but a merchant in Edinburgh and Glasgow. An apothecary was a merchant in Edinburgh but often attached to the barber craft elsewhere. Is it possible to talk of conflict between merchants and craftsmen when some burghs, like Brechin, had no incorporated craft guilds or when many burghs, like Dumfries, had no incorporated merchant guild until the seventeenth century? If the relative numbers of the two groups varied from burgh to burgh can conflict between them be said everywhere to have taken the same form? The use of the terms 'merchants' and 'craftsmen' to analyse the complex society of the early modern town could be likened to using bulldozers where what is needed is trowels.

The most serious objection to the notion of a conflict of merchants and craftsmen is that the terms in fact overlapped. One of the most cherished examples of the argument that a sharp social divide had come to exist between the two groups is the case of Robert Vernor, an Edinburgh skinner, who in 1588 was admitted to the merchant guildry on condition that he renounced his 'trade' and that his wife and servants did not appear carrying meat dishes in the streets 'with their aprons and serviettes', as ill-befitted the household of a guild brother.[33] The case was an isolated one, not because it marked a rare transition from craftsman to guild brother, but because Robert Vernor's wife needed such a sharp reminder of the social graces attached to membership of the guildry. There are, in fact, large numbers of examples of Edinburgh craftsmen being admitted to the merchant guildry throughout the sixteenth century. In Perth the guildry book also shows, from the point at which it opens in the 1450s, considerable numbers of craftsmen – dyers, skinners, furriers, even baxters – being admitted to the merchant guildry.[34] In Edinburgh there was a fairly sharp increase in the third quarter of the sixteenth century, reflecting the rise of craft aristocracy of tailors, goldsmiths, skinners and surgeons. By the 1580s this kind of craftsman had gained more power, both in burgh affairs and over his fellow craftsmen; he was also paying the tax which befitted his status. The transition which took place was not quite that of craftsman to merchant. It was more often that of master craftsman to craft employer and guild brother.

The full extent of the activities of these craftsmen entrepreneurs is as yet unknown but their admission to the guildry often seems to have given them new opportunities for wider investment[35] as well as political or social advancement. Often they were probably sons of merchant guild brothers. It was quite common in Edinburgh for one son to inherit the family business, a second to enter the law and a third to enter one of the more prestigious crafts. The family often cut across the supposed divisions within burgh society. The point has a general importance since it is the so-called 'merchant classes' which 'tend to be synonymous with urban growth and progress'.[36] These classes may have been rather wider and more flexible by 1600 than has hitherto been suspected in most of the larger burghs. The freer atmosphere which has been associated with the rise of Glasgow and which stemmed from its constitution of 1605 may have been a more general phenomenon in the larger burghs.[37] If the merchant guild was not as narrow an enclave of privilege – outside Glasgow – as many have thought, the preparations for the breaking free of privilege and restrictionism which has been taken to mark the Restoration period may in fact have been laid down for fully half a century or more. There seems often little difference in the general stratagem of mercantile investment at the beginning and end of the seventeenth century; money lending, secured by heritable bond, the buying and selling of tenement properties and even investment in small-scale manufactories can all be found in early seventeenth-century Edinburgh.[38] To borrow the phraseology of the Industrial Revolution of the late eighteenth century, the 'prelude to the take-off' of the growth of internal and external trade may need to be extended back half a century before 1660. It is a task which has been made more difficult by the intervention of the severe political crisis which engulfed Scotland in the twenty years before 1660. The detailed effects of the Scottish Revolution on any of the burghs remains unexplored. In the larger perspective the Revolution may better be seen as an interlude in the growing confidence and widening patterns of investment and opportunity which characterized the economies of many early seventeenth-century Scottish towns.

The alleged wholesale friction between merchants and craftsmen in the Scottish burghs in the early modern period is largely a fallacy. It has affected not only the way these groups have been examined but also analysis of many of the other elements of burgh society. The fundamental divisions in burgh life lay not so much between merchants and craftsmen as between masters and men, employers and employees, rulers and ruled. These were the divisions which were being renegotiated in Edinburgh's decreet of 1583. One of the provisions of this new constitution was that craftsmen chosen to serve on the town council should come only from 'the best and worthiest' of the crafts.[39] As a result only seven of the burgh's fourteen incorporated crafts were represented on the council. The decreet was a highly conservative rearrangement of political power, designed to perpetuate the old ideal of the medieval burgh that the more substantial citizens took the lead in burgh affairs. Exactly the same intention had lain behind the much-quoted legislation of the parliaments of James III.[40] The acts, such as 1487 c 13, which tried to draw a dividing-line between the respective economic spheres of merchants and craftsmen, are too often cited together and out of their particular context. Each of the parliaments of this reign had, it is now clear, a distinctive character of its own and its own *bêtes noires*.[41] The act of 1487 is only understood properly if it is considered alongside the act which immediately followed it and made clear its disapproval of the tinkering in certain unnamed burghs with the old arrangements guaranteeing hierarchy and consensus.

> It is statut and ordanit that the Act of parlment anent the chesing of officiaris in borowis be ratifiit and apprufit and put to execucioun in tym to cum to be obseruit and kepit sa that the eleccioun of the officiaris micht be of the best and worthiest induellaris of the toun and not be parcialite nor masterschip quhilk is undoing of the borowis quhare masterschippis and requestis cummis.[42]

There was an essential continuity in all this legislation. The 1583 decreet was designed to deal with trouble which had broken out at the annual elections of incorporated crafts. The parliamentary legislation of 1469 and 1487 was designed to counter the disturbances at municipal elections which took place at Michaelmas head courts. All of them reflected a traditional desire, reflected in the recurrent use of the same phrase, to protect the position of the 'best and worthiest' amongst the burgesses, including the craftsmen. The act of 1469, which bemoaned disturbances at burgh elections, had been linked to the subsequent appearance in many burghs of charters of incorporations for craft guilds. These had obvious advantages for the craftsmen.[43] But what advantages did incorporation bring to the town councils which granted them? The answer lies in the old idea of the medieval burgh as a community, which was coming under increasing strain as its population expanded. Incorporation of the groups within burgh society did two things: it continued to restrict power to a hierarchy; and it preserved the myth of the burgh community, now redrawn as a series of communities within one community. The Edinburgh decreet claimed that it had reunited merchants and craftsmen in 'one society'.[44] The true mark of the post-medieval burgh was not the opening-up of a division between merchants and craftsmen but the growing divide between the guild brother, whether overseas merchant or *rentier*, and the humbler merchant burgesses; or the divide between the guild brother, who like the tailor or goldsmith was part of a new craft aristocracy, and the ordinary master craftsman. Burgh society was in process of becoming more elitist and more oligarchical but the elite was not composed solely of merchants. This was part of the common pattern of towns in the early modern period, outside Scotland as well as inside – the larger a town grew the more consolidated its ruling oligarchy became and the tighter the grip of that oligarchy over the inhabitants.[45] The entry of significant numbers of craftsmen to the merchant guild was part of the more general story of the growing delegation of authority made by town councils to craft deacons and governing councils of craft guilds. This, in its turn, was part of the general revision of the traditional arrangements by which the medieval burgh had been governed, a change made necessary by population increase.

The most difficult item to dispose of in the thesis of merchant-craft rivalry is that of craft riots. Yet the evidence is often, when tested, suspect. Purely political demonstrations have, at times, been mistaken as craft riots.[46] Usually a craft riot was a riot involving only one craft and very often that craft was either the baxters or fleshers, the crafts most directly affected by the deliberate policy of town councils to hold down the prices of basic foodstuffs. So the Edinburgh baxters rioted in 1551 and the fleshers in 1553; in Dundee the baxters took the town council to the Court of Session in 1561 to protest at its policy of holding down the price of bread to an artifically low level in time of shortage.[47] There were no bread riots in sixteenth-century Scotland.[48] There were instead fairly frequent minor riots involving the producers of bread and other basic commodities against town councils which ruthlessly implemented a cheap food policy at their expense. It is here that it is useful to remember the broader context. The rulers of the Scottish burghs used a cheap food policy as an alternative to a proper poor rate in a period of sharply rising prices, recurrent food shortages and generally increasing population. There is a stark contrast if Edinburgh and Norwich, towns of nearly equal size, both of which had suffered from an outbreak of the plague in the 1560s, are compared. Norwich established an elaborate poor rate in 1571. Edinburgh had devised eight separate schemes in the course of the 1560s to meet the combined burden of its ministers, schools and poor. All had foundered. Efforts to implement the Act anent the Poor of 1574, which was modelled on the English poor law, were also abandoned by 1576.[49] The victims of the failure to establish a poor rate were the food producers. If there was a typical revolting craftsman in the sixteenth-century burgh it was a baxter apprentice – in a trade with a low level of technical skill and a high proportion of apprentices or journeymen, and subject to arbitrary interference in its profit margins so that real wages in it were falling sharply. The kind of craft riot to which such a victim of economic circumstances might resort illustrates a general point; if there was a politics of resentment in sixteenth-century burgh life, it had more to do with the combined economic pressures on the burgh than internal rivalries. The attraction – and the danger – of the notion of the craft riot and a self-generating struggle between merchants and craftsmen is that it imposes meaning on disparate scraps of information which are otherwise difficult to evaluate.

There is a temptation, which follows on from the notion of a merchant oligarchy, entrenched in power and answerable only to itself, to read the voluminous but extremely repetitive burgh records of this period too cynically. It is true that the same municipal regulations were re-enacted year after year in a head court and it is easy enough to find examples in which council elections became a ritualized reselection process. Head courts, nonetheless, could often remain as an important and genuine forum of burgh opinion. In Perth the political interventions in town council elections were usually ratified by the 'great council' of the burgh. The burgesses of Perth met in a head court in the summer of 1560 to elect the burgh's commissioner to the Reformation parliament. The protestant reformers in Edinburgh chose the forum of a head court in 1561 to give greater force to proclamations banning catholic priests from the burgh. In the capital every council election between 1561 and 1567 and between 1578 and 1585 saw a genuine contest for power; each election in those periods brought about shift in policy and the balance of power within the ruling oligarchy.[50] These examples tend to show that power in the burghs rested in a real sense on consent. Head courts continued to act as a regular re-expression of consensus. Neither burgh oligarchies nor neighbouring nobles and lairds could demand power and expect it to be rendered up without question. Even the grip of the Gordons of Huntly or of their surrogates, the Menzies family, over the burgh of Aberdeen wavered from time to time before it was eclipsed in the early 1590s.[51] It may be that historians have reduced burgh affairs to a far too predictable struggle for place, profit and power. Political issues, including among them the issues which stemmed from noble or lairdly patronage, need to be put back into burgh politics.

It is possible that historians, in their eagerness to seek out divisions within burgh society, may have missed the real issues, which lay instead between the burghs and the outside world which surrounded them. There are always dangers in reading the monotonous special pleading in the records of the Convention of Royal Burghs. Yet, if looked at closely, they reveal rather more references to disputes between royal burghs and local nobles or lairds than to internal disputes between merchants and craftsmen. Peebles was in serious dispute in 1580 with the commendator of New-battle. Elgin complained in 1587 of 'the great oppression committed by sundry lairds and gentlemen . . . violently to bereave them of their liberties'. Forfar raised an action in the Court of Session in 1591 against the Master of Glamis. Inverkeithing was only one of several burghs in dispute with the Scrymgeour family in the 1590s.[52] There seems to have been an increasing chorus of protest as the sixteenth century drew to a close. The struggle, it seems, between royal burghs and burghs of barony for an expanding internal market was already under way. Here and elsewhere – in widening patterns of investment, greater social mobility and the complex effects of population increase – the mould of later seventeenth-century Scottish urban history was firmly set before the first quarter of the century was over.

NOTES

1 G .Gordon and B. Dicks eds, *Scottish Urban History* (Aberdeen, 1983).

2 T. M. Devine, 'The merchant class of the larger Scottish towns in the later seventeenth and early eighteenth centuries', in Gordon and Dicks, *Scottish Urban History*, pp. 92–111, and 'The Scottish merchant community, 1680–1740', in R. H. Campbell and A. S. Skinner, eds, *The origins and Nature of the Scottish Enlightenment* (Edinburgh, 1982), pp. 26–41; I. Whyte, *Agriculture and Society in Seventeenth Century Scotland* (Edinburgh, 1979).

3 M. H. B. Sanderson, *Scottish Rural Society in the Sixteenth Century* (Edinburgh, 1982), pp. 188–90.

4 See, for example, Gordon and Dicks, *Scottish Urban History*, pp. 10–11, 62–70, 107–08.

5 As examined, for example, in P. L. Clark and P. Slack (eds.), *Crisis and Order in English Towns, 1500–1700* (London, 1972).

6 J. Wormald, *Court, Kirk and Community: Scotland 1470–1625* (London, 1981), p. 173; W. C. Dickinson and A. A. M. Duncan, *Scotland from the Earliest Times to 1603* (3rd edn, Oxford, 1977), pp. 400–01.

7 S. Reynolds, *An Introduction to the History of English Medieval Towns* (Oxford, 1977), p. 159.

8 See A. A. M. Duncan, *Scotland: The Making of the Kingdom* (Edinburgh, 1975), pp. 465–501.

9 W. Coutts, 'Social and economic history of the Commissariot of Dumfries, 1660–1665, as disclosed by the registers of testaments' (unpublished M Litt thesis, University of Edinburgh, 1982), pp. 94, 143; M. H. B. Sanderson, *Scottish Rural Society*, pp. 184–5, 'The Edinburgh merchants in society, 1570–1603: the evidence of their testaments', in I. B. Cowan and D. Shaw, eds *The Renaissance and Reformation in Scotland* (Edinburgh, 1983), p. 185.

10 T. C. Smout, 'The development and enterprise of Glasgow, 1556–1707', *Scot. J. Pol. Econ.*, vii (1960), pp. 195–6.

11 Edinburgh City Archives, MS Moses Bundles, no. 195, doc. no. 7029; see also M. Lynch, *Edinburgh and the Reformation* (Edinburgh, 1981), pp. 10, 14. The total of examinable persons is a corrected one. The scheme as outlined was abandoned. In 1598 four separate parishes, based on the existing four quarters, were created; a further two were added in 1641. It is noticeable that Glasgow was divided into four parishes by 1648 and into six in 1701, by which time the total of examinable persons was 9,994, so that each parish had charge of between 1,607 and 1,777; see A. MacGeorge, *Old Glasgow* (Glasgow, 1880), pp. 193–4. This is a subject which deserves fuller investigation.

12 Cf. S. G. E. Lythe, *The Economy of Scotland in its European Setting, 1550–1625* (Edinburgh, 1960), p. 110, and W H Makey, *The Church of the Covenant, 1637–1651* (Edinburgh, 1979), p. 3.

13 Lythe, *The Economy of Scotland*, p. 30.

14 See Sanderson, 'Edinburgh Merchants', pp. 184, 194.

15 I. B. Cowan, *The Scottish Reformation* (London, 1982), pp. 110–14.

16 Wormald, *Court, Kirk Community*, pp. 28–9, 161.

17 G. G. Simpson, 'The use of documentary sources by the archaeologists: a viewpoint from Scotland', *Archives*, xiii (1978), p. 208.

18 I am grateful to Mr Harold Booton for this point. His thesis on the development of political power among the landed and burghal families of the north-east, 1400–1550, should open up the important question of patronage and clientage in the burghs.

19 I am grateful to Fr Allan White, who is working on a PhD on the Reformation in Aberdeen, for bringing a number of examples to my attention.

20 I. Flett, 'The conflict of Reformation and democracy in the Geneva of Scotland, 1443–1610' (unpublished M Phil thesis, University of St Andrews, 1981), p. 105.

21 Wormald, *Court, Kirk and Community*, p. 119.

22 Sandeman Library, Perth, MS Burgh Court Books B59/12/2, fos. 34–60; Pitcairn, *Trials*, ii, 192–208. See also M. Lee, *Government by Pen: Scotland under James VI and I* (Chicago, 1980), p. 15.

23 Wormald, *Court, Kirk and Community*, p. 159.

24 *Edin Burgh Recs*, iii, p. 14; iv, pp. 325–6.

25 Lynch, *Edinburgh and the Reformation*, pp. 64n, 373, 378.

26 D. Macniven, 'Merchant and trader in Aberdeen in the early seventeenth century' (unpublished M Litt thesis, University of Aberdeen, 1977), pp. 96–100.

27 Devine, 'Merchant class', p. 99.

28 Aberdeen Town Council Archives, MS Stent Rolls (1592–1639); Edinburgh City Archives, MS Stent Rolls, vols i-ii; The Edinburgh tax roll of 1583 is printed in Lynch, *Edinburgh and the Reformation*, pp. 378–92.

29 Lynch, *Edinburgh and the Reformation*, pp. 63, 161, 378; the tax rolls of 1565 and 1583 are printed in apps xi and xii.

30 Cf. Reynolds, *History of English Medieval Towns*, pp. 140–1.

31 J. Brown, ed, *Scottish Society in the Fifteenth Century* (London, 1977), p. 71.

32 *Ibid.*, 71–2.

33 See Dickinson and Duncan, *Scottish from the Earliest Times*, p. 287, and T. C. Smout, *A History of the Scottish People, 1560–1830* (London, 1969), p. 160.

34 I am grateful to Mrs Marion Stavert, who is preparing an edition of the guild book for publication, for this information.

35 T. C. Smout. 'The Glasgow merchant community in the seventeenth century', *Scot. Hist. Review*, xlvii (1968), pp. 59–60.

36 Gordon and Dicks, *Scottish urban History*, p. 7.

37 Smout, 'Glasgow merchant community', pp. 68–70. Macniven in his study of Aberdeen has tried, with some success, to minimise the differences between the workings of the burgh constitution of Glasgow and Aberdeen; see 'Merchant and trader', pp. 290–7. More success might be had elsewhere.

38 These points all come from the researches of Mr James Brown whose thesis on the Edinburgh merchant community, 1600–1638, will provide the first detailed analysis of early seventeenth-century mercantile enterprise. Cf. Devine, 'Merchant class', pp. 104–07.

39 The phrase was used both in the decreet and its ratification by parliament; see *Edin. Burgh Recs.*, iv, 267; *Acts of the Parliament of Scotland* (APS), iii, p 361.

40 See G. Donaldson, ed., *Scottish Historical Documents* (Edinburgh, 1970), pp. 84–5.

41 N. Macdougall, *James III: a Political Study* (Edinburgh, 1982), p. 202.

42 *APS*, ii, 178, c 14.

43 Dickinson and Duncan, *Scotland from the Earliest Times*, p. 285.

44 *Edin Burgh Recs*, iv, p. 272.

45 W. G. Hoskins, 'The Elizabethan merchants of Exeter', in S. T. Bindoff, J. Hurstfield and C. H. Williams, eds, *Elizabethan Government and Society* (London, 1961), p. 165.

46 Such as the riot in Edinburgh in 1543. See Lynch, *Edinburgh and the Reformation*, pp. 68–9.

47 *Ibid.*, 70; A. J. Warden, *Burgh Laws of Dundee* (London, 1872), p. 338.

48 Wormald, *Court, Kirk and Community*, p. 46.

49 P. H. Ramsey, *Tudor Economic Problems* (London, 1966), pp. 160–61; Lynch, *Edinburgh and the Reformation*, pp. 19–21.

50 M. Lynch, 'From privy kirk to burgh church: an alternative view of the process of protestantisation', in N. Macdougall, ed., *Church, Politics and Society in Scotland, 1450–1929* (Edinburgh, 1983), p. 88.

51 I am grateful to Fr Allan White for this information.

52 *Burghs Convention Recs*, i, pp. 89, 262, 362, 388; ii, 35.

Early Modern Rural Society and Economy

ARTICLE 34A
IN THE BEGINNING: THE TENANTS OF SCONE ABBEY IN THE EARLY SIXTEENTH CENTURY

Extracted from MHB Sanderson 2002 *A Kindly Place? Living in Sixteenth Century Scotland*, East Linton (Tuckwell Press), 13–17.

The [early] rentals, of which those for the fifteenth century are fullest, cover the period 1466 to 1566. They are the record of the setting of the ground, naming the tenants and stating the conditions of their tenure. The land was set in various portions, from halves down to eighths, portions varying in size on the same settlement. Holdings were commonly granted for three, five or nineteen years, for several terms of three or five years, and even in the fifteenth century for life, or for life and to an heir afterwards. Some of the life-leases were said to have been granted by Abbot Thomas de Camera who died in 1465. By contrast land was occasionally held 'by tolerance' or 'at the abbot's will' without a formal tack (lease).

Share- or joint-tenancies might exist side by side on the same fermtoun. In 1466 half the Kirktoun of Blair was set to John Salmond and the other half to John Herries and William Chalmer; three separate quarters of Cambusmichael were set to three individual tenants and the remaining quarter to two. A number of settlements were set jointly 'to the husbandmen therof', who were named in some years and not in others.

There was nothing static about the pattern of tenancy, the number of tenants, their names and the size of their holdings changing in some fermtouns from time to time. In 1466 the Mains of Clien was set to eight husbandmen jointly 'at the abbotis will' but by 1520 it was leased in eighths to individuals, some of whom in 1543 received life-leases with power to create subtenants. After a reversal in their fortunes in 1548 when the land was leased for life to one of the Commendator's sons (probably with compensation to the occupants), the tenants recovered their possession (no doubt with compensation to Hepburn this time) and at least five families were eventually able to take feus of their holdings. As happened elsewhere tenants exchanged land, compensating one another for their resignations, in effect operating a local property market at tenant level. Changes in tenants' names on a settlement need not always indicate the end of a family's interest or presence there; land passed to relatives such as sons-in-law, nephews, nieces and cousins as part of the arrangements for family provision. When the landward line of the family failed, a burgess relative from Perth or Dundee might inherit.

Life for the tenants of Scone abbey in the century covered by the early rentals was a mixed experience of continuity and change, uncertainty and opportunity. Some who disappear for a time turn up again in the same location, others elsewhere, probably as a result of the exchanges which were always possible with the superior's consent. Tenants who had been long in possession might become fairly prosperous. The Small family as single tenants held the lands of Fotherans by life-leases 'and one heir' from at least 1465 until William Small feued the land in 1560 together with the walkmill [fulling mill] which his family had leased since 1481. When he died in 1584 his moveable goods were worth nearly £2,000 and he owed no debts. His 29 drawing oxen and £100 of household plenishings suggest a prosperous living. He was able to write, subscribing a deed of 1564 with his own hand. Thomas Small one of four feuars of that surname at Kinnochtry, who died in 1592 also in a prosperous condition, came from a branch of the Small family who held their portions of Kinnochtry from at least 1465 when Andrew Small received a life-lease from Abbot Thomas along with his neighbours the Thanes who also survived to become feuars. It is customary to see the coming of feu-ferm as bringing the tenants who could afford it the kind of security which would encourage them to develop their farms and so prosper. However, it may also be that tenants-turned-feuars like William Small of Fotherans and Thomas Small portioner of Kinnochtry also built on the advantages of long-term possession and a knowledge of the land which their families had worked for a hundred years. And there were others like them.

However, the early rentals reveal the presence of others besides the tenants with an interest in the land. Over the years a number of lairds and their relatives took leases of abbey property. Some of these tacksmen were more influential than others, from lairds – and lords – themselves to the dependent members of their extensive kin-networks. Under non-resident tacksmen the inhabitants would become sub-tenants. Sometimes the tacksman may have wanted to remove them to make way for subtenants of his own choice. Legally the existing tenants could not be removed until their current tacks had run out, and they would expect compensation for their *kindness*. These rights were not always respected, which led to many court actions against alleged wrongful eviction.

ARTICLE 34B
THE FARMING TOWNSHIP

Extracted from RA Dodgshon 1981 *Land and Society in Early Scotland*, Oxford (Oxford University Press), 146–51.

Whether a toun was held by one tenant or whether it was in the hands of a number greatly affected its character. In the case of the former, the tenant was confronted only with the problem of how best to farm the land. In the latter, the tenants faced a wider range of problems, not least of which was the problem of how best to divide their respective interests in the toun. Two strategies were adopted. Some farmed the township as a single unit and then divided the produce. The majority, however, preferred to divide the land. Again, by far the majority of those who divided the land did so on a strip basis, each tenant having his share subdivided into strips that were scattered across the arable land of the toun, intermixed cheek by jowl with those of his co-tenants. This systematic intermixing of each tenant's strips across the arable of the toun was called runrig or rundale.

Of course, the intermixture of land in the form of strips was common throughout medieval Europe. This being so, the use of a special term of description, or runrig, to describe open fields in Scotland has led many writers to conclude that there must have been something different about their character to justify such a mark of distinction. A number of possible distinguishing features have been proposed. They range from the parallel alignment of strips or their sequential allocation to the periodic reallocation of strips between the various landholders. The last mentioned has been especially popular, partly because it could be used to reinforce the old notion that runrig was a primitive system of landholding, an institution which relates back to the days when society was organized on a tribal basis and private property did not exist. In such a scheme, runrig seems to capture perfectly the midway stage between the decay of communal property and the rise of private property. There can be no doubt that each of the aforementioned characteristics – the parallel alignment of strips, their sequential allocation or their periodic realloca- tion – have some basis in fact. However, none of them is entirely convincing. When estate plans depicting runrig become available in the eighteenth century, they show that not all strips by any means were laid out in a parallel fashion, nor had they been doled out in a strict sequence. At the same time it is clear from a number of sources that not all runrig systems were subject to reallocation. Many were reallocated only occasionally. More serious, in the case of those examples which involved feuars and landowners, there was an undoubted stability of layout.

A way out of this dilemma of runrig's meaning is to focus on its tenurial background. Briefly, two types of tenure can be recognized in respect of multi- ple-tenant touns. The least common form was for tenants to hold by a joint tenure, each tenant being 'severally and conjointly' responsible for the management and rent of the entire toun and not just a portion of it. Alongside such touns, but far more numerous, were touns in which each tenant held a separately defined share. These separate shares are manifest either because they held 'per tak partes' each having a separate tack for his share, or because they were each accorded a separate share or portion of rent in a rental. Logically, since runrig was an intermixture of each person's separate holding and not a common or undifferentiated possession of a toun, then it must surely relate to this second form of multiple tenure.

The significance of this *share*holding system of tenure was twofold. First, it meant that tenants or landowners had to divide their notional shares into actual holdings on the ground before they could take up possession and begin farming. This is the reason why runrig holdings give the appearance of being re-divided or re-allocated periodically. Furthermore, linking re-allocation with the need to divide shares into actual holdings at the start of each new lease-set or when new landowners were introduced into a share of the toun helps to explain why the frequency of re-allocaton appeared to vary so much from toun to toun. Thus, if the shares of a toun were held on a year to year basis, then it was possible for re-allocationto take place every year, as some definitions suppose of *all* runrig touns. However, where shares were held on a long tack, or where feuars and landowners were involved, re-allocation would occur less frequently, perhaps only at the outset of the tenure and no more. However, in many parts of the Lowlands, the formal division of shares into holdings on the ground did not always accompany their leasing or conveyancing. Instead the problem was circumvented by tenants or landowners being given shares already laid out as holdings and identified through the name of their previous occupier.

ARTICLE 34C
ENCOURAGING IMPROVEMENT

Extracted from ID Whyte 1995 'Before the Improvers: Agricultural and Landscape Change in Lowland Scotland *c.1660–c.1750*', *Scottish Archives*, I, 33–4.

The changes which occurred in Scottish agriculture during the later seventeenth and early eighteenth centuries were underpinned by a series of acts passed by the Scottish Parliament between 1661 and 1695. It is not clear exactly which land-owners were responsible for drafting and promoting the various statutes but, taken together, they represent a sustained effort at encouraging improvement on a scale and at a pace that was realistic in the contemporary economic climate. The earliest act in 1661 was designed to encourage enclosure for tree planting, crops and livestock by means of tax concessions, facilitating the diversion of roads and sharing the cost of enclosures on estate marches. In 1669 this act was supple-mented by provisions for the exchange of parcels of land to straighten property boundaries. In 1685, the tax concessions on enclosed land were renewed. That the legislation was actually used is shown by a number of applications to the Privy Council to divert roads to allow enclosure. Agreements for straightening marches to aid enclosure are also known. In addition the acts are cited in the records of some Barony Courts. This indicates that the statutes were not dead-letter legisla-tion, as has sometimes been assumed, but were widely-known and actively used, by proprietors. The programme of legislation culminated in 1695 in two well-known acts relating to the division of commonties and lands lying runrig. The legislation used straightforward legal processes involving the Court of Session and Sheriff Courts.

    It is easy to make too much of this late seventeenth-century legislation. The act relating to runrig was not the general enclosure act some writers have claimed. It only involved land which lay runrig between different proprietors; not, as was more common, between tenants of the same landlord. Tenant runrig could be consolidated by proprietors at any time without recourse to any statutes or legal processes.

In terms of immediate impact on the rural landscape the most marked change in the later seventeenth and early eighteenth centuries was the enclosure of series of fields or 'parks' on the policies surrounding the castles and mansions of many Lowland landowners. There are indications that this trend may have started earlier in the seventeenth century, during the prosperous 1620s and 1630s, but it did not become widespread until after the Restoration, with improvement of existing fortified houses or their replacement by neo-classical style mansions.

ARTICLE 34D
WAS IMPROVEMENT SLOW?

Extracted from RA Dodgshon 1981 *Land and Society in Early Scotland*, Oxford (Oxford University Press), 264–5.

Recent papers by Whittington and Whyte have suggested that the changes wrought over roughly the period 1650 to 1760 may have anticipated the Improvers' Movement of the late eighteenth century to such an extent that it questions the neat chronology of the latter. Whilst accepting the importance of these changes, the present writer hesitates to see them as in any way invalidating the concept of a discrete post-1760 Improvers' Movement. The changes which occurred before then are best seen as achieving gains by adjustment rather than improvement. The fact that more tenants were drawn into market transactions can be put down to the conversion of multures [proportion of grain due to the miller] or grain rents. The fact that more grain was being marketed can be put down to tenant reduction, a concentration of resources in the hands of a few. The expansion of cattle production can be seen as a redirection of these resources. From out of such changes there emerged farmers and estates tied firmly to the market and in a position to start the long process of accumulating the capital necessary for improvement. The laying out of new policies and the building of stone farmsteads over this period may represent the first signs of this capital being conspicuously invested. However, this commercial sector of farming must be kept in perspective. With less than half of all touns in the hands of single tenants, and therefore a high proportion of holdings per tenant on the small side, it would be optimistic to see the number of farmers with commercially viable units as constituting more than a third of the total. If we add those factors which inhibited the strategy of farmers, then the number actually engaged wholeheartedly in production for the market may have been as little as a quarter. Not until the spurt in tenant reduction and holding amalgamation during the closing decades of this period, or during the 1730s, 40s and 50s, is the balance likely to have been finally tipped towards a market-orientated system.

ARTICLE 34E
POVERTY OR PROSPERITY? – COMPARING INTERPRETATIONS

Extracted from ID Whyte 1998 'Poverty or Prosperity? Rural Society in Lowland Scotland in the Late Sixteenth and Early Seventeenth Centuries', *Scottish Economic and Social History*, 18, 19–32.

What was happening in agriculture and rural society in the decades between the Reformation and the outbreak of Revolution in 1638? There is no doubt that rural society experienced a range of pressures from the mid-sixteenth century onwards, even leaving aside purely political and religious issues. The course and scale of the sixteenth-century price rise has now been accurately charted by Gibson and Smout while Brown has examined in detail its impact on the nobility. Sanderson has put the feuing movement into perspective, showing that some sitting tenants benefited by acquiring feus of their holdings while those who did not may have suffered from insecurity, rack renting and, in some cases, displacement. However, the long-term impact of the feuing movement on rural society is still far from clear; for example, its effects on the land market in the late sixteenth and early seventeenth centuries remain to be explored.

The end of the sixteenth century seems to have been a bleak period. On the other hand, arguments have been put forward suggesting that the later sixteenth and early seventeenth centuries were not a bad time for everyone on the land. The idea that tenant families who obtained feus of their lands are likely to have prospered in the long term as inflation steadily eroded the real value of their mainly cash feu duties is a familiar one. But even tenants who did not get feus may have prospered. This case has been forcefully made by Makey. He suggested that, in the Western Lowlands, where principal rents were mostly in money, rents lagged behind price increases or even remained static, despite inflation. He points out that while there was nothing, in theory, to prevent landowners from raising rents, there were major inhibiting factors which may have prevented this. These included the power of custom inherited from a pre-inflationary era, especially the survival of various forms of customary tenure, the censure of the church, and the inability of landowners to perceive the long-term scale of price rises operating behind the smokescreen of sharp inter-annual fluctuations.

Under these conditions, Makey considers that many tenants in the western Lowlands were able to prosper and accumulate considerable cash reserves. This leads naturally to the question of tenure and leases, a topic on which there is more apparent disagreement than on any other relating to rural society at this period. Sanderson has suggested that in the early and mid sixteenth century long leases were common on ecclesiastical estates and, she presumed, on lay ones. However, on crown estates like Southdean annual leases appear to have been normal. Wormald, following John Major, believed that there was a predominance of short leases in the early sixteenth century, while Grant believed that short leases were normal right into the early seventeenth century. Brown has followed Sanderson in suggesting that in the troubled mid sixteenth century there were incentives for landowners to grant longer leases to secure manpower on their estates. When these leases ran out in the early seventeenth century, he considers that landowners then seized the opportunity to raise rents. This argument implicitly shifts rent increases backwards from the 1630s, as Makey suggests, to the first decade of the seventeenth century. Moreover, if leases granted in the mid sixteenth century were only running out half a century later they must have been at least liferent tacks, perhaps ones for two lives. The widespread existence of such leases has yet to be demonstrated. Gibson and Smout, on the other hand, have argued for a policy of short leases and tenancies at will taking over in the later sixteenth century from longer leases granted in earlier decades. Devine and Lythe, following Donaldson, took the contrary view that there was a change from short to long leases in the early seventeenth century.

These conflicting suggestions can perhaps be resolved in part by suggesting that each represents one piece of a complex jigsaw which incorporated a good deal of variation locally as well as through time. The most interesting revision of ideas regarding what was happening in rural society in Lowland Scotland at this period has come from Macinnes. First, he believes that the nobility and gentry in the western Lowlands managed their estates efficiently and rigorously to maximise income as a response to inflationary pressures. Unlike Brown, who believes that agricultural improvements were few in the early seventeenth century, Macinnes suggests that real improvements in agricultural productivity were achieved in the first quarter of the seventeenth century in the western Lowlands. While it has been widely acknowledged that the early seventeenth century, until the famine of 1623, was a more favourable period for rural society than the 1590s, as shown indirectly by improvements in the finances of the nobility, Macinnes paints an altogether more positive picture. The improvements which he identifies included the commutation of services and rents in kind to money payments, the use of written leases, and the rationalisation of farm structures including reductions in the numbers of tenancies on multiple-tenant farms, a shift towards single-tenant farms, and the consolidation of land from runrig. He is not convinced that landowners were as hard hit by the effects of inflation as Makey believed. Macinnes agrees that rents did rise in the 1620s and 1630s, but claims that much of this was more apparent than real. The process of holding amalgamation might have pushed some former tenants or their sons downwards into the ranks of cottars, but some elements of the tenantry at least seem to have been responding positively until economic conditions started deteriorating during the mid-1630s. The picture is of a society with less stress and more co-operation between landlord and tenant than Makey described.

Books and articles mentioned in this text

Gibson, A.J.S. and Smout, T.C. 1995 *Prices, Food and Wages in Scotland, 1550–1780*, Cambridge (Cambridge University Press).

Brown, K.M. 1989 'Noble Indebtedness in Scotland between the Reformation and the Revolution', in *Historical Research*, 62, 260–75; 'Aristocratic Finances and the Origins of the Scottish Revolution', *English Historical Review*, 104, 46–87.

Sanderson, M.H.B. 1982 *Scottish Rural Society in the Sixteenth Century*, Edinburgh (John Donald).

Macinnes, A.I. 1991 *Charles I and the Making of the Covenanting Movement*, Edinburgh (John Donald).

Makey, W. 1979 *The Church of the Covenant*, Edinburgh (John Donald).

Wormald, J. 1981 *Court, Kirk and Community: Scotland 1470–1625*, London (Arnold).

Devine, T.M. and Lythe, S.G.E. 1971 'The Economy of Scotland under James VI: A Revision Article', *Scottish Historical Review*, 50, 97.

Grant, I.F. 1930 *The Social and Economic Development of Scotland before 1603*, Edinburgh.

Donaldson, G. 1965 *Scotland: James V to James VII*, Edinburgh (Oliver and Boyd).

ARTICLE 34F
LANDLORD–TENANT RELATIONS IN THE ISLANDS

Extracted from FJ Shaw 1980 *The Northern and Western Islands of Scotland: their economy and society in the seventeenth century*, Edinburgh (John Donald), 197–201.

Despite the adoption many generations before of the feudal rule of primogeniture for landholding and the associated emergence of the chiefs as owners of the land as well as rulers of the people, society in the Western Isles was still undeniably rooted in the old Celtic kin-based tradition. At the foot of the social scale, the ordinary tenant or subtenant was seen as more than simply an agricultural labourer. Since the power and prestige of a chief was judged largely in terms of the sheer numerical strength of his following, the number of loyal tenants even at the humblest level was seen as a matter of considerable importance. Thus in Hebridean society there was still a sense that each class had a distinctive and traditional function as part of an organic whole, and that each had something essential to contribute to the wellbeing of the whole community.

The old traditions of hospitality, entertainment, and support for many of the time-honoured Gaelic professions were being continued, albeit on a reduced scale. There is also evidence of the survival well into the seventeenth century of another Celtic social custom involving the chiefs – the practice of sending some of the children of the family out to be fostered by respected members of the clan.

Between chiefs and the ordinary labourers of the soil there is also evidence of a relationship beyond that of master and rent-paying tenant. For the tenant it meant that if the prospect of improving his lot were small, he could at least look to his landlord for help in difficult times.

There is no doubt, however, that the old values and relationships were beginning to suffer some erosion, and most of all in the islands of the south-west. By the end of the seventeenth century not only Lewis, Islay and Jura, but also most of Mull as well as Tiree, Colonsay and a number of smaller islands, had passed out of the hands of the old ruling families; and in Lismore and one or two of the other inshore islands off the coast of Argyll there had been a good deal of relatively small-scale feuing. All this was bound to lead to some weakening of the traditional bonds between landlord and tenant, and this was most noticeable in the seventeenth century in the more commercially minded attitude being taken by landlords like the Campbells of Cawdor towards the granting of tacks, with its ominous implications for the future of the middlemen of clan society. But even where lands had not changed hands, the old relationships were under threat from the gradually changing tastes and rapidly deteriorating financial position of most of the chiefs.

Even before the times of the Stewart earls of Orkney and the abrogation of the Norse laws in 1611, society in the Northern Isles had nothing like the degree of unity that is evident within the clan structure of the Western Isles. The relationship between the larger landowners in the Northern Isles and their tenants was also a very different one. There was no feeling that together they constituted a community in which each fulfilled an essential social as well as economic role. On the contrary, in most cases the landowning families had no lengthy historical association with their estates; they were not looking to their principal tenants as local administrators, professional servants or military organisers, and they had no particular interest in the sheer numbers or sense of loyalty of their tenantry as a whole. Their primary interest in their tenantry was in their ability to pay rent. Tacks granted to larger tenants contained few if any financial concessions.

For the ordinary labouring tenant who proved unable to pay his rent the outlook was bleak. Plainly this was not a society where the majority of tenants could rely on their landlords as a source of help in time of need. Instead they depended almost entirely on the assistance of their family and friends. For odallers, of course, this had always been the case, and what is known about provisions for old age and infirmity in seventeenth-century Orkney and Shetland seems to have derived largely from odal practices.

In the later years of the seventeenth century the situation seems to have been worst among the tenants on the various lands belonging to the crown. Their landlords at this period were themselves tacksmen on short leases, and to make any appreciable profit on the hard bargains driven by the crown, they could not afford to take a long-term view of their relationship with the tenants.

There may not have been much to choose between the material standards of the average small tenant in the Northern Isles and his counterpart in the Hebrides, and certainly, during the famines of the 1690s, there was severe hardship in the west as well as the north; but in the background and social philosophy of their major landlords, and indeed in the complete landowning structure, the differences between the Hebrides and the Northern Isles could hardly have been more marked.

ARTICLE 34G
THE FORTUNES OF THE FEUARS ON TAYSIDE

Extracted from MHB Sanderson 2002 *A Kindly Place? Living in Sixteenth-Century Scotland*, East Linton (Tuckwell Press), 25–31.

For those tenants [of Scone abbey] who became heritable proprietors the feu charters which brought increased security also brought many burdens and expenses. Initial outlay included the down-payment; the cost of confirmation at Rome and/or from the crown, a considerable expense which was often deferred to the next generation and in some cases was jointly borne by the feuars-portioners of the settlement; the annual feu-duty which was usually asked for in money and which, although it did not increase in the long term, represented an increase on the old rent; as well as periodic *grassums*. Then there were the expenses incurred when the heir succeeded: double feu-duty, the cost of recognition and *serving* of the heir and obtaining new instruments of *sasine*. Many families must have found recovery from the initial outlay difficult and in some cases impossible. A feu charter was not a safeconduct to prosperity for all, though it was for some.

The pattern of landholding was not more static among the feuars than among the tenants. Financial and other difficulties caused many new proprietors to exploit their heritage as they had formerly used their customary rights, temporarily or irrevocably. Financial problems, particularly debt, among the rural population existed before and apart from feuing. Testaments and other legal records show the ceaseless borrowing and lending of money among neighbours, and the debts incurred through failure to repay borrowing in kind, such as the hire of work animals and equipment, seed, victual and other necessities. The situation continued among feuars as among tenants. The records of chancery and Perth sheriff court contain evidence of lands being *apprised* from feuars of Scone and *adjudged* to their creditors and others who had taken them to law. The sources do not always state the reason for the apprising but it was most likely for debt. A number of creditors were burgesses and professionals with money to lend to struggling rural proprietors. This predicament was no more common among feuars of kirklands, however, than among other heritable proprietors, as the huge quantities of legal papers relating to debt in the archives of landed families make plain. There is illuminating if incomplete evidence of the expedients resorted to by the feuars in an attempt to survive. Besides receiving the rents of subtenants they might provide themselves with additional income by subfeuing the land, a prevalent and complicated practice which was well underway on the kirklands by the late sixteenth century. The land might be subfeued to friends, neighbours or fellow-portioners. In 1596, for example, John Sharp, whose father and widowed grandmother had taken a feu of a quarter of the Mains of Clien and six additional acres in 1561, subfeued part of his inheritance called Pitlowybank and Lathouse to James Hunter of Over Pitlowy, whose father William Hunter had feued Pitlowy in 1562 with its responsibility for flocks of sheep. In 1618 John Ogilvy, second-generation portioner of a third of the Weltoun of Creuchies, subfeued his portion to Alexander Ashunder, while a fellow-portioner, Thomas Wichtand resigned his to Thomas Cuming, Wichtand's forebears had leased the land since 1481.

Another means of raising money, normally in order to borrow, was by the endemic practice of *wadsetting* which pledged the land or an annual rent lifted from it annually, to the creditor until the money was repaid. The papers relating to the creation and final cancellation of a wadset – and in many cases its transfer to a third party – must have swelled the contents of many a new proprietor's kist of *evidents*.

Of the two versions of pledging the grant of an annual rent in return for the loan was the more popular with the feuars of Scone. Where the land itself was pledged it often remained unredeemed for years, the creditor adopting the designation *wadsetter*. Many a wadsetter became the proprietor through the ultimate inability of the debtor to repay. On 12 July 1650 Patrick Martin, portioner of Newmill (on the former Scone abbey estates), and his son borrowed 2100 merks from Thomas Meek in Ledcassy (on the former Coupar Angus abbey estates) in return for which they wadset him an annual rent of 120 merks from the rents of their part of Newmill, and from a quarter of Craigmakerran. Patrick's forebear and namesake had feued half of the Newmill and its lands from Scone in August 1560, and the family had acquired the quarter of Craigmakerran some-time during the early seventeenth century. David Elliot, heir to his maternal grandfather John Sanders who had feued a third of the Weltoun of Blair in 1559, postponed having himself entered heir for four years before being ordered by the court to do so in 1662 in order that his creditor William Haliburton of Buttergask might receive a charter of the land apprised from him for a debt of £2134 13s 4d. The land was under wadset and Elliot reserved the right to redeem it in spite of his inherited financial problems.

As a last resort in desperate circumstances there was the alienation of the land, or at least moving out; there is rarely a clue as to where those who sold out went. In May 1586 John Watson in Balbarrow 'sometime in Innergowrie' sold his part of Invergowrie to Patrick, brother of Lord Gray. [In] 1593 David Morris, 'sometime portioner of Innergowrie' leased his house and yard there to his daughter and son-in-law, in terms of their marriage contract, presumably having himself gone to live elsewhere.

Many feuars of Scone appear to have lived above subsistence level. Both feuars and tenants handled money and had enough surplus in cash and kind to lend to neighbours. Surviving testaments give some indication of how well they fared in the second half of the [sixteenth] century. The amount of net estate depended on the level of debt due to and owing by the testator. John Watson in Balgey who ended up with only £14 17s 6d free gear [i.e. net estate] had an inventory of £1483 16s 8d. His 24 oxen, 82 sheep and £88 worth of household plenishings suggest a sizeable farm and comfortable home for someone of his status. He was obviously struggling financially, however, since he owed over £1500 to other people. He was just saved from insolvency by the fact that a few people owed him some money . . .

[One] feuar whose debts exceeded his assets, Thomas Dog, had acquired two eighths of Craigmakerran in 1560 on the resignation of the initial feuar Patrick Martin. Yet his family also survived for some time, his great-grandson and namesake being served heir in 1621. Ranald Robertson who took feus of two quarters of Sherifftoun in 1561 seems to have given up farming by the time he died in 1588, having no goods but his household plenishings and clothes, and is designated, 'sometime portioner of Sherifftoun' . . . Much more prosperous were William and John Soutar at Wester Banchory who survived Sir John Bellenden's land-speculation to feu their long-established holdings in 1563, and Thomas Small at Kinnochtry and William Small at Fotherans, whose families, like that of the Soutars, had been in possession since mid-fifteenth century. [These feuars left over £800, over £1200, over £1300 and over £1900 respectively.] The family circumstances of some feuars are revealed in the marriage contracts of the next generation. Some fathers purchased land from other feuars in order to provide for sons and daughters. In 1618 John Cumming, portioner of the Weltoun of Blair, acquired a third of these lands from another feuar, Thomas Wichtand, already mentioned, in order to settle it on his future daughter-in-law, Elspeth, daughter of William Donaldson in the Cottoun of Ruthven. In 1620 Constantine Scott portioner of Kinnochtry purchased another quarter there which he granted to his son Patrick and his wife. Successful feuars' children might marry outwith their social background, like Elizabeth daughter of Patrick Blair portioner of Liff who married a son of Andrew Rollo of Duncrub in 1593. Perhaps we should think of tenant families of long-standing, many of whom became feuars in the sixteenth century and 'bonnet lairds' in the seventeenth, as akin to yeomen, who in the kin-based networks of Scottish society were not so removed socially from the gentry and cadets of noble families as their descendants were to become. Certainly, intermarriage 'upwards' is a phenomenon among the feuars of kirklands in other parts of the country besides Perthshire.

There are no complete rentals or estate accounts for the Scone estates listing all proprietors in the late-seventeenth or early-eighteenth centuries. There are no [relevant] Poll Tax records for Perthshire. The general impression from those rentals that do survive is that of the amalgamation of small properties into unified estates. A rental for 1667–8 which lists outstanding dues only, names more tenants than proprietors, but it does name John Herries, portioner of the Weltoun of Creuchies, George Soutar, portioner of Wester Banchory, Edward Montago at Liff, Alexander Martin at Newmill, John Scott at Cambusmichael, Constantine Snell at Balgarvie and Limpotts, and Patrick Anderson at Ardgilzean, all of whom were descendants of those who feued these lands one hundred years before. The memory of the early feuars is long enshrined in legal documents. A crown charter to Robert Patullo commissary clerk of Dunkeld in 1725, as heir to his father in the lands of Kinnochtry, identifies the four component portions, even naming their 'former'(i.e. sixteenth-century) owners, among them John and Robert Small whose forebears had ploughed the land before the battle of Flodden.

ARTICLE 34H
THE OLD ORDER: LOOKING BACK

Extracted from TM Devine 1994 *The Transformation of Rural Scotland: Social Change and Agrarian Economy, 1660–1815,* Edinburgh (John Donald), 2–4, 15–16.

The 'Revolution in Manners' of the eighteenth century was still in the future but domestic accounts for the later seventeenth century indicate growing purchases of clothing, furniture and paintings, and increased spending on building and travel. The new concerns with the economic potential of landed estates was in large part a direct result of these rising levels of expenditure. Landed property had to be made to yield more cash income.

The capacity of the rural economy to produce this has also been address in recent scholarship. Traditionally, Scottish agriculture before the era of Improvement in the eighteenth century has had a bad press. It was seen as inert in structure, primitive in technique and wasteful both of land and labour. It is now recognised, however, that much of this criticism reflected the views of the 'improving' writers of the later eighteenth century.

Modern scholarship has gone a long way to rehabilitate the rural economy in the era before improvement. There have been two parallel developments. First, the bias in much improving writing has been recognised and an effort made to understand the old system within its own terms rather than by the standards of a later and quite different type of society. Second, most recent work has depended on the sifting of original material from the seventeenth century.

The conclusion that is emerging as a result of the enquiries completed to date is that the older agrarian economy was more successful than previously thought. The achievement of recent research has, therefore, been to present the old agrarian economy in a more positive light and to demonstrate its flexibility and capacity for change.

In every social system there exists a tension between the forces of change and continuity. Rural Scotland in the later seventeenth century was no exception . . .

The tenant class, already a minority in the rural population, albeit a substantial one in certain regions, seems to have contracted even further. The legal right to land, as guaranteed by a verbal or written lease, was probably confined to fewer individuals in 1700 than in 1600. By corollary, the majority of the country population, while having for the most part access to the land at some time in their lives, had only a tenuous connection with it and could relatively easily be displaced through the decision of proprietors or principal tenants. Everywhere there was an intricate hierarchy connecting the various gradations of the social structure.

Yet the evidence presented here suggests that it would be an exaggeration to conclude that the rural Lowlands in general were on the move by 1700. Movement occurred but it was essentially *within* rather than *of* the prevailing structure. It would appear that the forces of continuity were still more powerful than the forces of change. There were several indicators of this. First, the vast majority of the population were heavily dependent on the land and land-related employment. Second, recognition of the existence and growing importance of a market sector cannot obscure the continuing significance of subsistence relationships. In an important sense this book is about the triumph of commercial forces and relationships in Scottish rural society in the eighteenth century. In 1700 that process, in so far as it was to affect and mould the social structure below landlord level, was only in its early stages.

James VI's Architects and their Architecture

A MacKechnie 2000 *in* J Goodare and M Lynch (eds), *The Reign of James VI*, East Linton (Tuckwell Press), 154–69.

> Watch towers and thundr'ng walls vain fences prove
> No guards to monarchs like their people's love.
> Jacobus VI Rex, Anna Regina, 1606.[1]

Documentation casts little light upon James VI's thoughts on architecture, possibly because his cultural interests were mainly literary and philosophical. But important architectural investments were made both during his minority, and in his adulthood, when palace-building was revived (albeit not on the scale of some of his predecessors). James recognised architecture's propagandist potential, utilising it to broadcast his image of Stewart majesty. Consideration, though, of his architecture is hampered: mostly visual, fragmentary, primary or analogous evidence has to be pieced together, because iconoclasts savaged his chapels, Holyrood was rebuilt, and the other palaces spoiled through destruction, inappropriate usage or neglect.

The royal works contained a developed organisational structure, but it has not been clear who was responsible for architectural design. The following discussion stems partly from a seeming contradiction in past interpretations: that in the 1590s, the king's master of works designed royal palaces, while by the 1610s, this responsibility is said to have lain with the king's master mason.[2] Reconsideration of available evidence suggests that, by our period, it was the former of these whose role was central in palace design. Masters of works also became important as disseminators, through architecture, of royal propaganda, so some ways in which architecture related to James's kingship are also suggested. Because the masters of works are still hardly known, yet seem now to be crucial in formulation of architecture in this period, it seems worthwhile to highlight their names and something of their careers. But first, some contextualisation is required.

I

Edinburgh's developing role as 'capital' increasingly associated aristocracy and government with the burgh. Satellite houses for lairds were built round about, while the royal palaces were also in the east-central region. All this encouraged a distinction between court (and courtier) architecture, centred in these parts, and derivative regional variations where local schools of mason-architects operated.[3]

These are most evident in the west and north-east – a pattern still visible in the early twentieth century, though by then any sense in the west of derivativeness was gone.

James inherited a brilliant – arguably, sometimes, precocious – series of royal palaces, the legacy essentially of James I and his successors until James V.[4] Mary had refitted interiors at Holyrood, but built no great new palaces. During James's earlier years, palaces were sometimes neglected. A major palace-building programme was unnecessary, and little royal building was done until the 1590s, when Dunfermline was rebuilt for Queen Anna. But others – including the Regents Mar and Morton – were to build, sometimes on a large scale.

James's birth-date, 1566, is inscribed over the rusticated entrance to the apartment in Edinburgh's royal palace in which he was born. The reconstruction presumably related to this event, and thus a consideration of the architecture of James's time might commence here.[5] James, of course, had no influence on architecture for some years to come. Yet the element of continuity in architecture was as marked as in music or literature; consideration of the architecture of a given period requires appreciation of the context from which it derived. As in other areas of culture, reference was made to the national, the classical and the Biblical past to inform and to legitimise the present.

Continuity has to be set against a constant programme of innovation, as new ideas were devised or imported. Any important new building had to be innovative. The Marian court – which used imagery from the two most culturally progressive European centres of the age, France and Italy – might have been cosmopolitan, but in many respects it was essentially modelled upon that of France. By James VI's time, politics had lessened the direct French link, validating a readier interest in and interchange with Protestant northern Europe, notably England and Denmark, while a growing emphasis upon classical scholarship was reflected in the young king's own outlook. Classicism was also to serve as a model for the post-1603 'British' Stuart monarchy. Perhaps this was an extension of the imperial symbolism seen in the architecture of James IV, for a vastly-enhanced new 'empire'.

The dismantling of Mary's court, iconoclasm and diminution of ecclesiastical patronage of the visual arts represented a cultural reversal. It was perhaps counterbalanced by a new stress upon intellectualism and more developed interest in classicism, that was to manifest itself in architecture, which already had a tendency towards unadorned monumentality.[6] James's reign witnessed consolidation of the process begun after 1542 (and completed post-1689) when rural aristocratic houses became the touchstone of fashion, supplanting the role held formerly by the church and the royal palaces. Church architecture also broadcast messages: the classicism of Burntisland (1589), related to contemporary Dutch presbyterian plans, while the pseudo-antique neo-Gothic of Archbishop Spottiswoode's Dairsie (1621) asserted the antiquity of episcopalianism.[7]

The earlier decades of James's reign saw a vastly increased volume of building, funded primarily through secularisation of church property. This developed the existing aesthetic of externally plain, dignified, stone-built or harled massiveness, but now with a balanced asymmetry. By 1600, another new courtly fashion existed:

a surer classicism combining symmetrical elevations and outline plans. From about 1620 fashion again changed, introducing more extensive applied decoration – a fashion whose spectacular swan-song was Glasgow College, on the point of becoming artistically old-fashioned when completed *c.* 1660, albeit forward-looking in terms of promoting tenemental street architecture. Attempting to identify the mainstream at any point is not straightforward. It was a web of overlapping tendencies, survivals, revivals and innovations. The verticality and monumentality exemplified by Drochil may have remained dominant throughout our period, but the horizontalising seen at Falkland also reappeared, for instance at Pinkie (1613). Maitland's Lethington (renamed Thirlestane; *c.* 1590) represents something of a hybrid, with the vertically divided façade exemplified by Falkland, but set on a massive, vertically-emphatic structure.

This was the architectural context into which James was born, and which he left behind at his death: a mainstream European tradition, yet distinctive and unique, constantly seeking modernisation.

II

Who, then, was responsible for palace design? Was it (as had been suggested in the case of Dunfermline) the master of works, or was it (as suggested at Linlithgow) the master mason?

Today, the term 'architect' applies to one trained to design buildings and to supervise their erection. In Renaissance thought, the concept of an architect had been set out by Vitruvius, in the first century BC. An architect not only created buildings for clients, but was the Renaissance ideal, the 'universal' individual, whose studies embraced literature, drawing, geometry, arithmetic, philosophy, music, medicine, law and astronomy.[8] The balance of available evidence suggests that this Vitruvian concept of an architect applied in appointment of royal masters of works. James Murray, for instance, as royal master gunner, presumably required surveying skills (including geometry and arithmetic) necessary for architects.[9] Masters of works had expertise in structural technicalities: Murray made official reports on bridges, such as Lasswade.[10] In preparation for an abortive visit by Charles in 1630, he was commissioned to 'assist . . . with his advice . . . anent the preparatiouns requisite to be made and perfytted within . . . [St Giles'] . . . kirk towards his Majesteis coronatioun'.[11] King Charles referred to Murray and to his partner, Anthony Alexander, by the term 'surveyor' ('generall surveyaris and principal maisteris of all his hienes werkis and buildinges' – the English equivalent both in terminology and – in Charles's perception – in post.[12] Alexander studied architecture abroad to qualify him for the mastership.[13] Just as Inigo Jones designed royal buildings for James in England, so at least one of his Scottish counterparts (Murray) is documented as having done likewise. The term 'architect[us]' was used of royal masters of works.[14] In the context of an intellectually based court culture where education centred upon the humanities, the word, surely, was understood in its Vitruvian sense.

William Schaw was a personal friend of royalty, and his being one of two people chosen in 1585 by Sir James Melville of Halhill to negotiate with a Danish delegation demonstrates a special regard. Yet this did not set Schaw apart from the artisan or tradesman. At Doune, in 1581, Robert Drummond was 'his majesties maister of wark, agrear with all the warkmen', duties subsequently performed by Schaw and Murray.[15] The king's master of works is seen – indeed, in his professional capacity, is only ever seen – operating between the patron, on the one hand, and the operative, or artisan, on the other. This was crucial for the Vitruvian role to be fulfilled. Although only for James Murray is there powerful documentary evidence to suggest an architect in the Vitruvian sense, the argument might tentatively be extended to include other masters of works. So who were they?

III

The first master of works in James's reign was Sir William MacDowell (or MacDougall), who in 1536 was overseer at Salisbury quarry. Subsequently (from 1551 at least) master of works, he was probably dead when replaced in 1579, for the post was usually given for life.[16] A cleric, he had the vicarages of Dalmeny, Inch and Leswalt in Galloway.[17] In 1548 he had presentation of a Magdalene chapel at Whitehill, near Musselburgh.[18] His works included James's gallery of 1576–7, comprising the northern 'pile' of the Holyrood north quarter,[19] but he was busier at Edinburgh Castle, where his interventions included the 1566 palace reconstruction for Mary, notable for the above-mentioned doorway and innovative, long, scale staircase within.[20] He was engaged in the post-siege reconstruction from 1573 – 'bigging and reparing of the castell of Edinburgh'.[21] This included the Half-moon Battery and 'bigging of the inner yett within the castell' (the Portcullis Gateway). Its unorthodox main opening contrasted with its 'correct' overdoor aedicule, a formula almost suggestive of Michelangelo's Porta Pia (1562).[22]

This reconstruction was done for the Regent Morton, for whom Drochil was built and Aberdour enlarged, raising the possibility of MacDowell having been involved with either or both these houses. The Portcullis Gateway arch-springer detailing is similar to that at Mar's Wark (dated 1570 and 1572), the Regent Mar's Stirling town house. Each also has an understated overdoor pediment (reduced at Edinburgh to a plinth), and armorial over. Mar and Morton, like Governor Arran at Kinneil in the 1550s, were well-placed to exploit the services of the best architects and craftsmen. The distinctive shafted detailing seen at these two buildings matched that at Carnasserie, begun in the later 1560s for John Carswell, bishop of the Isles. Carswell was also linked with the court, having been chancellor of the Chapel Royal from perhaps 1558 until his death in 1572.[23] Similarities of detail exist at Carnasserie and Torwood (1566). This small group of buildings can be associated with one another and, mostly, with the court. The possibility exists of the same architect influencing some or all of these. Might this be MacDowell?

IV

On 6 April 1579, MacDowell's successor, Sir Robert Drummond of Carnock, was appointed 'maister of all . . . [James's] . . . werkis and places, biggit and to be biggit'.[24] He held office until 1583. A seventeenth-century family history tells that he died in 1592, aged 74, and that he was 'Master and surveyor of all the King's works to King James'. He was grandfather of William Drummond of Hawthornden.[25] Alexander Montgomerie's epitaph is illuminating:

> All buildings brave bids DRUMMOND nou adeu;
> Quhais lyf furthsheu he lude thame by the laiv.
> Quhair sall we craiv sik policie to haiv?
> Quha with him straiv to polish, build, or plante?
> These giftis, I grant, God lent him by the laiv.[26]

God-given gifts of architectural and landscaping skills were his 'by the laiv' – in abundance. This could have applied only to an operative (which Drummond, an aristocrat, was not) or else to a designer or architect. It could hardly have been said of a lay administrator or accountant.

In May 1583, still during the period in power of the Ruthven regime, Drummond submitted an estimate of 'Outlays for Repair of Royal Palaces'. In it, he addressed past neglect and proposed ambitious new ideas. He had a sensitive eye – for instance, at Stirling, the 'westqwarter' was to be dismantled and rebuilt

> In the maist plesand maner that can be dewyssit; quhilk qwarter off the said paleys is the best and maist plesand sitwatione off ony of his hienes palayes be ressone it will have the maist plesand sycht of all the foure airthis, in speciall perk and gairdin, deir thairin, up the rawerais of Forthe, Teyth, Allone, and Gwddy to Lochlomwnd, ane sycht round about in all pairtis and downe the rewear of Forthe quhair thair standis many greit stane howssis provyding thair be ane fair gallery beildit on the ane syd of the said work, and this forsaid gallerie and tarras to be beildit and bigit upone the heich pairtis off the foirsaid work.[27]

Drummond envisaged a substantial superstructure, its purpose being enjoyment of the view in all directions, like the *altana* of Italian Renaissance architecture.[28] This fitted into a pre-existing formula associated with Stewart monarchy, for at Linlithgow, the north-west tower is topped by a single viewing room, reportedly used by Queen Margaret as a lookout while awaiting the news of James IV's English campaign of 1513. That such an arrangement threw out the symmetry was evidently unimportant: in Rome, for instance, the Palazzo Venezia had a viewing tower at one end, as had Peruzzi's Villa Farnesina, commissioned in 1508.[29] Drummond's ideas and epitaph are important in demonstrating the link in perception between landscape, both natural and man-made, and architecture. The view from Stirling was of

James's kingdom – in the same way as, later, Louis XIV's great vista at Versailles was upon nothing specific: but upon France. The 'Scottish Historical Landscape' identified by Margaret Stewart[30] – the intentional visual exploitation of national history within a landscape, exemplified by the huge formal garden at Alloa planned by the earl of Mar *c.* 1701 – is perhaps illustrated here in embryo, for many of the great stone houses to be viewed from Drummond's high gallery were ancient, while nearby (and overlooked from the palace south front and terrace) lay Bannockburn, site of the military triumph still then central to royal and national propaganda. Such viewing platforms remained a feature of the royal works until the platforming of the towers at Charles II's Holyrood.[31]

Drummond's report was submitted to the lords of exchequer a month before the Ruthven regime ended in June 1583. Was it commissioned by that regime? Or was it prepared by Drummond as an action list for his successor? Although Drummond's appointment had been for life, a new master of works was created some six months after the fall of the Ruthven regime. Perhaps Drummond had become politically inappropriate, for after the Ruthven regime ended, 'certane of the Kingis seruandis, officiaris and utheris seruandis, fauoreris of the erle of Mar, war dischargit courti on namly Dounypace and Carnock maister steblaris'.[32] Patrick Drummond, younger of Carnock, held this post. By August 1584 he had been convicted of treason.[33] Drummond the elder possibly shared this unpopularity.[34]

Drummond's own Carnock is long gone, insufficiently recorded. Bannockburn House, which he also owned, was rebuilt in the seventeenth century, and his Stirling town house is unidentified.[35] Both in his own time, and in the seventeenth century, he was a highly-regarded contributor to architectural and to landscape design, but not enough survives to characterise this contribution.

V

On 20 December 1583 William Schaw was appointed 'grit maister of all and sindrie his hines palaceis, biggingis and reparationis, and grit oversear, directour and commandar of quhatsumevir palice devyset or to be devyset for our soverane lordis behuif and pleasure'.[36] He held office until his death in 1602. A modern account of Schaw's career exists so little is said here.[37] Of the Sauchie family, Schaw found favour with King James, and then Queen Anna, to whom he was chamberlain and for whom he rebuilt Dunfermline Palace, her dower house. He has been associated with the reconstruction of the Chapel Royal at Stirling.[38] In 1589, when James left for Norway and Denmark to fetch his bride, Schaw accompanied him, returning ahead of the royal party in march 1590 to prepare for the homecoming.[39] Schaw's epitaph, by his 'true-hearted friend', Alexander Seton (the future Chancellor Dunfermline), related that 'in his eagerness to improve his mind he travelled through France and many other kingdoms. Accomplished in every liberal art, he excelled in architecture. Princes in particular esteemed him for his conspicuous gifts'.[40] An English complaint described him as 'praefectum architecturae'.[41] The 'Dunvegan Armorial', compiled in 1582–4, had been his.

During Schaw's terms of office emerged the new fashion of houses symmetrical both in plan and elevation. Examples included Barnes (c. 1594), Duntarvie (1589; western angle later infilled), Thirlestane, Fyvie (c. 1596), Scone (post-1600) and Boyne. Perhaps Burntisland Kirk (1589) and the Chapel Royal (1594) should also be seen in this context. Might this be due to the classicism of James's court and to Schaw's influence upon architectural fashion, and even to his foreign travels to 'many kingdoms', as his epitaph claimed?[42]

Little survives of Dunfermline Palace. Slezer's seventeenth-century views suggest its scale and magnificence, showing a giant eastern quarter, long gone without proper record. But parts of the south quarter, including many of the cross-windows, and the three symmetrical western bays (an addition to the pre-existing work) seem likely to be by Schaw.[43]

Schaw served on a committee for rebuilding Perth Bridge, and he built the classical north-east quarter at Seton.[44] Fyvie, built for Alexander Seton, was conceived as a symmetrical corner-towered quadrangle, its turreted castellation reminiscent of James IV's triumphalism, but perhaps also to be regarded in the context of James's 1590s chivalric phase, which found elaborate expression in the baptismal ceremonies for Prince Henry in 1594.[45] The entrance tower has a high-level arch between paired turrets. This could be interpreted as a giant Roman or triumphal arch like that within the portico of the Pantheon in Rome, and, in the Renaissance period, at, for instance, Alberti's S Andrea in Mantua; while in Naples, the centre area of the arch of Alfonso (1452), is (like Fyvie) sculptural and in a contrasting material. Were Fyvie's arch a product of Seton's Italian travels, it would be tempting to suggest a covert allusion to Catholicism. It was reproduced at nearby Craigston (1607), and had been used previously at Saltcoats (1592). Did Seton use Schaw as his architect?

Direct Italian inspiration, noted in contemporary courtly literature,[46] is well-known from Crichton's north quarter (1581x1591), built for the fifth earl of Bothwell after his return from italy. Other near-contemporary examples of Italianising include Newark (1597) on the Clyde, with its Michelangelesque pediments derived from the Porta Pia, and possibly the Chapel Royal, Stirling (1594); while, after Schaw's time, Culross Abbey House (1608) may be a third.[47]

The Chapel Royal was built hastily for Prince Henry's baptism, and must have involved Schaw. It was already anticipated that Henry might become king of a united Britain, so a great Renaissance festival was held, with foreign ambassadors present. Despite the crow-steps, at a glance the building looks Florentine, with paired round-arched windows set in round-arched frames (on the tympanum of each the ghost of a painted roundel). The doorway is a triumphal arch, which was originally more complex, with a superstructure, but sufficiently intact to denote it as Scotland's first known building based upon formal 'correct' use of classical Orders.[48]

However, might we expect William Schaw, re-creator of freemasonry, to be associated with more complex propagandist ideas, for an event otherwise crammed with allusions? James had many personae: the chapel proclaimed him as Solomon. As described in I Kings 6, Solomon's Temple had three components: the porch ('ulam) at one end, the Great Chamber (hekhal or cella) and, beyond, the Holy of Holies (devir), producing a total length : breadth ration of 3.5:1; as used also on Constantine's Old St Peter's, Rome.[49] These are also the proportions of the Chapel Royal.[50]

Moreover, the centre door is flanked on each side by three windows, containing six apertures – totalling twelve lights plus a door.[51] This one plus twelve formula represented Christ and his apostles. When this image was visually expressed, Christ was typically placed exactly central, the apostles in sixes, flanking, as in Leonardo Da Vinci's *Last Supper* (1495–8). The formula was later used by James VII at his Thistle Chapel (1688), and by Louis XIV in his pavilion disposition at Marly (1679). Round-arched windows of the type used at Stirling had been illustrated, also in groups of three, in sixteenth-century religious commentaries, in connection with Ezekiel's visionary replacement of the first temple.[52] Not only – the architecture asserted – had James the God-given virtues of Solomon, and the semi-divine status his philosophical tracts claimed, but also Biblical legitimacy for his theology. And there were also, no doubt, allusions to Henry's status.[53] The Ezekiel allusions, if intentional, would show the new prince as symbolic almost of the new Messiah, of a new Jerusalem, and a new Solomon in a new Temple.[54]

James loved and used symbolism. For him, rapid completion of the chapel was so important that not only had he 'the supply of the greatest number of artificers in the whole country, convened there of all craftes for that service', but he personally undertook the function of 'dayly overseer, with large and liberall payment'.[55] The interior was lavish, with cloth of gold and tapestries; the sense of drama was heightened by partitioning, and James's throne at the north-east end. The ceremony was delayed until the English ambassadors arrived. It was important that they witnessed the regal grandeur and scholarly sophistication of this event and heard a recitation of royal pedigrees, in which the closeness of the Scottish and English dynasties was emphasised, and Patrick Galloway's sermon on Genesis 21; possibly to verse 13, or more especially, verse 18: 'Arise, lift up the lad, and hold him in thine hand; for I will make him a great nation'. The allusion to anticipated regnal union, made before a select, international audience, can hardly have been blunter or louder. This sophisticated, classical and Biblically-inspired building was the venue in which James could impress the world, and legitimately and publicly stake his dynastic claim. Stewart architectural patronage and iconographically-laden classicism were now wedded. Clearly, Schaw's sophisticated design made the chapel a paradigmatic work of the Scottish Renaissance, important both for James's kingship and the history of freemasonry. Schaw himself may have been an important disseminator of classicism and architectural intellectualism throughout Britain.

VI

Sir David Cunningham of Robertland, master of works between 1602 and 1607, was the son and namesake of a man who fled to Denmark after his part in the murder of the earl of Eglinton in 1586. Cunningham the elder was received at the

Danish royal court, was pardoned when King James visited Denmark, and returned to Scotland. He became one of the royal stablers.[56] Here again is a Danish link, and it is tempting to wonder whether Danish court architecture might have been studied by the younger Cunningham.

No Scottish buildings have a documented association with Cunningham, though a single pediment at Robertland, bearing the monogram of James and Anna and evidently from the long-demolished house, may date from his time. He presumably worked on William Schaw's monument in Dunfermline (c. 1605), for it was raised at Anna's instruction. The monument bears an extraordinary number of mason's marks, all (except on the monogram stone) of one design. An identical mason's mark is seen on the Glencairn monument at Kilmaurs, together with the inscription 'WROCHT BE DAVID SCWGAL MASSON BURGES IN CAREL [Crail] 1600'. There can be little doubt that Scougal was responsible for both monuments, and perhaps he also worked on a similar monument at Ballantrae to Kennedy of Bargany. Is it significant that of these three related designs, one was a royal work, presumably involving the master of works, while the other two monuments are in Cunningham's native Ayrshire?

Cunningham went to England with his king, indicating that James required an architect familiar with the royal agenda. In June 1603 he was given the post equivalent to that of master of works in England, that of Surveyor, which he held until April 1606.[57] His contribution there has yet to be properly assessed.[58] In 1606, his new year gift to King James was 'a platt of an upright' (an architectural drawing), indicating the ability to make architectural compositions.[59] The term 'architectus' was used of him, posthumously, in 1614.[60]

Tantalisingly little is known of Cunningham, but perhaps he was talented. Two English designs are associated with him in his capacity as Surveyor: the Banqueting House at Whitehall (predecessor of Jones's better-known survivor) and a hunting lodge at Ampthill. In England, both designs are considered unusually forward-looking: the latter described as 'for 1603 [?recte 1605] a remarkably classical conception', the former as 'a rather advanced plan'.[61] This might be consistent with an architect coming from a land whose associations with classicism differed from those of England. Ultimately though, we pass Cunningham by, uncertain yet as to his architectural contribution. A reappraisal of his career is required.

VII

James VI's last master of works was Sir James Murray of Kilbaberton, who held the post between 1607 and 1634. He was of the Falahill family. His father and namesake (d. 1615), a master wright, was in royal service from at least 1575, and in 1601 was appointed master overseer.[62] Murray the younger is first on record in the royal works in 1594, as a wright, but by 1597 he was engaged in the first of a series of special duties for the crown, 'transporting of xxviii deir' to Falkland.[63] Friends of Murray included Sir William Dick, the wealthiest of Edinburgh's merchants, and Sir Henry Wardlaw of Pitreavie, receiver of crown rents (Murray was godfather to a Wardlaw child). To Sir Gideon Murray of Elibank, he was (albeit not necessarily a blood relation) 'nevoy' (nephew). In December 1607 he was appointed 'principall master of all his majesties warkis and buildingis'; he held this post until his death in 1634.[64] In 1628, he was conjoined in post with Sir Anthony Alexander, son of Sir William, one-time poet friend of James, subsequently Charles's secretary for Scotland.

The orthodox view that William Wallace (d. 1631), the king's master mason, was the outstanding royal architect of this period, now seems doubtful. Reappraisal of the evidence produces nothing to substantiate that reputation; he was probably a skilled designer, but as regards the *royal* works, Wallace is found only in the role of operative, being paid for specific tasks.[65] Where, in the royal works, he is given a further designation, it is that of 'carver' – again, hardly suggestive of the role of architect.[66] Murray, who recommended Wallace for the post of master mason, is on the other hand seen only in the role of supervisor, having supreme authority over works, and generally fulfilling the role of architect. He is known to have designed two major buildings: the earl of Dunbar's colossal, though long-gone house in Berwick (work abandoned 1611), and Parliament House, designed in 1632.[67] He was regarded by the captain of Berwick as potentially suitable for building a new stone bridge there, where technical complexities suggested the work to be beyond local expertise.[68] Perhaps he had an input to other great courtier houses, such as Culross Abbey House and Pinkie.

Murray's royal works included preparation of the palaces for the 1617 royal visit, notably reconstruction of Edinburgh (1615–17), where Wallace was engaged as master mason and carver, and Holyrood, where (presumably as a preamble to what became the Five Articles of Perth) the royal chapel was set up for what seemed to many to be Anglican-style worship, with English craftsmen employed. At Edinburgh Castle, symmetry was impossible because it incorporated the pre-existing palace, including James's birth-room, which was given an elaborate commemorative painted decoration by James Anderson, underlining its role as historical artefact; but the additions were given the same restrained classicism introduced at the Chapel Royal and the aedicule-windowed Culross Abbey House. Murray's eastern façade, set in the only spot overlooking the High Street, had square bartizans like those at Pinkie and Parliament House. Also like Parliament House, the roof was flat and leaded (as Culross appears to have been) as a viewing platform. Fronting the courtyard and on the north end flank were half-projecting polygonal stair turrets, each containing a main entrance: an arrangement seen previously at royal palaces elsewhere, such as Kronborg and, more famously, Blois.

Linlithgow's north quarter collapsed in 1607, through official neglect. James, who did not visit there in 1617, instructed that it should be rebuilt. Murray began work in 1618. The courtyard façade is symmetrical, dropped down from end towers, a central stair turret of the kind noted at Edinburgh set between smaller openings – an arrangement paralleled on the flanks of Heriot's Hospital, begun in 1628.[69] The different floors are essentially uniform, enabled by stacked apartments in near-symmetrical disposition, a formula important in the genesis of tenement design. At first floor level, a north-facing gallery, with sophisticated classical chimney-pieces, extended near-full length. Fenestration would have emphasised its presence externally before the palace was burnt.

Despite the losses, something of the fine quality of interior ornament of James's palaces is known from fragments of paintwork, plaster, timber and stonework, and from similar decoration in non-royal architecture. At Edinburgh in 1617 'paper and floore' were supplied to the painters, presumably wallpaper; John Anderson was also paid for 'furneisching of all sortis of cullouris and warkmanschip with marble dures and chinnayes' (paint marbling of doors and chimneys).[70] The new work at Linlithgow involved

> Johne Binning and James Warkman painteris . . . for furnisching all sortis of cullouris and gold . . . and lykwayes . . . for painting and laying over with oyle cullour and for gilting with gold the haill foir face of the new wark with the timber windowis and window brodis staine windowis and crownellis.[71]

These palaces must have been astonishingly beautiful.

The 1620s saw development of the new style, exemplified by Heriot's (1628), while both Parliament House and the Moray House gatepiers (mid-1620s) introduced hints of an 'antique' Roman monumentality. Influenced by North European Mannerism, some English references are also identifiable: Winton's parapet, for instance, is a version of that at Haddon Hall. Murray's own house, Kilbaberton (with 1622 and 1623 datestones) survives, its flank aligned upon Edinburgh Castle: another illustration of the Scottish Historical Landscape. A symmetrical U-plan, it is compellingly similar to Wardlaw's Pitreavie and to the apparently very dissimilar (because of the return to the ideas of asymmetry and of unequal sized end towers) Winton. All share a repertoire of ornament.[72] Visual links confirm, or extend, the documentary possibilities.

James died during Murray's term in office. But the fashions of his reign continued to develop, with new ideas and responses to new situations – for instance, at Glasgow College. With Alexander's death in 1637, and political strife thereafter, the mastership of works, despite being temporarily revived from 1671 as a 'surveyorship' for Bruce and Smith, was headed towards irrelevance, becoming a sinecure. The court, especially after 1689, would never again be resident, and the permanent post of royal architect to supervise 'palace [work] devyset or to be devyset' was hardly necessary.

VIII

Architectural commissions for the crown served far more than the private requirements of James or Anna. Each work spread propaganda about James's kingship, including political and theological messages. Translation into architecture of the ideas conceived by or for James was the responsibility of his architects – who, it is now suggested, were his masters of works. James Murray, it is increasingly clear, was the driving force behind the new architecture of the second and third decades of the seventeenth century. Others must have contributed to design; masons and other tradesmen, of course, but presumably royal advisers and intellectuals, theologians and classicists, and surely – in enormous measure – James himself, at the Chapel Royal if not elsewhere. A significant input may have been made by Chancellor Dunfermline, who, reportedly, was skilled in architecture, building himself an astonishingly sophisticated classical villa at Pinkie (1613) – which, like the royal works, was crammed with imagery.[73] We have also seen similar work used in high-status, non-royal architecture, indicating the existence of a group of court designers and craftsmen being employed by others of high rank. The resident court had been generous in providing architectural patronage, and ready to exploit its allegorical potential; the absentee court similarly so.[74] Only with the Covenanting wars of the mid-century did this royal investment stall, and only after 1689 did it cease, until the nineteenth century.

NOTES

1 Inscription, James VI statue, Netherbow Port, Edinburgh; quoted (translated from Latin) in J. Grant, *Old and New Edinburgh*, 3 vols (London, n. d.), i, 218.

2 R. Fawcett, *The Abbey and Palace of Dunfermline* (Historic Scotland, 1990), pp. 15, 26; D. Pringle, *Linlithgow Palace* (Historic Scotland, N D), p. 19. The uncertainty is noted by I MacIvor, *Edinburgh Castle* (London, 1993), p. 72.

3 Spectacular exceptions exist, such as Carnasserie: court architecture in rural Argyll.

4 M. Glendinning, R. MacInnes and A. MacKechnie, *A History of Scottish Architecture from the Renaissance to the Present Day* (Edinburgh, 1996), chapters 1 & 2; I. Campbell, 'A Romanesque revival and the early Renaissance in Scotland, *c.* 1380– 1513'; *Journal of the Society of Architectural Historians*, liv (1995); I Campbell, 'Linlithgow's "Princely Palace" and its influence in Europe', *Architectural Heritage*, v (1995).

5 Sometimes said to date from 1615–17, with retrospective datestone. But the monogram commemorates Mary and Henry, while the architecture differs from that of the identified 1615–17 work. The calligraphic evidence also indicates a sixteenth-century date.

6 M. Lynch, 'Scottish culture in its historical perspective', in P. H. Scott (ed.), *Scotland: a Concise Cultural History* (Edinburgh, 1993), pp. 17–18.

7 Revived Gothic was similarly promoted at Wurzburg in 1573–1617 by Bishop Julius Echter von Mespelbrunn for comparable, symbolic reasons, as part of his Counter-Reformation activities: E. Hempel, *Baroque Art and Architecture* (Harmondsworth, 1965), p. 13.

8 Vitruvius, *The Ten Books on Architecture*, trans H. Morgan (Dover, NY, 1960).

9 R. S. Mylne, 'Notices of the king's master gunners of Scotland', PSAS, xxxiii (1898–9).

10 *Register of the Privy Council of Scotland* [RPC], eds J. H. Burton *et al.* (Edinburgh, 1877–), first series, xii, p. 710.

11 *RPC*, 2nd ser, iii, p. 498.

12 R. S. Mylne, 'Masters of work to the crown of Scotland', *Proceedings of the Society of Antiquaries of Scotland*, xxx (1895–6), p. 57.

13 *The Earl of Stirling's Register of Royal letters, 1615–1635,* 2 vols, ed C Rogers (Edinburgh, 1885), I, pp. 69, 319.

14 e.g. *Register of the Great Seal of Scotland [RMS]*, vii, p. 689.

15 R. S. Mylne, *The Master Masons to the Crown of Scotland* (Edinburgh, 1893), 60; *Accounts of the Masters of Works for Building and Repairing Royal Palaces and Castles [MWA]* eds H. M. Paton *et al.* (Edinburgh, 1957–82), i, p. xxviii.

16 *MWA*, i, p. xxvii.

17 C. H. Haws (ed), *Scottish Parish Clergy at the Reformation* (SRS, 1972), pp. 59, 108, 160.

18 *MWA*, i, p. xxvii. Whitehill was later owned by a successor in post, James Smith (*c.* 1645–1731).

19 *Accounts of the Lord High Treasurer of Scotland [TA]* eds T. Dickson *et al.* (Edinburgh, 1877–1978), xiii, pp. 150–1. The interior was painted by Walter Binning, 1577; *ibid.*, 166. This gallery was rebuilt by Bruce and Mylne in the 1670s, possibly incorporating much 1570s work not now visible. MacDowell also built a gallery within the abbey kirk; *ibid.*, 187.

20 *MWA*, i, p. xxvii, citing *TA*, xii, 514.

21 *TA*, xiii, p. 33.

22 *TA*, xiii, p. 187. Also known as the Regent Morton Gateway.

23 D. E. R. Watt (ed.), *Fasti Ecclesiae Scoticanae Medii Aevi* (SRS, 1969), p. 338.

24 Mylne, 'Masters of work', p. 54.

25 W. Drummond, *The Genealogie of the Most Noble and Ancient House of Drummond* (Edinburgh, 1831), pp. 71, 250, 267.

26 Alexander Montgomerie, *Poems*, ed J Cranstoun (STS, 1887), p. 221.

27 *MWA*, i, p. 310.

28 Cf. V. Vesey, 'Una nuova attribuzione a martino Longhi il Vecchio: la villa Caraga, oggi Grazioli, di Grottaferrata', *Opus*, v (1996).

29 Other roof-top or high-level viewing structures of the general period include both internal spaces (e.g. the oriel-windowed topmost room at Maybole) and external platforms (e.g. Craigievar).

30 M. C. H. Stewart, 'Lord Mar's Plans, 1700–1732' (University of Glasgow M Litt thesis, 1988), p. 66; Glendinning *et al, History of Scottish Architecture*, pp. 104–5.

31 Conceivably, the 'over gallerie' referred to in 1628 represents that particular proposal by Drummond fulfilled: *MWA*, ii, p. 240. The same document also proposed (among much else) a two-storey dwelling for the captain of the castle over the 'new yett' at Edinburgh, to protect the portcullis mechanism from rain (a scheme carried out by William Schaw in 1584; MacIvor, *Edinburgh Castle*, 7) and rebuilding of the Chapel Royal. MacDowall assembled materials 'to mak the new galry in the castell of Striviling' in 1576; *TA*, xiii, p. 149.

32 D. Stevenson, *The Origins of Freemasonry* (Cambridge, 1988), 28; D Moysie, *Memoirs of the Affairs of Scotland 1577–1603* (Bannatyne Club, 1830), 45–6; cf. *RPC*, iii, p. 648.

33 *Registrum Secreti Sigilli Regum Scotorum (Register of the Privy Seal of Scotland)*, viii, pp. 883, 2359. Another son, John (father of Hawthornden) was also suspect for a time in 1584: *RPC*, iii, p. 664. He was restored to favour, and by 1587 was 'ane of the yshearis of his majesteis chalmer': *RPC*, iv, p. 199.

34 An armorial from Gowrie House, now in the Scottish National Portrait Gallery, is dated 1582. If Carnock was turned out of his post, perhaps Montgomerie's friendship with him

impeded his readmittance to the court. While in prison after the regime ended, the earl of Gowrie wrote, 'What a pitie it were to take me from my parks and policie', and at Ruthven he had a gallery 'newly built and decored with Pictures': D. Pringle, *Huntingtower* (Historic Scotland, 1996), 7. Did any of this work involve the subsequently displaced Drummond?

35 *RPC*, iv, 229. Carnock is described in D. MacGibbon and T. Ross, *Castellated and Domestic Architecture of Scotland*, 5 vols (Edinburgh, 1887–92), ii, pp. 490–6. Similarities to other work may be significant: for instance, the ground plan had a latitudinal corridor fronting three rooms out of the four, as at Carnasserie. At first floor the hall was central, with a room either side, as at Melgund and (in its pre-1581 form) Airth. A staircase was set forward at either side of the entrance front, as at Carnasserie and Melgund. But evidence that Drummond worked at Carnock is lacking.

36 Stevenson, *Freemasonry*, p. 26; *MWA*, i, p. xxviii.

37 Stevenson, *Freemasonry*, pp. 26–32.

38 Stevenson, *Freemasonry*, p. 93.

39 Moysie, *Memoirs*, p. 82.

40 Translation in *Inventory of Fife*, p. 112; repr Stevenson, *Freemasonry*, pp. 26–7.

41 Stevenson, *Freemasonry*, p. 28.

42 Schaw left for France in 1584 in the company of Lord Seton, whose son, Alexander, might well also have travelled with them: Stevenson, *Freemasonry*, pp. 28–9.

43 John Slezer, *Theatrum Scotiae* (London, 1693), plates 45–6.

44 *RPC*, v. 532; Stevenson, *Freemasonry*, p. 29. Schaw – possibly in the role of James's Vitruvian architect – was also commissioned to demolish the 'place and fortalice' of Strathbogie in 1594; *RPC*, v p. 186.

45 Scottish National Portrait Gallery, *Treasures of Fyvie* (exhibition catalogue, 1985), fig. 3; M. Lynch, 'Court ceremony and ritual during the personal reign of James VI', Chapter 4 above.

46 R. J. Lyall, 'The literature of Lowland Scotland, 1350–1700', in Scott (ed.), *Cultural History*, p. 94.

47 The near identical, console-bracketed Newark and Spedlins chimney pieces are likewise Italianate, possibly derived from Sebastiano Serlio, *Architettura et Prospettiva* (Venice, 1619; repr Farnborough, 1964).

48 There was a 'pirament at the chaippell dore' (*MWA*, ii, 239), and a reference to 'the foir entrie of the chaippill with the pillaris and haill ordour thairof with the armes housingis crownellis [pediments] and siferis with tua new tafrellis [decorative panels?] to the housing' (*ibid*., p. 256). Is the pyramid an allusion to the pinnacle of Solomon's temple which featured in the Temptation of Christ? Cf. Luke 4–9.

49 T. C. Bannister, 'The Constantinian Basilica of Saint Peter at Rome', *Journal of the Society of Architectural Historians*, xxviii (1968).

50 Interior measurements of 31.685 × 9.03 m give a ratio of 1:3.5 (9.03 × 3.5 = 31.605, a discrepancy of 0.8 m; alternatively 31.685/3.5 = 9.0528; a discrepancy of 0.0228). I am grateful to Graeme McMorran of Historic Scotland for providing such precise dimensions. The distance between floor and underside of tie-beam is 0.75 that of the width and half the overall height, giving a width : full-height ratio of 1:1.5. David Stevenson argues that seventeenth-century masonic lodges represented a notional re-creation of Solomon's Temple; D Stevenson, *The First Freemasons* (Aberdeen, 1988), p. 7. Perhaps the partition at the east end of the chapel created a square, alluding to James and the great dignitaries occupying a notional 'Holy of Holies'. A dedication (1500) to James IV at King's College

Aberdeen – with its imperial crown spire – stated the commencement date as 2 Apr, which was computed as the commencement date of Solomon's Temple: Stevenson, *Freemasonry*, 24. The King's College plan appears likewise to use proportions derived from the Temple. The 1:3.5 ratio relates to internal breadth : length from doorway to steps beyond founder's tomb (which area, significantly, is divided into double-square nave – square choir – half-square, beyond); the ratio may also apply externally, to overall breadth : length). Plan in F Eeles, *King's College Chapel Aberdeen* (Edinburgh, 1956), p. 271.

51 Did the columns represent the four evangelists? Had the doorway royal symbolism? Compare John 10:9, 'I am the door; by me if any man enter in, he shall be saved'.

52 Ezekiel 40:1, H. Rosenau, *Vision of the Temple* (London, 1979), 50 and *passim*. I am grateful to Ian Campbell for drawing my attention to these illustrations.

53 For example, Christ was brought as an infant to the Temple, 'to present him to the Lord': Luke 2:22, 27. He was aged twelve when he went missing, and was found in learned discussion with the theologians in the Temple: Luke 2:42–9.

54 The dimensions of Solomon's Temple were 70 × 20 cubits. At Stirling, this would result in a cubit length of about 0.45 m (17.7 inches) – within the known range of ancient cubit measurements, between 17 and 21 inches. *Cambridge Companion to the Bible* (Cambridge, 1997), p. 147.

55 'A true reportaire of the baptisme of the Prince of Scotland', in H. W. Meikle (ed.), *The Works of William Fowler*, 2 vols (STS, 1936), ii, p. 171.

56 *The Historie and Life of King James the Sext*, ed. T Thomson (Bannatyne Club, 1825), pp. 239–40.

57 H. Colvin (ed.), *The History of the King's Works*, 6 vols (London, 1963–82), iv, p. 105.

58 M Girouard, 'Designs for a lodge at Ampthill', in H. Colvin and J. Harris (eds), *The Country Seat* (Harmondsworth, 1970), 15 and *King's Works*, iii, 105–6, both dismiss him.

59 J. Nichols, *The Progresses, Processions and Magnificent Festivities of James I . . .*, 4 vols (London, 1828), i, p. 596.

60 *RMS*, vii, p. 986.

61 *King's Works*, iv, p. 46; J. Harris and G. Higgot (eds), *Inigo Jones: Complete Architectural Drawings* (New York, 1989), p. 108.

62 This was given in succession to the late Sir William MacDowell, suggesting that the post may have been dormant since his time; *TA*, xiii, p. 81; *MWA*, i, p xxxvii.

63 *Extracts from the Records of the Burgh of Edinburgh*, ed. J. D. Marwick *et al.* (Edinburgh, 1869–1967), v, 113; *Letters to King James the Sixth* (Maitland Club, 1835), p. lxxiii.

64 *MWA*, i, p xxix.

65 e.g. for making a horn for the unicorn of an armorial: *MWA*, ii, 81. Wallace had to transport his 'warklumes', indicating his need to do manual labour: ibid., 134. In 1625, Wallace had two days 'attending', at Ravelston quarry because 'nyne great stanes for the kingis badges [were] to be wrocht in for the rigging of the great hall' at Stirling – where a carver had a particular interests in overseeing: ibid., p. 170.

66 *MWA*, i, p xxxv.

67 *King's Works*, iv, p. 771; *Edin Recs*, vii, p. 119.

68 *King's Works*, iv, p. 771.

69 This was also paralleled in vernacular form at Lamb's House, Leith, and in half-width at Caerlaverock (1634) and Gladstone's Land, Edinburgh.

70 *MWA*, ii, p. 79, 81.

71 *MWA*, ii, p. 269.

72 The chimney-piece at Kilbaberton is evidently a stripped version of that at Winton; the chimney-pieces of the Linlithgow gallery were reproduced in variant form in the Argyll Lodging chamber; the pediment sculpture of the palace within Edinburgh Castle is near-identical to pediments at Pitreavie, Parliament House and Kilbaberton.

73 M. Bath, 'Alexander Seton's painted gallery' in L. Gent (ed.), *Albion's Classicism* (New Haven, NY, 1995); Stevenson, *Freemasonry*, 29. Dunfermline is said to have designed old Somerville House (renamed Drum) part-incorporated within the existing pavilion. Architectural study was also a gentlemanly pursuit later in the century, as demonstrated by Sir William Bruce and the eleventh earl of Mar.

74 An important legacy of James's pre-1603 patronage would appear to have been Stuart commissions after 1603 to Inigo Jones, which for a time, through precocious buildings such as the Banqueting House, Whitehall (from 1619), placed England at the forefront of architectural accomplishment north of the Alps.

A National Style

Extracted from M Bath 2003 *Renaissance Decorative Painting in Scotland*, Edinburgh (National Museums of Scotland), 1–27.

In his standard history of *Scottish Art* (1990) Duncan Macmillan writes, 'The decorative painting of the reign of James VI and the early years of his son would, by its very quantity alone, be a striking feature of Scottish culture, but it also seems to be quite specific to Scotland'(p 56). Such painting survives, or is recorded, in more than one hundred different buildings throughout Scotland, ranging from royal palaces and the castles of the nobility to modest burgess houses of the increasingly affluent middle class. Nor is such painting confined to domestic buildings since, despite the wholesale destruction of Scotland's medieval inheritance of religious painting following the Reformation, new schemes of decoration were executed in a number of churches and chapels. Indeed, perhaps the most surprising thing about this tradition of decorative painting is that it should have coincided with a period of such intense religious iconoclasm. In 1559 the Reformation breaking of images was described by a witness as follows: 'The manner of reformation is this – they pull down abbeys, cleanse parishes of all images – and prohibit all masses.' In the following year the *First Book of Discipline*, which laid down the law on the regulation of the reformed church in Scotland, required 'all idolatry . . . to be utterly suppressed'. Yet the new style of decorative painting uses images which are far from being simply decorative; more often its subjects – secular and religious, classical, emblematic, historical, or heraldic – are iconographically significant, full of meaning: speaking pictures. Understanding what they were saying and how they were functioning in this Scottish climate of Renaissance iconology and Reformation iconoclasm would seem to be a task worth pursuing.

As Macmillan says, 'The sheer quantity of such painting and the social range of those for whom it was executed clearly reflect the establishment of a new standard of civil life' (p 56). It therefore has to be understood as part of a wider development in Scottish culture that includes the architectural revival of the late sixteenth and early seventeenth centuries. What a contemporary observer describes as the 'fair new fabric and stately edifices' (cited Howard 1995, p 48) which had arisen out of monastic properties, not only served to define their owners' social status but were also designed to express a new sense of national identity. It is now more widely accepted than it used to be that the castellated style of building, and particularly the use of a native style of flamboyant bartizans, skewputs, and corbels, represents a conscious stylistic choice, rather than any kind of defensive necessity. These Renaissance castles and tower houses are making stylistic statements before they are doing anything else, and their internal decoration has to be seen as contributing to such statements.

Much of this painting was carried out for the class of person described by William Lithgow in 1628: 'as for the nobility and gentry of the kingdom, certainly, as they are generous, manly and full of courage; so are they courteous, discreet, learned scholars well read in the best histories, delicate linguists, the most part of them being brought up in France or Italy' (cited Howard 1995, p 49). We shall certainly see that much of this painting assumes a certain level of literacy, both verbal and visual, in its viewer, which undoubtedly reflects not only the humanism of the court of James VI but also the level of general education that was available to virtually all social classes who had access to the Scottish universities. Moreover, many graduates of Scottish universities in the late sixteenth and early seventeenth centuries went on to further study abroad, in the Netherlands, France, Italy and as far afield as Poland. There they would have had direct access to buildings that exhibited the latest trends in the European decorative arts. Scottish connections with continental Europe had, of course, been much closer throughout the sixteenth century than England's, and we should not make the mistake of regarding this northern tradition as some kind of regional extension of an English fashion. It is, rather, a fully independent national tradition with its own European connections. Its failure to attract the kind of scholarly attention it manifestly deserves is a symptom of the marginalisation of Scottish culture in a British context and the traditional neglect of the applied arts by conventional 'fine art' historians.

Painted decoration in royal palaces was the responsibility of successive masters of the King's Works, who were periodically charged with restoring or refurbishing one or other of the five palaces between which the royal household regularly migrated. After the Union of the Crowns in 1603 such redecoration was most likely to be required in anticipation of projected royal visits, which James and his successor made to their northern kingdom in 1617 and 1633. Undoubtedly royal tastes influenced architectural styles in the houses of the nobility, and some of the most outstanding examples of decorative painting are to be found in the houses of noble families whose names figure in the history of Scotland – the Gordons, Hamiltons, Ruthvens, Hays, Setons, Stewarts, Kerrs, Drummonds, Lindsays. Both the ancient members of the Scottish nobility, and the more recent 'lords of erection' who played such a significant part in the increasingly competent administration of James VI, had taken over the estates of the Catholic church (which had owned about a third of the land in Scotland before the Reformation). Younger sons of the nobility were regularly appointed as lay 'commendators' to ancient abbeys, thus securing their family's title to the property and income of the ecclesiastical estates which they tried to consolidate by affirming the antiquity of their lineage and titles through the heraldic and dynastic iconography that often predominates on both the external sculptured stonework and internal painting of their houses. Often this dynastic iconography, however, is intent not so much on establishing the particular lineage and antiquity of the owner's own family – though it may be doing so – as on defining a more extended scheme of European monarchy and/or Scottish nobility, which normally includes direct or implied statements of loyalty to the Scottish crown. Such heraldic schemes help to define the relation of the Scottish nobility to its monarchy, and it seems likely that important reconstructions of the nation's relation to its history were also at play in these architectural and iconographic programmes, reconstructions which have at least some similarities with the revival of medieval chivalry (in the work of Edmund Spenser and Philip Sidney, for instance) which took place at this period in Elizabethan England.

The architectural context in which this painting flourished does not consist, however, solely of this exploitation of a native style, for its vocabulary includes some elements, or developments, which one can only describe as classical. The rebuilding of the Chapel Royal at Stirling in 1594 saw one of the earliest Scottish examples of a purely classical design, with its entrance portal based on continental models illustrated by Serlio (Howard 1995, pp. 31–3). Its interior was treated to an elaborate programme of decoration, including the surviving decorative painting. The paintings executed for Alexander Seton at Pinkie House, Musselburgh, are similarly contained in a building that insistently declares its aspiration towards an ideal of classical humanism. We need to beware, however, of assuming that 'classicism' is a matter of unswerving commitment to Vitruvian models. Historians sometimes write as though architecture in Britain at this time was holding its breath for the belated arrival of Inigo Jones, but the visual arts in both England and Scotland employed more diverse classical elements long before any strict adherence to classical models became de rigueur. As Lucy Gent argues, 'twentieth-century perceptions of the classicism embodied in the Italian Renaissance are inappropriate to sixteenth- and seventeenth-century Britain' (Gent 1995, p 3 and see Christy Anderson, 'Learning to Read Architecture . . .' in Gent, pp 239–86). Even before the arrival of a thoroughgoing neoclassical revival, which in Scotland means the period of William Bruce or of William Adam, Scottish buildings will be found to be signalling, however sporadically and indistinctly, their aspiration towards those standards of taste and cultivation which traditionally adhered to the classical. Those signals represent an international dimension which complements the more verna-cular vocabulary of the castellated Scottish baronial style, a style which itself turns out to have more continental analogues than was sometimes thought. Both are essential, and complementary rather than opposed, elements of a local renaissance.

Scottish decorative painting conforms to this pattern in its inclusion of both vernacular and more cosmopolitan elements. While Duncan Macmillan's claim that this was 'specific to Scotland' has much to be said for it, decorative painting of various kinds can be found throughout Europe in buildings of this period, and the Scottish school demonstrably draws on a decorative vocabulary of wider prove-nance. The identification of some of its analogues and antecedents will, perhaps, help us to define the international context within which it was working. A national style need not be parochial.

The question of how far this style of painting was regionally or geographically distinctive is closely linked to the related question of its historical termini. There are good reasons for claiming that it is both geographically and historically distinct, with the Reformation as a clear enough starting point, and the Civil Wars of the 1640s signalling its close. A near-contemporary description of the work of a painter called Andrew Bairhum, who was working at Kinloss Abbey as early as 1538, described some of his work as in 'the lighter style of painting which is now customary throughout Scotland' (Ferrerius, *Historia Abbatum de Kinloss*, cited Macmillan 1990, 35), and this highly suggestive comment has been taken as an indication that 'the fashion for painted interiors, that we know from surviving painted ceilings, was already established in the reign of James V' (*ibid.*, p 36). The earliest paintings we can identify as belonging to the new tradition, however, are those executed for the Earl of Arran at Kinneil, which date from the 1550s. Arran was Regent of Scotland from 1542–54, and these are predominantly religious subjects, but the next-earliest datable example, the remarkable scheme of grotesque painting executed for Mark Kerr at Prestongrange, is dated 1581 and could certainly be described as 'in the lighter style', including, as it does, Priapic figures copied from a book ascribed to Rabelais. The majority of its grotesque motifs are copied directly from the *Grottesco: in diversche manieren* (*c.* 1565–71) of Jan Vredeman de Vries, and the style of this ceiling has to be seen as the earliest Scottish example of that Renaissance ornamental vocabulary which began to spread across northern Europe from its Flemish sources in the second half of the sixteenth century. The painted ceilings at Delgaty Castle record their own dates as 1592, 1593 and 1597, whilst those at Crathes similarly have the dates 1599 and 1602 painted on the beams. We know that the painting in the Chapel Royal, Stirling, was executed for the baptism of Prince Henry in 1594, the painting in James VI's birthroom in Edinburgh Castle was of 1617, and the redecoration of Falkland Palace was ordered for the royal visit of 1633. Painted ceilings at Gladstone's Land bear the date 1620; at The Dean, Edinburgh, 1627; at Ballachastell, 1634; at Gala House, Galashiels, 1635; and at Skelmorlie Aisle, 1638. The dating of other examples depends on what we know about the history of the building, or may be inferred from dates carved on lintels, from owners' initials, or from armorial bearings elsewhere in the building. It seems likely that most of the painting at Culross, for instance, was executed for George Bruce shortly after one or other of the dates, 1579 and 1611, carved on the respective wings of his house, the latter being the date when he was knighted.

Some examples, however, have been included which fall outside these historical boundaries. Around 1520 Gavin Dunbar, Bishop of Aberdeen, had the nave of St Machar's Cathedral decorated with a series of carved and painted coats of arms which includes the shields of the Scottish bishops, of the nobility of Scotland, and of the European (or terrestrial) monarchies. This scheme is unlike anything else to be found in British churches, and its connections are almost certainly with an armorial tradition that descends from the later Middle Ages and was taken up by a number of the armorial ceilings of the later period. The St Machar's decoration therefore constitutes an important precursor of a type of painting that concerns us in this book. There are also at least a few examples of more traditional painting in Scottish churches that escaped the destruction of the image breakers. Two of the best known examples are the paintings at Foulis Easter, near Dundee, and at Guthrie Aisle, near

Brechin, which represent clear survivals, dating as they probably do from the late fifteenth century. Other ecclesiastical painting which is more difficult to date, such as that in the cathedrals at Elgin and Dunkeld, and in the abbey at Dunfermline, may well represent a survival of pre-Reformation art in Scotland and should not be included in the Renaissance decorative tradition which is our subject. But it is not easy to supply a precise date for most of these, and it seems worth giving some account of them for the sake of completeness.

A few examples, likewise, can be assigned dates which might seem to call into question Duncan Macmillan's statement that this type of painting 'stopped abruptly with the Civil War' (p. 52). The painted gallery at Cullen, for instance, includes not only the royal arms of Scotland on the wall at one end but also the arms of Charles II, clearly ascribed in the painted initials 'CR2', forcing us to assign both coats of arms to the Restoration period. The stellar painting, with its planetary and other deities on the soffit of the same ceiling, appears to have been executed by the same hand and is almost certainly of the same date, unlike the classical subjects – the Sack of Troy, the Calydonian Boar-Hunt, and Diana and Actaeon – painted on the two side panels, which are evidently earlier work. Such later work would include a barrel-vaulted ceiling in the remains of the town house of General Thomas Dalziel, commander of the forces of Charles II, persecutor of the Covenanters, and victor in the Battle of Pentland, 1666. According to Daniel Wilson in his *Memorials of Edinburgh* (1848, vol. ii, p. 70), 'The chief apartment was a hall of unusually large dimensions, with an arched or waggon-shaped ceiling adorned with a painting of the sun in the centre, surrounded by gilded rays on an azure ground. The remainder of the ceiling was painted to represent sky and clouds and spangled over with a series of silvered stars in relief.' It would appear that this was similar to the type of stellar ceiling we find at Innerpeffray Chapel, at Liberton House (Edinburgh), and in Linlithgow. The nineteen *trompe l'œil* Corinthian pilasters in Argyll's Lodging in Stirling were executed as late as 1675 – these are one of the few commissions for which a surviving contract enables us not only to date the work but also to identify the artist, namely the painter David McBeath, who had been apprenticed to Joseph Stanefield in Edinburgh in 1671. Though there may be a few such precursors or remnants of this decorative tradition, all its major examples nevertheless belong in the reigns of James VI and Charles I. The tradition is, we may claim, both geographically and historically discrete.

It has sometimes been said that the demise of decorative painting coincides with and, by implication, was a consequence of, the development of a taste for decorative plasterwork in the later seventeenth century. We should, however, beware of assuming a clear break between the fashion for tempera painting on boards and the new taste for decorative plasterwork that undoubtedly spread north from England. Some of the decorative plasterwork in Scotland is quite early and is associated with the same patrons, families, and buildings where painted decoration is found. The plasterwork at Muchalls, Aberdeenshire, for instance, was carried out for Thomas Burnett, whose main residence was just twenty miles away at Crathes, where his father Alexander had executed the most extensive programme of painted decoration to be found anywhere in Scotland only twenty years previously. The early plasterwork at Pinkie House is almost certainly contemporary with the decoration of the painted long gallery, using the same personal devices of Alexander Seton that we find in his decorative painting. Seton was a cousin and close friend of Alexander Burnett, as it happens. The delicate mouldings at Pinkie are copied at Winton Castle, East Lothian, where documents record 'John Quytte' as the plasterer. The English plasterers Richard Cob and Ralph Rawlinson travelled to Scotland to do plasterwork, and almost certainly a taste for decorative plasterwork was acquired by the large number of Scots who migrated to London in the years immediately following the Union of Crowns. Moulds used in England were also employed in Scotland; the cycle of heads of the nine Worthies which is found at Merchiston, Edinburgh, and at Balcarres, Fife, for instance, has been shown to use the same moulds as the heads from Bromley-le-Bow in London (1606), now in the Victoria and Albert Museum.

Decorative painting is found on plaster, stonework, the walls of houses, window embrasures, overmantels and vaulting, but by far the greater part of this work is painted on wooden boards on the ceiling; indeed decorative painting in Scotland is commonly described in the phrase 'painted ceilings'. This alone makes the Scottish tradition somewhat exceptional. Sometimes, it is true, the painting is carried onto the plaster to create a decorative frieze, as at Gladstone's Land, Earlshall, or Crathes, but the rest of the walls tended to be left bare. This was probably because they would normally be covered with tapestry or painted cloths. The ceilings themselves tend to be of two kinds. Most common is the type we call open *board-and-beam* ceilings. In these the supporting beams are likely to be painted on all three sides and between them are the undersides of the floorboards of the room above. Such a surface places severe constraints on design possibilities, consisting as it does of a series of long, narrow compartments between beams. It favours linear, repetitive, or elongated images: rows of heraldic shields, flower and plant forms, winged cherubs, and animals and grotesque figures in fixed or, more often, in seemingly random sequences. That there were several such compartments lying side by side occasionally suggested its suitability for such fixed and conventional sequences as the nine Worthies or the Cardinal Virtues (both at Crathes), one per section. The beams themselves are generally given a purely decorative treatment, though their sides may be covered in writing, usually texts from the bible or proverbial sayings, sometimes versified. These images often assume a viewing angle that changes as one moves about the room. Sometimes it is not easy to make much sense of the way such viewing angles articulate the spaces which the decoration fills, though much may depend on the position of the doors, windows, or fireplace, and the uses to which the chamber was put.

These problems of articulation become, if anything, greater in the second, the *barrel-vaulted* or *coved* ceiling, whose surface is entirely covered with wooden boards suspended from the roof, creating an unbroken surface upon which the painter has a free hand. Nothing much can be done on such a surface, however, until it has been divided up into sections – until it has been articulated. Often the solution is to treat it to some false architecture, divide it up with *trompe l'œil* coffering, with the illusion of moulded rib-work or with false vaulting. Such divisions of the surface space create a number of smaller compartments that can be filled with images.

The medium for most of this painting is tempera colour. The painting was normally executed *in situ*, with the artist working above his head. The surface was first prepared by laying on a white ground, made up of a mixture of chalk and size, and the design was drawn onto this in a black outline, which was then filled in with colour. The black outlining remains visible and should not be seen as the sign of crude and unskilful work; in cases where the colour has since decayed or faded it remains our only clue as to what was represented. As Schomberg Scott says, 'The drawing of the outline and the infilling of colour were not necessarily done by the same hand. There are indications in certain instances that when more than one room in a house was being done at the same time, the master would draw in all the outline designs and then, in the less important places, leave the infilling of colour to his assistants' (Scott 1971, pp. 33–4). There are two places, Aberdour and Northfield, where the ground is not white but black, and at Prestongrange the grotesque designs are all executed on a ground that was originally a bright red.

Glue tempera is a type of water-based distemper, in which the pigment is suspended in a glue-based size. The pigments used are natural materials: lamp-black, chalk, lead- or iron-oxide for red, copper verdigris for green and a crushed azurite for blue. Though subject to discolouration as a result of damp or dirt, such pigments do not fade appreciably on exposure to light, but because they are water-based are badly damaged by water penetration. Many of the vanished examples fell victim to leaking roofs and gutters, and many survivors show signs of such damage. Several of the ceilings including some of the more important ones, only survived as a result of last-minute rescue operations. Since the 1950s, however, there has been a growing body of technical expertise devoted to their conservation and restoration at the Stenhouse Conservation Centre (now Historic Scotland Conservation) in Edinburgh. Many of the original ceilings were later plastered over; perhaps the best thing that could have happened to them since it afforded protection until paintings came to light during more recent alterations. As Schomberg Scott notes, 'No protective coat of varnish was ever applied by the original artists so that the finished surface should be absolutely matt, almost chrystalline. Where this has survived it can be appreciated how important it is to the general character. Unfortunately there are cases where varnish has been applied in the present century in a mistaken attempt at preservation and it has always proved wholly disastrous'. With some examples, particularly those that came to light in the nineteenth century, restoration consisted largely of heavy overpainting, so that much of the paint one sees at Crathes, at Stobhall, and at Gala House, for instance, is not original. Conservation techniques applied to the earliest property to come into the safe-keeping of the National Trust for Scotland, Culross, in 1937, turned out to be inappropriate to the tempera medium and, rather than conserving the paint, have destroyed most of it. Early pre-conservation sketches and photographs now represent the best record we have of some of this decoration. These include the colour sketches by the nineteenth-century architect, Thomas Bonnar, who drew a number of the schemes in the 1840s and 1850s as patterns or precedents for some of his own designs for the decoration of Victorian neo-baronial interiors. Bonnar's drawings, now conserved in the National Monuments Record in Edinburgh, not only offer a record of some of the surviving ceilings before more recent restoration or overpainting, but also represent the unique record of a number of examples, such as Dalcross and Borthwick castles and Pitcairn Church, which have since been destroyed. Early restorers did not scruple to supply missing detail or missing letters from an inscription, even managing in some cases to get the Latin grammar wrong. In looking at these paintings, therefore, we need to bear in mind that what we are looking at is not always what was originally painted or, at least, may not be the original paint.

Oil paint is sometimes used rather than tempera – for instance at Skelmorlie Aisle, or the panels from The Dean, Edinburgh – but was normally reserved for external use; indeed the accounts written in 1628–9 by the Master of the King's Works, James Murray, specify oil for external and tempera for internal surfaces at Stirling Castle, 'the window brodis to be layit over without with oyle cullour and within in Temper cullour and the articles weill set af' (*Maitland Club Miscellany* 1843, p 372). These instructions, and payments, are recorded specifically to the painter Valentine Jenkin, and they allow us a rare chance of identifying the actual painter responsible for the work. Valentine Jenkin also worked in Glasgow at this time, where he gilded the cock and painted the civic and royal arms above the Tolbooth, and in 1629 he was also being paid for work at Falkland Palace. In 1634 the accounts of Lady Hamilton record payments to the same artist for work at Hamilton and at Kinneil, allowing us almost certainly to ascribe the surviving painting of this period at Kinneil to him. It is seldom possible, however, to identify the artist who carried out the painting in specific buildings. We do know that in preparation for King James's return to Scotland in 1617 John Anderson (fl. 1599–1649) was summoned from Huntly Castle to carry out work at Falkland Palace, and at Edinburgh Castle, where he painted the room in which the king had been born fifty years earlier. George Jamesone, afterwards to become the most celebrated Scottish portrait painter of the seventeenth century, was Anderson's apprentice in 1612. Sir John Grant of Freuchie regarded Anderson as the only artist good enough to paint the ceiling of his gallery at Ballachastell. The only paintings to be signed by the artist are at Delgaty, where the initials 'JM' have been taken to be those of John Melville (or Mellin), who worked in Aberdeen, and the Skelmorlie Aisle at Largs, where one of the compartments is signed 'J Stalker fecit 1638'. This has to be the James Stalker who was registered apprentice to John Sawers in Edinburgh in 1632. Sawers, his master, was appointed Snowdon Herald in 1643 and compiled a manuscript armorial (National Library of Scotland, Advocates Manuscripts 31.4.4) and it may be Sawers and not his pupil who was responsible for the fine heraldic painting in the aisle at Largs. Other herald painters are worth recording, since they are very likely to have been responsible for decorative painting. Perhaps the most interesting of these is James Workman (fl. 1587–1633) who was appointed Marchmont Herald in 1597, and has left us an illustrated armorial manuscript which contains what look like sketches of biblical scenes for decorative use. We know that he, too, was paid for work at royal palaces, Edinburgh, Holyrood, Linlithgow, at various times between 1616 and 1633. Since he owned a house in Burntisland, Fife, it seems not unlikely that he was responsible for the two surviving painted ceilings at Burntisland, at Rossend Castle and at Mary Somerville's House.

There were no Painter-Stainers Guilds in Scotland as there were in England, and painters belonged to the same trade guild as the Wrights and Masons. Payment accounts confirm that they were normally expected to carry out not only artwork in the form of figure and scene paintings, but a whole variety of other types of work: John Sawers, for instance, was paid in 1618 for colours 'for painting of his majesties bed that wes sent up to London'; James Workman was paid for work on the ship that took the king to Denmark to bring home his queen in 1589, and for gilding and painting of the decorations that greeted Queen Anne on her ceremonial entry into Edinburgh (Apted and Hannabuss 1978, p 108). Use of the English term 'limners' is unknown in Scotland before the late seventeenth century and there seems to have been no distinction between what we would think of as 'art' painting and routine decoration. The painting we are looking at in this study is all the work of tradesmen; journeymen artists.

The surviving corpus of painting from the sixteenth and seventeenth centuries in Britain, though not exactly meagre, should nevertheless be regarded as small enough for us to want to preserve and document the whole surviving corpus. A primary aim of this study has been, therefore, to offer as exhaustive an account of Renaissance decorative painting in Scotland as possible.

Even before we have established the corpus, however, we need to ask various questions of these paintings, questions which we might distinguish under the separate headings of content and context. Under content, I assume that we want to know what the painting represents. In many cases that may seem obvious enough, though accurate description will often reveal significant details even in images that appear to be self-evident. But some of this painting represents subjects by no means obvious or commonplace and which have remained unidentified, or sometimes misidentified, by previous viewers. Allegorical and emblematic images, for instance, draw on the iconological systems of their day and can only be properly explicated once their iconology has been recognised. Such description and explication is fundamental; before we do anything else with this painting we need to know what we are looking at and what it represents.

Iconology is largely a matter of identifying sources and analogues for particular images. The best book on the decorative arts of this period in England, Anthony Wells-Cole's *Art and Decoration in Tudor and Jacobean England* (1997), concentrates on identifying sources in contemporary English and continental prints. Wells-Cole's pioneering study has shown just how derivative the decorative arts were at this period; very little appears to be original work. That sets it apart from many of our modern assumptions about 'creative' design and artistic originality – instead we probably need to bear in mind those much older Renaissance doctrines which saw the close connection between imitation and invention. Scottish decorative painting can be shown to be equally indebted to continental prints, and much of the discussion that follows will be taken up with an exploration of the relationship between specific paintings and particular prints which supplied their patterns.

Woodcuts and copperplate engravings circulated both in printed books – illustrated Bibles, natural histories, fable and emblem books – and as commercial prints which might be sold either in single sheets or in 'sets' which could be bound up. The printing of multiple copies from woodcuts developed in the late fourteenth century and the use of intaglio prints, where the ink lies in the grooves scraped out of a copper plate, developed in the late fifteenth. This technology helped to secure the circulation of multiple copies of the same image with consequences for the visual arts that were, arguably, almost as momentous as the invention of movable type was for the printed book. In the early sixteenth century there were still a few artists – of whom Dürer is probably best known – who excelled both in the art of painting and as engravers, but by the mid-sixteenth century a gap had opened between the artist who drew the pictures and the engraver who executed the print. That gap helped to foster the growth of a separate trade of professional craftsmen who made their living from the production of commercial prints. By the mid-sixteenth century there were leading European centres for printmaking in Italy (Rome, Florence, Venice, Bologna); France (Paris, Lyon); Germany (Augsburg, Frankfurt, Nuremberg); and the Netherlands (Antwerp, Rotterdam). As Wells-Cole says, 'It would be virtually impossible to list all the types of prints being produced by the middle of the sixteenth century. The range was vast, from illustrations to the Bible, Classical and modern literature, scientific discoveries, through title pages and page borders, printers' devices and emblems, to a whole range of popular printed ballads and broadsheets' (p. 5). They include subject prints and a specific genre, or genres, of ornament prints designed as patterns for the use of craftsmen in the design of jewellery, ceramics, needlework, armour, wood-carving, and interior decoration.

There were few printmakers in Britain before the late seventeenth century and fewer, if any, in Scotland, but continental prints are known to have been imported by merchants or purchased abroad by travellers. The cheapest single-leaf woodcuts would be sold by itinerant pedlars, and such prints have been shown to have been used for decoration by quite modest householders in England (Watt, 1991), but they are among the most ephemeral of such sources and there does not appear to be any place in Scotland that corresponded to the area of London, around St Paul's and Blackfriars, which became the recognised centre for London booksellers. Scholars such as Lucy Gent have begun the difficult work of trying to identify copies of particular prints in the inventories of English households at this period, so that we can begin to understand how popular they were among different social classes, but this work has hardly begun in Scotland. Nevertheless, the sheer number of different sources identified leaves no room for doubt that Scottish householders, or their painters, owned or had access to a large number of continental prints and regularly used them as patterns for decorative painting. It is not my purpose in this book to provide an exhaustive list of such print sources – I have not scoured the major

European prints collections for unknown sources and the extent of Scottish painting's indebtedness to early decorative prints remains to be fully researched.

Such source hunting helps us to define the context within which such images circulated and allows us to place national traditions in their international context. Source identification can also help us with problems of interpretation. Commercial prints and engravings in books of this period tend to identify their subject and comment on its significance. Emblematic decoration in buildings can be impenetrably obscure until one discovers its source in particular emblem books; then the accompanying epigram or commentary will generally explain what it is and what it means. The same is often true of biblical, classical, and more loosely allegorical images.

However, as with all source studies, it is important not only to identify the patterns that are used by decorative artists, but also to show exactly how they are used. This was, after all, a period when *imitatio* occupied a central place in the process of *inventio*. In some cases, certainly, we shall find the pattern functioning simply as a cartoon, to be copied exactly, but more often we shall find the Scottish patron, or his artist, adapting his source, changing significant details, or combining different sources to produce a new synthesis. This would suggest that some, at least, of this painting is engaging in an inventive process of original composition. Such composition at this period always used received materials.

Those materials constitute the pictorial vocabulary within which painting and the visual arts operated and it would seem to be worth documenting this corpus if only to clarify the different systems of representation, the particular visual economies, which were available to people living in Scotland at this time. They were quite rich, diverse, and complex. They have both native roots, in such areas as proverbial wisdom or national heraldry for instance, and specific lines of connection with foreign fashions such as European grotesque or 'antique' painting, continental mannerism, and Renaissance emblematics.

The appropriation of foreign styles and received images to a specifically Scottish tradition needs to be read in context. Better knowledge of how an image functioned in its source may clarify how it was understood in its Scottish application, but we also need to recognise that it may function differently in its new context from the way it functions in its source. Emblems were symbolic pictures teaching a generalised moral, applicable to any observer. They were often distinguished from personal devices, or *imprese*, which signalled the moral and political aspirations of their bearer. These more personal devices had been adopted – like the heraldic badge, which they closely resemble – by individual courtiers, nobles, churchmen and scholars from the later middle ages onwards, and in the sixteenth century they were often collected in printed anthologies that closely resemble the illustrated emblem books. When a painter takes images from Claude Paradin's *Devises heroúques*, however, to decorate ceilings at Rossend, at Nunraw, at Blyth's Close or the outside of houses in Edinburgh, it is by no means certain that they retain their original function as personal *imprese*. A lot depends on the way they are used, and on how they relate to the overall decorative programme and to the larger architectural statements made by the building of which they are now a part. The meaning of an image is likely to involve not only its received iconology but also the specific purpose it has in its new setting. The attempt to reconstruct a patron's or artist's motives for the selection of particular subjects and images is always likely to be speculative, however. It helps to find out as much as we can about the religious beliefs and social standing of the patron and, sometimes, the occasion of the original commission. We know, for instance, that the chapel of Stirling Castle was rebuilt and decorated to celebrate the baptism of prince Henry in August 1594, at a cost of £100,000, and that it brought together 'the greatest number of artificers in the whole country'. But in many cases information on the occasion and motivation for the painting has disappeared without trace.

Much may depend on where the decoration was located in the actual building. The work of modern scholars such as Mark Girouard or Maurice Howard has improved our understanding of the way buildings of this period were designed, where their main offices were located and how they were used. The changing architectural functions of the great hall and of the 'great chamber', the 'withdrawing chamber', closets, saloons, and galleries are increasingly well understood, at least in England. Some of the outstanding examples of decorative painting in Scotland – at Pinkie House, at Earlshall, at Cullen – are, indeed, to be found in that most characteristic of Renaissance apartments, the long gallery. The decorated long gallery in Scotland can tell us a lot about the way this well-known and much-studied feature of the early modern country house was designed and used. Hitherto, however, these impressive Scottish painted galleries have remained largely unknown to architectural historians.

We need to bear in mind that the buildings that were decorated with painting in Scotland were of many different kinds, ranging from royal palaces and fortified tower houses to modest town houses, merchant and burgess houses, private chapels and funerary aisles. Even when we know what kind of building contained the painted decoration, we do not always know what kind of apartment it decorated or what the apartment was used for. It has been suggested, for instance, that the wing of the Earl of Arran's house at Kinneil containing painted decoration was for the use of his wife and that its religious and heraldic iconography was designed to suit the needs of Lady Hamilton. If this were true it might be interesting evidence of the importance of gender in the choice of decorative subjects at this period, but I believe the assumption that this wing of the building was for her exclusive use is not as well established as it needs to be before embarking on a gendered reading of its iconography. In some cases where painted boards have been removed from their original locations for conservation it is no longer easy to establish which rooms in a house they originally came from – records have not always been as scrupulously kept as they ought to have been, and even where the painting remains in its original setting, subsequent alterations to buildings can make their original layout difficult to reconstruct.

A potentially useful distinction might be between public and private apartments. The decoration of public apartments is often seen as making statements about the social status, doctrinal or ethical values of the owner. Alexander Seton's painted gallery is an extended exercise in public self-fashioning, depicting its owner (literally, since it includes a rather remarkable portrait of him) as a neo-Stoic. Its programme of classical apophthegms and emblems lays great stress on modesty, moderation, friendship, and fortitude in adversity. Those values, so strongly exemplified in the long gallery, extend to the neoclassicism of the house as a whole, with its claim to be viewed as a Scottish *villa suburbana*. It is, indeed, surprising how many of the inscriptions that Seton placed on his house at Pinkie, both inside and out, talk about the building of which they are part. Here is a house which keeps telling us what it means, a building that, quite literally, speaks.

Other decoration is more private, located in rooms seldom, if ever, open to visitors. Private oratories, bedrooms, or withdrawing chambers used only by the occupants and their immediate family are more likely to offer texts and images for private devotion. The programme of emblems from Hawstead Hall in Suffolk, traditionally known as 'Lady Drury's Oratory', has now been shown to realise some of the emblematic images that are strongly implied in the *Occasional* and other meditations of her chaplain at Hawstead, Joseph Hall. Though we do not know exactly where these painted panels were located in the house, it is beyond doubt that they were designed to serve as emblems for private meditation (Mantz, Gardner and Ramsden 1997). There is nothing quite so specific or original of this kind in Scotland, and although the room decorated with Sibyls from Wester Livilands in Stirling has been described as an 'oratory', it is difficult to be sure what this small, very narrow room, subsequently converted into a stairway and cupboard, was really for, or how such images would have been used in any kind of spiritual exercise.

Painted images, particularly of a striking and memorable kind, were often recommended as suitable vehicles for use in the construction of a private memory theatre. The traditional *ars memorativa* was taught and practised in Scotland in the sixteenth and seventeenth centuries; indeed the Art of Memory became one of the skills to be mastered by craftsmen in the new Masonic lodges instituted and regulated by the architect and master of the King's Works, William Schaw (Stevenson, 1988). But though some of the cycles of imagery found in Scottish decorative painting at this period would have been well adapted for such use, I have found no evidence that they were actually designed for such purposes, and such memory schemes did not have to be located in a private apartment, they simply had to be committed to memory.

Traditional memory theatres not only made use of the types of imagery we find in Scottish houses but were often used to help memorise precisely the type of sententious wisdom frequently inscribed along the beams and elsewhere in their schemes of decoration. Any attempt to understand the function, or functions, of such schemes needs to come to terms with the conventions that influenced the manifold combinations of work and image in the art and culture of this period. The use of proverbial or sententious inscriptions in the decorative arts at this time is by no means unique to Scotland; indeed Tessa Watt has shown how prevalent was the use of 'Stories for Walls' among the applications of popular prints in England during the seventeenth century (Watt, 1991, ch. 5). But the sheer volume of writing inscribed on ceilings and murals from an early date in Scottish houses does seem to be something of a special phenomenon.

Such inscriptions take a variety of forms, in Scots and Latin. They vary from strict biblical quotations, often taken from the Geneva Bible (though the King James version is also used), through versified Scots proverbs, to Latin *adagia* and learned *sententiae*. Sometimes they have a discernible connection with adjacent images, as with the inscriptions voiced by the nine Worthies or the nine Muses at Crathes, but often seem to have no relationship at all with the surrounding iconography, as with the verse proverbs from the 'Green Lady's Room' at Crathes. Some of these Scottish cycles of proverbial inscriptions have the appearance of a private commonplace book writ large, and they were almost certainly influenced by some of the rhetorical functions which commonplace books traditionally served – they were compiled by students in order to master and memorise a number of classical or moral apophthegms, out of which written exercises could be composed. We need to be on our guard against the modern assumption that popular proverbs are an unsophisticated commodity whose natural home would have been the kitchen. Proverbial wisdom was collected, and memorised, by both the learned – students of rhetoric – and the unschooled at this period. Hence it probably makes no sense to insist on a clear break between vernacular proverbs, so often set out for us in spelling that suggests their native Scots pronunciation, and the kind of Latin learning represented by the *Adagia* of Erasmus, that great collection of Latin proverbs which spawned innumerable similar anthologies used as textbooks for Latin composition in schools. When George Bruce used the English epigrams to Geffrey Whitney's *Choice of Emblems* (1586) on his ceiling at Culross, he adapted their spelling to reflect his Scots pronunciation, making them sound like bits of native proverbial wisdom indistinguishable from the versified Scots proverbs we read on beam after beam, for instance at Delgaty. However, the mottoes to these same emblems at Culross are all in Latin. We cannot make anything of the choice of language in our, probably misguided, attempts to make hard and fast distinctions between popular and learned styles of decoration; this is not kitchen wisdom. Nevertheless, the Renaissance tradition of commonplace rhetoric is closely involved, as Walter Ong has shown, with a 'residual orality' which long outlasted the growing dominance of the print medium (Ong 1974, p 94), while the readiness of Scottish householders such as George Bruce or Alexander Hay to adapt the spelling of the (English) printed commonplace or emblem books to reflect Scots pronunciation almost certainly reflects the assumption that proverbial sayings are predominantly a spoken form. Whatever their printed sources, these painted inscriptions are strongly voiced.

Emblems, or emblem books, represent probably the most important vehicle through which the connections between work and image were regulated in Renaissance culture, which is why their prevalence in Scottish decorative painting needs to be acknowledged and accounted for. Although Scotland produced no emblem books or emblem writers of its own (with one or two possible exceptions),

Scottish culture was deeply infused with an emblematic mentality, and its material culture was deeply impregnated with applied emblematics. This whole context needs to be explored in order to understand how these emblems may be functioning in decorative painting in Scotland. Emblem books combine word and image in a closely regulated format that normally assumes their interdependence – the words explain the picture, the picture illustrates the words. However, we find not only schemes of decoration combining word and image in formats that preserve the tripartite combination of *inscriptio* (motto), *pictura* (image), and *subscriptio* (verse), but also schemes which simply appropriate emblematic images without accompanying text. Moreover, at least one example – Gardyne's House at Dundee – appears to have used lines taken from Francis Quarles's *Emblemes* (1635) with no accompanying pictures.

Emblems are by definition speaking pictures: ideographic images which call for interpretation, but the question of how much significance was retained once they were adapted to 'decorative' schemes is one to which I shall keep returning. Indeed, whether they had any significance once they had been stripped, as at Nunraw or at Rossend, of their accompanying texts, has to be open to doubt. Much depends on how familiar we can assume their viewers to have been with the received iconography. There are grounds for thinking that at least some of the patrons who commissioned the schemes were familiar with their sources and that, just as a biblical quotation would have called to mind for its early readers its biblical context, so at least a few of these emblems would have recalled their contexts. Some of the emblems of Paradin certainly became part of the stock-in-trade of the artisans who carried out the painting and sculpture that adorns these buildings; the reduplication of one or two of the more familiar designs at several different places (Paradin's *Spes altera vitae* device, for instance, which shows corn stalks growing out of a heap of bones) suggests that such emblems had become part of the painters' acquired design vocabulary with a received meaning that would have been easily understood by contemporary viewers.

That there was such an acquired vocabulary is beyond doubt. Decorative schemes were drawn on at site after site, where the patron evidently commissioned established styles of decoration used in buildings owned by his friends and neighbours. The garlands of fruits and flowers, with occasional animals, at Gladstone's Land are typical of a style of ornamental painting found in burgess houses of this period all down the Royal Mile in Edinburgh. Versions of it are found elsewhere too – at Galashiels, Stobhall, Aberdour, Northfield House and in St Andrews. The sides of beams are often divided into rectangular framed sections, each of which is filled with a stencil-like arabesque motif. The underside of the beams is sometimes decorated by a repeated motif which is difficult to characterise, but which I propose to call 'trailing tassel' since it takes the form of a tassel or pan-shaped object that diminishes or fades into its successor all along the beam. Vine scrolls with swags of other fruit, gourds, flowers and foliage can be elaborated at random or in repetitive sequences. Though close similarities sometimes suggest the work of a single painter (at Northfield House and Gladstone's Land, for instance), this was a design vocabulary easily taught to apprentice craftsmen and, once learned, could be applied by the yard.

It will become clear that heraldic painting was also of this type, part of the stock-in-trade of more than a few of the artists responsible for this decorative work, several of whom (James Workman, or John Sawers, for instance) were either official Heralds or had close connections with the Court of the Lyon King of Arms in Edinburgh, whose job it is to regulate the award of coats of arms (Scotland has no need of the English College of Arms; heraldry is a legal rather than academic discipline in Scotland). In some places (Kinneil, Collairnie and Pinkie, for example) herald painters were required to execute armorial schemes which had specific relevance to the dynastic connections of the owner; but elsewhere (at Balbegno, Nunraw and Linlithgow) they were called upon to execute extended armorials which could include the arms of the Scottish nobility, of royalty, of the nine Worthies, or of the 'Kings of Collene' (the Magi); arms which make no reference to the family connections of the patron. Clearly the execution of such a scheme called upon the artist's own mastery of the science of arms and of the specific heraldic achievements of the Scottish nobility. Such mastery must have been acquired through prior study at the Lyon Court, and what we find painted on such ceilings is very close to the extended armorial manuscripts, sometimes by the same painters, that have survived at the Lyon Court and elsewhere. Sometimes they made mistakes, and at least one, James Workman, compiled a manuscript (National Library of Scotland, Advocates MS 31.3.5) which a later Lyon King took to task for the frequency of its errors. When we examine some of these schemes of heraldic decoration it is instructive to put them alongside the illustrated armorial manuscripts they so closely resemble.

However, although the artists brought with them their own repertoire of styles and subjects on which a house-owner could draw, it will become clear that in many cases the patron had a major input into the design of the programme and the details of its execution. It is inconceivable that Alexander Seton's gallery at Pinkie does not call upon a depth of classical erudition way beyond the competence of a journeyman artist. Its emblems and inscriptions are demonstrably indebted to rhetorical skills its patron would have mastered in the course of his education by the Jesuits in Rome. Other schemes may well be informed by the humanistic tastes their patrons had developed as part of their education in the Scottish universities. The illustration of scenes from classical literature and mythology – at Cullen House and Monymusk, and in the Abbot House, Dunfermline – is likely to owe at least something to the educated tastes of their owners. The inclusion of the nine Muses and the nine Worthies at Crathes, and of the other commonplace schemes such as the Cardinal Virtues at Crathes and also at Earlshall, may owe something to the popularity such schemes gained from their depiction in prints and other familiar sources, but it is also likely to have been a deliberate choice on the part of the patron rather than simply part of the stock-in-trade of the artist.

Religious subjects, such as the Old Testament scenes at The Dean, the Passion cycle at Provost Skene's House, the *Veritas et Vita* panel from Blyth's Close,

Edinburgh, the Good Samaritan cycle at Kinneil, or the Last Judgement and four Evangelists at Grandtully, also have to be seen as decisions which were too important, not to say too controversial at a time of widespread religious iconoclasm, to have been left to the choice of the artist. Such choices can be assumed to reflect the particular doctrinal and sectarian convictions of the patron. It has often been claimed that the Reformation purged Christian iconography of representations of the Passion, the Virgin, and the saints, but we find instances of all of these in Scottish decorative painting of this period. For example, the merchant John Watson (or possibly his son Andrew) included not just the pagan Sibyls on his ceiling at Burntisland ('Mary Somerville's House'), but also images of the Agnus Dei and of the Virgin Mary with her name 'MARIA' inscribed on a label. Around 1620 Matthew Lumsden decorated the ceiling of his house in the centre of Aberdeen with scenes illustration the Annunciation, Nativity, Crucifixion and Entombment of Christ, together with the instruments of the Passion and the Stigmata. Lumsden belonged to an Aberdeen family several times persecuted for its recusancy; in 1629 the Register of the Privy Council records a complaint against Dr William Lumsden 'for hearing mass and resetting Jesuits', and in 1650 he was imprisoned; in 1656 his son, Patrick, was 'excommunicate for poperie' (Forbes Leith, 1909, III, p. 369).

The remarkable range of styles and types of subject matter that were available to decorative artists in England at this period is suggested by two extraordinary manuscripts executed in 1608 and in 1616 by Thomas Trevilian (or Trevelyon). Long known, at least by repute, to English art historians, their actual contents were familiar, until quite recently, only to scholars able to consult the originals, of which the 1608 volume is in the Folger Shakespeare Library, Washington DC. The larger 1616 version, which duplicates nearly all of the material from its predecessor, can now be consulted in Nicolas Barker's exhaustively researched edition (Barker, 2000). A glance at its contents will immediately suggest how much of the subject matter which we have already identified in Scottish decorative painting corresponds to the decorative vocabulary which was also favoured by English designers at this period. Consisting of 531 leaves comprising 1014 numbered pages, the *Great Book* includes a variety of material. The two hundred pages of what Barker identifies as 'the central part of the work' (Barker, vol. I, p. 10) include the twelve degrees of the world, the twelve tribes of Israel, the twelve apostles, the prophecies of the twelve Sibyls, the nine Muses, nine Worthies, seven Deadly Sins, seven Cardinal Virtues, seven Liberal Arts, seven points of humanity and inhumanity, five senses, four Ages of Man, and four continents. Then there are Old Testament subjects, moral tags and wise saws, and New Testament subjects which provide what Barker rightly describes as 'some unexpected images' – including the Annunciation, Nativity, Circumcision, Temptation, Crucifixion and Ascension, and the martyrdom of St Sebastian (although Trevilian makes his own anti-Catholicism quite clear elsewhere in the manuscript). Many of these images, which Trevilian depicts in vivid watercolour sketches, often with explanatory texts, have now been shown to copy woodcuts and engravings, including a number of the very same prints which – as we shall see – are also used by the decorative painters in Scotland.

Almost everything we know about Trevilian derives from what he tells us, or what he shows us, in these two manuscripts. Born in 1545, probably in Cornwall or the West Country, he almost certainly worked as an embroiderer or as a draughtsman for embroiderers, probably in London. The large number of embroidery patterns were for many years the only part of these books to have been reproduced (Nevinson, 1966–8); and until recently scholarly attention has largely been pre-occupied with attempts to identify actual embroideries of the period which use Trevilian's patterns. These identifications have had only modest success, and it remains the case that very few surviving artefacts in the material culture show any direct relationship with Trevilian's pattern books; indeed the very status of the books as pattern books is open to doubt and their function and purpose remains one of the greatest mysteries about them. They are, as Barker stresses, utterly unique: 'No other picture book of the period, manuscript or printed, is so large, in either the size or number of pages; none provides so large and diverse a profusion of visual imagery . . . What purpose the two books served, and why he made them, are questions to which there is no obvious answer' (p. 4). Subjects which we find both in Trevilian's books and in Scottish decorative painting include: the Sacrifices of Cain and Abel, copying the same print by Johannes Sadeler after Maarten de Vos that was used at Dean House, Edinburgh; the five Senses as depicted also by Sadeler after de Vos at Dean House; Judith and Holofernes at Dean House; the badges of the tribes of Israel at Skelmorlie Aisle; the nine Worthies at Crathes; the Cardinal Virtues at Earlshall; the parable of the Good Samaritan at Kinneil; and caryatids from Vredeman de Vries, also used at Prestongrange. Trevilian also has a fifty-page section of animals copied from Topsell's *Foure-Footed Beastes*, source of many of the animals at Earlshall (and widely used in decorative arts elsewhere in Britain at this time). Perhaps the most telling overlap between Trevilian's designs and Scottish painting is the set of pagan Sibyls which Trevilian has copied from a set of prints by de Passe which is also copied at Mary Somerville's House at Burntisland; but the verses which Trevilian has inscribed below the half-length portraits of the Sibyls in the *Great Book* are not found in any known print series; however they do correspond, word for word, to the sets of verses we find inscribed beneath another set of Sibyls from the house known as Wester Livilands, Stirling. This overlap confirms the case, which Barker and others have argued persuasively, for the widespread indebtedness of the decorative arts in Britain to ephemeral, popular prints, of which no copies may have survived. As it is very unlikely that Trevilian's books were the actual source or pattern for any of these Scottish examples, it must be the case that they go back to a common source.

What we perhaps need to recognise at the moment is the more general evidence that these examples provide of a shared vocabulary of styles and subjects between the decorative arts in both England and Scotland at this time. Although we can certainly make a strong case for the distinctiveness of the Scottish tradition, we need to recognise that there was at the same time a strong community of taste between the two countries.

Grotesque painting represents a style that certainly became part of the stock-in-trade of practising decorative artists. Originating in the antiquarian excavations of Nero's *Domus Aurea* in Rome in the late fifteenth century, it was adopted by Raphael for the decoration of the Vatican Loggia, and by imitators at major sites like the Escorial, Fontainebleau and the Doge's Palace, so that by the later sixteenth century it had become recognised across Europe as the authentic style for decorative painting *à l'antique*. Subsequent artists acquired their knowledge of the style both directly from actual buildings, some of them very famous, and from the growing body of prints and pattern books which supplied them with models, in particular the work of such Netherlands engravers as Cornelis Bos, Nicholas de Bruyn and Jan Vredeman de Vries. Their engravings supplied the patterns for decoration in several English houses of the sixteenth and seventeenth centuries (Wells-Cole 1997) and were also known in Scotland. The style is characterised by the fantastic transformation of images into monstrous and imaginary shapes, challenging that principle of truth to nature generally seen as the test of Renaissance art. Metamorphosis – of plants into humanoid or monstrous figures, of the animate into the inanimate, of the familiar into the strange – is fundamental to the style. Decorative painters quickly learned to elaborate their leaf scrolls into grotesque faces and to incorporate hybrid shapes of fantastic beasts – a woman with a fish's tail, a man's head upon a horse's neck (as Horace satirised in the opening lines of his *Ars Poetica*), so that we should not always assume that such designs copy a printed pattern, however often they do so. The narrow boarded sections of Scottish board-and-beam ceilings lent themselves to the transformation of one object into another in a continuing interplay of animate and inanimate shapes; we find some notable examples on the ceilings at Delgaty, at Nunraw, at Prestongrange, at Rossend, and at John Knox House in Edinburgh. Though some of the most accomplished of these copy continental prints, others appear to be original compositions.

By the mid to late seventeenth century such a style had become *démodé*, dismissed in 1658 in a telling comment by an English writer as 'ale-house' painting, but it always appears to have retained something of the prestige which attached to all manifestations of the antique in many of the highly prestigious buildings (castles and palaces, not ale-houses); this re-established its position in modern European architecture. What we may need to recover in a Scottish context is, indeed, some sense of precisely what status it held – what its recognised antecedents and associations were – for those who were redesigning and redecorating their houses, baronial or otherwise, in the remarkable flowering of Scottish domestic architecture of the late sixteenth and early seventeenth centuries.

Antique, or grotesque, painting had strong links with the wider development of European Mannerism in the visual arts. 'False architecture' is an expression that usefully describes the tendency of so much of this painting to reinterpret the architectural spaces it fills. Time and again we see how such painting remodels the surfaces and spaces it occupies in order to make them look like something they are not. The Montgomery Aisle at Skelmorlie, for instance, suspends a barrel-vaulted ceiling from its sloping roof, which it covers in boards painted with ribs, rising from false corbels, to imitate a stone-built vault; it then carries this rib-work across the soffit of the ceiling to divide the surface into panels in a kind of false coffering. Seton's long gallery at Pinkie does something similar. None of these buildings uses such *trompe l'œil* conventions with anything like the assurance of such places as Fontainebleau, but the questions we need to ask have less to do with the relative sophistication of this false architecture in comparison with acknowledged masterpieces than with what such practices imply about the cultural aspirations of builders and owners in a Scottish context. That they imply some kind of aspiration towards European models of architectural sophistication seems more than likely. Such aspiration does not depend wholly on the relative skill or finesse of their execution.

Trompe l'œil effects are certainly omnipresent in the decorative painting we shall be looking at, whether in the use of *trompe* pilasters to break up and articulate architectural spaces (Provost Skene's House, Argyll's Lodging), false corbelling, false coffering, or the extraordinary *trompe* lantern at Pinkie which, it can now be shown, copies a print from one of the most influential books of its time on the theory and practice of perspective, Jan Fredeman de Vries' *Artis perspectivae* (1st edn, Antwerp, 1568). The tendency to decorate ceilings with deities, radiant suns, angels, putti, moon and stars, may seem to be nothing more than naïve painting that never attains anything resembling the splendour of the European baroque, but the taste for ornamental strapwork, in which the painted surface is richly elaborated in outward-curving and receding segmented forms resembling leather-work (hence the name), clearly appealed to a decorative taste in which two-dimensional surfaces are interpreted as three-dimensional. Such strapwork is widely used in the ornamental cartouches that frame both texts and images on these surfaces, where the boundaries between frame and image may easily be rendered ambiguous. The design of such cartouches was, evidently, something on which an artist could exercise his inventive skills, which is why cartouche patterns were printed and sold by the same engravers who devoted their energies to grotesque patterns and caryatids.

Scottish use of continental engravings as patterns is evidence of its close connection with continental tastes and fashions. More work needs to be done before we can claim to have identified all the commercial prints which Scottish decorative painting copies, but enough sources have now been identified to leave no doubt that decorative prints and engravings circulated widely in Scotland at this period and constituted a major resource for decorative artists. Grotesque patterns from Verdeman de Vries were not only copied at Rossend and Prestongrange but incorporated in embroideries by Bess of Hardwick; prints by Etienne Delaune supplied the patterns for Mannerist decoration at Skelmorlie Aisle. Much of the stencil-like scrollwork that is everywhere painted along the beams of these Scottish ceilings closely resembles the type of 'arabesque' ornament marketed in numerous decorative pattern books by artists such as Virgil Solis, Jost Amman, Pierre Flötner and Theodore de Bry in Germany; by Androuet Ducerceau and Etienne Delaune in France; and by Frans, Jacob and Cornelis Floris, the Collaerts and de Vries in the Netherlands, though no particular sources have yet been identified.

Decorative painters did not confine themselves to such purely ornamental prints and patterns, for many of the classical, biblical and allegorical subjects depicted on these ceilings also go back to continental engravings. Often these are treated with some freedom. The Old Testament scenes from The Dean, for instance, rework engravings by Philips Galle after Maerten van Heemskerk (Judith and Holofernes), by Wierix and by Johannes Sadeler after Maarten de Vos (Abraham and Isaac, Cain and Abel), whilst its personifications of the five Senses owe something to engravings of the same subject after designs by Maarten de Vos. The Provost Skene's House Annunciation also has a number of details that must go back to one or other of the prints of this subject after designs by de Vos. Perhaps the most important of the printed books they used were the illustrated emblem books, and the way they copy, adapt, or reinvent the images from these provides us with the clearest evidence of the working methods of these artists. An examination of emblematic sources soon reveals the close relationship between imitation and invention in the decorative painting of this period in Scotland.

Books and articles mentioned in this text

Anderson, C. 1995 'Learning to Read Architecture in the English Renaissance' in L Gent (ed.) *Albion's Classicism: The Visual Arts in Britain, 1550 1660*, New Haven (Yale University Press).

Barker, N. (ed.) 2000 *The great book of Thomas Trevilian : a facsimile of the manuscript in the Wormsley Library*, 2 vols, London (Roxburghe Club).

Howard, D. 1995 *Scottish Architecture, Reformation to Restoration 1560–1660*, Edinburgh (Edinburgh University Press).

Macmillan, D. 1990 *Scottish Art 1460–1990*, Edinburgh (Mainstream).

Miscellany of the Maitland club : consisting of original papers and other documents illustrative of the history and literature of Scotland, 1840, A. MacDonald and J. Dennistoun (eds) 2 vols, Edinburgh (Maitland Club).

Scott, H.S. 1971 *Crathes Castle: An Illustrated Account*, Edinburgh (National Trust for Scotland).

Wells-Cole, A. 1997 *Art and Decoration in Elizabethan and Jacobean England: The Influence of Continental Prints*, New Haven (Yale University Press).

Wilson, D. 1848 *Memorials of Edinburgh in the Olden Time*, 2 vols, Edinburgh (Hugh Paton).

Music in the Courts of Mary Queen of Scots and James VI

Extracted from DJ Ross 1993 *Musick Fyne: The Art of Music in Sixteenth Century Scotland*, Edinburgh (Mercat Press), 129–39.

> *SCOTORUM TERNA NOMEN CUM LAUDE TRIUMPHA;*
> *SIT GENS PRO TITULIS NOBILITATA SUIS.*
> *VIRIBUS INDULGET, MULTOQUE INFRACTA LABORE*
> *DURA SUBIT, VERBIS PARCA, SED ALTA CUPIT*
> *SUBDOLA SIMULET FRAUDES INIMICIS, AMICUM*
> *PLURIS HABET REBUS, PATRIA CARA MAGIS.*
> *DURATURA DIU CRESCAT SUB SIDERE FAUSTO*
> *SCOTIA, CRISTICOLIS TERRA BEATA VIRIS.*
> *O SUA SEMPER AMES JACOBUM SCOTIA QUARTUM,*
> *QUO DUCE TE CELO FAMA SECUNDA FERET*

> Triumph with threefold praise, O name of Scots;
> May thy folk for their own merits honoured be!
> Proud of their strength, unbowed by heavy loads,
> They endure; few their words, yet they seek the heights.
> Though to foes it may seem they use deceit, yet their friends
> They value more than any thing, even than their native land.
> Long may Scotland thrive, beneath a favouring star,
> And lasting be the blessings on this folk that worships Christ.
> O thou, his Scotland, shouldst love James the Fourth
> By whose aid fair fame will carry thee to heaven!

> (From a '*carmen elegium*' written in July 1512 by James
> Foullis, procurator of the 'Scottish nation' at the University of
> Orleans. Translated into English by Jamie Reid Baxter.)

Hé! Quelle Musique! The Court of Mary

During her formative years at the French court, Mary had become both an accomplished poetess and an able performer on the lute and on that other seemly instrument of feminine recreation, the virginals. She is also reputed to have played the harp, but that instrument was already in sharp decline in Lowland Scotland, where people now looked to the south for the latest cultural trends, and where things Gaelic were regarded with growing contempt. Mary also had a fine singing voice (a French contemporary had described it as 'très douce et très bonne') and it is entirely possible that she sang to her own accompaniment on the lute or even took a line in the ensemble singing that is described for the first time during her reign. She maintained expressly for this purpose a ground of 'sangsteris' who doubled as *valets de chambre*.

The Queen also kept a group of 'violaris' (as many as seven at one stage, but settling down to four) and apparently all Scotsmen, to judge by their names. These may have been joined on occasion by any of the three lutenists in her employment, while recorders and reed instruments (increasingly the more refined 'hautbois', probably already very similar to the two-keyed Baroque oboe) played an active role. The obligatory trumpeters were occasionally replaced by cornetists, probably guests from England or the Continent, while Italian musicians also frequented the court.

Against this lively musical backdrop, one or two individuals stand out, and not always by reason of their musical prowess. David Rizzio (Riccio) came to Mary's court in the entourage of the visiting ambassador of Savoy, and seems at once to have caught the eye of the young Queen. He was invited to sing bass with her three valets, 'to be ther fourt marrow, in sort that he was drawen in to sing somtymes with the rest', and presently received a permanent post as her secretary. In addition to singing, he seems also to have played stringed instruments including the fiddle, and he possibly also composed, although no music which can be attributed to him has survived. Although undoubtedly 'a merry fallow, and a good mucitien', he almost certainly did not play the seminal role subsequently credited to him in later accounts of Scottish musical history, and his main claim to fame remains his gory death at the hands of a group of Scottish nobles, led by Mary's estranged husband Darnley, in Holyrood Palace. Darnley, a neurotic and sickly young man, undoubtedly suspected that Riccio had taken advantage of his privileged position as Mary's secretary, but there is no evidence to back up the claim made in Francis Osborne's *Traditionall Memoyres* that James VI, the child whom Mary almost miscarried as a result of Rizzio's murder, was 'David the Fiddler's son'. There was surely enough of the impetuous and devious Darnley in James to scotch that libel!

Less colourful than the ill-fated Rizzio were father and son James and John Lauder. James Lauder (*c.* 1535–*c.* 1595), composer, singer and performer on the organ and the virginals, studied music both in England and in France, and took up a position at the Scottish court early in the 1560s as one of Mary's *valets de chambre*, composing consort music and part-songs. Both he and his son John accompanied Mary on her flight to England in 1568, and the latter, a player of the 'base violin', stayed with Mary until her execution in 1587. By this time his father was back in Scotland, composing and playing, and a number of pavens from this period which are recorded by the eclectic Thomas Wode may well be his work.

The paven is a sedate processional dance in four, or occasionally three beats in the bar, which (usually coupled with the more vigorous galliard) was in considerable vogue in the sixteenth century, both at the English court and on the Continent.

Prince Edward's Paven, recorded by Wode, appeared in a five-part setting in a collection of dances printed in Paris in 1555 by Claude Gervaise, and a number of related pieces were copied and set elsewhere in Europe. It is possible that the *Prince Edward's Paven* is a Scottish contribution to this body of music.

If the original paven melody is Scottish (although there is no evidence that it is), it possibly belongs to the period when Prince Edward, the son of Henry VIII, was being considered as a spouse for Mary Stuart, before the ascendancy of the French party at the Scottish court ensured that the two-year-old Mary 'jilted' the infant Prince in 1543, in favour of the Dauphin and the bonds of the Auld Alliance. The four-part setting recorded by Wode is almost certainly later in date than this, but its static harmony suggests that it is one of the earliest of the pavens recorded by Wode, in a style which directly anticipates that of James Lauder.

Another of the pavens, described by Wode as 'Ane uther paven verray gude', also demonstrates features similar to Lauder's later work and is perhaps one of his early compositions. It displays a solid rather than inspired approach to counterpoint, but the composer does take scrupulous care that rhythmic initiative is shared among the four voices and that a constant forward momentum is maintained. There are even traces of motivic development in the final section, which explores the potential of a rising figure comprising two quavers and a crotchet, itself a development of the initial figure of the paven.

In the *Dublin Virginal Book* (*c.* 1570) this paven is coupled with a pleasant galliard which seems closely related in material and style. While Wode records only pavens, it is possible that many of them were originally composed in tandem with galliards, in accordance with English and Continental practice.

In 1584 James Lauder was commissioned to write a paven to celebrate the assumption in 1580 of the title of Earl of March by Robart Stewart, son of the third Earl of Lennox. This was the same Robart Stewart who as Commendator of St Andrews Priory had commissioned David Peebles' motet *Quam multi Domine* some eight years earlier. The resulting *My Lorde of Marche Paven*, the only piece which can definitely be attributed to James Lauder, is the finest consort work of this whole period, a masterpiece of precision and invention written by a mature composer in complete control of his medium. Thomas Wode records the melody and the alto part, while *David Melvill's Bassus Part-Book* (1604) provides the bass, and other sources indicate that the piece was originally in four parts.

The first three bars establish a dotted crotchet-plus-quaver rhythm, while bar four covers the same ground in diminution and extends the phrase. The ensuing section is dominated by a syncopated figure, proposed by the upper voice, imitated immediately by the bass and which gradually pervades the texture with the help of the alto part. This quaver-plus-crotchet-plus-quaver figure is passed from voice to voice and is juxtaposed with a dotted quaver-plus-semi-quaver figure, which springs directly from the diminution of bar four. The syncopated figure is further explored in the concluding section, where in the penultimate phrase it undergoes diminution, simultaneously recalling bar four and leading through a tightening of the syncopation to a satisfactory cadence – a crowning stroke of inspiration.

This rhythmic sophistication is complemented by a new eloquence of phrase, making *My Lord of Marche Paven* a joy to play and to listen to, performed either by a mixed or a full consort, especially of viols.

By 1584, when Lauder composed *My Lord of Marche Paven*, much water had passed under the bridge. On 10 February 1567 Mary's second husband, Henry Stewart, Lord Darnley, estranged from her since the murder of Rizzio, had himself been brutally murdered at the age of twenty-one by a band of conspirators, who almost certainly included James Hepburn, Earl of Bothwell, whom Mary married three months later on 15 May. Bloody civil war was only averted by Mary's surrender to a group of Protestant Lords at Carberry Hill on June 15. Bothwell fled and on 24 July Mary was forced to abdicate in favour of her thirteen-month-old son, James VI.

Such were James Lauder's musical skills that his reputation survived Mary's fall (and his son's continuing association with her), and by the time he had fulfilled Robart Stewart's commission in 1584, the turmoil of the 1560s was a distant memory. James VI, now a precocious adolescent of eighteen, had assumed personal control over court and nation and had established his cultural circle, the Castalian Band, a group of talented practitioners of all the arts, whose influence would bring secular music at the Scottish court to new pinnacles of excellence.

With Most Delicate Dulce Voices: The Court of James VI

In the period from 1567 to 1578 when the child James was little more than the political pawn of his Protestant nobility, he was assigned the great scholar George Buchanan as tutor and four English 'violaris' for his entertainment. Buchanan was one of the most consummate intellectuals that Scotland has ever produced, a poet (in the opinion of his contemporaries 'poetarum sui saeculi facile princeps') an unrivalled master of Renaissance Latin, a political thinker far in advance of his time and a formidable linguist, who spoke Gaelic and whose analysis of the Celtic languages modern research has done little more than confirm. He had once been Queen Mary's Latin tutor, and portraits of him bear the legend:

> *Sic Buchananus ora, sic vultum tulit: Pete scripta et astra, nosse si mentem cupis*
> (Thus Buchanan wore his features, thus his face: if you would know his mind, ask for his writings and the stars.)

The 'violaris' were Thomas, Robert, James and William, the brothers Hudson, 'sangsteris, inglismen, violleris' and much more besides, who had reached the Scottish court in the entourage of Lord Darnley and weathered the ensuing chaos and bloodshed to emerge with the young king into a new flowering of the arts.

Two consort pieces by John Blak, preserved in seventeenth century sources but probably written in the 1560s, give some idea of the sort of music the king's 'violaris' might have played. *Black called fyne musick* displays an inventive approach to melody with an assertive chordal section midway through suggesting a verse and chorus structure, while *Blak major* presents a more restive and insistent aspect with deft handling of motivic development within a consistently contrapuntal texture.

By March 1578 James had achieved some degree of autonomy, and a part-song probably written to celebrate his triumphal entry into Edinburgh in October 1579, *Nou let us sing*, reflects the optimism which greeted yet another emergence from minority. Chordal throughout, and not unlike *O Lusty May* in its robust simplicity, this drinking song is probably connected with the revels of this carefree time, praising the young king, calling upon Bacchus to grace the company with his blessing through the ministrations of the 'Deame' or hostess, and amusingly introducing in turn each of the voices, the 'Treble', the 'Counter', the 'Tenor' and the 'Basse', who list their own distinctive qualities and extol their own virtues, each in his own verse. The thirst of the performers is regularly reaffirmed, and in the final verse they unite forces in a mock-desperate plea to the hostess:

> Deame, ye are sweir that lets us cry
> Once fill the stoop and let us rest.

Also from this period is a delightful piece of consort music, *Ane Exempill of Tripla*, probably composed as an academic exercise especially for *The Art of Music*. It consists of a vigorous *cantus firmus* in compound time, perhaps a popular melody, to which a complementary bass and two lively upper parts have been added. The piece exploits delightfully a continuous ambiguity between compound 6/8 time (two groups of three quavers) and simple 3/4 time (three groups of two quavers) with catchy syncopations and dancing dotted rhythms – in short, it is a charming little gem which belies its rather prosaic title.

It is perhaps frank frivolity and pleasure-taking of this kind, as much as the King's renewed cultivation of the Catholic French connection in the person of the dashing Esmé Stuart, Lord d'Aubigny, whom James created Duke of Lennox in 1581, which stampeded his Protestant nobility into seizing him and controlling his policies until 1583. Only after this was James able to determine fully the direction he wished to follow, and there ensued the culturally prosperous years of the Castalian Band, which derived its name from the spring in Mount Parnassus frequented by the muses and Apollo himself. The rather pretentious analogy is obvious.

This exceptional circle, grouped around the gifted young James and comprising the greatest artists of the age, produced a lively ferment of creativity and interaction, which led to the production of some of the finest of all Scottish Renaissance works. The most accomplished of these artists was the poet Alexander Montgomerie, a militant Catholic who had accompanied the charismatic Esmé Stuart to Scotland in 1579, and who survived his expulsion to lead a precarious artistic existence at court, only ever as secure as the volatile religious politics and the whim of the young King would permit – his poetry occasionally rails at the King's inconstancy with the sort of petulance normally associated with a Romantic poet crossed in love.

Although Montgomerie's poetry displays some knowledge of music and he seems to have chosen musicians for his personal friends, no music by him has been identified, and it is entirely possible that his musical gifts lay rather in the direction of performance and in producing song texts either to fit pre-existent melodies, or so well crafted as to be a joy to set to original music – and there was no shortage of capable composers in the Castalian Band on hand to do just that.

Kenneth Elliott recognises features of the style of James Lauder in the settings of Montgomerie's *Evin dead behold I breathe* and *What mightie motion*, and the settings of his lyrics *No wonder is suppose*; and *In throu the windows of myn ees* may also be Lauder's work. Thomas Wode credits Andro Blakhall with setting Montgomerie's *Adieu, O desie of delyt* to a new harmonisation of a pre-existent melody, and the harmonisation of Nicholas de la Grotte's quirky melody which matches Montgomerie's equally quirky lyric, *Lyk as the dum Solsequium*, could also be by Blakhall, or perhaps by another of the prominent composers of the Castalian Band, such as Thomas Hudson, his brother Robert (a particular friend of Montgomerie), or William Kinloch.

The beautifully measured setting of Montgomerie's *Evin dead behold I breathe* is among the finest part-songs of this period, almost thoroughly chordal, except for the occasional detail of rhythmical variance in one of the parts. But it is in the subtleties of harmony that one detects the advance from earlier part-songs and which calls to mind the name of James Lauder. The opening phrase displays the type of High Renaissance suspension which religious composers had been employing for a generation by this time, and some of their facility with harmonic shading is apparent in the juxtaposition of é natural and é flat in the second phrase. All of this marks a radical departure in the art of part-song composition.

What mightie motion carries this a stage further with the sophistication of its striking refrain, 'alace, alace, that ev'r I leirnd to love', where again the gentle shading of an e´ flat is juxtaposed with the expected e´ natural, this time in a way which is nothing short of masterly.

Particularly in vogue at the Scottish court at this time, thanks to the admonitions of James VI, was alliterative verse, where the poet attempted to string together in each line of his poem a series of words beginning with the same sound. To the uninitiated this at first sounds rather peculiar, particularly when viewed from an age which has been more inclined to concentrate on end-rhymes and to relegate alliteration to the role of a special effect. But alliterative poetry has a long history in the oral traditions of most of the Germanic languages, and before Chaucer, English poetry was alliterative too.

Montgomerie carries the alliterative style of writing, already fundamental to the very earliest Scottish part-song texts such as *O lusty May*, to extremes in such lines as:

> A frentick fevir through my flesh I feill;
> I feill a passion can not be expresst;
> A feill and byll with my bosum beill;
> No cataplasme can weill impesh that pest.

The composer again intelligently responds with a rhythmically simple setting, chordal with occasional syncopation, allowing the poetry to speak for itself. The effect is all the more impressive when the seemingly inexorable flow of words and music is brought to a standstill on the first syllable of the refrain.

More contrapuntal in texture is the part-song *In throu the windows of myn ees*, where Montgomerie's imaginative text is conducted through a rich forest of musical invention, led by the tenor part in the manner of the finest French chansons. Syncopated and harmonically varied, it complements the text pleasingly as it relates the melodramatic tale of a lover who has taunted Cupid and now reaps the whirlwind. Montgomerie's use of alliteration and his uncanny ability to breathe life into the most improbably scenarios through dialogue and description make this a most rewarding part-song text – and the anonymous composer fulfils his role discerningly and unobtrusively.

Adieu, O desie of delyt demonstrates a more elaborate interplay of music and words. Montgomerie's text used the elaborate Helicon stanza, while Blakhall's setting, part of a general striving on the part of the Castalian Band towards the perfect synthesis of words and music, is the ultimate in High Renaissance simplicity, largely chordal in texture, with the tenor and treble parts moving in parallel thirds against a backdrop of contrary motion in the other parts. And yet from its first to its last perfect open fifth, this part-song is perfection indeed, exemplifying in its calm restraint and moderation that Golden Mean so highly prized in the Renaissance.

Also written in Helicon stanzas, Montgomerie's *Lyk as the dum Solsequium* draws an analogy between the sunflower drooping its head when the sun goes behind a cloud and the lover hanging his head when his mistress is absent. The revitalisation of the flower when the sunlight returns is given erotic undertones when applied to the lover. The poem is matched with a setting of a melody by Nicholas de la Grotte, which alternates simple and compound time, even and dotted rhythms and major and minor chords in a dazzling showpiece of flair and sweeping confidence. The survival of even one galliard by James Lauder or of consort music by Andro Blakhall might have helped us to attribute this piece of exquisite craftsmanship – or perhaps, after all, Alexander Montgomerie's skills extended further than has been supposed.

From the pen of another of the Castalians, William Kinloch (*fl.* 1582), comes the earliest surviving Scottish music for keyboard, recorded in *Duncan Burnett's Musicbook* of around 1610, but probably composed in the latter decades of the sixteenth century. Ranging from simple dances (with ornamented versions or divisions written out in full) to more elaborate programme pieces, such as the *Batell of pavie*, this body of music is fascinatingly informative as well as being fine original music.

Although Kinloch's is the first Scottish music for the instrument to survive, we know that there was a strong tradition of virginal playing at the Scottish court and that Mary, Queen of Scots was an enthusiast. It is entirely possible that the leading composer of her reign and a player of the virginals himself, James Lauder, composed for the instrument, and his survival to 1595 would have allowed him to influence the style of William Kinloch.

Of particular interest in Kinloch's work are the divisions, which largely follow the tenets of the English virginal masters as exemplified by the *Fitzwilliam Virginal Book*, with cascades of running scales, often with flattened sevenths at their peaks, and recurring sequential figures. While these examples of ornamentation are clearly in a keyboard idiom, they provide some picture of how Scottish musicians in general might have been ornamenting consort music in performance – clearly the florid muse of Carver was still alive and flourishing at the end of the century.

Fine examples of this rich decoration occur in *Kinloch his Lang pavane*, and the *Galliard of the Lang paven* which, in addition to displaying a fine disdain for spelling conventions, demonstrate a particularly high degree of invention. As the magisterial *Lang pavane,* with its major/minor ambiguity, unfolds section by section, the interposed divisions each seize upon and elaborate one particular aspect with a Carveresque thoroughness and inventiveness. Related material is given still more varied treatment in the *Galliard*, with sections in triplets, double diminutions and syncopation enhancing the virtuosic impression as detailed in the section on 'prolation' in *The Art of Music.*

Duncan Burnett (*fl. c.* 1615–1652), who recorded Kinloch's works in his music books, continued the tradition of Scottish keyboard composition into the seventeenth century, but by that time the magic of the Castalian Band had been broken. Alexander Montgomerie drifted further and further from his royal patron and into the arms of Catholic conspiracy. He died in 1598 in his late forties, having spent the last year of his life as an impoverished outlaw. The first-generation Castalians were growing older, and James' attention was increasingly taken up with the tantalising prospect of a United Kingdom of Great Britain and the seemingly inexhaustible coffers of England. By the time he eventually secured his prestigious prize, the output of the Band had become fitful. The withdrawal of patronage in 1603 left the second generation of Castalians with an interrupted tradition and a flagging impetus. These youthful talents dispersed themselves around the castles of the aristocracy, where they prepared to write an epilogue to Scottish Renaissance culture.

Early Modern Literature

ARTICLE 38A
SCOTTISH CULTURE IN ITS HISTORICAL PERSPECTIVE

Extracted from M Lynch 1993 *in* PH Scott (ed.) *Scotland: A Concise Cultural History*, Edinburgh (Mainstream), 15–45.

The major events or themes in Scottish history – such as the coming to power of Kenneth mac Alpin in 843, the Wars of Independence which afflicted Scotland for almost a hundred years from 1296 onwards, the Reformation of 1559–60, the Union of 1707 and the Enlightenment of the mid-eighteenth century – are easy to list, even if historians' lists would vary a little. The impact of such landmarks on Scotland's cultural history is less easy to evaluate. Each of those listed above, it is possible to argue and it was argued at or near the time, was a turning point, at which the concern of contemporaries was less the past than the present. A series of anonymous chroniclers were intent, after 843, at making Kenneth mac Alpin the symbol of a new kind of kingship as well as the founder of a new dynasty; John Knox, in his *History of the Reformation*, devoted only 300 words to the centuries of Scottish history before the arrival of its first Protestants, the Lollards of Kyle; within a couple of pages he had reached the tragic account of Scotland's first Protestant martyr, Patrick Hamilton, burned at St Andrews in 1528; a long line of later Presbyterian historians would pass over the Middle Ages in a quest for their own roots in the primitive Christianity of the Columban Church. In a similar vein, William Robertson, in his *History of Scotland*, first published in London in 1759, which celebrated the present age of politeness as an escape from a trouble and barbarous past, cast off the centuries of Scotland's history before 1500 as unworthy of consideration. The present 'enlightened' generation was the 'historical age' of David Hume; the 'historical nation', in the words of two distinguished modern historians of the Enlightenment, moved 'almost overnight' in the 1750s from a position of cultural isolation to being the 'centre of the thinking world'. In 1929 Robert Boothby, then a promising young Conservative politician, in turn dismissed Scottish history before the Union of Parliaments:

> Prior to 1707 the Scottish people were a pack of miserable savages, living in incredible poverty and squalor, and playing no part in the development of civilisation. Since 1707, they have been partners in the greatest undertaking the world has ever seen.

This was a view which surfaced again during the general election of 1992, which in Scotland provoked a historical debate about the effects of the Union which might have taken place in the polite salons of mid-eighteenth-century Edinburgh. When Sir Nicholas Fairbairn, Conservative MP, opined: 'Look at the food – oatcakes, haggis, broth – it's all peasant fare. This was a peasant country before the Union', it was clear that the wheel had again come full circle: North British rhetoric was *redivivus*.

One of the oddities of the position taken by Conservative politicians such as these is that it owes more to a Whig interpretation of history than a Tory one; the past is seen as a struggle between progressives and reactionaries with the progressives eventually winning. Although the crudities of the Whig position have generally rendered it out of favour with most modern historians, it nonetheless persists – in various forms – in assessments of Scotland's cultural history. Knox, Robertson and the Unionist view of Scottish history are all examples of it, highlighting a decisive turning-point which suddenly brought Scotland into a new godly, 'modern' or more civilised age. Various schools of Scottish history – Presbyterian, Enlightenment and Unionist – have a vested interest in the construction of a major watershed somewhere in Scotland's past.

During the past generation, there has been a distinct tendency amongst historians to stress the overarching continuities – in social and economic history especially – which give some coherence to the complex story of Scotland's past. In every century until the nineteenth, it has been asserted, the forces of continuity outweighed those making for change. In recent years, the same features have notably marked studies of the major components of Scotland's culture – in art, historiography, music and philosophy, and, to a lesser extent, in architecture and literature. David Allan, for example, has traced a 'compelling moral vision', based on a philosophical core of 'Presbyterian humanism', which ran as a consistent thread linking the historical writings of John Knox and George Buchanan not only with half-forgotten seventeenth-century philosopher historians such as the mathematician Thomas Crauford and the lawyer and linguist Sir Robert Spottiswoode but also with the giants of the Enlightenment, including David Hume, Adam Ferguson and William Robertson. Alexander Broadie, focusing on the intellectual ferment of the opening decades of the sixteenth century, has similarly linked the circle of John Mair in the 1520s and 1530s with the philosophers who formed the school of Francis Hutcheson in the generation after 1720.

The Reformation was in a number of significant ways, and not least in culture and learning, less of a watershed than is often assumed. John Durkan has shown how developments in both the universities and grammar schools in the pre-Reformation period prepared the ground for the primacy given by the Protestant reformers of 1560 to establishing a godly, educated society. John Purser has shown that music did not entirely disappear after 1560 and that some of the notable early successes of the new Protestant religion in evangelising society depended on the blunt instruments of new, simple words being set to existing popular tunes. Duncan Macmillan has demonstrated that the power that painting had as public propaganda was too valuable a weapon to be abandoned after the Reformation, by the Crown and even, to an extent, by the Reformed Church. The Protestant reformers, confronted by an instinctively conservative society, faced the most formidable obstacles in the spheres where they argued for a new society; the first generation of Protestant preachers, hampered by the insistence on the purging of 'idolatrous' paintings, statues and images and faced by congregations where typically less than a quarter of adult males could read, had less evangelical tools with which to fight the good fight than the parish priests and chaplains of the pre-Reformation Church.

The Reformation, as a result, for a time succeeded most readily in the areas where it could draw on the cultural treasury of the late medieval Scotland. Pre-Reformation song schools were not disbanded but refounded as vernacular schools, practising godly psalms, sung to a small batch of common tunes. The inculcation of the simple truths of the Gospel took generations to achieve in a semi-literate society, and the most potent weapon in the Kirk's armoury was the psalter rather than the catechism or bible. As late as the mid-seventeenth century, many congregations relied on a precentor to sing tune, pitch and words, to be repeated line by line; the psalms of David, which had been central to the worship of the Scottish Church since at least the twelfth century, continued, with a new purpose and vigour after the Reformation.

Four other initial sets of points are worth making. Throughout Scottish history, it will be seen, the culture of the present has been informed by a highly developed, self-conscious sense of the past. Even the Reformation, after the first flush of iconoclastic enthusiasm was over, was not an exception to this rule. In 1633, when an elaborate, formal entry was prepared to mark the first visit of Charles I to his capital, one of the centrepieces was a huge, timber Parnassus, built in the middle of the High Street, near where the Tron Kirk now stands. On it, amidst a double-topped mountain 'stopit full with books' were displayed representations of the 'ancient worthies of Scotland for learning'. The contents of this three-dimensional cultural history of Scotland were significant: they featured Duns Scotus, Scotland's most celebrated academic philosopher; Robert Henryson, schoolmaster and the greatest poet of the age of James IV; William Elphinstone, bishop of Aberdeen, a rector of Glasgow University and founder of Scotland's third university, at Aberdeen, doyen of the late medieval class of churchmen who were simultaneously distinguished scholars and skilled administrators of the Crown; Hector Boece, chronicler, who had returned from Paris to become the first rector of Aberdeen's new university; John Mair, logician and historian, a teacher at Glasgow and Paris before he became principal of the new College of St Leonard's at St Andrews; Gavin Douglas, bishop of Dunkeld, royal tutor and translator of Virgil's *Aeneid*; Sir David Lyndsay, royal herald, tutor to James V, poet and playwright; and George Buchanan, another principal of St Leonard's, one of the most celebrated humanists in sixteenth-century Europe, and author of the most widely published history of Scotland to date. The Parnassus of 1633 is clear evidence of the status then given to learning: the 'worthies' included five academics and a schoolmaster; it celebrated three of Scotland's recent and most influential historians; it mirrored some of the best-selling printed works of the early seventeenth century, which included Lyndsay's collected words and Henryson's *Testament of Cresseid*; and it reinforced the justification which Elphinstone had himself given for his new university, founded '*pro patria*'.

The conclusion to be drawn from this temporary national monument, constructed for the benefit of Scotland's first fully absentee king, are clear enough. The works of the Renaissance, fostered in the Courts of James IV and V, had reached, through the new medium of the printing press and a wave of patriotic publishing which marked the three-quarters of a century after 1570, a new and much wider audience. The importance attached to learning and the need for a national system of schooling formed a bridge across the troubled waters of the Reformation century. The continuum of Scotland's culture and learning were perceived to be part of the very fabric of its historical identity. This was a view which remained unchallenged until the polite historians of the Enlightenment.

A Long Renaissance?

The fifteenth century should not be thought of as the 'end of an auld sang' but as the first act in a series of cultural patterns which would, for the most part, lead to the Enlightenment of the eighteenth century. In this century, Scotland's first three universities were founded: at St Andrews in 1412; another college (St Salvator's) erected at St Andrews in 1450 to teach theology and philosophy; a College of Arts founded in Glasgow in 1451, and the setting up at Aberdeen in 1495 of the College of St Mary in the Nativity (or King's College). Further colleges shortly followed at St Andrews: St Leonard's, erected in 1513 as a 'college of poor clerks' based on the austere model of the College of Montaigu in Paris, was fuelled by Augustinian piety; St Mary's, first mooted in 1525, given formal foundation in 1538 and reorganised in 1544, would become the centre of the movement for internal reform of the Church in the late 1540s and 1550s. All these foundations were the acts of bishops, who placed them at the centre of their dioceses, and were clerically endowed. Even if the number of graduates was still modest, amounting to perhaps a hundred a year by the 1540s, all this amounted to a national programme for higher learning – Elphinstone referred to his university as being built for the 'glory of the fatherland'.

The most talented and ambitious of these graduates who wished to pursue their studies further, usually by specialisation in those passports to ecclesiastical preferment – canon and civil law – continued to go abroad, to the great universities of Western Europe, as Scots, such as Duns Scotus (d. 1308) who had gone to Oxford and Paris, had done for centuries. Yet not the least of the achievements of the new university foundations was that they partly reversed the academic brain drain: Hector Boece, lured home by Elphinstone from the College of Montaigu to become the first Principal of Aberdeen University, was a close friend of the great Erasmus and a devotee of the new learning; and John Mair (or Major), who had gained a European-wide reputation while at Paris, returned to become Provost of St Salvator's College in 1534. This was the generation of scholars which brought the 'humanist revolution' to Scotland: it was based on the study of classical languages, Greek and Hebrew as well as Latin, and a new understanding of Aristotle. Far less is known of the other two sectors of the medieval education system – the grammar schools and the variety of 'little', song and vernacular schools. Duns Scotus had gone to a grammar school at Haddington and it seems likely that the upsurge in university education reflected an increase in the number of grammar schools, which were based mostly in towns. Many were associated with cathedrals or with collegiate churches. Some religious houses, too, had monastic schools which opened their doors, like the Cistercian abbey at Kinloss, to a wider intake of boys. Some friaries had their own 'lector' in theology or arts, and the Dominican house at Ayr had a tutor in grammar in 1420. By the time of the Education Act passed by parliament in 1496, which encouraged the attainment by the sons of barons and freeholders of 'perfyte latyn', it seems likely that the growing demands of the state for administrators and lawyers may have been threatening to outstrip supply. The course of the sixteenth century would see the increasingly heavy hand of state intervention in both the grammar schools and the universities, but the curriculum remained much the same as in 1530. The nature of the training of the intellect changed before the Reformation rather than after it.

The sixteenth century brought a Reformation, but it came late to Scotland and this is immensely significant. The Reformation needs to be set alongside but disentangled from the two other phenomena with which it was intimately connected: the humanist revolution and the arrival of the printing press. Without these twin props, the effects of the Reformation are easily exaggerated or dated too early. There was only a modest return of Scots Protestant exiles from abroad to provide clerical leadership and impetus.

The Reformation is better understood as one part of a three-headed revolution, much of which had already been set in train more than a generation before 1560. When combined with the rise of humanism and access to the new print culture, the impact of Protestantism was startling. It benefited immeasurably from the spread of the new learning in academic circles and from the growth of a new reading public amongst the 'middling sort'. The new humanism continued Scotland's intimate links with the universities of Western Europe. The printing press had by 1600 already become the instrument of a mass culture, which would in the course of the seventeenth century create a new intelligentsia, largely made up of the professions and lairds. For them, printed sermons like those of the Edinburgh minister, Robert Bruce, were best-sellers in the 1590s, and by the 1620s a contemplative piety, seen in the vogue for spiritual autobiographies and manuals of practical divinity, had grounded itself in the psyche of Scottish Calvinism. But the other best-sellers of Jacobean Scotland were histories and works of vernacular literature from the late medieval period. Barbour's *The Brus* and Blind Harry's *Wallace* vied for popularity with George Buchanan's *History*, first published in 1582. Similarly, the works of the poets of the Renaissance Courts of James IV and V, such as Henryson's *Testament of Cresseid* and Gavin Douglas's *Palace of Honour*, were more popular in the revival from the 1570s onwards of the literary masterpieces of Middle Scots than they had been when first written. It was the first example in Scottish history of a patriotic publishing campaign; it would be repeated at regular intervals, most notably in the works of the printer, Thomas Ruddiman, between 1707 and 1715.

The rationale of the wave of historical works produced after the Reformation owed a good deal both to the philosophical tradition established by John Mair and to the vogue for collecting historical documents, which had been seen, for example, in the register of Cambuskenneth Abbey assembled in 1535 by its abbot, Alexander Mylne, scholar, canon lawyer and first President of the newly created Court of Session. The national tradition of historical scholarship became a moral duty and an empirical science in the process. The philosophical tradition, which would culminate in Stair's *Institutions of the Law of Scotland* (1681), also underlay the growing systematisation of the law, where the first milestone was the printed collection of *Acts of Parliament* (1566), the work of a little-known legal circle at the court of Mary, Queen of Scots; by the 1590s collections of legal precedents or practicks had become common. The study of history and law, both of which traced their provenance to the fifteenth century, became the core of Presbyterian humanism which would culminate in the self-styled 'new' philosophical history of Hume and Robertson.

The vital difference which distinguished the seventeenth century from the centuries which preceded it was the loss of the role as cultural patrons of both the Church and the royal Court. The scope of ecclesiastical patronage narrowed after the Reformation, but Presbyterian ministers quickly continued and strengthened the long tradition of the clergy as the guardians of the national memory and university teachers bound to a patriotic programme of learning. The effects of the removal of the Court to London in 1603 are often exaggerated. Poets and chroniclers had already learned to survive in a cold climate; half of the sixteenth century had been taken up with royal minorities. The *Bannatyne Manuscript*, a huge collection of Middle Scots verse assembled in the mid-1560s by an Edinburgh lawyer, George Bannatyne, is ample testimony to the widening circle of literary patronage and interest taking place well before 1603.

For some, the century of the Covenants, conventicling, state repression and the witch hunt produces a dismal story and little literary culture of interest, but if the same standards were applied to the eighteenth century, recent historians would produce a picture of an age of deep anxiety, riven by rebellion, popular riot and a church at odds both with itself and a growing body of Presbyterian dissent. There was, it is true, less creative writing of quality, in Scots or English, in the seventeenth century than in the sixteenth. The focus of culture, however, had shifted to a wider Renaissance of letters, involving architecture, heraldry and music. What Charles McKean has termed the 'Scottish architectural renaissance', manifested in a galaxy of baronial tower houses in both town and country, was only just beginning in 1603. In this century, Latin, still the language of scholarly communication, was the favoured medium of the intellect rather than Scots. The new cultural patrons were the landed classes and the professions. Their contribution did not replicate the previous roles played by Church and Crown, but established new patterns of cultural interests which would be of great significance for the future. The great libraries were no longer those of religious houses or bishops but of individual lairds and lawyers or the collections of the new professions. This was the age of the collector and the virtuoso. One model of his age was Lauder of Fountainhall, who had amassed 536 books by the time he was admitted as an advocate in 1668 at the age of twenty-two; they straddled the classics, modern histories of European countries as well as of Scotland, and both French and English literature. The most impressive collection of all was that in the Advocates' Library, founded in 1689, which had a catalogue of 158 pages; sixty-nine of them were devoted to non-legal works.

The pursuit of the intellect gathered in pace after 1600, but its rationale was to rediscover Scotland's links with its past, interrupted by a generation of civil war. If there was a break marked by the Restoration of 1660, it came in the universities, where there was a calculated purge of dissident clergy. Newton's theories of light and colour and Harvey's discoveries about the blood were being taught at Edinburgh University from the 1670s onwards. There was a broad-based advance among the Scottish universities in the study of mathematics, law and some of the physical sciences between the 1670s and the 1720s. The schemes for a new medical school at Edinburgh, eventually realised in 1726, built on at least three successive attempts made in the previous century. Enlightened ideas did not burst upon a bare stage in the 1730s; they had been gathering momentum in the universities since at least the 1670s.

The main dynamic in the Restoration period, however, was provided by the professions. Between 1679 and 1688 an astonishing number of institutions and offices were founded; they included the Royal College of Physicians (1681), the Order of the Thistle (1687), the Advocates' Library (1689) and the offices of Royal Physician, Geographer-royal and Historiographer-royal, all introduced between 1680 and 1682. Even if there was no dramatic declaration of the birth of a new age, such as the publicists of the Enlightenment would make in the 1750s, the achievement of the Restoration age was a very real one: it drew together the threads which linked the long Renaissance stretching back to the late fifteenth century with the Enlightenment of the eighteenth. The most lasting effects of the Enlightenment – and not least the growth of the medical profession – were those which depended most heavily on a long tradition.

ARTICLE 38B
REX STOICUS: GEORGE BUCHANAN, JAMES VI AND THE SCOTTISH POLITY

Extracted from RA Mason 1982 *in* J Dwyer, RA Mason and A Murdoch (eds) *New Perpsectives on the Politics and Culture of Early Modern Scotland*, Edinburgh (John Donald), 9–33.

Between 1570 and his death in 1582, Buchanan presided over the formal schooling of the king.[1] During those same years he prepared the *De Jure Regni*, the *History of Scotland* and the politically significant play *Baptistes* for publication.[2] While there is no clear evidence that the two activities were strictly related, it does seem probable that the one would have exerted some influence on the other. Certainly, all three of these works bear dedications to James VI which clearly suggest that, if they were primarily designed to justify rebellion, they were also seen by Buchanan as manuals of political guidance and instruction for his pupil. In the dedication to the *Baptistes*, for example, he wrote that the play

> may seem of particular interest to you as it clearly displays the torments and miseries of tyrants even when they seem to flourish the most. This I consider not only useful but also necessary for you to understand, so that you may begin at once to dislike that which you must always avoid.[3]

In the same way, just as the *Baptistes* provided a model of tyranny to eschew, Buchanan thought his *History* contained many examples of kingship worthy of emulation. In dedicating it to James he commented on the ill-health which had kept him from his charge and hoped the deficiency could be supplied 'by sending to you faithful monitors from history, whose counsel may be useful in your deliberations, and their virtues patterns for imitation in active life'.[4]

The king cannot be set free of the law, Buchanan tells us later in the *De Jure Regni*, because 'within a man two most savage monsters, lust and rage (*cupiditas & iracundia*), wage perpetual war with reason (*ratio*)'. This basic presupposition about man's nature, never discussed at any length in his writings and never defined with any precision, is nonetheless the keystone of his political philosophy. The closest Buchanan approaches to a definition of it occurs in a passage towards the end of the *Dialogue*. There Maitland is led to remark that 'there is no monster more violent and more pestilential than man when . . . he has once degenerated into a beast', prompting Buchanan to reply that

> You would say this much more emphatically, if you considered how many-faceted an animal man may be and out of what a variety of monsters he is made . . . It would be an infinite task to describe the nature of each one, but certainly two most noisome monsters, anger and lust (*ira & libido*), are clearly apparent in man. And what else do laws do, or strive after, but that these monsters be subjected to reason (*ratio*)? And when they do not comply with reason, may not the laws restrain them with the fetters of their sanctions? Whoever, therefore, loosens these bonds from a king, or anyone else, does not merely release a single man, but lets loose against reason two exceptionally cruel monsters and arms them to break down the barriers of the law. Aristotle seems to have said well and truly that he who obeys the law obeys God and the law, he who obeys the king, obeys a man and a beast.[5]

The language of this passage and the citation of Aristotle clearly indicate that Buchanan is drawing directly (albeit crudely) on the psychological theory of the ancient world. That is, he is describing man's nature in terms of the classical distinction between reason and the passions in the human soul. This language, however, is not merely descriptive of psychological faculties, it is also, indeed for

Buchanan primarily, an ethical vocabulary in which the passions are uniformly vicious and reason (or prudence or wisdom[6]) the essence of virtue. With his king-centred conception of politics, moreover, Buchanan invariably sees the conflict between reason and the passions, virtue and vice, being waged most significantly in the soul of the ruler. For Buchanan, therefore, the right functioning of the body-politic depends on the moral predilections of its head, and underlying both the *Dialogue* and the *History* is the fear that the passions of the ruler will overcome reason and unleash the moral anarchy – the tyranny – that inevitably accompanies the unrestrained indulgence of a ruler's sensual instincts.

There is nothing at all unusual in Buchanan's use of this 'psycho-ethical' language or in his application of it to political theory. It was a common device in the *specula principum* and was further popularized by sixteenth century humanists who exploited the antithesis of reason and the passions (as did Buchanan) to emphasize the significance of education in the attainment of virtue. Ultimately, the distinction derives from Plato and Aristotle, but it was developed as a central tenet of Stoic philosophy and, despite his reference to Aristotle, it is with Stoicism that Buchanan seems to have associated the doctrine. For Buchanan's ideal king, the prudent ruler impervious to the demands of his passions, is *Rex Stoicus*, the Stoic King. This conception, furthermore, he explicitly associates with the Roman Stoic, Seneca. Twice in the *Dialogue* when discussing the ideal ruler Buchanan refers Maitland to Seneca's tragedy *Thyestes*, on both occasions saying that therein is portrayed a model of the perfect prince (23, 47). Moreover, the particular lines he had in mind are appended as a tailpiece to the *Dialogue* under the heading *Rex Stoicus ex Seneca* (104). Put briefly, Seneca's portrait merely emphasizes that the true king is in-corruptible and self-sufficient, unmoved by either riches or honour, ambition or the favour of the mob. It hardly matches the expectations generated by Buchanan's encomiastic references. But Seneca's tragedies as a whole could hardly be bettered as examples of the dire and vicious consequences following upon the unbridled indulgence of man's sensual appetites. The lesson was apparently not lost on Buchanan who presented young King James with a volume of 'Senecae Tragoediae' to complement his copy of Synesius.[7] Presumably he wished to impress upon James that only the Stoic King, ruthlessly subjecting his passions to the rule of reason, could be a virtuous individual and a worthy ruler.

For Hector Boece, the domestic history of Scotland consisted of the valiant efforts of her virtuous kings to stem the tide of luxury and restore the ancient discipline. While, conversely, those vicious tyrants who succumbed to their passions were disposed of by those of the nobility who remained uncorrupted. King-centred, ethically orientated and dependent on a very crude theory of the passions, the appeal of such an historical framework to Buchanan should be readily apparent. Not surprisingly, he adopted it almost wholesale. More sceptical and more restrained, Buchanan's *History* is for the most part simply a revision and continuation of that of Boece.

Although common enough in sixteenth century Europe, it seems likely that the paradigm of luxury and corruption used by Boece was appropriated from Livy's *Ab*

Urbe Condita. The passage in the preface to Book I of Livy's work, in which he laments that 'avarice and luxury' have gradually corrupted the ancient Roman spirit, finds countless echoes in Boece and thence in Buchanan. Livy, moreover, was a favourite author of Buchanan and in the more tranquil days before 1566, Mary would read 'daily after her dinner, instructed by a learned man, Mr George Bowhannan, somewhat of Lyvie'.[8] Given his preconceptions, it is safe to assume that Livy's appeal for Buchanan transcended purely stylistic interest. It has, for example, been argued that the dynamic of Livy's history 'is above all attributable to the Stoic ethical influence', and that he 'looks at the past as a battlefield of manners, and seeks to illustrate the moral qualities needed for a state to thrive . . .'[9] Precisely the same words might be applied to Buchanan, who similarly saw Scottish history as 'a battlefield of manners' and was equally concerned with those 'moral qualities' which, exemplified by the ancient Scots, had sustained the nation through so many centuries of trial and tribulation. For Buchanan, indeed, by virtue of the pervasive norm of natural law, on these moral criteria depends the correct functioning of the polity. Just as the essence of moral worth is the subjection of the passions to reason and conformity thereby with nature and nature's law, so the harmony of the body-politic, its 'justice' or 'temperance', depends on the ruler's conformity with reason and the free play of natural law which must thereby ensue. Given a Stoic King, conforming to reason and the law, the people will emulate his virtuous manners and the well-being of the polity will be assured.

Despite the evidence of Mary Stewart's deposition, however, Buchanan remained fearful that luxury and avarice were corrupting the ancient discipline beyond redemption and obscuring the efficacy of the natural laws on which the Scottish polity was founded. It was only in the Highlands and Islands that the pristine discipline of the ancient Scots was still to be encountered, and only among the clans that chieftains were still unquestioningly elected and bound to follow the advice of a council.[10] Uneducated, but as yet uncorrupted by luxurious living, the clansmen still adhered to those laws of nature implanted in man by God. Describing the primitive island of Rona, Buchanan suggests that its temperate inhabitants have an innate grasp of those laws which the corrupt majority of mankind can only learn through hard study:

> . . . and here alone in the universe, I imagine, are to be found a people who know no want, among whom every necessity of life abounds even to satiety. Unacquainted alike with luxury and avarice, they find in their ignorance of vice, that innocence and tranquillity of mind, which others laboriously search for in the discipline and precepts of wisdom.[11]

Buchanan's admiration of the islanders was no doubt tempered by his knowledge that their virtuous manners were not adopted voluntarily but imposed by the impoverished environment in which they were condemned to live. Nevertheless, he would have the more sophisticated and corrupt Scottish Lowlanders take note of their untutored virtue and aspire to emulate them. It was to the Celtic west that Buchanan looked for inspiration and guidance. If he had a vision of the Scottish polity of the future, one may guess that it was based on the temperate manners of the Gaels enriched by the language and culture of the Romans. 'I can perceive without regret', he wrote,

> the gradual extinction of the ancient Scottish language, and cheerfully allow its harsh sounds to die away, and give place to the softer and more harmonious tones of the Latin. For if, in this transmigration into another language, it is necessary that we yield up one thing or other, let us pass from rusticity and barbarism, to culture and civilisation, and let our choice and judgment, repair the infelicity of our birth.[12]

Himself of Celtic descent and possibly also a native Gaelic speaker,[13] Buchanan was, above all, a humanist.

NOTES

1 Buchanan shared responsibility with Peter Young, but there is no doubt that he was the senior partner, at least until his health began to fail in 1578. For details of James's schooling, see P Hume Brown, *George Buchanan: Humanist and Reformer* (Edinburgh, 1890), pp. 249–63.
2 For a detailed study of when Buchanan's major works were composed, see H. R. Trevor-Roper, 'George Buchanan and the Ancient Scottish Constitution', *English Historical Review*, supplement 3, 1966, *passim*. As he makes clear, there is no means of ascertaining precisely when the *Dialogue* in its final form was written. The earliest possible date is 1567 and MS copies were circulating in England by at least 1576. Nevertheless, the extent to which it was revised – if at all – before publication is impossible to determine. With the *History* more precision is possible. It seems likely that the bulk of it was written between 1566 and 1572 and extensively revised between 1576 and its publication in 1582. The *Baptistes* was written as early as 1540 but not published until 1577.
3 *Georgii Buchanani . . . Opera Omnia*, ed Thomas Ruddiman and Peter Burmann, 2 vols (Leyden, 1725), ii, p. 217.
4 *History*, i, civ. The edition used throughout is the *History of Scotland*, trans. James Aikman, 4 vols (Glasgow, 1827).
5 The reference is to Aristotle, *Politics*, III, xi, 4, but cf *Nichomachean Ethics*, V, vi, p. 5.
6 I have been unable to detect Buchanan distinguishing in any consistent manner between *ratio, prudentia* and *sapientia*. He appears to use them interchangeably and all imply a high degree of moral excellence.
7 G. F. Warner (ed.), 'The Library of James VI 1573–1583', *Scottish History Society Miscellany, I* (Edinburgh, 1893), lxix.
8 Brown, *George Buchanan*, p. 180.
9 P. G. Walsh, *Livy: His Historical Aims and Methods* (Cambridge, 1961), 4, 66 and passim.
10 *History*, ii, 602; cf. *De Jure Regni*, p. 65.
11 *History*, i, p. 55.
12 *Ibid.*, i, p. 9.
13 On this point, see Brown, *George Buchanan*, pp. 8–9.

ARTICLE 38C
THE NEW HISTORICISM IN RENAISSANCE STUDIES

Extracted from JE Howard 1986 in *English Literary Renaissance* 16, 13–43.

A new kind of activity is gaining prominence in Renaissance studies: a sustained attempt to read literary texts of the English Renaissance in relationship to other aspects of the social formation in the sixteenth and early seventeenth centuries. This development, loosely called the 'new history', and flourishing both in Europe and America, involves figures such as Stephen Greenblatt, Jonathan Dollimore, Alan Sinfield, Kiernan Ryan, Lisa Jardine, Leah Marcus, Louis Montrose, Jonathan Goldberg, Stephen Orgel, Steven Mullaney, Don E Wayne, Leonard Tennenhouse, Arthur Marotti, and others.[14] Journals such as *ELH, English Literary Renaissance, Representations*, and *LTP: Journal of Literature Teaching Politics* regularly publish 'new history' pieces. In short, a critical movement is emerging, and in this essay I want to look at the new historicism both to account for its popularity and to try to define what, if anything, is new about its approach to the historical study of texts and then to examine some instances of new historical criticism.

I

Historical scholarship linking Renaissance literary works to various non-literary historical contexts is not, of course, in and of itself, new, although in the last thirty years in particular, formalist approaches have been in the ascendancy in some quarters of Renaissance studies. This is partly due to the importance of the lyric and partly due to the importance of Shakespeare in the English curriculum. For quite different reasons, formalism has dominated the study of both. In America, the lyric poems of the Renaissance provided many of the set texts, the verbal icons, used by New Critics to demonstrate their critical methods, and several generations of students trained in the New Criticism now teach today's students. And in both England and America, the plays of Shakespeare have often been treated not as products of a particular moment but as works for and of all times: universal masterpieces.[15] Consequently, until quite recently formalist studies of theme, genre, and structure dominated the criticism of these texts. History, when broached at all, usually meant the history of ideas, as in E. M. W. Tillyard's famous study of the importance to Renaissance literature of the 'Elizabethan world picture'.[16] In part, then, the new historicism is a reaction against formalism, though one must note that certain very contemporary formalisms – particularly structuralism and deconstruction – have not been enormously influential in Renaissance studies. The novel and the Romantic and modern periods have more often provided the exemplary texts for these movements. By contrast, the new historicism has been taken up with particular intensity, in part has been created, by Renaissance scholars.[17]

Why is this so? In part, I believe, many teachers of Renaissance literature simply have grown weary, as I have, of teaching texts as ethereal entities floating above the urgencies and contradictions of history and of seeking in such texts the disinterested expression of a unified truth rather than some articulation of the discontinuities underlying any construction of reality. Yet a purely formalist pedagogy should be debilitating for those who teach *any* literature, not just that of the Renaissance. Why, then, is it critics of Renaissance texts who have found in a new historicism an answer to their dissatisfaction?

The answer, I believe, lies partly in the uncanny way in which, at *this* historical moment, an analysis of Renaissance culture can be made to speak to the concerns of late twentieth-century culture. For a long time the Renaissance as cultural epoch was constructed in the terms set forth by Jacob Burckhardt; it was the age of the discovery of man the individual, the age of the revival of classical culture, the age of the secularization of life. How enmeshed this picture was in nineteenth-century ideology is now clear, but it may be less clear what the *current* revival of interest in the Renaissance may have to do with twentieth-century concerns. Consider, for example, the work of Jonathan Dollimore, who is particularly interested in the way in which what he calls essentialist humanism has both dominated the study of English literature in the twentieth century and also has prevented recognition of the fact that man is not so much possessed of an essential nature as constructed by social and historical forces. Looking back at the seventeenth century, Dollimore sees it as a sort of privileged era lying between the Christian essentialism of the Middle Ages – which saw man as a unitary being who took his essence from God – and Enlightenment humanism – which first promulgated the idea of man the individual: a unified, separate, and whole entity with a core of identity emanating from within. For Dollimore, the late Renaissance was the age of skepticism in which in the drama in particular one finds recorded a recognition of the discontinuous nature of human identity and its social construction.[18] It is not hard to see affinities between this picture of the Renaissance and certain contemporary understandings of our own historical moment as the post-humanist epoch in which essentialist notions of selfhood are no longer viable.

I will return later to the theoretical issues raised by the fact that when a new historian looks at the past he or she is as likely as an old historian to see an image of the seeing self, not an image of the other. But for the moment I want to continue to pursue further the way in which 'the Renaissance' is being re-understood within that configuration of periods which constitutes the framework by which literary historians make the past intelligible. Within this framework the Renaissance has usually been assigned a transitional position between the Middle Ages – held to be encumbered with a monolithic Christian ideology and a static and essentially unhistorical view of itself – and the modern era – marked by the rise of capitalism with its attendant bourgeois ideology of humanism, progress and the all-important interiority and self-presence of the individual. Almost inevitably, this construction of the past has produced the question: just *how* modern and *how* medieval was this transitional period?[19] Burckhardt, looking back at Renaissance Italy from mid-nineteenth century Germany, stressed the modernity of the Renaissance, its sense of itself as definitively different from prior periods of history. Others have insisted on the fundamental continuity between the Renaissance and the Middle Ages. But now, as critics and historians sense the modern era slipping away and a new episteme inchoately emerging, the Renaissance is being appropriated in slightly different terms: as *neither* modern nor medieval, but as a boundary or liminal space between two more monolithic periods where one can see acted out a clash of paradigms and ideologies, a playfulness with signifying systems, a self-reflexivity, and a self-consciousness about the tenuous solidity of human identity which resonate with some of the dominant elements of post-modern culture.

In short, I would argue that the Renaissance, seen as the last refuge of pre-industrial man, is of such interest to scholars of the post-industrial era because these scholars construe the period in terms reflecting their own sense of the exhilaration and fearfulness of living inside a gap in history, when the paradigms that structured the past seem facile and new paradigms uncertain. Clearly this emerging reading of the Renaissance is made possible by the traditional emphasis on the Renaissance as an age of transition. Previously critical emphasis was on continuity – on the way the period linked to the past or anticipated the future. Now the emphasis is on *dis*continuity, seen most clearly perhaps in Dollimore's insistence on the early seventeenth century as a kind of interperiod standing free of the orthodoxies of the Middle Ages and the Enlightenment. But the difference between prior and past conceptions of the Renaissance is also clear in the way the new historical critics so often make the period intelligible by narratives of rupture, tension, and contradiction, as, for example, when Greenblatt talks about the gap between the Renaissance ideology of human freedom and the actuality of Renaissance man as the subject of determining power relations[20] or, as we shall see, when Louis Montrose stresses the enormous contradictions in the social formation which Renaissance literature attempted to mediate.[21] And, as I have been hinting, these narratives of discontinuity and contradiction are narratives which owe much to the way late twentieth-century man construes his own historical condition.

To answer these questions, I want to sketch what must of necessity be a simplified picture of some of the assumptions underlying the historical criticism of a figure such as Tillyard. These assumptions include the following: that history is knowable; that literature mirrors or at least by indirection reflects historical reality; and that historians and critics can see the facts of history objectively. (This last assumption is particularly paradoxical since it rests on the premise that while literature is implicated in history, historians and critics are not.)[22] The criticism resulting from these premises often led to the trivialization of literature: to its reduction to a mere reflection of something extrinsic to itself, and to the trivialization of criticism; its reduction to a mode for explaining (not reading) texts in terms of their relationship to a fixed ground, such as James I's monarchical practices, English imperialism, or Puritan theology. At its worst, such criticism reduced literary study to the search for topical references; at its best it illuminated particular texts in relationship to great men or events or ideas of a period, but its distinguishing mark was always the assumption that literature was a mirror reflecting something more real and more important than itself.[23]

Contemporary theoretical work, it seems to me, has seriously put in question a number of these assumptions. For example, much reception and reader-response criticism has directly challenged the idea that a reader/interpreter can ever escape his or her own historicity in order to encounter objectively the historical difference encoded in texts. Consequently, one must question the status of that 'knowledge' about the past produced either by the historian or the historically minded critic. Similarly, Saussurian linguistics has challenged the premise that language functions referentially. One mode of historical criticism assumes that literature is connected to history in that its representations are direct reflections of historical reality, but one must ask what happens to that assumption when the referentiality of language itself is questioned. If literature refers to no ground extrinsic to itself, what can be the nature of its relationship to an historical context or to material reality? In fact, if one accepts certain tendencies in post-structuralist thought, is the possibility of an historical criticism even conceivable?

It is only by addressing these and a number of other equally urgent theoretical issues that a new historical criticism can distinguish itself from an older, more positivistic critical practice. The new historicism may well turn out to be an important extension of the theoretical ferment of the past two decades, a movement which will fundamentally rethink how we study texts in history. On the other hand, there is a real danger that the emerging interest in history will be appropriated by those wishing to suppress or erase the theoretical revolution that has gone on in the last several decades.

NOTES

1 Stephen Greenblatt is perhaps the central figure in the American branch of this movement; see *Renaissance Self-Fashioning From More to Shakespeare* (Chicago, 1980). In his introduction to a volume entitled *The Forms of Power and the Power of Forms in the Renaissance* (Genre 15 [1982], 3–6), he outlines what he sees as a few of the distinguishing features of the 'new historicism'. This essay is primarily concerned with what motivates the turn to history and with the theoretical problems posed by such a move, rather than with defining what are clearly emerging as differences among those now doing historical criticism.

2 For a provocative discussion of the way Shakespeare has been constructed in twentieth-century British culture as the writer who best reveals the timeless elements of the human condition see Derek Longhurst, '"Not for all time, but for an Age": an approach to Shakespeare studies' in *Re-Reading English*, ed Peter Waddowson (New York, 1982), pp. 150–63.

3 E. M. W. Tillyard, *The Elizabethan World Picture: A Study of the Idea of Order in the Age of Shakespeare, Donne and Milton* (London, 1943).

4 I do not mean to suggest that *only* Renaissance scholars are interested in historical approaches to texts. At the 1983 MLA convention Jonathan Culler devoted a major presentation to an attack, by way of Terry Eagleton, on the reification of history in much

contemporary criticism. Culler's attention to this issue I take as an indication of the crucial professional space historical studies are now assuming in many quarters of the discipline. Critics as diverse as Eagleton in *Literary Theory. An Introduction* (Minneapolis, Minn, 1983) and Frank Lentricchia in *After the New Criticism* (Chicago, 1980) have led the way in arguing that the most serious flaw of the major critical movements of the last several decades has been their failure to acknowledge history, and it is that failure which is now being redressed.

5 Jonathan Dollimore, *Radical Tragedy*, especially Chap 10, 'Subjectivity and Social Process', pp. 153–81.

6 Consider, for example, the lengthy debate surrounding Sir Thomas More and whether or not his *Utopia* reflects an essentially medieval and monastic conception of life (see R. W. Chambers, *Thomas More* [London, 1953]) or an enlightened anticipation of modern socialism (see Karl Kautsky, *Thomas More and his Utopia*, trans. H. J. Stenning [1888; reprinted New York, 1927]).

7 Greenblatt, *Renaissance Self-Fashioning*, especially pp. 1–9.

8 This idea is present in many of Montrose's early essays. See, in particular, 'The Place of a Brother' in '*As You Like It*: Social Process and Comic Form', *Shakespeare Quarterly*, 32 (1981), 28–54.

9 For a useful critique of naïve historicism see David Carroll's essay, 'Mimesis Reconsidered: Literature, History, Ideology', *Diacritics* 5 (1975), 5–12.

10 Perhaps the most notorious example of a critic reducing a Renaissance text to the contours of its supposed historical referent is Josephine Waters Bennett's *Measure for Measure as Royal Entertainment* (New York, 1966). But even in a work as recent – and as interesting – as Philip Edwards's *Threshold of a Nation. A Study in English and Irish Drama* (Cambridge, 1979), one can still see operating the idea that literature is the mirror reflecting the social realm and that an historical approach to literature means retrieving that social ground.